GREGG SPEED BUILDING FOR COLLEGES DIAMOND JUBILEE SERIES

JOHN R. GREGG

CLYDE I. BLANCHARD
ADMINISTRATIVE MANAGEMENT CONSULTANT
FORMERLY PROFESSOR OF BUSINESS EDUCATION
UNIVERSITY OF TULSA

WOODROW W. BALDWIN
DIRECTOR, SCHOOL OF BUSINESS ADMINISTRATION
SIMMONS COLLEGE

ESTELLE POPHAM
CHAIRMAN, DEPARTMENT OF BUSINESS EDUCATION
HUNTER COLLEGE

SHORTHAND WRITTEN BY
CHARLES RADER

gregg SPEED BUILDING

FOR COLLEGES
DIAMOND JUBILEE SERIES

GREGG DIVISION McGRAW-HILL BOOK COMPANY

NEW YORK ST. LOUIS DALLAS SAN FRANCISCO TORONTO LONDON SYDNEY

Title Page Photograph: Werner Wolff

Design: BARBARA DU PREE KNOWLES

GREGG SPEED BUILDING FOR COLLEGES, DIAMOND JUBILEE SERIES

Library of Congress Catalog Card Number 65-26167.

23456789 RRD-66 5432109 24610

preface

Gregg Speed Building for Colleges, Diamond Jubilee Series, is the latest book in the successful Gregg Speed Building series, the first volume of which appeared in 1932.

The authors have retained, with slight modifications, the five-lesson shorthand skill development and transcription cycle that has been a distinctive feature of all editions in the Gregg Speed Building series. At the same time they have upgraded the speed building and transcription programs to give them collegiate status.

SPEED BUILDING FEATURES

Isolated drills to build dictation speed and transcription facility precede connected matter in each unit. Built-in reviews of English, spelling, and punctuation provide material for teaching, testing, reteaching, and retesting these essentials throughout the course. Progressive speed building materials are followed up by sustained speed builders. Shorthand speed and transcription facility are developed concurrently, and provision is made for testing progress in each area in the last lesson in each unit.

The most far-reaching improvement in the revision, however, is the opportunity it gives for teaching applications of business principles and practices studied in business administration and economics courses. The material in most of the dictation and transcription lessons patterns that dictated by executives representing the organization within which most company activities are coordinated and controlled. *Gregg Speed Building for Colleges, DJS,* complements college courses in management. The interoffice memorandums in particular reflect management thinking prior to policy decisions.

IMPROVED ORGANIZATION

Gregg Speed Building for Colleges, DJS, justifiably stresses the importance of secretarial work and prepares the college student for some of the decision-making aspects of the "executary's" job.

PART ONE • BRIEF-FORM DICTATION AND TRANSCRIPTION

Part One (5 lessons) contains a review of brief forms and many of their derivatives. Each of the lessons in this section contains a brief-form chart for reading and writing drills and a group of short letters, loaded with brief forms, for speed building practice.

PART TWO • GENERAL DICTATION AND TRANSCRIPTION

Part Two (55 lessons) is the core of the book. It contains dictation of executives in eleven departments of NATIONAL PRODUCTS, INC., a large corporation with headquarters in St. Louis, Missouri, and plants and branches located in several states and foreign countries. The context reflects the interrelationships among the various departments and shows the methods of dealing with customers and vendors.

In Part Two, each department of NATIONAL PRODUCTS is treated in a separate unit consisting of five lessons. Each of these units follows a five-lesson plan for speed and transcription development.

Secretarial Assignment • The student is introduced to the work situation with which the part deals and is provided with definitions of new terms and spelling-transcription practice.

Lesson 1 — Building Transcription Quality • Transcription pointers are stated and illustrated. Sentences in shorthand illustrate these pointers and provide immediate learning reinforcement. Connected matter in shorthand for reading, writing, or taking dictation is provided for speed building needs.

Lesson 2 — Mastering Shorthand Theory • Word beginnings and word endings are presented in word families for reading and writing, providing a complete review of shorthand theory. Connected matter for dictation and transcription complete the lesson.

Lesson 3 — Building Phrasing Skill and Office-Style Dictation • In Units 2 through 9, shorthand phrases are stressed; in Units 10 through 12, special attention is given to office-style dictation. In all units, connected matter for reading, writing, and dictation is provided for speed building needs.

Lesson 4 — Progressive Speed Building • There are three one-minute speed-forcing drills preceded by a vocabulary preview in shorthand. Each drill is to be dictated 10 words a minute faster than the last. The first speed-forcing drills are counted for dictation at 50, 60, and 70 words a minute. The one-minute "takes" are given at progressively higher speed ranges in each unit — from 50 to 140 words a minute. Reinforcement and control dictation follows each speed-forcing sequence. In addition, there are business letters or memorandums in shorthand, the last of which is counted for production typing.

Lesson 5 — Building Transcription Speed • Dictation material is provided for sustained dictation at successively higher speeds. Students can practice this material at home, and the class period can be used to test their ability to take sustained dictation. Spelling and punctuation rules covered in the unit are reintroduced in the material, and marginal word counts are included so that transcription production rates can be determined.

PART THREE · SPECIALIZED DICTATION AND TRANSCRIPTION

Part Three (20 lessons) provides dictation and transcription materials in four specialized areas: Medical, Legal, Technical, and International Trade. In this part the correspondence and professional records are not limited to one company. Students can learn to recognize, spell, and use appropriately an extensive list of specialized terms and to some extent gain insight into the nature and significance of specialized secretarial positions.

In Part Three, each specialized area is treated in a separate unit consisting of five lessons. Although these units basically follow the five-lesson plan for speed and transcription development used in Part Two, modifications of the plan permit a greater emphasis on specialized terminology. At the same time, an effort is made to encourage the development of some shorthand facility and transcription competency when working with highly specialized material. Portions of the shorthand section of the Certified Professional Secretary Skills Examination are reproduced in the final lesson of *Gregg Speed Building for Colleges, DJS.*

OTHER ENRICHMENT MATERIALS

A *Student's Transcript* is available so that students can have a counted key to all the shorthand in the text for out-of-class practice.

A *Workbook* is also available to provide additional practice in the English conventions necessary to help the student become a master transcriber. The last lesson in each unit focuses attention on the meaning of the dictation and the business practices with which the dictation is concerned.

ACKNOWLEDGMENTS

The authors express their gratitude to the many teachers whose suggestions have been so helpful and to Mr. Charles Rader for the beautiful shorthand notes.

CLYDE I. BLANCHARD
WOODROW W. BALDWIN
ESTELLE L. POPHAM

contents

to the student

The exercises and drills in this text are designed to help you become a stenographer who can take dictation at a high rate of speed and transcribe rapidly and accurately at the typewriter. The extent to which these exercises and drills will contribute to your shorthand speed development and your ability to transcribe dictated material, however, will depend on how efficiently you practice them. Unless your instructor directs you otherwise, follow the procedures suggested here for practicing the various drills and speed building exercises.

BRIEF-FORM DERIVATIVES DRILLS

Most of the high-frequency brief forms, with many of their derivatives, are found in Part One, Brief-Form Dictation and Transcription. Because mastery of these words is essential to shorthand skill, you should read through each list aloud as rapidly as you can; then, cover the shorthand outlines and write each brief form and derivative in shorthand several times, pronouncing each word aloud as you write the shorthand outline. Observe the reading and writing goals that have been provided, always matching or improving upon them before reading and writing the speed building practice letters that follow each drill.

SECRETARIAL ASSIGNMENTS

Each of the eleven units in Part Two, General Dictation and Transcription, contains the dictation of executives who represent the organization of a business within which most business activities are coordinated and controlled. After reading the unit opening statements, studying the specialized terms and their definitions, and transcribing the spelling and transcription practice sentences, you will gain a better understanding of the interrelationships that exist among departments in a business enterprise and the methods used by business executives in dealing with people, solving problems, and making decisions.

BUILDING TRANSCRIPTION QUALITY

A wide assortment of transcription pointers deal with the troublesome details of punctuation, the use of the hyphen, the writing of numbers, the formation of possessives, and various points of grammar. You will find the following procedure helpful in getting the most out of each pointer and its accompanying transcription exercise and in finding answers to many of the puzzling questions that constantly arise in your endeavor to turn out acceptable transcripts and mailable letters.

1. Read the explanation of each pointer to be sure you understand its application.
2. Read the illustrative examples.
3. Transcribe the practice sentences. Reinforce any pointer not mastered by transcribing incorrect sentences correctly several times.

MASTERING SHORTHAND THEORY

In the second lesson of each unit you will find a list of words illustrating a major word-building principle of Gregg Shorthand; in Part Three, Specialized Dictation and Transcription, there are exercises on combining forms and specialized terminology. Before reading and writing the transcription speed building letters and memorandums that follow these word lists, be sure to (1) read through each list aloud as rapidly as you can (refer to the key that follows the drill the moment you cannot read an outline), (2) write each outline rapidly, saying each outline as you write it, and (3) repeat each outline until it can be written smoothly and without hesitation.

BUILDING PHRASING SKILL

In the third lesson of Units 2 through 9, phrase builder skills are introduced. You should read through each drill aloud as rapidly as you can and then make a shorthand copy of each drill before reading and writing the transcription speed builder letters and memorandums that follow and before transcribing the transcription pacer.

Office-Style Dictation is substituted for phrase builder drills in Units 10 through 12. Your instructor will dictate these letters in the manner that is more natural in the business office.

PROGRESSIVE SPEED BUILDER

In the fourth lesson of each unit you will find three speed-forcing letters for one-minute dictation and one two-minute letter for reinforcement and control. First, however, practice the vocabulary preview that precedes the speed-forcing practice, reading each outline aloud and making repeated shorthand copies until each can be written smoothly and without hesitation. Be sure to attain the two-minute reinforcement and control speed goal before reading and writing the transcription speed builder letters that follow. A transcription pacer, with a marginal word count, is the final activity in each progressive speed building lesson. Keep a record of your transcription progress by dividing elapsed time into total words transcribed for each such practice.

BUILDING TRANSCRIPTION SPEED

Your instructor will no doubt give you specific directions on how to handle the sustained speed builder in each fifth lesson. You may be asked either to make a shorthand copy of the letters and memorandums that are in type or simply to practice the previews and then to take them in dictation in class the next day. In any event, practice the vocabulary previews (the more difficult words and phrases that appear in the sustained speed builder) so that you will be able to write the speed builders from dictation without difficulty. Here is the way you should practice previews:

1. Read the outlines in the preview aloud.
2. Make repeated shorthand copies of each outline, saying each word or phrase aloud as you write it.

The transcription checkpoints that follow the sustained speed builder practice review the transcription pointers, shorthand theory, and terminology presented in the four previous lessons. Your instructor will either dictate the letter and ask you to transcribe from your shorthand notes or instruct you to transcribe directly from your text.

SPECIALIZED DICTATION AND TRANSCRIPTION

In Part Three you will become acquainted with the types of material and many of the terms and expressions that are peculiar to medicine, science and technology, law, and international trade. Learn to recognize, spell, and use appropriately the lists of specialized terms and to some extent gain insight into the nature of specialized vocabulary and develop some proficiency in writing special shorthand forms for higher frequency specialized terms. Compare your general dictation reinforcement and control speed with the dictation speed you achieve when the specialized transcription reinforcement practices are dictated.

You cannot, of course, hope to remember all of the specialized terms; however, you can develop an acquaintanceship and a base for further study if you will:

1. Spell each term aloud.
2. Read the definition.
3. Write the shorthand outline repeatedly.
4. Read the outlines you have written.

FURTHER SPEED BUILDING

The personal use of shorthand will do much to increase your dictation speed. You will find that you can keep longhand out of your mind when you hear words dictated to you if you write most of the things you normally write during the day in shorthand. If you will write, for example, all your personal memorandums in shorthand, you will soon be thinking in shorthand and you will find that your shorthand speed will increase.

PART ONE Brief-Form DICTATION AND TRANSCRIPTION

Part One, consisting of Lessons 1 to 5, reviews intensively those brief forms and many of their derivatives having a high frequency of business use. Each of the five lessons also reinforces your grasp of word-building principles and the major points of Gregg Shorthand theory. Mastery of the challenging drills, as well as practice in reading, writing, and transcribing the shorthand material given in the form of business correspondence, will ready you earlier for the next phase of your shorthand program—general dictation and transcription.

The drills and speed-building practice in this unit are designed to help you become a secretary who can take dictation at a high rate of speed and transcribe rapidly and accurately at the typewriter. The extent to which these speed-building exercises will contribute to your professional growth, however, will depend on how efficiently you practice them.

In practicing the brief-form drills, (1) read through each list aloud as rapidly as you can and (2) make a shorthand copy of the list, saying each outline aloud as you write it. You should match or, better still, improve upon the reading and writing goals that are provided.

In reading and writing the speed-building practice portion of each lesson, (1) always read, aloud if possible, all shorthand before you copy it; (2) refer promptly to the Student's Transcript when you come across an outline you cannot decipher after spelling the shorthand characters in it; (3) use the Student's Transcript for self-dictation, reading a convenient group of words—aloud, if possible—and writing that group in your notebook as rapidly and as legibly as you can; and (4) read what you have written.

unit 1

BRIEF FORMS AND DERIVATIVES

Lesson 1

BRIEF-FORM REVIEW

DERIVATIVE PRACTICE

This chart contains 60 brief forms and derivatives. Read the entire list of shorthand outlines. Then cover the shorthand outlines and write each word in shorthand from the key (or get somebody to dictate the words to you).

READING GOAL: 60 SECONDS — WRITING GOAL: 65 SECONDS

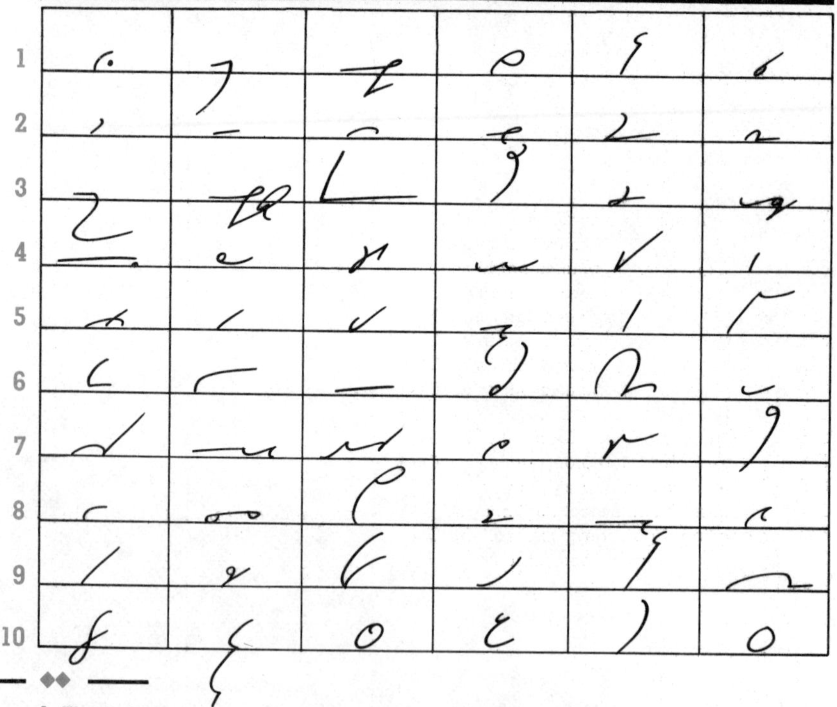

1 Think-thing, never, merchant, that, such, yet. 2 His-is, in-not, can, next, from, one-won. 3 Envelope, merchandise, gentlemen, several, send, request. 4 Morning, were-year, situation, railroad, should, shall. 5 Quantity, at-it, what, newspaper, which, during. 6 Upon, them, am, very, difficult, are-our-hour. 7 Could, Mrs., throughout, they, street, ever-every. 8 Than, immediate, about, soon, must, those. 9 Would, yesterday, between, and, subject, gone. 10 Particular, publication-publish, why, opportunity, have, I.

1▸ 

(164)

2▸ 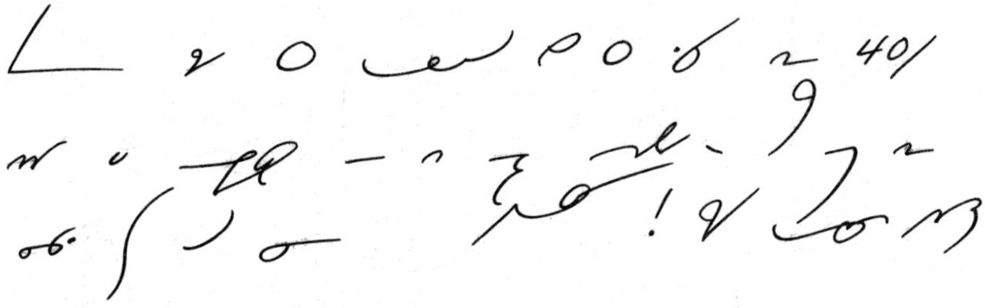

(101)

3

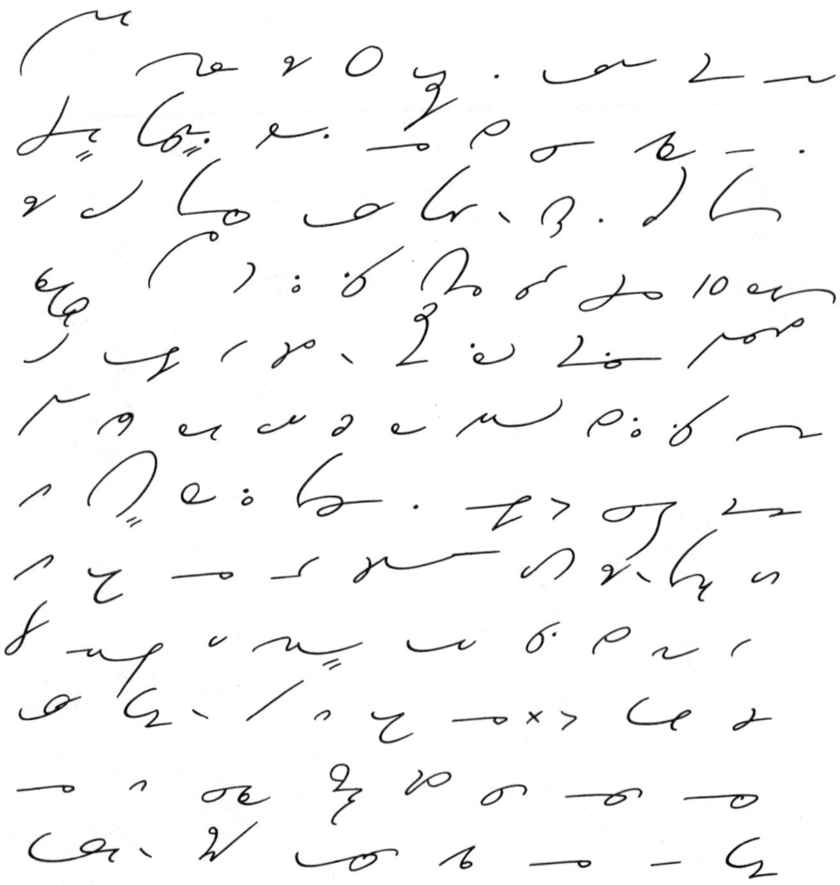

 (141)

4  (108)

5 

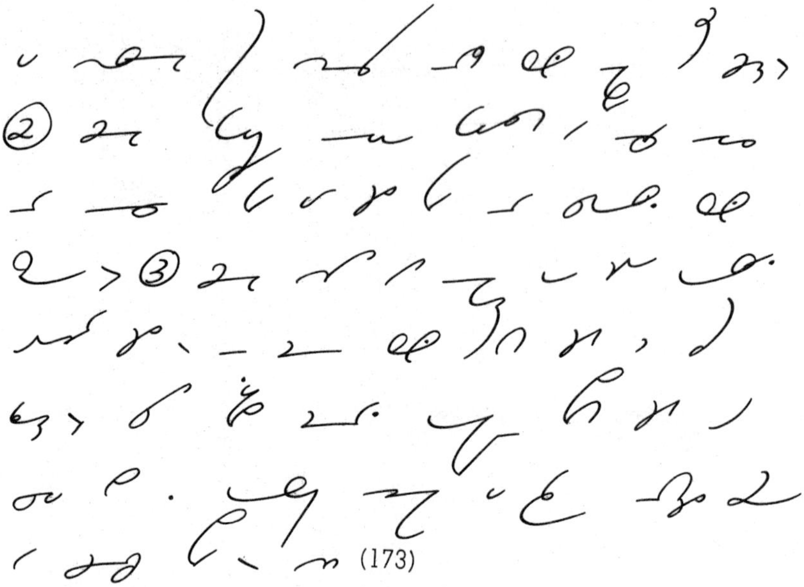

(173)

6 

(114)

lesson 2

BRIEF-FORM REVIEW

DERIVATIVE PRACTICE

This chart contains 60 brief forms and derivatives. Read the entire list of shorthand outlines, and then write each word in shorthand as rapidly as you can.

READING GOAL: 60 SECONDS WRITING GOAL: 65 SECONDS

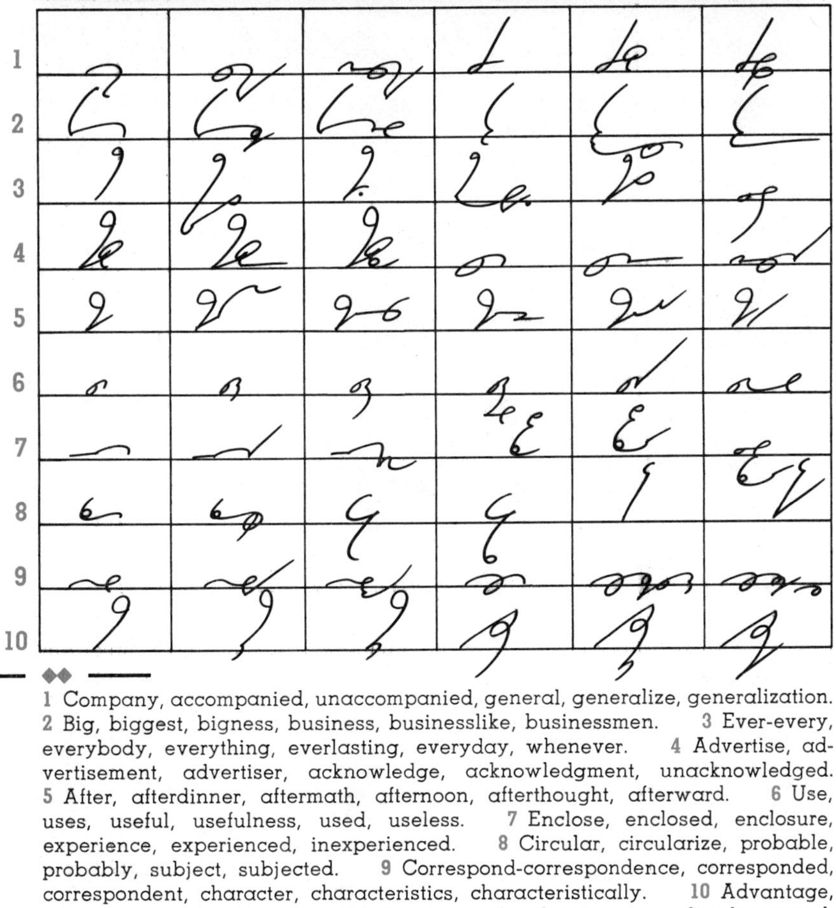

1 Company, accompanied, unaccompanied, general, generalize, generalization. 2 Big, biggest, bigness, business, businesslike, businessmen. 3 Ever-every, everybody, everything, everlasting, everyday, whenever. 4 Advertise, advertisement, advertiser, acknowledge, acknowledgment, unacknowledged. 5 After, afterdinner, aftermath, afternoon, afterthought, afterward. 6 Use, uses, useful, usefulness, used, useless. 7 Enclose, enclosed, enclosure, experience, experienced, inexperienced. 8 Circular, circularize, probable, probably, subject, subjected. 9 Correspond-correspondence, corresponded, correspondent, character, characteristics, characteristically. 10 Advantage, advantages, advantageous, disadvantage, disadvantageous, disadvantaged.

7

(147)

8

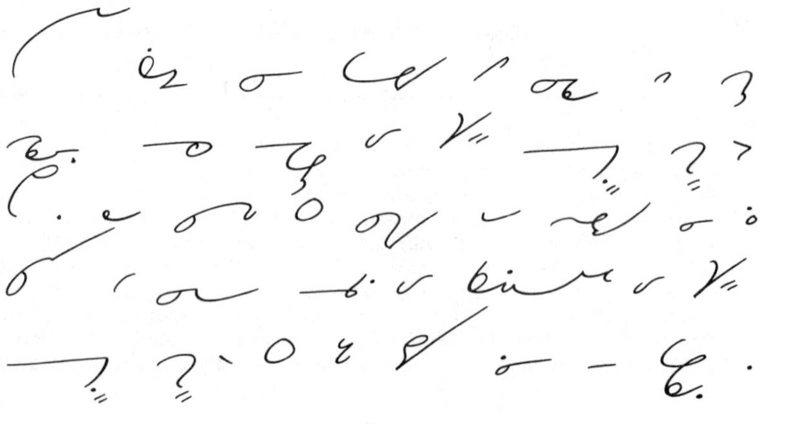

(150)

9 

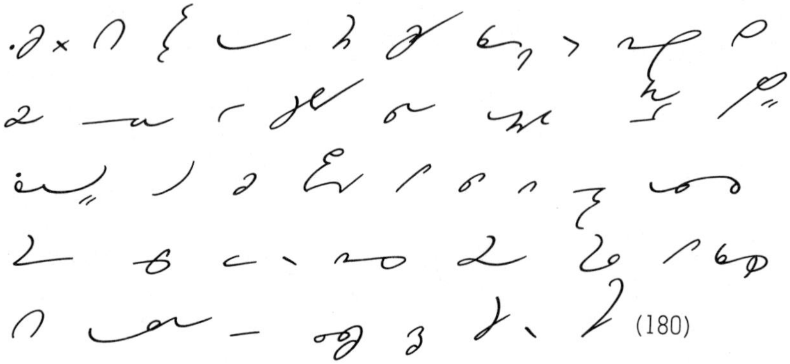

(180)

10 

(140)

11 

(114)

12 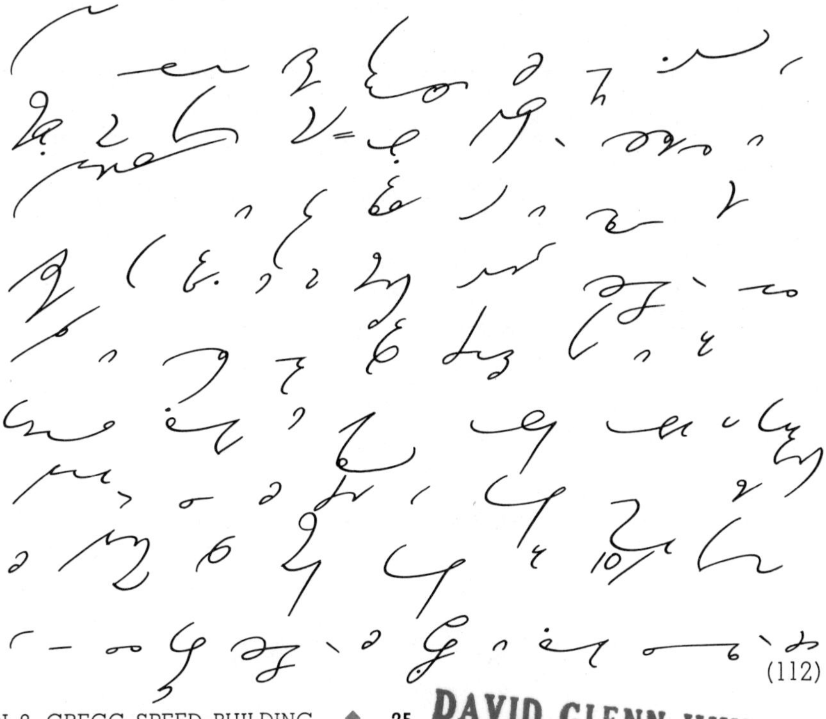

(112)

lesson

3 BRIEF-FORM REVIEW

DERIVATIVE PRACTICE

This chart contains 60 brief forms and derivatives. Read the entire list of shorthand outlines, and then write each word in shorthand as rapidly as you can.

READING GOAL: 50 SECONDS **WRITING GOAL: 55 SECONDS**

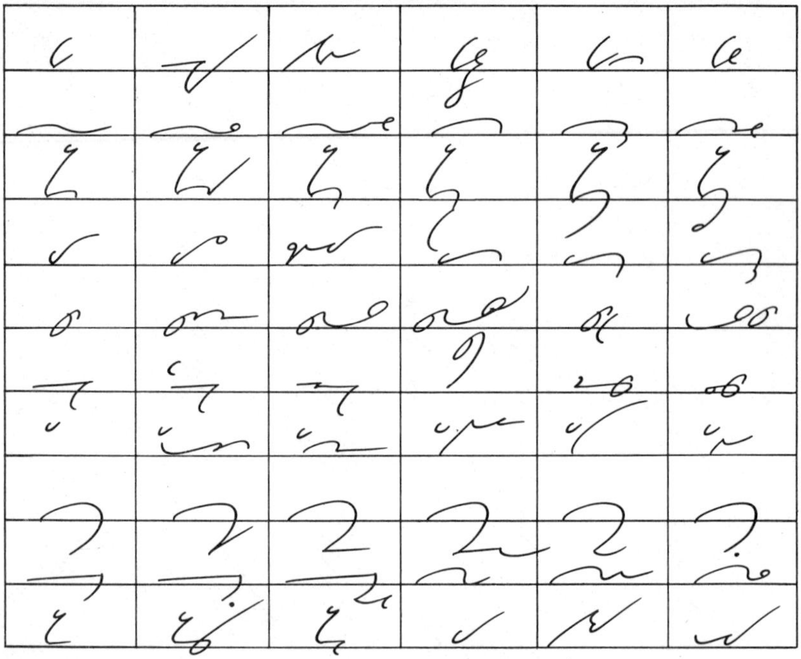

1 2 3 4 5 6 7 8 9 10

1 Part, imparted, departure, participate, particle, parties. 2 Glad, gladly, gladness, good, goods, goodness. 3 Object, objected, objection, objectionable, objective, objectively. 4 Ordinary, ordinarily, extraordinary, organize, organization, organizations. 5 How-out, outcome, outlay, outlined, output, layout. 6 Important-importance, self-importance, unimportant, however, somehow, anyhow. 7 Over, overlook, overcome, overdrawn, overtime, overture. 8 Govern, governed, government, governmental, governor, governing. 9 Manufacture, manufacturing, manufacturers, great, greater, greatly. 10 Opinion, opinionated, opinions, order, disorder, reorder.

SPEED-BUILDING PRACTICE

13

(222)

14 

(207)

15  (106)

16 

(155)

17

(141)

lesson

BRIEF-FORM REVIEW 4

DERIVATIVE PRACTICE

This chart contains 60 brief forms and derivatives. Read the entire list of shorthand outlines, and then write each word in shorthand as rapidly as you can.

READING GOAL: 50 SECONDS **WRITING GOAL: 55 SECONDS**

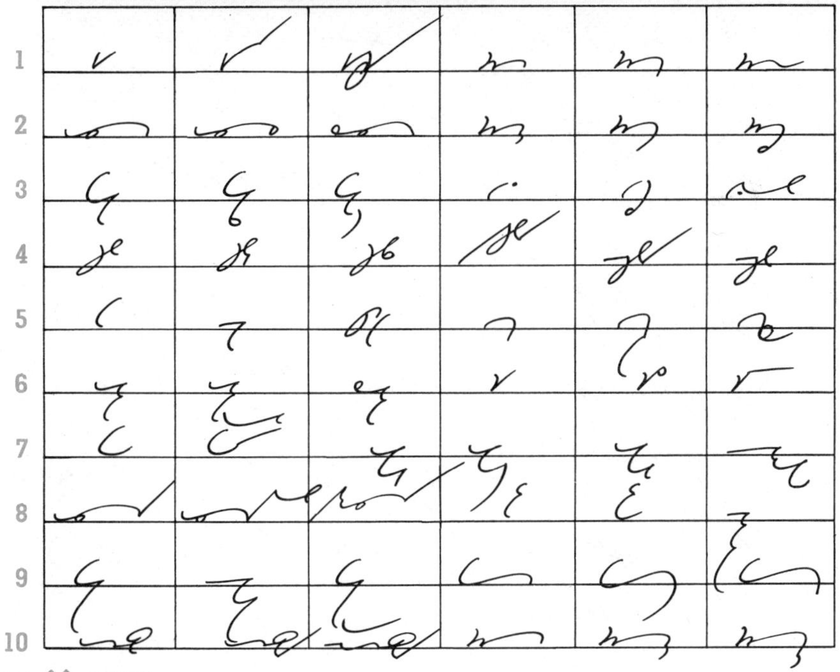

1 Short, shortened, shortsighted, success, succession, successor. 2 Regular, regularly, irregular, successes, successful, successfully. 3 Purpose, purposely, purposeful, thank, thankfully, thankless. 4 Satisfy-satisfactory, satisfaction, satisfactorily, dissatisfied, unsatisfied, unsatisfactory. 5 Put, input, output, question, questionable, questionnaire. 6 Responsible, responsibilities, irresponsible, state, stately, statement. 7 Present, presented, representation, representative, represents, misrepresent. 8 Regard, regardless, disregarded, speak, speaker, unspeakable. 9 Probable, improbable, probability, progress, progressive, progression. 10 Recognize, recognized, unrecognized, suggest, suggests, suggestions.

18 ▸

(283)

19

(120)

20

(156)

21 

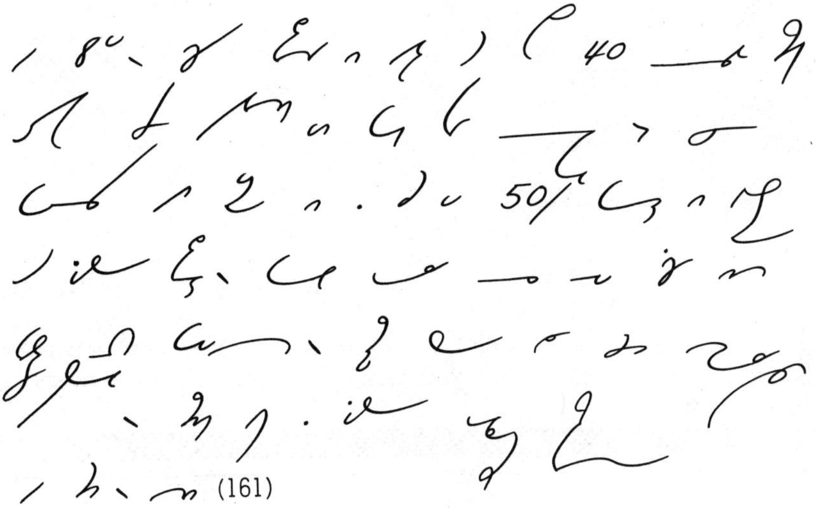

22 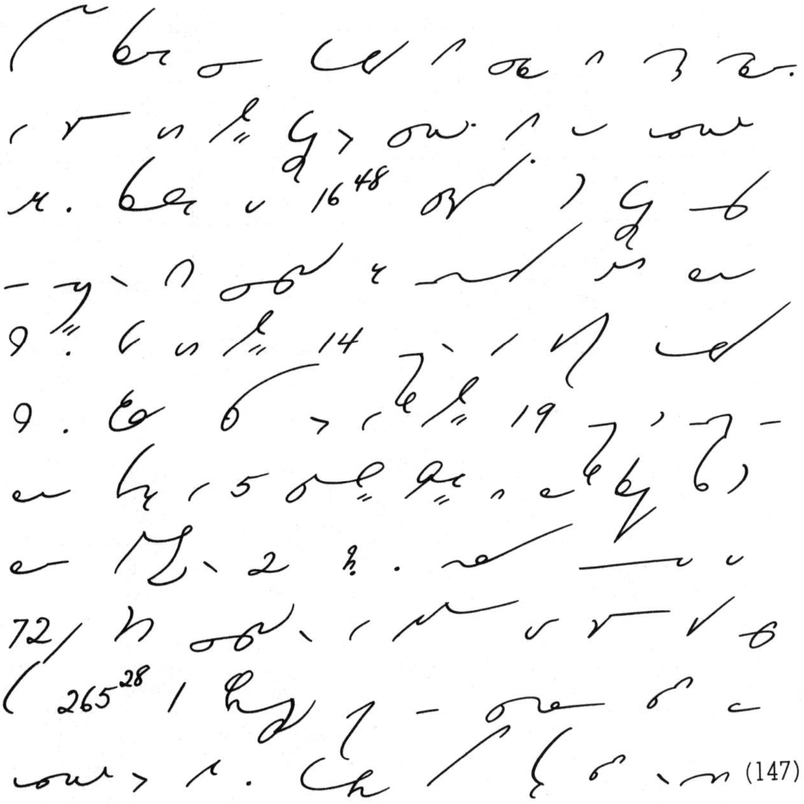

Lesson 5

BRIEF-FORM REVIEW

DERIVATIVE PRACTICE

This chart contains 60 brief forms and derivatives. Read the entire list of shorthand outlines, and then write each word in shorthand as rapidly as you can.

READING GOAL: 50 SECONDS   WRITING GOAL: 55 SECONDS

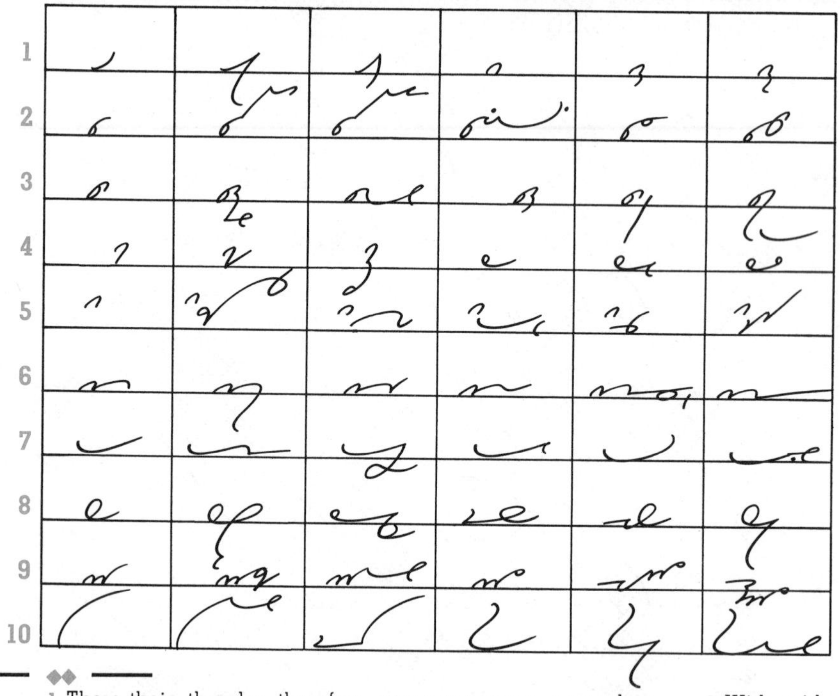

1 There-their, thereby, therefore, you-your, yours, yourselves. 2 With, withdrew, withdrawn, withholding, within, without. 3 Use, usefulness, useless, uses, usage, usability. 4 Wish, wished, wishfully, year-were, years, yearly. 5 Under, underestimate, undergo, underlings, underneath, understood. 6 Work, workable, worked, worker, workmanship, workmen. 7 Will-well, welcome, welfare, wills, willed, willingness. 8 Where, whereabouts, elsewhere, somewhere, nowhere, whereby. 9 Worth, worthiest, worthless, worthy, noteworthy, newsworthy. 10 Time, timeless, sometime, value, valuable, valueless.

23  (192)

24 

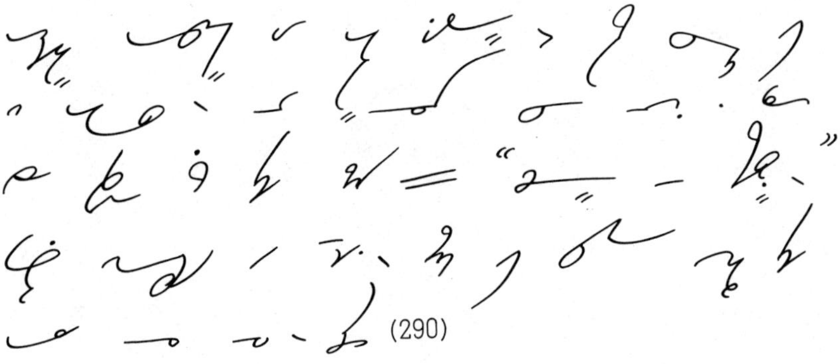

(290)

25

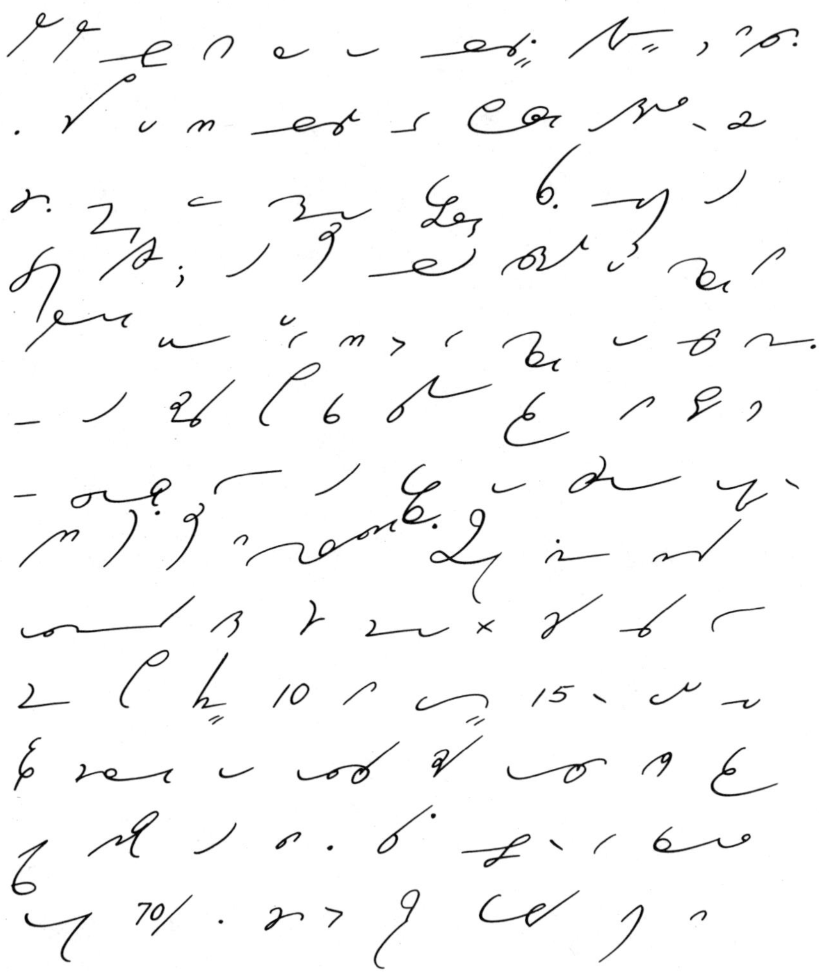

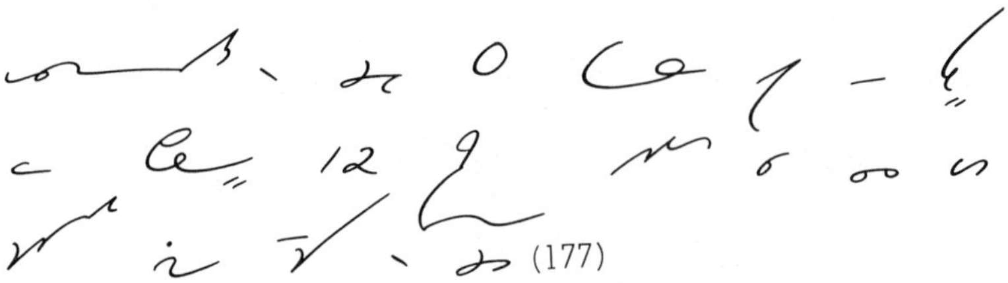
(177)

26 
(133)

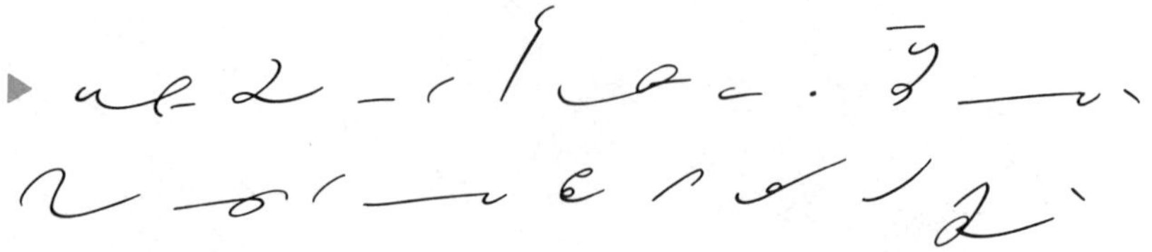

PART TWO General DICTATION AND TRANSCRIPTION

Part Two, consisting of Lessons 6 to 60, "samples" the type of material that a beginning secretary, employed by National Products, Inc., 211 Forest Avenue, St. Louis, Missouri 63100, would take from dictation and transcribe.

You will be given dictation by eleven executives, representing the organization of the business within which company activities are coordinated and controlled.

UNIT	ORGANIZATION	COMPANY EXECUTIVE
2	Administrative Services	John J. Parker
3	Credit and Collections	Harold C. Poling
4	Personnel	Edward R. Harmon
5	Public Information	Arthur C. Williamson
6	Finance	Henry P. Walters
7	Research and Development	Charles C. Haynes
8	Purchasing	David R. Monroe
9	Production	James W. Walsh
10	Advertising	Stuart P. Henderson
11	Sales	Ralph C. Akin
12	Traffic	James R. Russo

What is meant by administrative services? In a business enterprise it means a service—the planning, directing, coordinating, and interchange of information that permeates all business activity. It stems from the need for more and better factual information, and it involves the management of personnel and the implementation of systematic procedures.

In actual practice, administrative services is the management of company-wide activities. In terms of work, it is writing, filing, duplicating, calculating, mailing, analyzing, and telephoning—handling information so as to (1) process work within reasonable limits of time, energy, and cost expenditures; (2) supply reliable information to manage effectively; and (3) implement the performance of other functions of a business.

In the "office" that is the nerve center of a business, the administrative manager is the coordinator of all activity, whether it is done in or out of the office.

unit 2

ADMINISTRATIVE SERVICES

Secretarial Assignment

In this unit, you are secretary to John J. Parker, director of Administrative Services. All letters are signed by him over his title, General Manager.

SPECIALIZED TERMINOLOGY

You will transcribe Mr. Parker's dictation more efficiently after you are familiar with the specialized terms he uses.

Direct Mail • Advertising media, such as letters, catalogs, booklets, folders, or postcards, mailed directly to prospective buyers at home or at the office.

Duplicating Process • Any process (direct, offset, photocopy) used to prepare multiple copies of office records and messages quickly, easily, and cheaply.

Personnel Evaluation (Employee Appraisal) • Periodic efforts to estimate the degree of productivity and general effectiveness of employees.

Exit Interview • Conference conducted when an employee is leaving the company of his own free will in order to find out his reason for leaving.

Job Classification • The grouping together of several similar positions into a single bracket or class for purposes of determining wages and for transfer or promotion of employees.

Job Specifications (Job Description) • Written report based on the analysis of a particular job, including such statements as the job title, equipment used, description of materials used, skills required, working conditions, and responsibilities assigned to job.

Management Consultant • Expert who understands how to apply modern technology and recently developed managerial techniques in solving management problems.

Office Manual (Training Manual) • Compilation of employee duties and responsibilities in terms of specific jobs, company policies and practices, and job descriptions for use in training employees.

Office System • Work sequence and the various steps making up that sequence.

Service Contract • Agreement with a manufacturer or sales distributor to service his product, calling for regular inspection, cleaning, and adjusting.

Office Procedure (Office Practice) • Plan of action to simplify the use of material, equipment, time, energy, and space in the performance of office work.

Work Measurement • Data showing the amount of work done for purposes of distributing work fairly, defining job success, and analyzing employee performance.

Workshop • Study session designed to fill the gap between the ability a worker can supply and the ability the job requires.

This list contains 24 words that appear frequently in business letters.

accommodation	handling	procedures
appraisal	inaugurate	quantities
appropriate	innovations	recommendation
association	inquiries	reciprocate
beneficial	obsolescence	representative
convenience	personnel	schedule
cooperate	phases	similar
disappointed	probationary	undoubtedly

Transcribe the following sentences, preferably at the typewriter, until you master the spelling of the words that appear in the word list above.

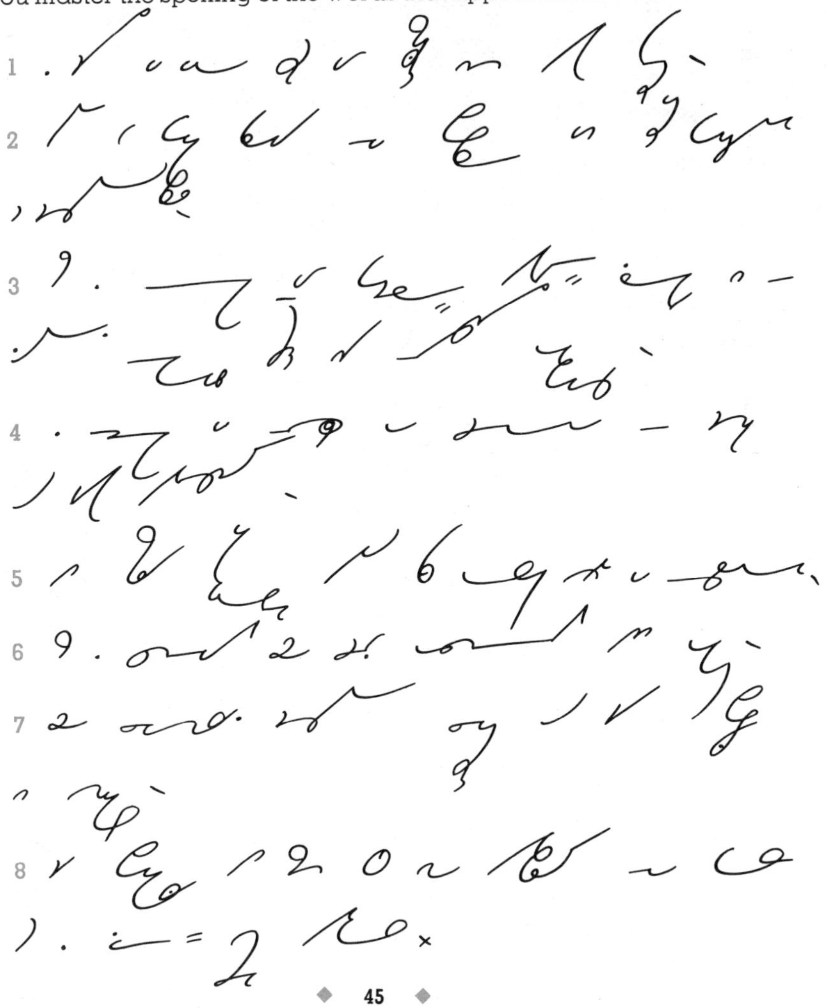

NATIONAL PRODUCTS, inc.

211 FOREST AVENUE
ST. LOUIS, MISSOURI 63100

May 26, 19--

Miss Mary Louise Lewis
2718 Sherman Avenue
Pittsburgh, Pennsylvania 15212

Dear Miss Lewis:

This letter is a sample of the form that has been adopted in Administrative Services here at NATIONAL PRODUCTS, INC. Since you will soon be working with us, you may wish to type your letters in this style while finishing your college program.

Note that we have adopted a letter with two features:

1. The use of standard punctuation, which requires a colon after the salutation and a comma after the complimentary closing.

2. The alignment of the date and the closing lines at the center.

For emphasis, we indent tabulated copy five spaces on each side. If you set a tab stop for such indentions before starting a letter, you will find this style easy to type.

Notice that we always capitalize NATIONAL PRODUCTS as an advertising technique. In addition, the initial letters of Administrative Services are always capitalized.

Enclosed is a memorandum for you to study. Plan for top and side margins of about an inch. Type headings as shown, using a tab stop 10 spaces from the left margin. Leave two blank lines between heading and message. Backspace the date from the right margin. Type the writer's name or initials a double space below the body, even with the date.

We are looking forward to having you with us!

Sincerely yours,

John J. Parker

John J. Parker
General Manager

hb
Enclosure

To: Edward R. Harmon, Director
Personnel Department

May 26, 19--

From: John J. Parker, General Manager
Administrative Services

Subject: Job Specifications

The new job specifications in the area of Administrative Services will be released at the annual meeting of the Administrative Management Society on May 28.

I suggest that we defer any decisions about changes within our own company until I can get a copy of this report, probably within the month.

JJP

NOTE An interoffice letter, rather than a memorandum, addressed to Mr. Harmon would contain a two-line inside address as well as a salutation:

Mr. Edward R. Harmon, Director
Personnel Department

Dear Mr. Harmon (or Dear Ed):

lesson 6

BUILDING TRANSCRIPTION QUALITY

TRANSCRIPTION POINTERS

Uses of the Compound Adjective

1 When a compound adjective precedes a noun, the adjective is hyphenated. Ask yourself the question, "Are the two words used as one modifier?"

The hard-fought proxy battle was finally won.

2 If the expression follows the noun, however, the adjectives are not hyphenated.

The battle between the two stockholders was hard fought.

NOTE: Do not confuse the adjective-adverb combination with the compound adjective. Also, remember that adjectives can end in *-ly*.

Very difficult situation, hardly credible excuse, friendly-appearing person.

3 The *self*-words are hyphenated.

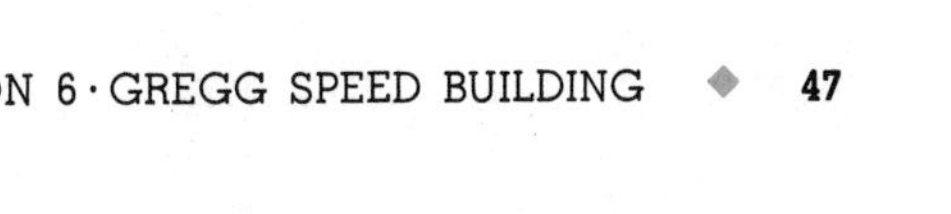

The message received was self-explanatory.

Check your understanding of compound adjectives by transcribing the following sentences, preferably at the typewriter.

1 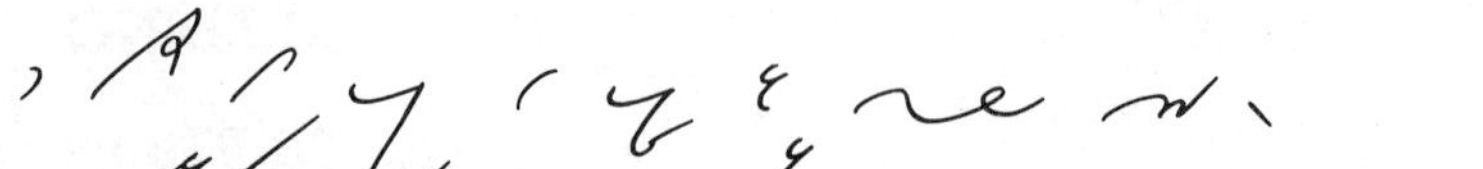

2 

3 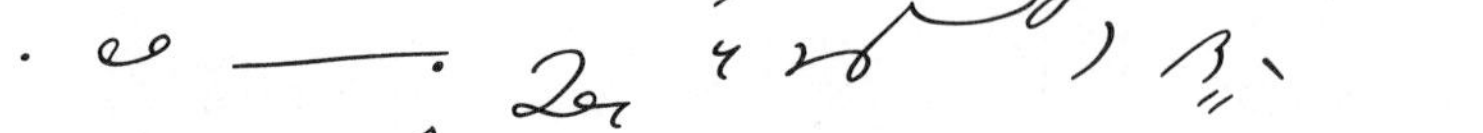

4 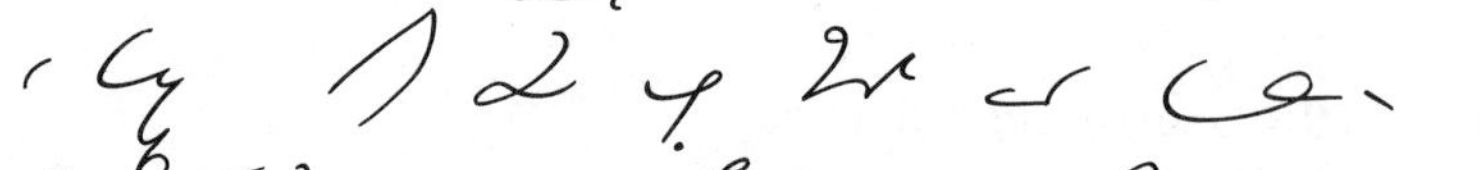

5 

6 

7 

8 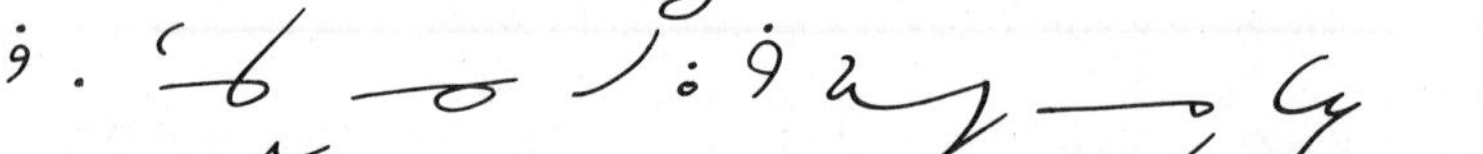

9 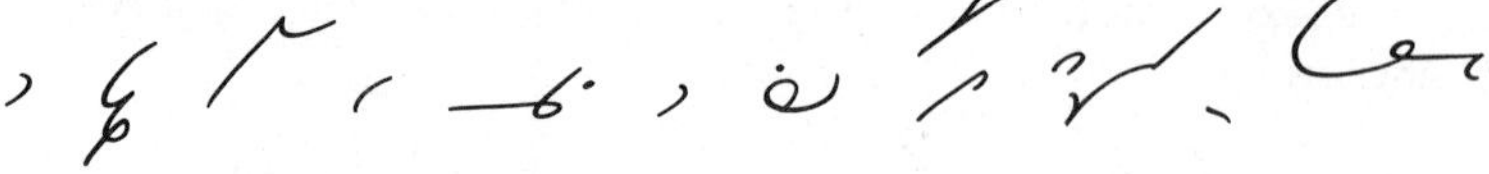

10 

TRANSCRIPTION SPEED BUILDER

27 Mr. William R. Browne, American Management Association, 135 West 50 Street, New York, New York 10019.

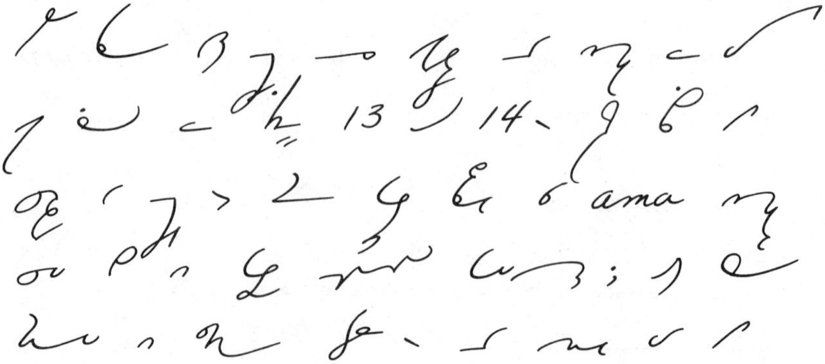

(218)

28▸ Mr. Harold P. Myers, Management Consultant, Hayes, Myers, and Wilson Company, New Rochelle, New York 10802.

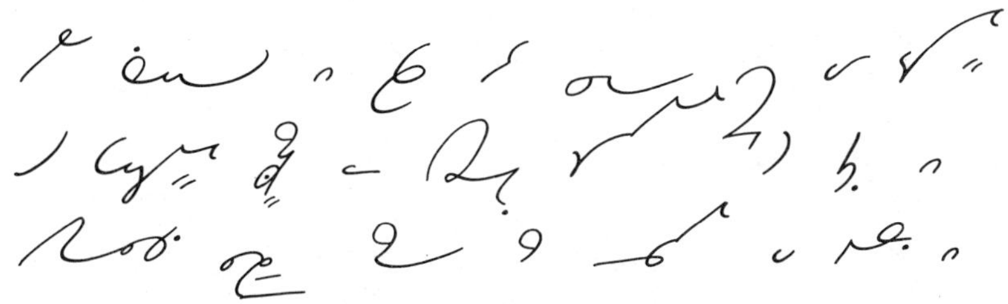

(257)

29 To: Edward R. Harmon, Director, Personnel Department.

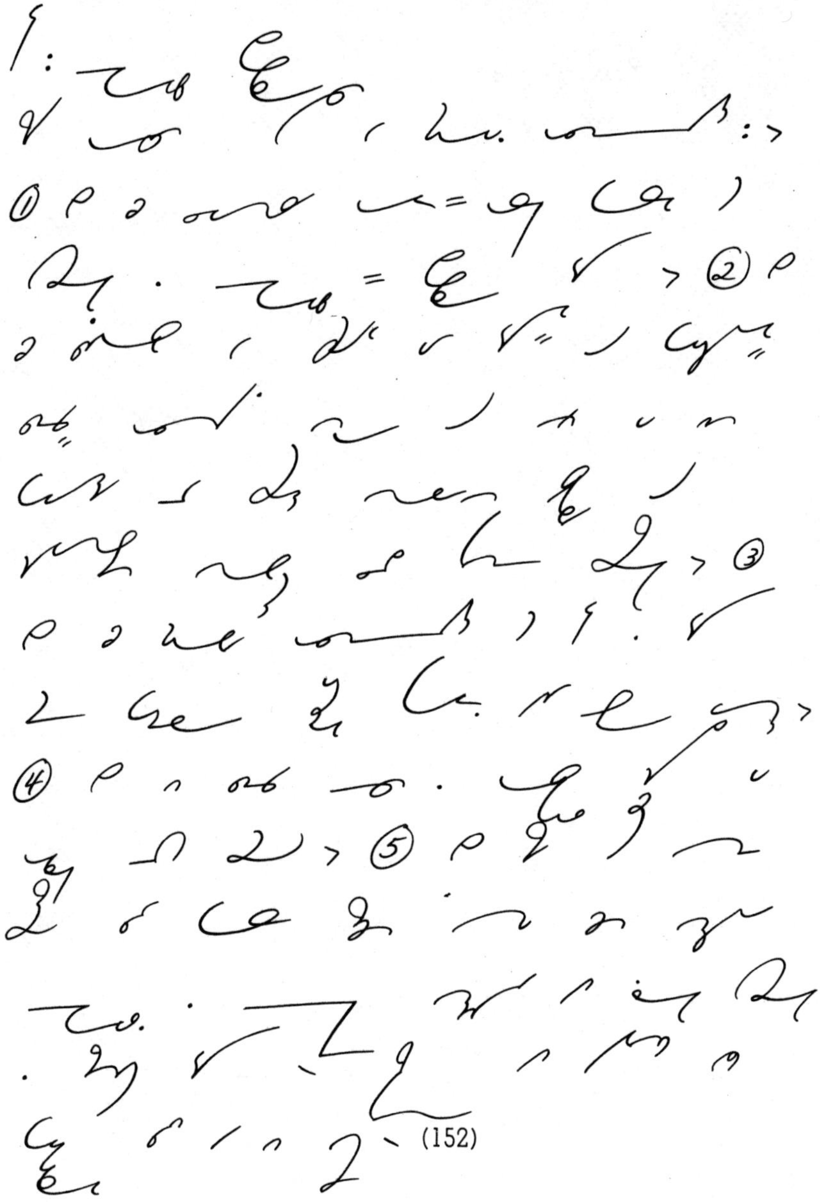

(152)

lesson

7 MASTERING SHORTHAND THEORY

WORD BEGINNINGS

En-, In-, Un- (followed by a vowel)

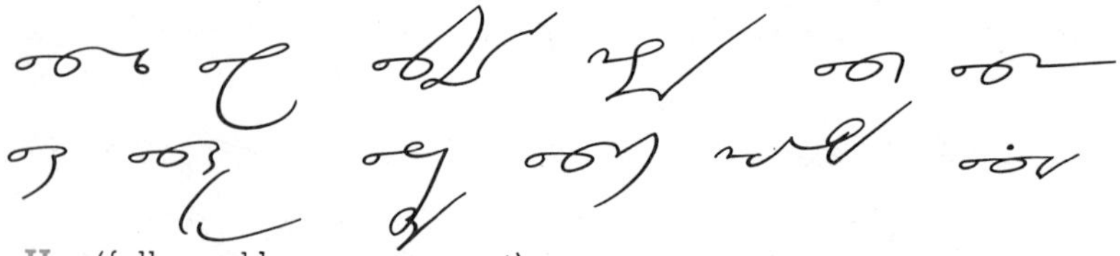

En-, In-, Un- (followed by a consonant)

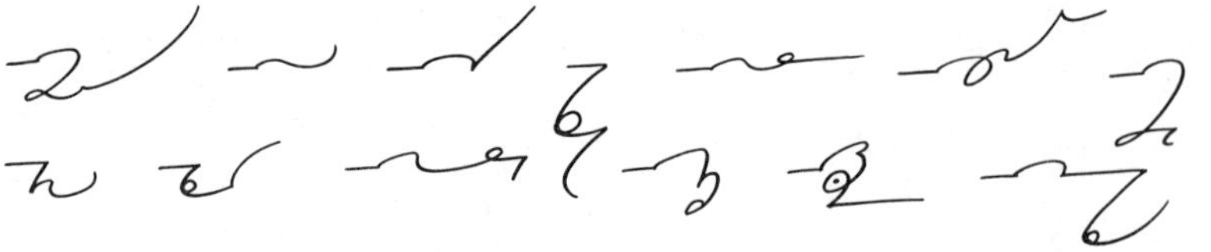

WORD ENDINGS

-lty, -lity

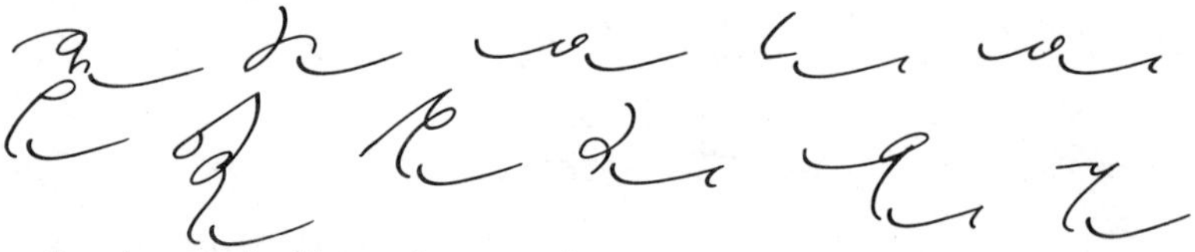

-ition, -ation (preceded by t, d, n, or m)

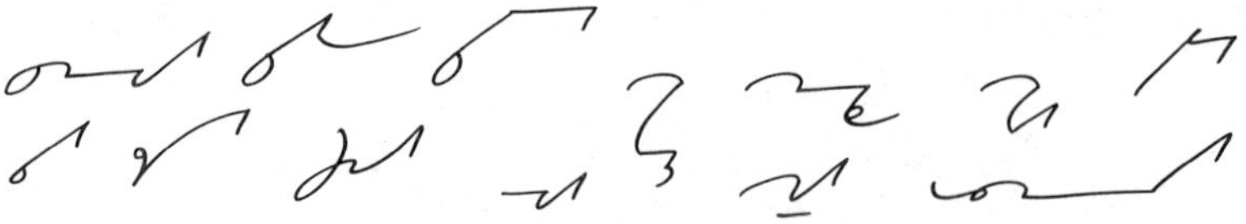

Inaccuracy, enabled, inadvertent, unaffected, inaction, enactment, enough, inaccessibility, energized, inactive, unauthorized, enhanced.

Unconfirmed, incurred, enclosed, unbearable, increment, encounter, inconveniences, insured, uncertain, inclination, unconsciously, enthusiasm, incumbent.

Casualty, faculty, loyalty, penalties, royalties, ability, advisability, disability, facilities, liabilities, nobility.

Accommodation, additional, admission, combinations, commissioner, competition, donation, edition, estimation, foundation, notation, quotation, recommendation.

TRANSCRIPTION SPEED BUILDER

30 ▸ The Acme Letter Service, 117 East Madison Street, Boston, Massachusetts 02178.

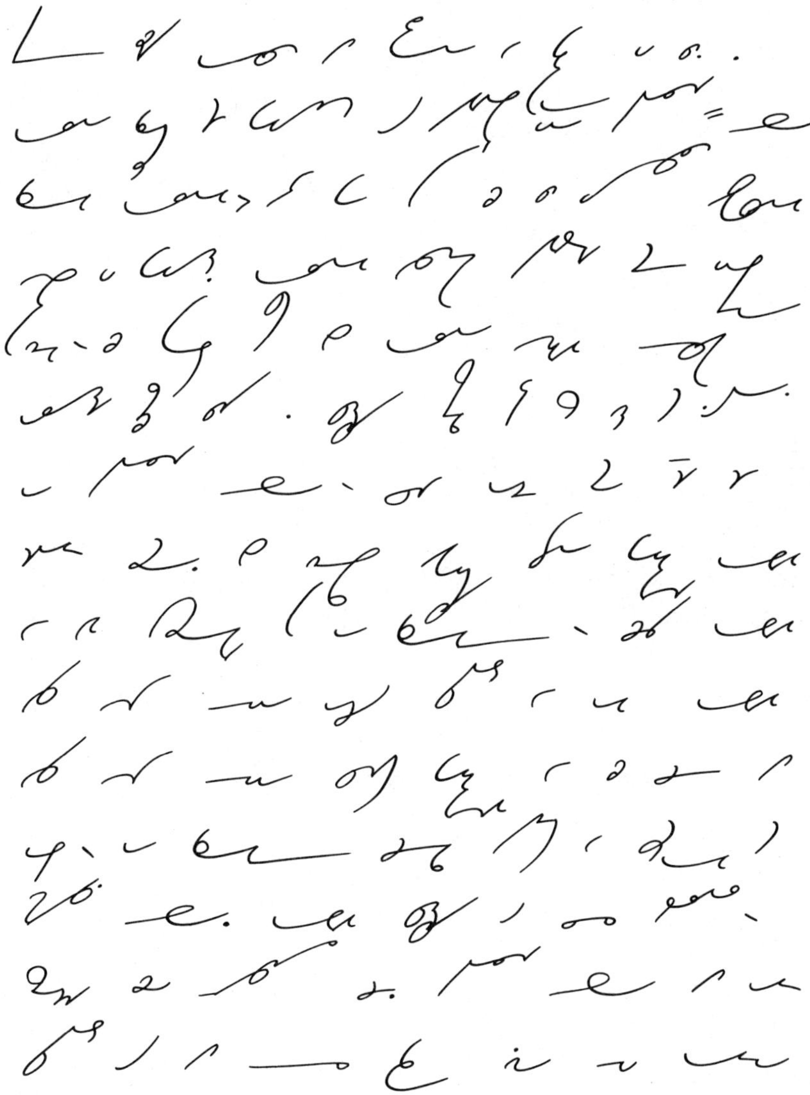

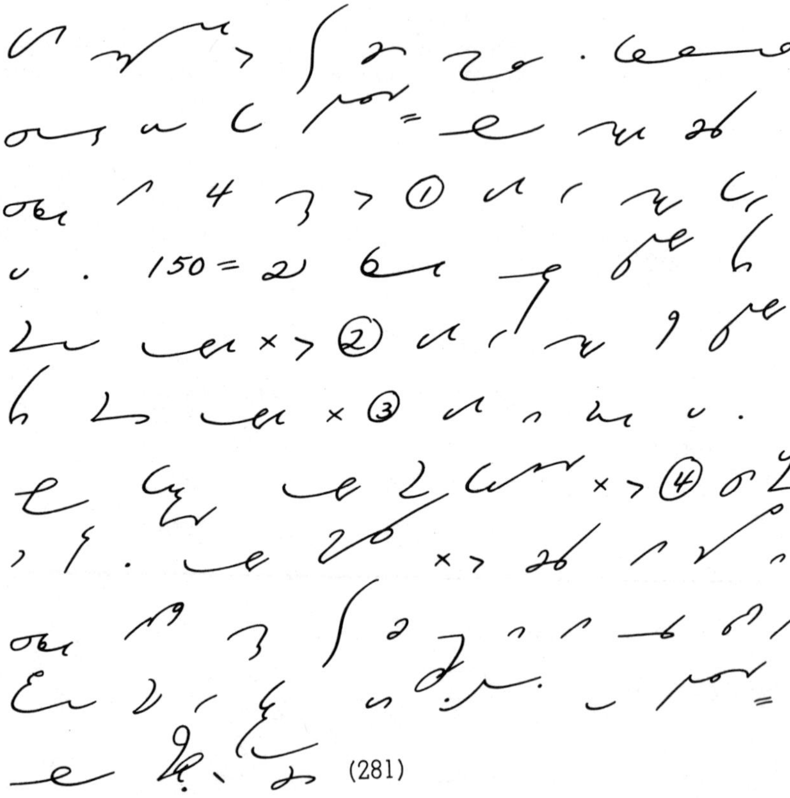

(281)

31▸ Mr. Harold K. Putnam, Office Manager, Springer Manufacturing Corporation, Wilmington, Delaware 19804.

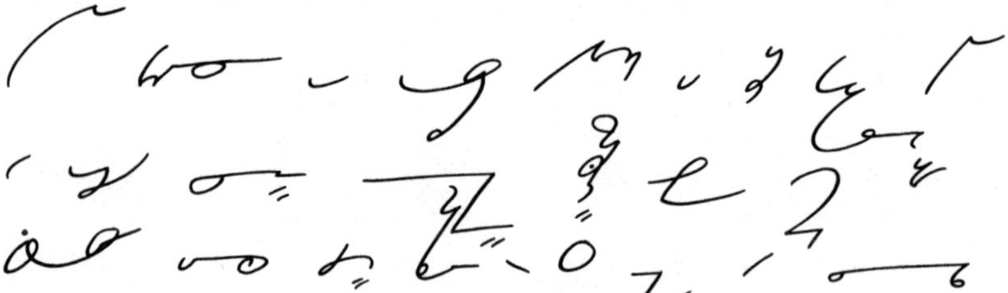

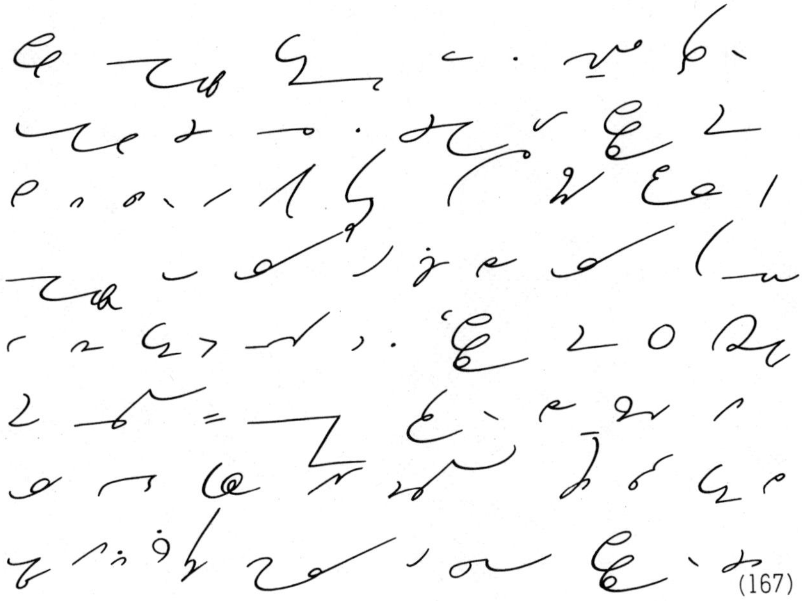

(167)

32 To: Director of Systems and Procedures.

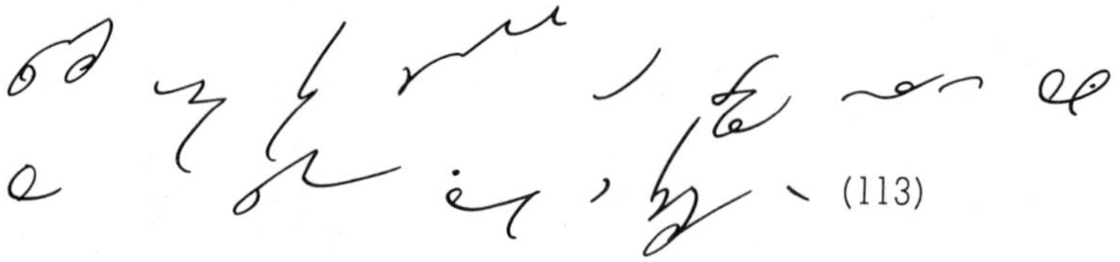 (113)

33 To: Mary Williamson, Supervisor, Women's Personnel Services.

 (174)

lesson 8

BUILDING PHRASING SKILL

PHRASE BUILDER

Drill 1

Drill 2

Drill 3

Drill 4

Drill 5

Drill 6

We can be, we can have, we can say, we cannot be, we did not, we have not been able, we mailed, we shall be able.

As you think, do you think, I do not think, I think, if they think, who think, if you think, he does not think.

He must be, he must have, I must be, I must have, she must be, we must have, you must be able.

Before us, by us, for us, gave us, give us, on us, send us, with us.

Thank you, thank you for, thank you for the, thank you for this, thank you for your, to thank you for, I thank you for, I thank you for the.

To be, has to be, to be sure, to blame, to change, to check, to choose, to promote, to ship.

TRANSCRIPTION SPEED BUILDER

34 ▸ To: Employees in Administrative Services.

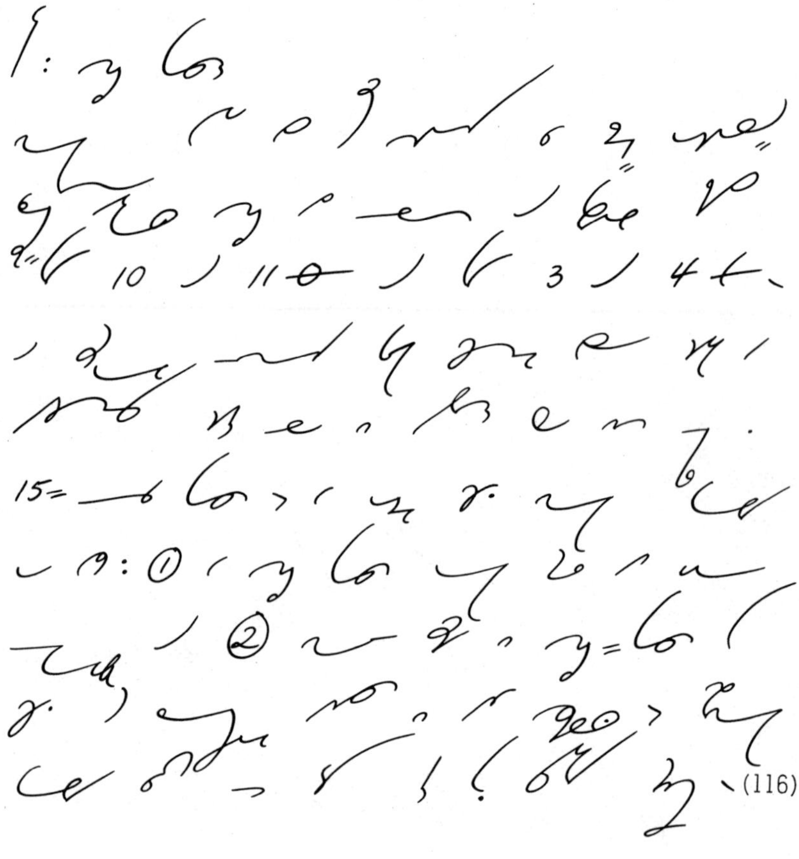

(116)

35 ▸ To: Mildred Emmons, Supervisor, Stenographic Pool.

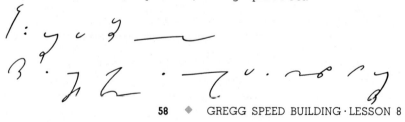

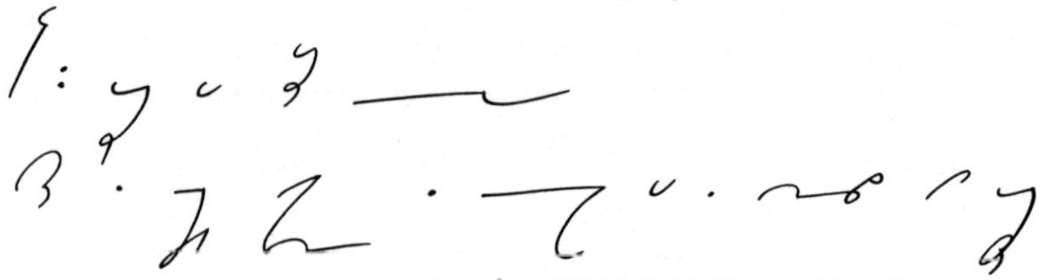

(176)

36 ▸ Mr. William Workman, Sales Manager, Consolidated Files, 220 State Street, Duluth, Minnesota 55803.

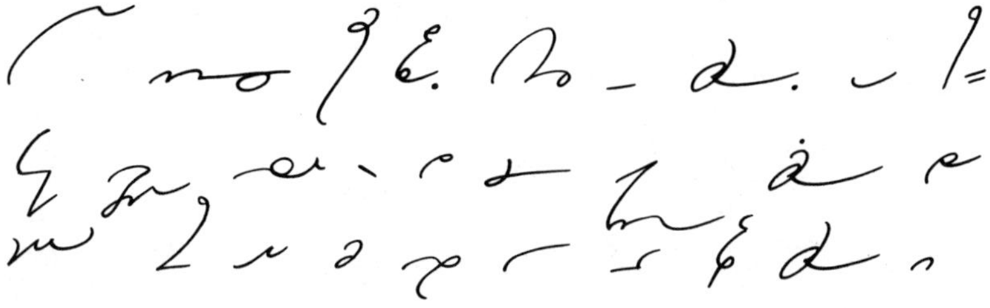

(201)

37▸ The Progressive Office Supply Company, 214 State Street, Chicago, Illinois 60610.

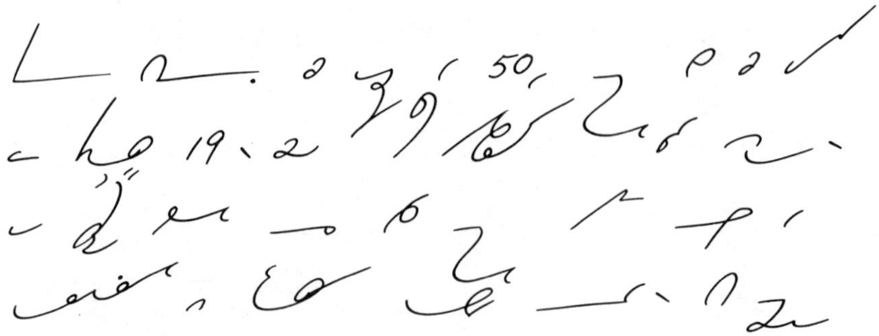

(112)

38 ▸ Reliable Typewriter Company, 4320 Madison Road, Hartford, Connecticut 06101.

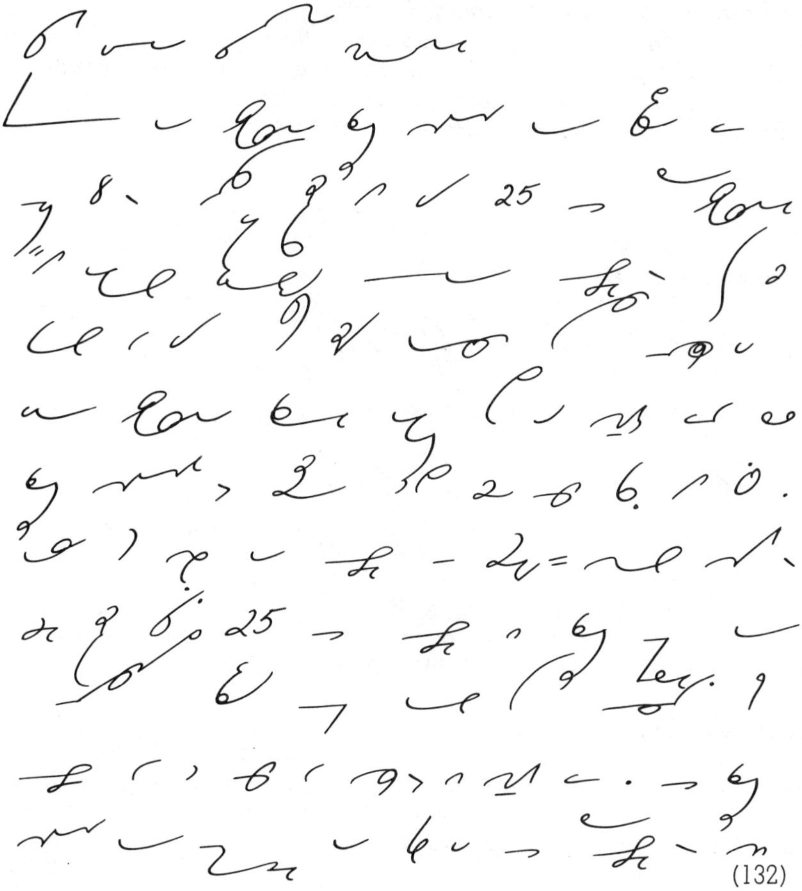

(132)

lesson

9 PROGRESSIVE SPEED BUILDING

In the fourth lesson of each unit you will find two types of progressive speed-building letters: three speed-forcing letters for one-minute dictation, and one two-minute letter for reinforcement and control.

In this lesson the one-minute speed-forcing letters will be dictated at 50, 60, and 70 words a minute. The two-minute reinforcement and control letter will be dictated at 60 words a minute.

Your first step should always be to practice the vocabulary preview that precedes the speed-forcing letters and review the specialized vocabulary presented at the beginning of each unit.

NOTE: In each letter, one diagonal indicates the end of a quarter minute's dictation; two diagonals, the end of a half minute's dictation; three diagonals, the end of a three-quarter minute's dictation; a number in parentheses, the end of a minute's dictation.

SPEED-BUILDING LETTERS

Vocabulary Preview

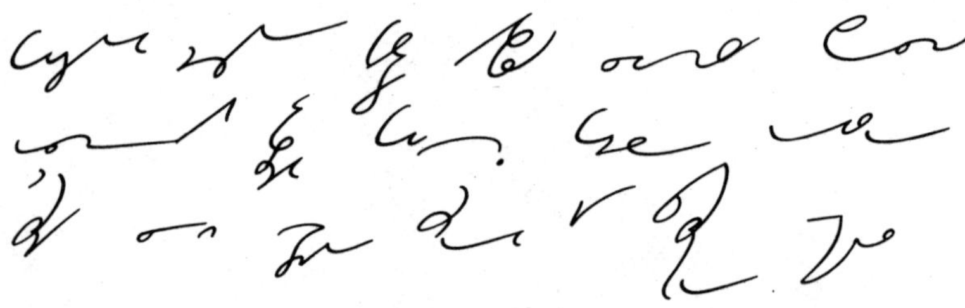

Procedures, schedule, participate, disappoint, inaugurate, applicants, recommendation, specialists, programming, personnel, loyalty, supervised, emulate, computer, facilities, shorten, advisability, inventory.

Speed Forcing

(1 Minute at 50)

39 Dear Mr. Jones: Thank you for inviting me to join the membership/ committee of the Office Procedures Association. I should like//to accept, but my schedule will not permit me to participate///in committee work.

I am sorry to have to disappoint you. Yours truly, (1)

(1 Minute at 60)

40▸ Dear Jim: I believe that we should inaugurate new procedures for testing applicants/for positions in Administrative Services. This recommendation//corresponds with suggestions outlined by almost all specialists in business management.///

Do you have suggestions for testing applicants for programming jobs? Sincerely yours, (2)

(1 Minute at 70)

41▸ Dear Bill: I have been told by Personnel that you are retiring at the end of June after thirty/years of service.

We shall all miss you, for you have been a valued member of the staff for many//years. Your loyalty to the company and your interest in those you supervised set a standard///for us to emulate.

Wherever you go, our good wishes go with you. Very truly yours, (3)

Reinforcement and Control

(2 Minutes at 60)

42▸ Mr. Lee: As you know, we automated our payroll operation as our first/computer venture. By means of our new facilities, our records have been successfully//converted to magnetic tape. We have been able, thereby, to reduce the ///personnel in that unit by 25 persons and still shorten by two days the time (1) schedule between the completion of weekly time cards and the issuance of checks./

I suggest that we now consider the advisability of using the//computer in our inventory control. Many systems men believe that this phase of///manufacturing represents the most valuable application of the computer. (2)

TRANSCRIPTION SPEED BUILDER

43▸ Professor Helen Norton, Chairman, Department of Business Education, Eastern University, Worcester, Massachusetts 01601.

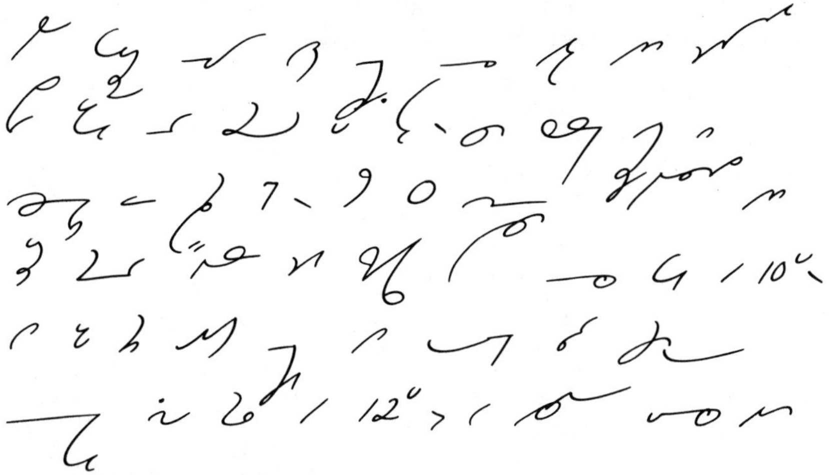

(224)

44 ▸ Mr. John Cramer, Manager, Progressive Office Employment Services, 3479 State Street, Chicago, Illinois 60626.

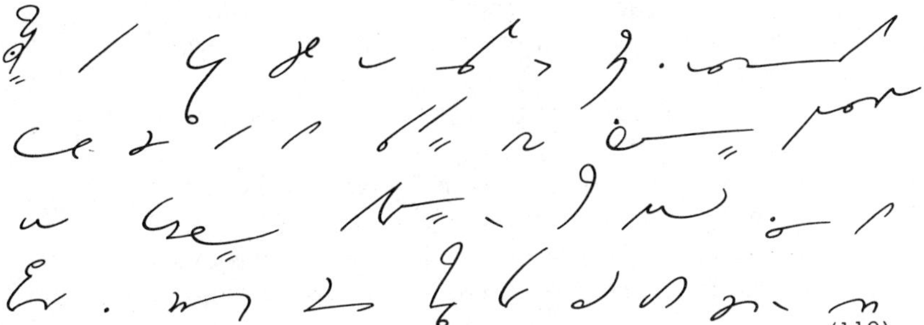

(118)

45▸ To: Edward R. Harmon, Director, Personnel Section.

(103)

TRANSCRIPTION PACER

The following letter and a letter in the fourth and fifth lesson of all the remaining units will help you to develop your ability to transcribe shorthand outlines at the typewriter at high speed and with accuracy. With this and the other transcription production exercises in this text, follow this procedure:

1▸ Read the entire letter, aloud, if possible.

2 ▸ Make a shorthand copy of the letter. Read a group of words and then write that group in your notebook as rapidly and as legibly as you can.

3 ▸ If time permits, read what you have written and insert punctuation.

4 ▸ Transcribe the letter from the printed shorthand at the typewriter as rapidly as you can.

5 ▸ Compute your transcription production rate (total words divided by elapsed time), using the 5-stroke word count that is provided.

46 ▸ Mr. Bernard Lange, World-Wide Office Equipment Company, 12
332 Randolph Street, Chicago, Illinois 60610. 21

35 47 58 69 80 90 101 111 127 138 149 163 173

lesson

BUILDING TRANSCRIPTION SPEED 10

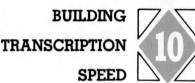

The purpose of the Sustained Speed Builder in the fifth lesson of each unit is to generate shorthand writing endurance.

The Transcription Checkpoint that concludes each unit summarizes the spelling, punctuation, and shorthand principles practiced in the four preceding lessons.

SUSTAINED SPEED BUILDER

The Sustained Speed Builder letter is dictated by Mr. Parker to Miss Alice Elizabeth Evans, supervisor of In-Service Training Department, National Products, Inc.

Practice the vocabulary preview, and then see whether you can sustain your reinforcement and control speed.

NOTE: Each small raised number represents 20 standard words.

Vocabulary Preview

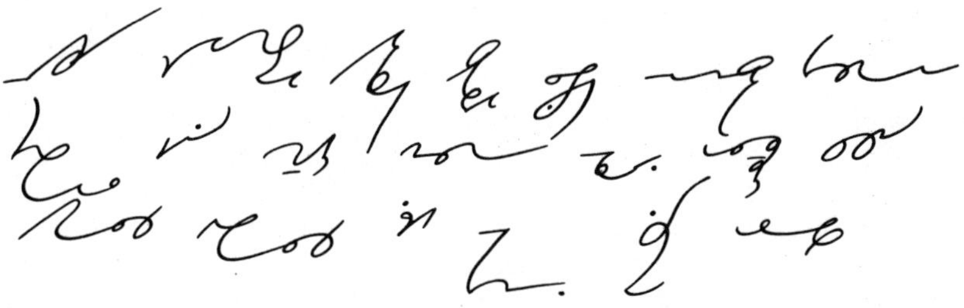

Undecided, stenographers, discharge, typists, initiative, unrecognizable, peculiar, vocabulary, shorthand, quotations, unequal, inserting, requisitions, account, duplicate, triplicate, hesitation, unbecoming, behavior, realization.

Speed Builder

47 Miss Alice Elizabeth Evans, Supervisor, In-Service Training Department.

Dear Miss Evans: Here are my suggestions for the development of training materials for secretarial[1] trainees.

Your best source of material is the files of the sections in which the trainees will eventually[2] work. Choosing appropriate items that are typical examples of work performed is difficult; and[3] at best, the selection is an arbitrary one. In any event, Miss Evans, I have chosen four kinds of[4] Administrative Services records for you to consider.

1. Correspondence dictated to secretaries[5] during the routine discharge of their duties.

2. Forms that our stenographers and clerical personnel[6] regularly process.

3. Form letters that serve as models when office workers compose replies to routine letters[7] on their own initiative.

4. Case problems involving personnel relations.

I would recommend that you[8] carefully edit all the correspondence before it is reproduced for trainee use. For instance, it might be[9] advisable to use fictitious names and to modify any statement that might reflect company action[10] in an unfavorable light, especially to a partially informed reader.

These letters and memorandums[11] are an excellent source of words for spelling and for shorthand theory drills. They also contain many examples[12] of superb punctuation usage that could be abstracted for use as punctuation reviews. It also[13] occurred to me that trainees will learn from these letters not only the vocabulary of our business but[14] also something about the methods used throughout the company to handle a number of business problems.[15]

Perhaps this kind of office correspondence could be used as a device to improve the trainee's rate of transcription.[16] Frankly, Miss Evans, too many of our secretaries take dictation at a rapid rate and then expend[17] a disproportionate amount of time attempting to transcribe their shorthand into usable typewritten copy.[18] Perhaps you can help secretarial trainees to become time-and-motion conscious with an appropriate[19] kind of transcription drill. Last but not least, you can use the letters as production copy to improve typewriting[20] speed.

The sample business forms are those that are used throughout the company – purchase requisitions, expense account forms,[21] telephone message forms, and stock requisitions. The variety of sizes will give the trainees valuable[22] practice in insertion, alignment, and making corrections at the typewriter, especially when carbon[23] packs are involved. When carbon packs are not provided, you may wish to prepare multiple copies of these forms so[24] that trainees will get needed experience in preparing duplicate or triplicate copies.

Form letters[25] comprise about 5 percent of our correspondence load.

Those selected will give your trainees practice in composing[26] responses to routine inquiries.

The case problems might be used for group discussions in which personnel policies[27] and problems are explored. Impersonal discussion of company practices and desirable[28] employee behavior might result in a more comprehensive grasp of employee-employer procedures.

I hope[29], Miss Evans, that these suggestions will be useful to you. Best wishes for an outstanding program. Sincerely yours,[30] (600)

TRANSCRIPTION CHECKPOINT

The purpose of the Transcription Checkpoint in the fifth lesson of each unit is to review many of the transcription pointers, the shorthand theory, and the terminology presented in the four previous lessons.

Practice reading and writing the letter to Mr. Howard. Review the spelling and punctuation pointers. Your instructor will either dictate the letter and ask you to transcribe from your shorthand notes or instruct you to transcribe directly from the text. Your efforts will be judged for correctness of transcript and for rate of transcription.

48 Mr. William C. Howard, Office Manager, Bedford Manufacturing Corporation, 4352 Washington Avenue, Bedford, Massachusetts 01730. 12 24 26

42 52 66 78 93 105 118 129 140

155
172
182
195
208
219
236
246
258
269
281
294
309
323
334
344
357
368
377

390
411
425
435
450
459
470
482
496
506
519
529
543

No doubt you are familiar with various credit plans offered by companies, such as the 30-day payment plan or the revolving payment plan. Have you ever stopped to think, however, about the efficient techniques and practices on which credit is established and maintained?

Before goods or services can be sold on credit, the purchaser must be approved by the credit manager. His ability to pay and his record of prompt payment must be established before he will be granted credit. The credit manager must also dictate an assortment of letters to collect past-due accounts and to discontinue credit privileges.

unit 3

CREDIT AND COLLECTIONS

Secretarial Assignment

In this unit you are secretary to Harold C. Poling, manager of Credit and Collections. All letters are signed by him over his title, Credit Manager.

SPECIALIZED TERMINOLOGY

An understanding of the credit and collection terms in the letters dictated by Mr. Poling will add to your understanding of credit and collection procedures.

Cash Flow • Movement of cash from the buyer to the seller (cash receipts) and from the seller to his creditors (cash payments).

Collection-Letter Series • Sequence of letters to credit customers at various stages of delinquency—reminder, payment plan, suspension of credit, and decisive action.

Computerized "One Write" Accounting • Placement of an order on paper tape, punched cards, or magnetic tape. Once written, information need not be retyped for shipping papers, invoices, and statements.

Cycle Billing • Billing groups of customers at predetermined intervals during the month according to alphabetic assignments instead of billing at the end of the calendar month.

Purchase Discounts • Cash discounts offered as an inducement for the prompt payment of bills.

Downtime • Time that equipment is out of use for maintenance and repairs.

Time Cycle for Credit Control • Schedule for controlling credit policy by showing delinquent customers how they can pay immediately rather than by dunning and threatening them.

SPELLING AND TRANSCRIPTION PRACTICE

This list contains 21 words that appear frequently in business letters.

accidentally	efficient	jeopardize
acknowledgment	exorbitant	maintenance
attorneys	explanation	occasionally
bookkeeper	extension	privilege
conscientious	financial	reimburse
courteous	incidentally	sizable
disastrous	indispensable	welfare

Transcribe the following sentences, preferably at the typewriter, until you master the spelling of the words that appear in the word list.

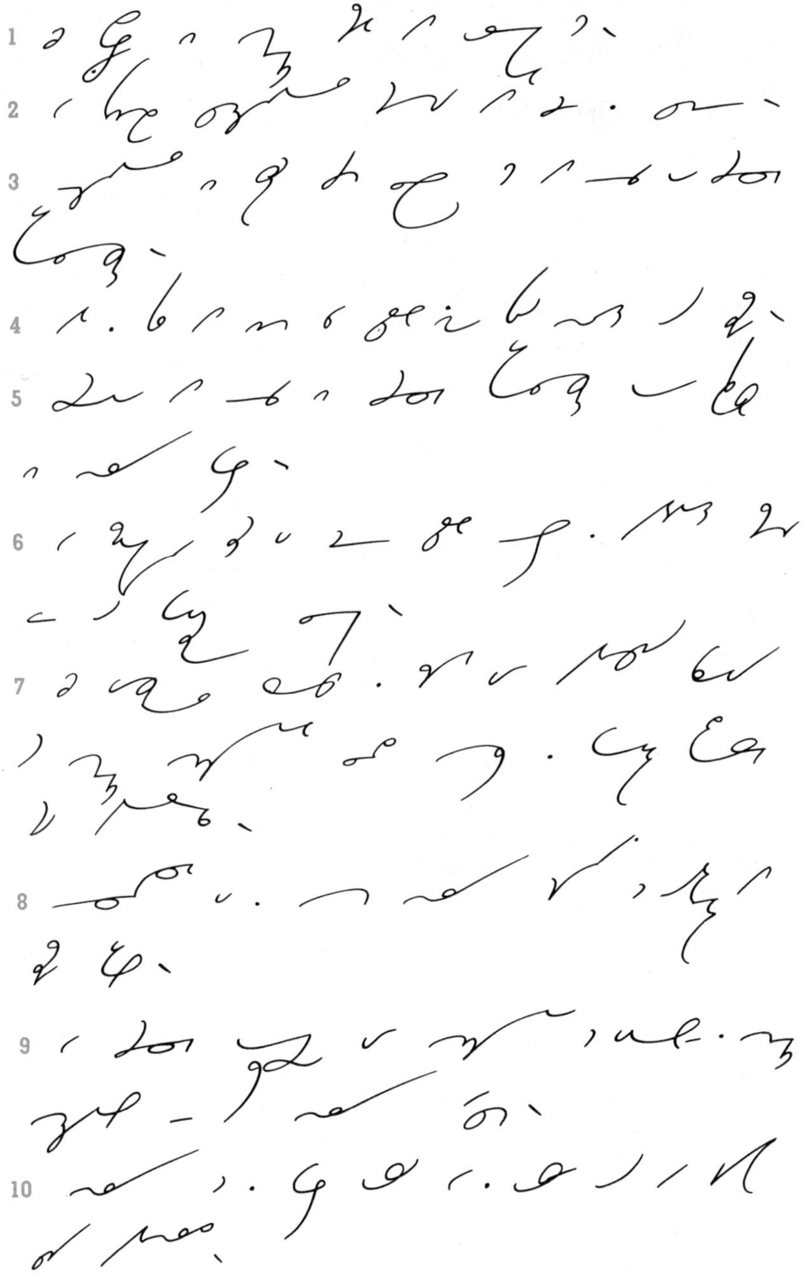

lesson 11

BUILDING TRANSCRIPTION QUALITY

TRANSCRIPTION POINTERS

Uses of the Comma

1 Use the comma to separate an introductory adverbial clause from the rest of the sentence.

If you have finished the report, leave it with the secretary.

If the adverbial clause follows the main clause and is restrictive, do not use the comma.

Leave the report with the secretary when you have finished it.

2 When two or more adjectives modify a noun, a comma separates the adjectives if each one modifies the noun alone. *Test:* If the word *and* can be inserted between the adjectives and if either adjective might occur first without changing the meaning, use the comma.

This is a logical, clear presentation of the advantages of the plan.

If, however, the second adjective and the noun form a unit that is modified by the first adjective, no comma is used.

He presented the difficult business report.

Check your understanding of comma usage by transcribing the following sentences, preferably at the typewriter.

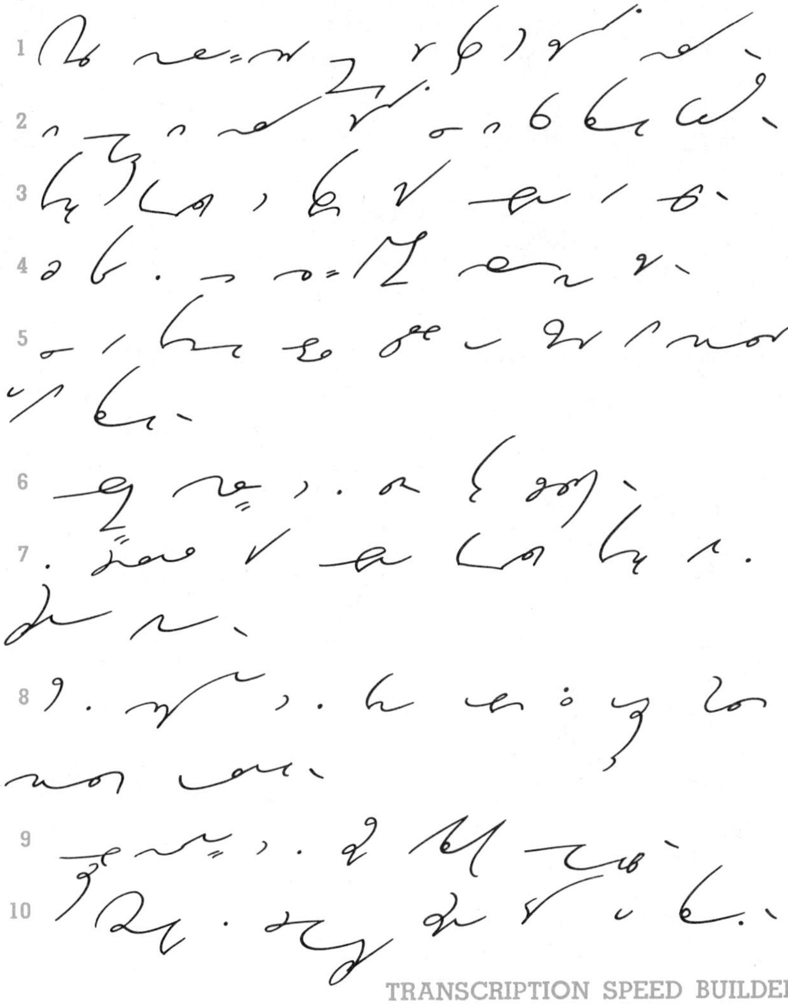

TRANSCRIPTION SPEED BUILDER

49 ▸ Mr. Harry Morris, President, The Morris Company, 144 Grand Avenue, Kansas City, Missouri 64100.

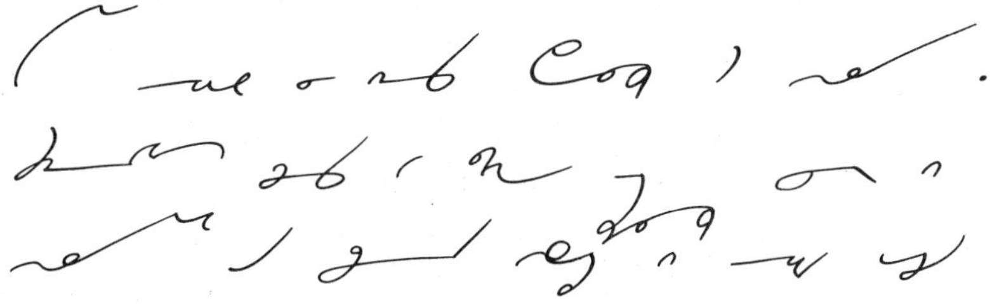

(247)

50▸ The Brownlee Company, Box 614, Tulsa, Oklahoma 74122.

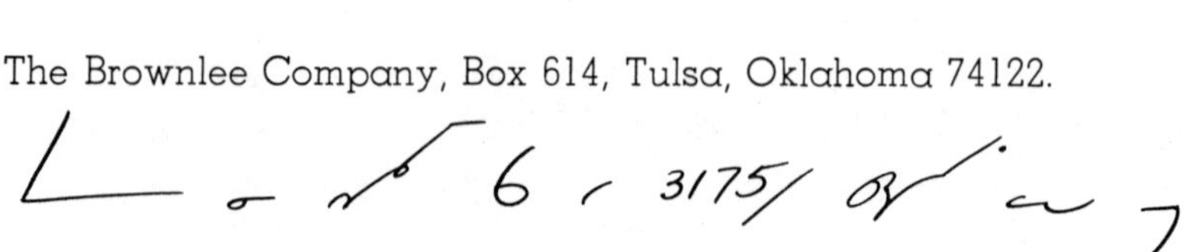

(231)

51▸ Mr. Edward Milbank, Milbank Mercantile Company, Bound Brook, New Jersey 08805.

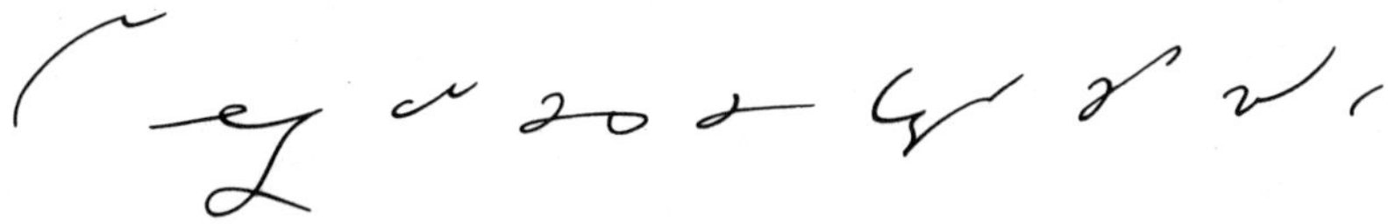

348

(237)

lesson

MASTERING SHORTHAND THEORY 12

WORD BEGINNINGS

Inter-, Intr-

Enter-, Entr-

Dis-, Des-

WORD ENDINGS

-cal, -cle

-ings

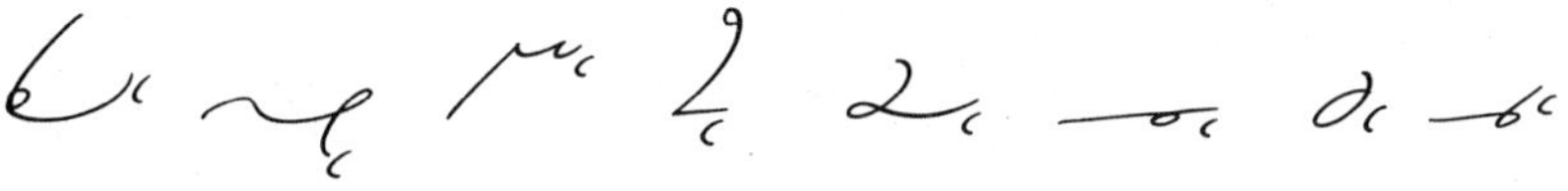

Interested, interchangeable, international, internally, interpretation, interruption, interval, interview, introduction, introspection, introvert, intrusion, intrusive.

Entertainingly, enterprising, entered, unenterprising, entrance, entrant, entertainment.

Dishonesty, discount, disenchanted, disturbed, despair, describe, destiny.

Geographical, logical, political, practically, pinnacle, theoretically, critical.

Buildings, clippings, drawings, evenings, feelings, meanings, sayings, meetings.

52 Ace Stop and Save, 161 Locust Street, Bowling Green, Ohio 43401.

(105)

53 The Goodman Manufacturing Company, 1411 Tenth Avenue, Amarillo, Texas 79104.

(144)

54 Mr. Todd F. Bradford, Bradford-Heaton, Inc., 3 East Willow Street, Bowling Green, Ohio 43402.

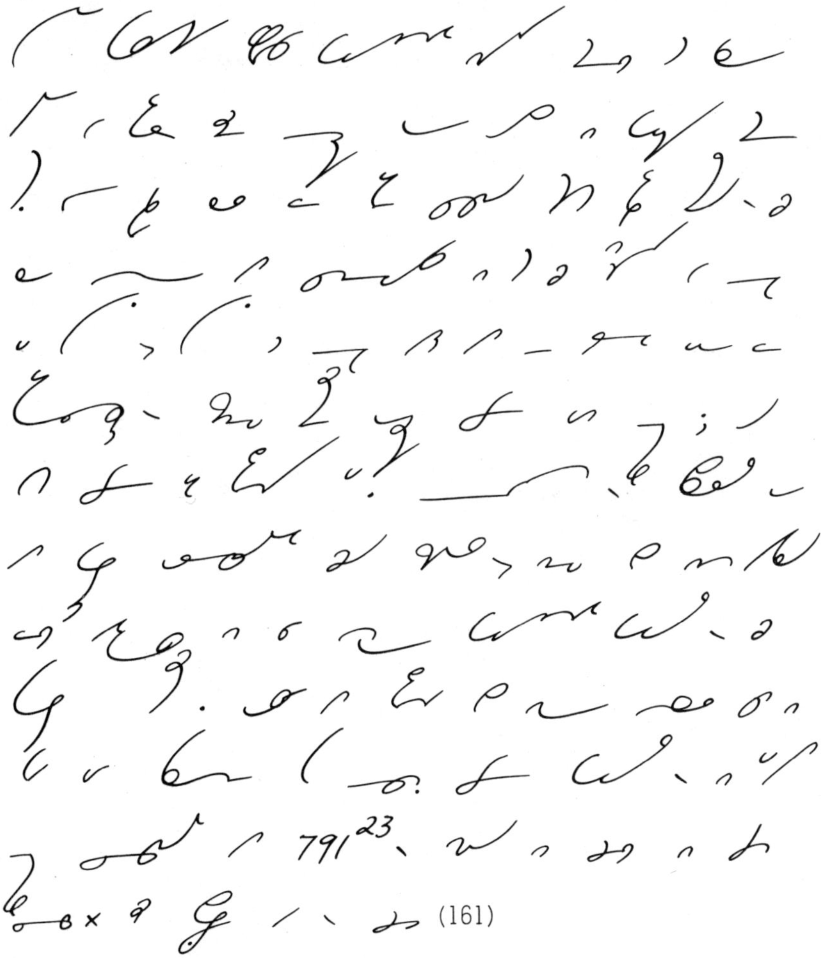

(161)

55 Mr. George H. Martin, Executive Vice-President, Martin-Simpson Company, Box 404, Trenton, New Jersey 08605.

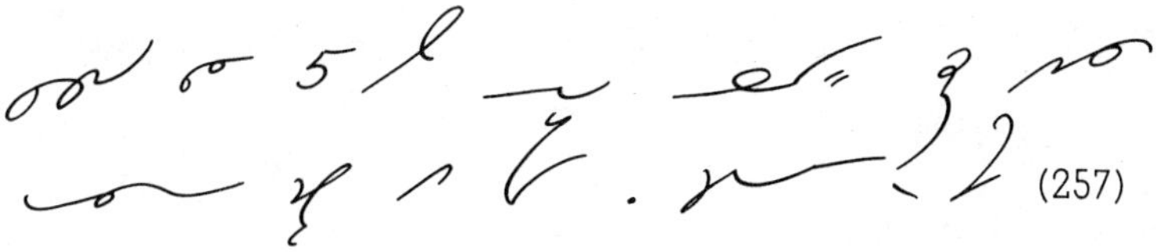
(257)

56 Mr. James C. Perry, Manager, The Associated Shops, 1411 Jefferson Street, Elgin, Illinois 60122.

(143)

lesson 13

BUILDING PHRASING SKILL

PHRASE BUILDER

Drill 1

Drill 2

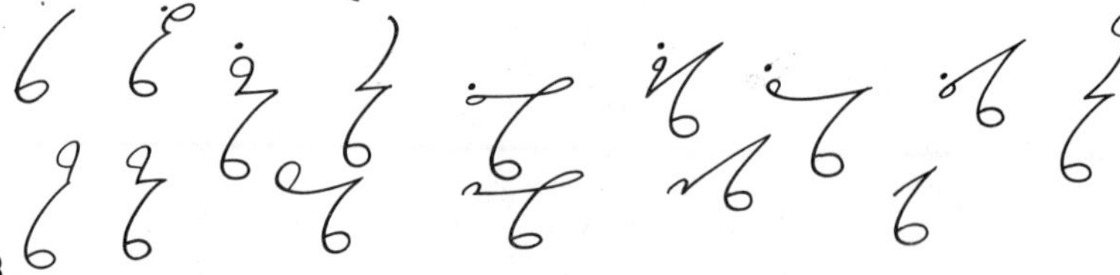

Drill 3

Drill 4

Drill 5

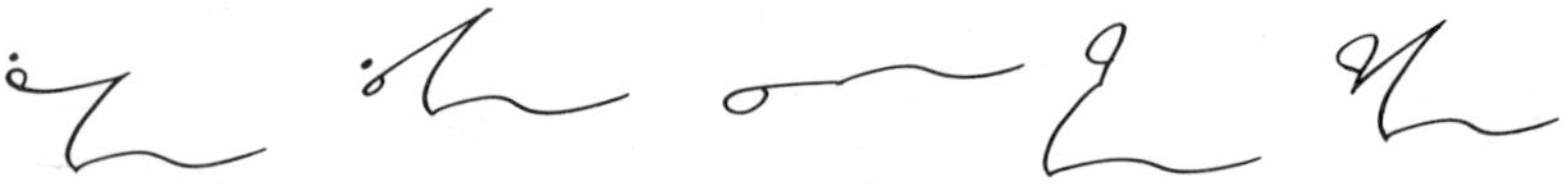

Could have been, had not been, has been, having been, I have been, should have been, had been, it has been, there has been, we have been.

Be able, has been able, has not been able, have not been able, he may be able, he should be able, he will be able, he would be able, I have not been able, I shall be able, I shall not be able, I will be able, you may be able, you would be able, to be able.

As they, as they are, before they, if they, if they are, if they are not, they may be, if they can.

He was, he wasn't, I was, if it wasn't, that it was, there was, this was the, which was.

He will be glad, he would be glad, I am glad, I shall be glad, I should be glad.

57 ▸ Memo to: Henry D. Walters, Vice-President—Finance.

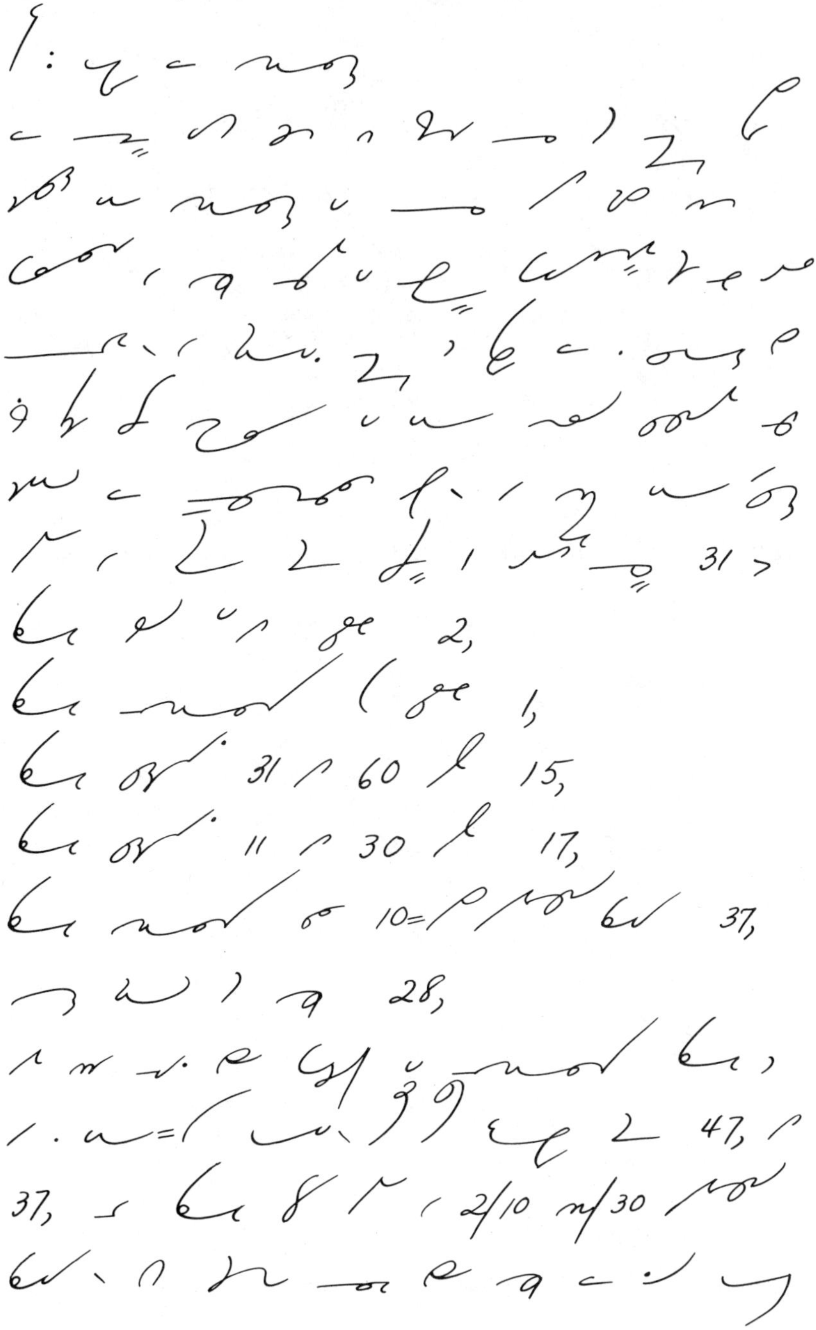

(274)

58 ▸ Memo to: John Parker, Director of Administrative Services.

(283)

59▸ Mr. Willard M. Ewing, Credit Manager, The Standard Chemical Company, 704 West Avenue, Milwaukee, Wisconsin 53289.

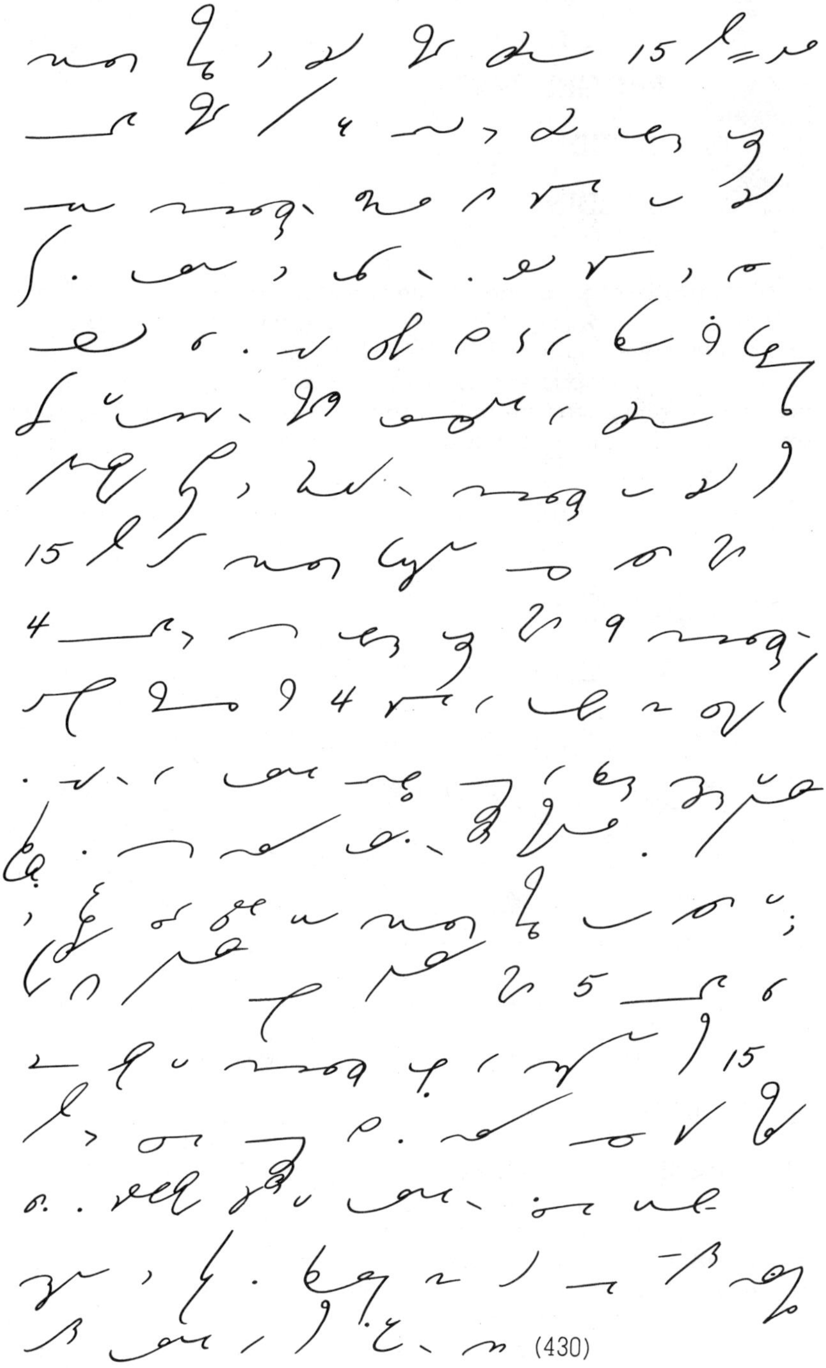

(430)

lesson 14

PROGRESSIVE SPEED BUILDING

In this lesson the one-minute speed-forcing letters are counted progressively at 60, 70, and 80 words a minute; the two-minute reinforcement and control letter is counted at 70 words a minute.

Your first step is to practice the vocabulary preview that precedes the speed-forcing practice and to review the specialized vocabulary presented at the beginning of this unit.

SPEED-BUILDING LETTERS

Vocabulary Preview

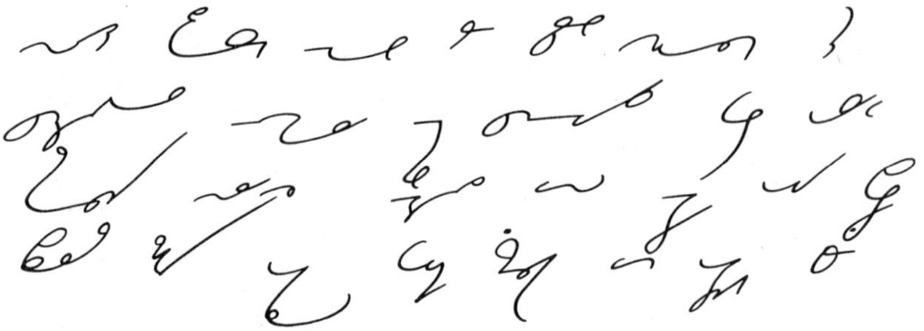

Courteous, explanation, unless, turn, attorneys, collection, force, accidentally, incomplete, invoice, accommodate, privilege, ratings, evaluated, critically, insistently, occurred, unpaid, reorder, appreciate, apparently, exhausted, rebuild, profit, has not yet been, of course, reputation, why not.

Speed Forcing

(1 Minute at 60)

60▸ Dear Mr. Lewis: We have tried to collect your long-overdue account through a/series of courteous letters; yet we have no explanation of the reasons you can't//pay.

Unless we receive your check by November 9, we shall turn the account over///to our attorneys for collection. Please don't force us to take this action. Yours truly, (1)

(1 Minute at 70)

61▸ Gentlemen: Did we accidentally do something wrong by either shipping an incomplete order/or filing an incorrect invoice?

If not, we are wondering why you have not replied to our//two requests for payment of our bill. We accommodated you by extending this credit, and///we think it only fair that you send us your check immediately.

Don't you agree? Sincerely yours, (2)

(1 Minute at 80)

62▸ Gentlemen: When you asked us for the privilege of handling your purchases on credit, we checked your ratings/and evaluated your earnings reports critically. We labeled you an excellent risk.

During the three//years you have used your account, you have maintained a consistently good record for prompt payment..

What has occurred? Your///January 10 invoice has remained unpaid for two months, and we have had no explanation. Cordially yours, (3)

Reinforcement and Control

(2 Minutes at 70)

63▸ Dear Mr. Lundberg: Your reorder for $542 worth of merchandise from/NATIONAL PRODUCTS has just reached my desk. We appreciate it.

The fact that your first supply is// apparently exhausted and that you need to rebuild your inventory tells us that sales must be///running high for our merchandise and that you must be making a good profit on it. Our accountant (1) tells me that payment for your first order has not yet been received, although it is 45 days/past due.

You know, of course, the value of a good credit reputation and the difficulty of//regaining a high rating once it has been lost. Why not send us your check for $350///today? If you take this action, you will enable us to rush your order to you. Cordially yours (2)

TRANSCRIPTION SPEED BUILDER

64▸ Memo to: Mr. Philip Irwin, Manager.

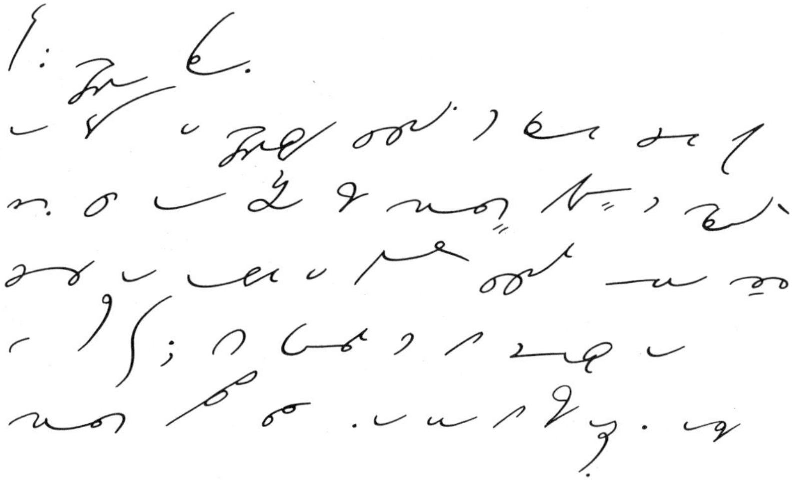

(190)

65 ▸ Mr. Donald Adams, The Adams Shoppe, Winchester Road, Mount Vernon, New York 10551.

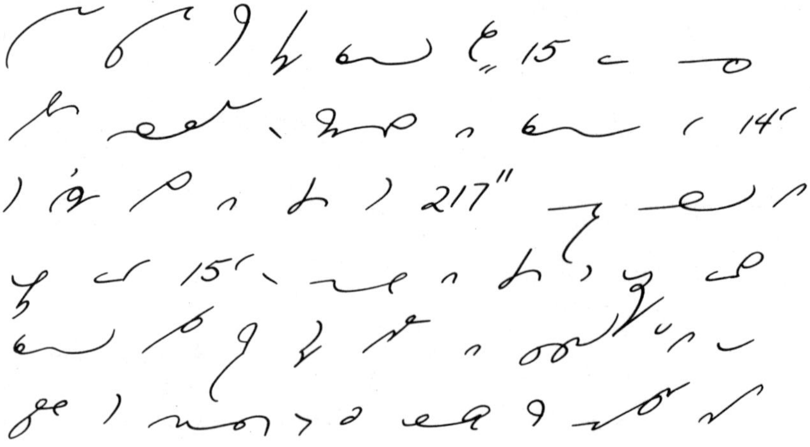

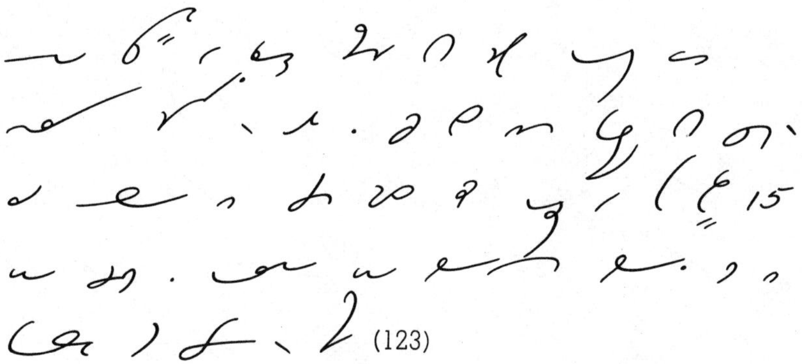

66 ▸ Mr. Harry R. Mason, Mason & Brown, 145 Shelton Drive, Wilmington, Delaware 19814.

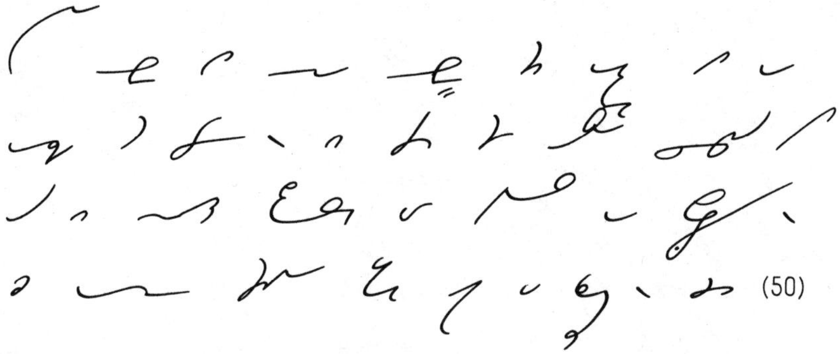

67 ▸ Mr. Walter C. Edgar, Edgar Retail Shop, Bowden Square, Portland, Maine 04110.

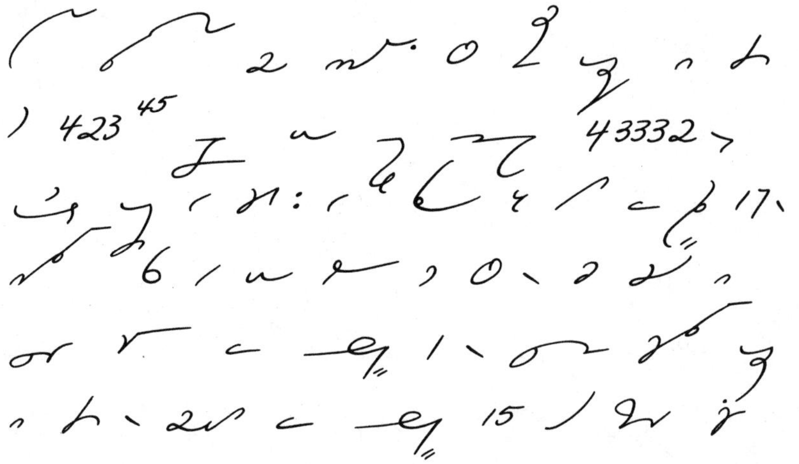

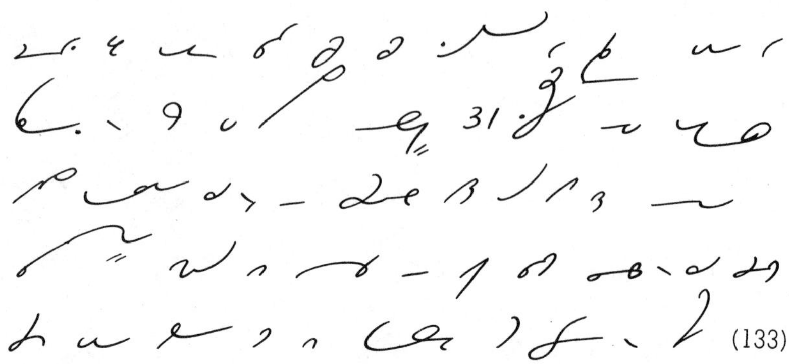

(133)

TRANSCRIPTION PACER

68▸ Alfred Williams, Inc., Fairfield Shopping Center, Phoenix, Arizona 85013. 13 15

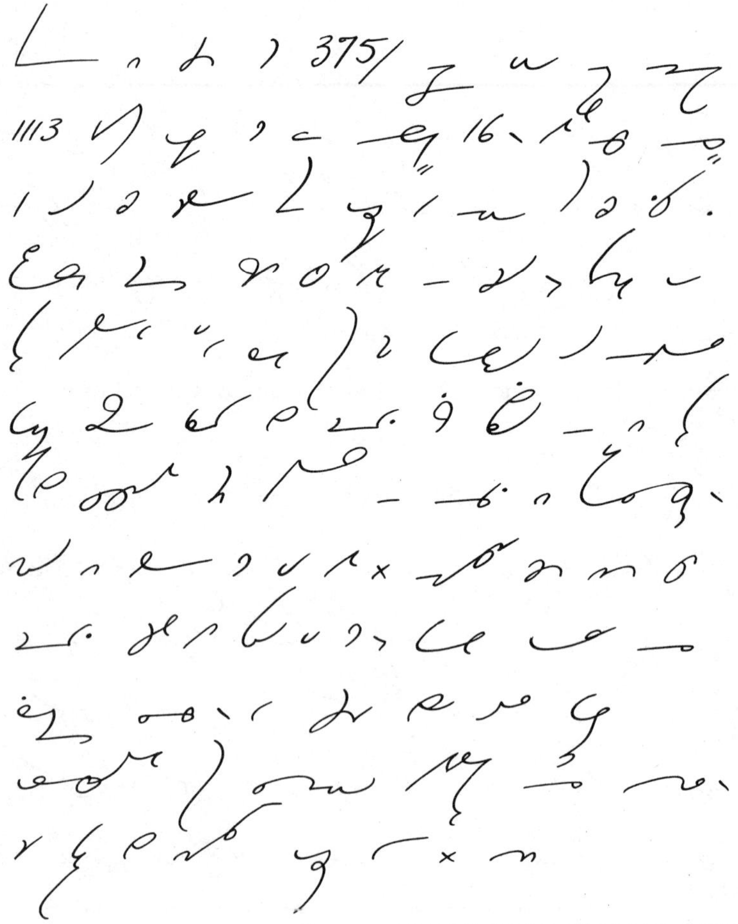

28
39
50
63
77
91
103
114
125
137
147
160

lesson 15

BUILDING TRANSCRIPTION SPEED

SUSTAINED SPEED BUILDER

Mr. Poling dictated the sustained speed builder memorandum to be sent to Kenneth Crowley, controller, National Products, Inc.

Practice the following vocabulary preview, and then see how well you can sustain your reinforcement and control speed.

Vocabulary Preview

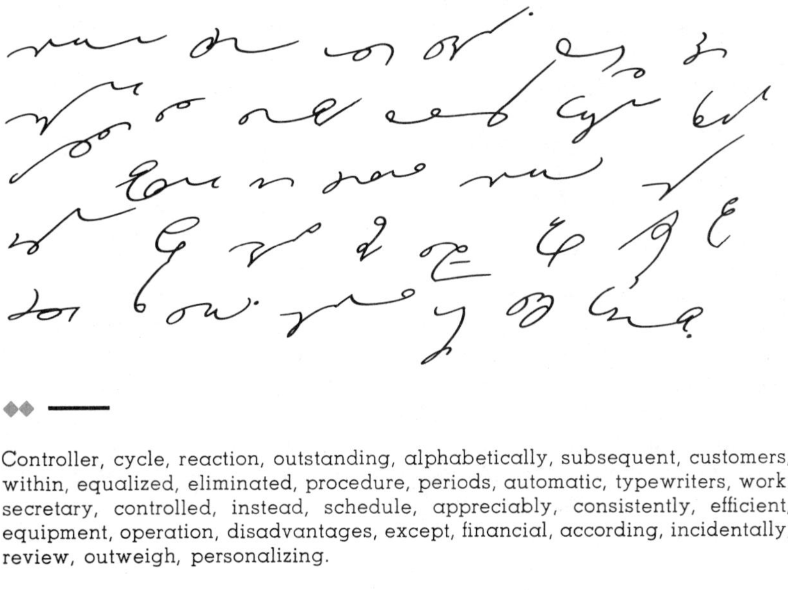

Controller, cycle, reaction, outstanding, alphabetically, subsequent, customers, within, equalized, eliminated, procedure, periods, automatic, typewriters, work, secretary, controlled, instead, schedule, appreciably, consistently, efficient, equipment, operation, disadvantages, except, financial, according, incidentally, review, outweigh, personalizing.

Speed Builder

69 To: Kenneth Crowley, Controller, Subject: Cycle Billing.

I have your memorandum of September 12, asking for my reaction to the proposal for adopting[1] cycle billing. Instead of mailing all statements on the first of the month, you suggest that we divide the list of[2] outstanding accounts into four groups alphabetically. Every Tuesday the statements for one of the four[3] groups would be mailed, and on the subsequent Tuesday the next alphabetic list of customers would be billed. Within[4] the cycle of a month all bills would be mailed, one-fourth each week.

As I see it, the advantages are these:

1. The[5] work of the billing clerks would be equalized, and present end-of-the-month peak loads would be eliminated. If[6] we adopt this procedure, we could reduce the number of clerks by two.

2. The work in my department would also[7] be equalized. Instead of sending collection letters on the first and fifteenth of the month, we would send them[8] at the end of 15- and 30-day periods of indebtedness, thus spreading work over the entire[9] month.

3. There would be a controlled flow of cash into National Products. Instead of receiving payments following[10] the old billing schedule, we would take in money on an everyday basis from all credit customers,[11] not just from those taking their discounts. This might appreciably reduce the amount of cash we would have to[12] borrow on short-term loans in order to take advantage of our own discounts.

4. We could make more efficient use[13] of our billing equipment. It would be in operation every day, even at night if we go on a[14] three-shift schedule of office work. The only time that our billing equipment would be out of operation[15] would be during downtime, while maintenance checks are being made.

I see only two disadvantages to cycle[16] billing:

1. Customers expect their bills on the first of the month, and they may have made their financial plans to[17] provide cash for paying according to this schedule. Making a change would require explanations and,[18] incidentally, reeducation of our credit customers.

2. More time would be required for scheduling[19] due dates of outstanding accounts. Review would be on a daily basis instead of twice a month.

In my opinion,[20] Mr. Crowley, the advantages of cycle billing far outweigh the disadvantages. Therefore, I[21] recommend that we adopt this procedure on December 1. That will give me time to work out with John Parker our[22] plan for using the automatic typewriters for routine collection letters. It would also give me an[23] opportunity to send a letter of explanation of the new system to our complete list of charge[24] customers.

Does this suggestion seem reasonable to you? (490)

TRANSCRIPTION CHECKPOINT

70▸ Mr. William Metzler, Metzler Variety Store, Meadowlark Shopping Center, Greeley, Colorado 80630.

(86)

TRANSCRIPTION PACER

71▸ Mr. Elmer L. Dewitt, Dewitt Manufacturing Company, 141 East 13
Chapel Street, Harrison, New Jersey 07029. 21

34
45
61
70
84
93

104
116
125
137
149
165
176
186
195
205
218
232
245
257
271
284
297
308
318

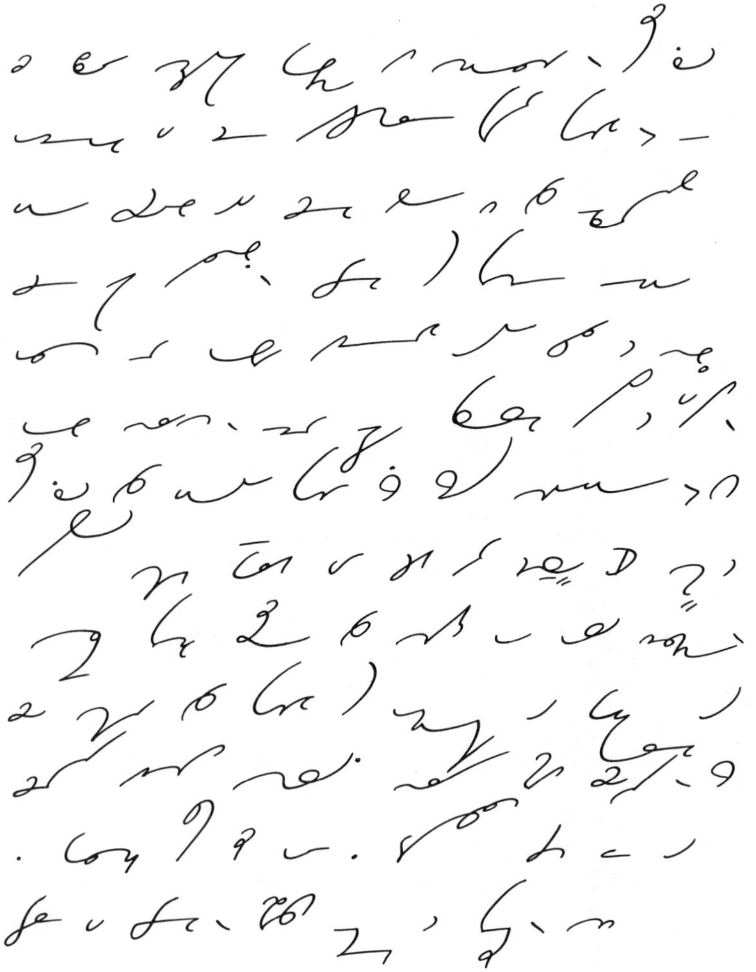

330
341
353
363
377
389
402
419
431
445
456
468
485

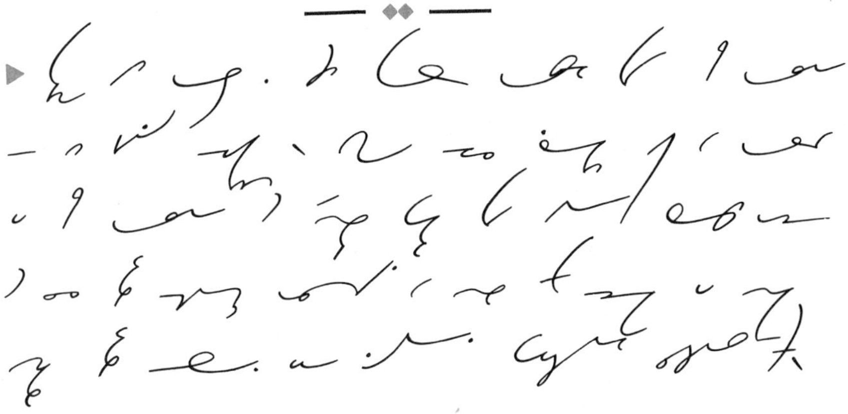

How would you respond if you were asked, "What is the most important resource a business possesses"? You might say material, equipment, and machines, for they are used to produce the goods or services that ultimately satisfy our economic needs and wants. However, they can be readily replaced or insured against loss. Perhaps you would name management, for it is an expression of all that is done to plan, organize, direct, and control the operation of a business. In the final analysis, however, it is people who make or break management.

The Personnel Department, usually consisting of a personnel manager and a staff of assistants, sees to it that a business obtains qualified people and that they are motivated favorably, develop their abilities, and find satisfaction in their jobs.

unit 4

PERSONNEL

Secretarial Assignment

In this unit you will take the dictation of Edward R. Harmon, director of personnel, National Products, Inc. All letters are signed by him over his title, Director, Personnel Department.

SPECIALIZED TERMINOLOGY

In transcribing Mr. Harmon's dictation, you will encounter the following terms:

Fringe Benefits • Advantages, such as group insurance, group hospitalization, retirement income payments, discounts on purchases, and loans, provided for employees by forward-looking companies.

Incentive Plan • Wage-payment plan that is designed to reward the worker with added compensation for exceptional performance.

Employee Motivation • Techniques, such as communication, suggestion systems, and merit ratings, that encourage employees to perform at more productive levels.

Employee Test • Interest, knowledge, special aptitude, and performance tests administered to workers to obtain an index of the degree of qualification for job selection and placement.

In-Service Training • Organized courses taught on the premises either by an employee or by an outside specialist to increase employees' skill and competence.

Performance Rating (Merit Rating) • The rating of an employee by systematic evaluation of his proficiency in his job. It usually involves a discussion between an employee and his supervisor in an attempt to define the employee's self-development and job objectives and to outline the means to achieve them.

Probationary Period • Trial period during which the employer decides whether to give a new employee a permanent position.

Stock-Purchase Plan • Type of fringe benefit that permits employees to purchase company stock at reduced rates.

Tuition Reimbursement • Plan for repaying employee tuition costs for successful completion of company-approved study at an accredited college or school.

SPELLING AND TRANSCRIPTION PRACTICE

This list contains 24 words that appear frequently in business letters:

absence	attendance	consensus
acceptable	career	eligible
advertisement	competitive	familiar

gauge	misspell	unanimous
initiative	optimistic	versatile
liaison	pamphlet	vicinity
mediocre	separate	vying
miscellaneous	supersede	wholly

Transcribe the following sentences, preferably at the typewriter, until you master the spelling of the words that appear in the word list above.

Lesson 16

BUILDING TRANSCRIPTION QUALITY

TRANSCRIPTION POINTERS

Uses of the Comma *(Continued)*

1 Use the comma to separate two independent clauses that are joined by a coordinate conjunction.

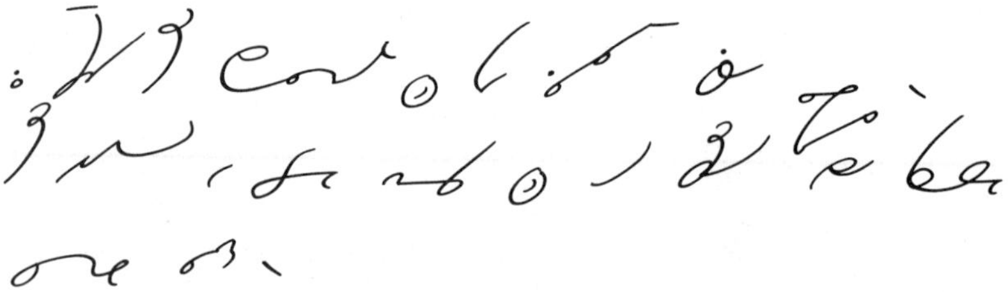

He interviewed several applicants, but he did not hire anybody.
We have totaled the payments you made, and we find that our balance agrees with yours.

Do not use a comma between two verbs comprising a compound predicate. Likewise, do not use a comma between two parts of a compound subject, compound object, or other compound construction.

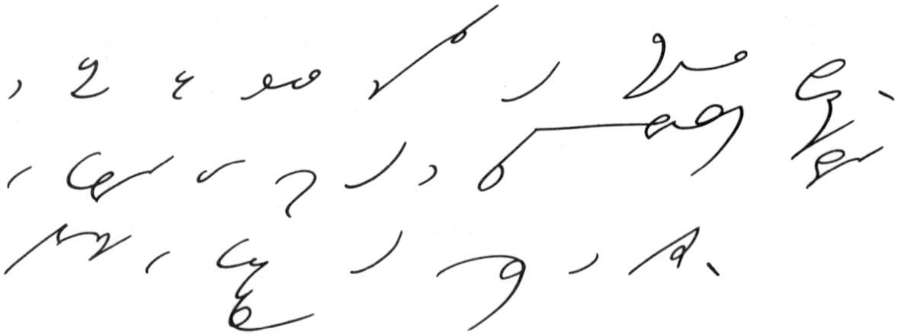

His offer was thoroughly studied and eventually approved.
The president of the company and his administrative assistant discussed the proposal and gave their decision.

2 In a series of three or more items, use a comma between the items and before the conjunction preceding the last item.

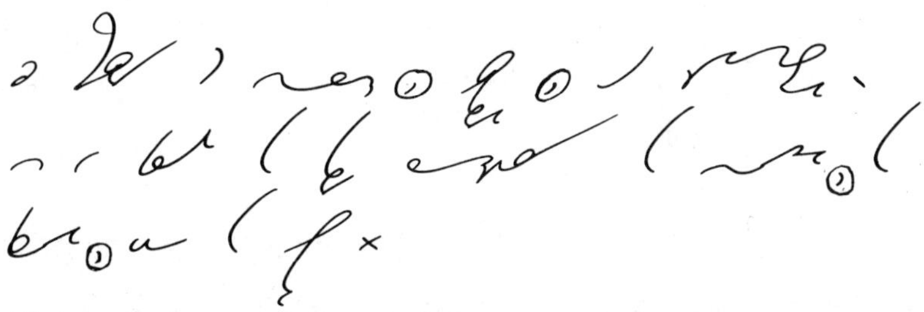

We advertised for clerks, typists, and stenographers.
Can the points be best illustrated by cartoons, by charts, or by tables?

Check your understanding of comma usage by transcribing the following sentences, preferably at the typewriter.

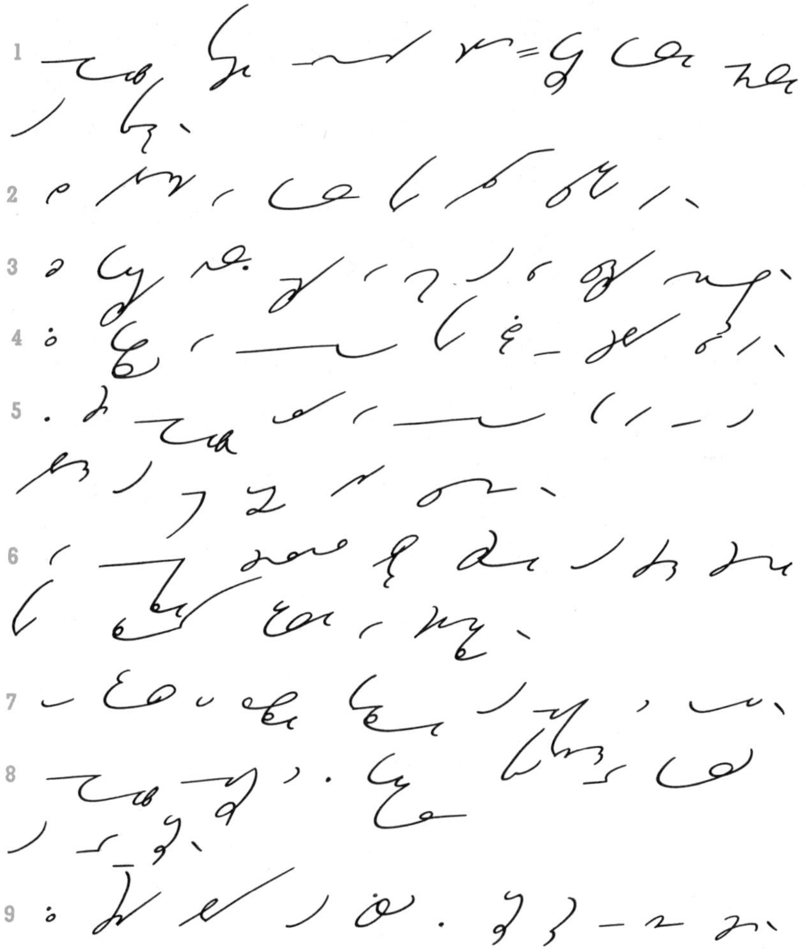

10 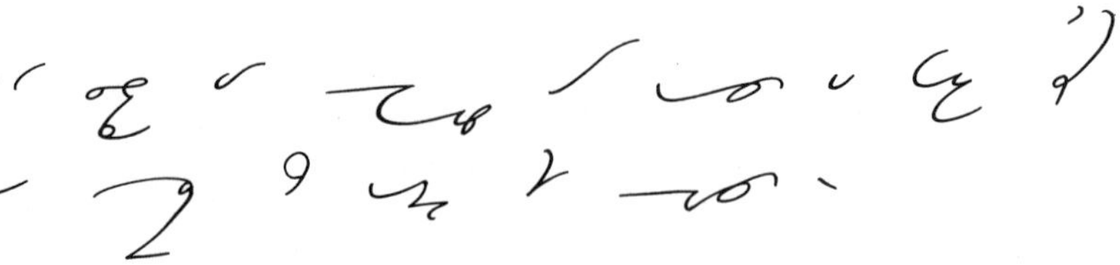

TRANSCRIPTION SPEED BUILDER

72▸ Mr. Richard D. Beatty, 1401 Sheridan Road, Wilmette, Illinois 60091.

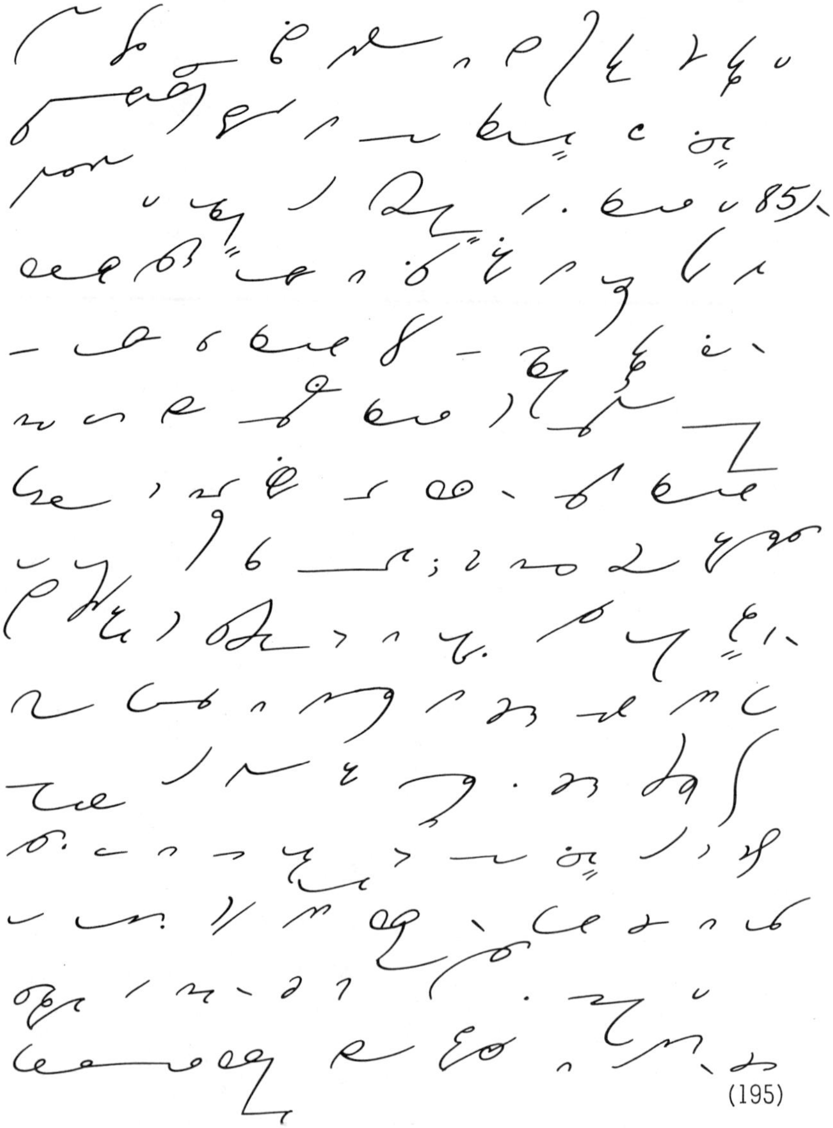

(195)

73▸ Miss Elizabeth Drew, 1411 Wacker Drive, Chicago, Illinois 60613.

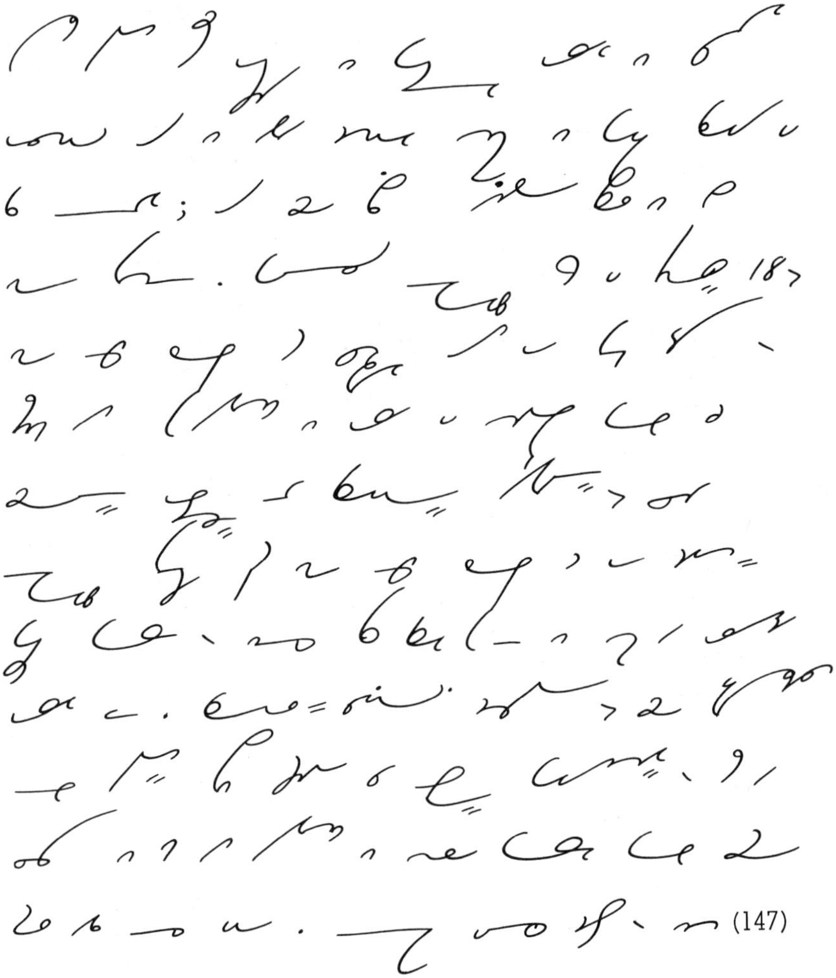

(147)

74▸ Mr. Robert E. Robinson, Howard Dormitory, University of Arizona, Tucson, Arizona 85721.

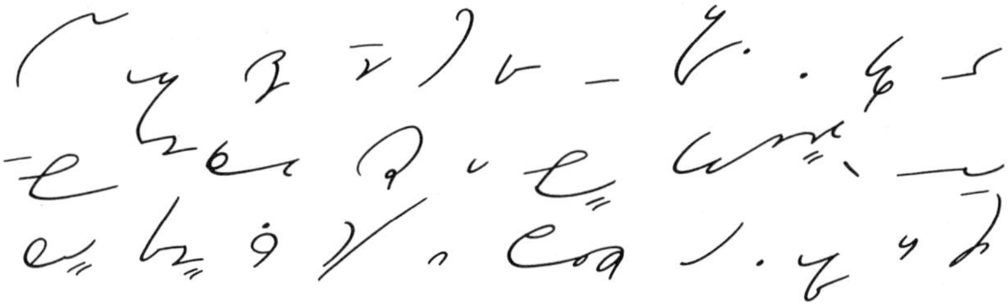

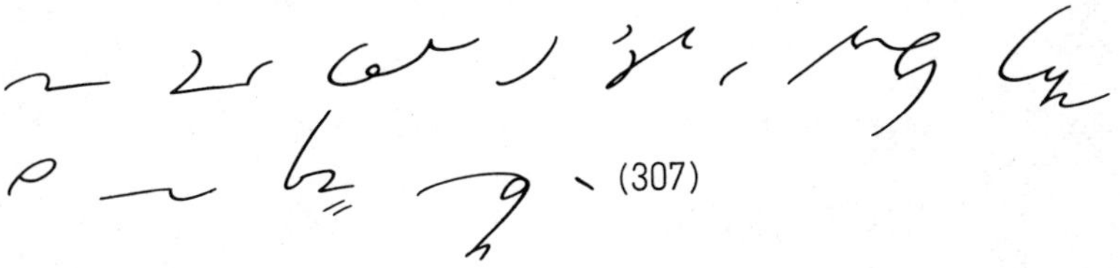

(307)

75 To: All Department Heads.

(168)

lesson 17

MASTERING SHORTHAND THEORY

WORD BEGINNINGS

Re- (before a downstroke or a vowel)

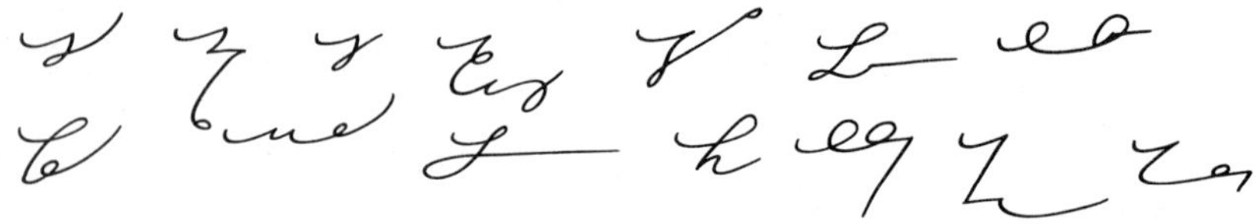

Per-, Pur-

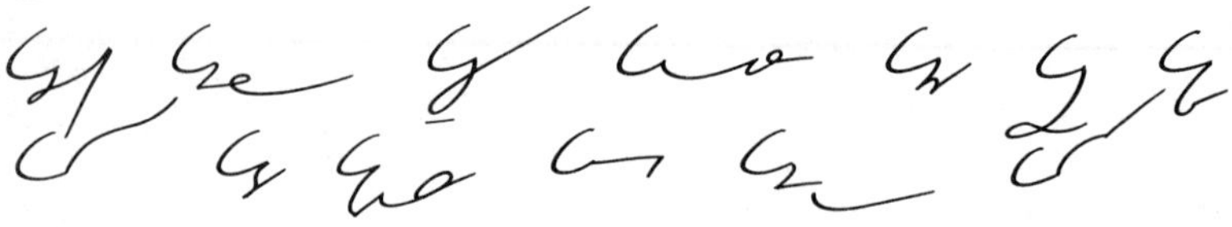

WORD ENDINGS

-ly

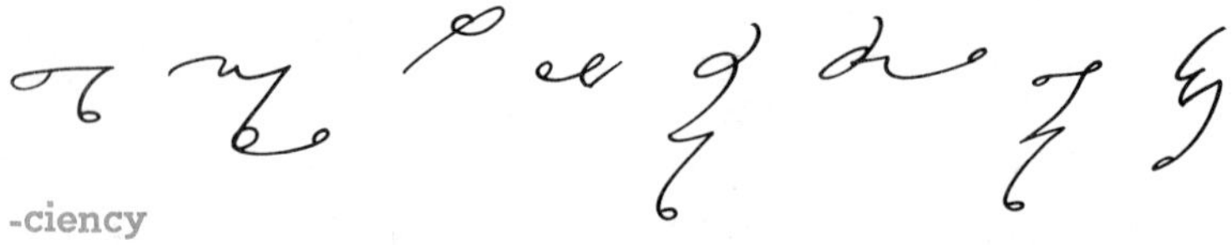

-cient, -ciency

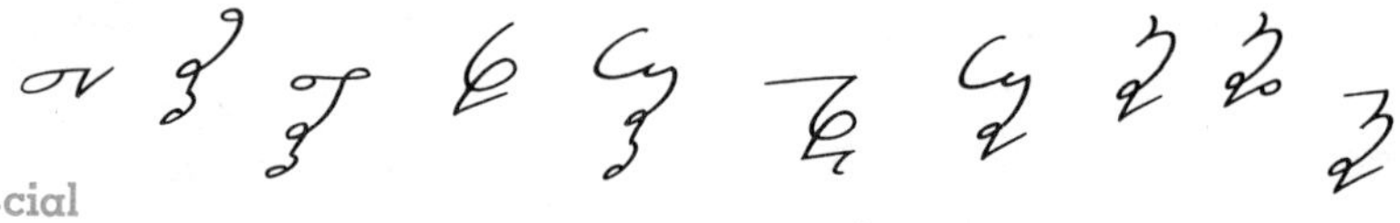

-tial, -cial

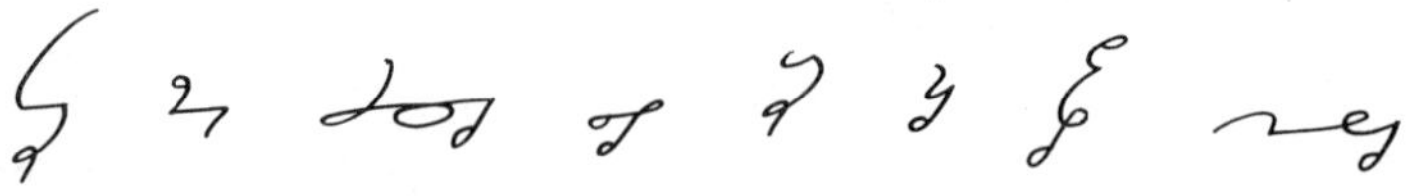

Rescind, reasonably, receipt, reciprocate, repeatedly, reaffirm, realign, reappoint, reorient, reexamine, reassure, rearrange, regional, replenish.

Percentage, personnel, persuaded, purloin, pursuit, purveyor, purport, pertinent, persist, perpetrate, permission, personality, pertained.

Amply, cordially, daily, earliest, favorably, finally, inevitably, positively.

Ancient, efficiency, inefficiency, patient, proficiency, impatience, proficient, sufficient, sufficiently, insufficient.

Beneficial, essential, financially, initially, official, socially, especially, commercially.

TRANSCRIPTION SPEED BUILDER

76 To: All Supervisors.

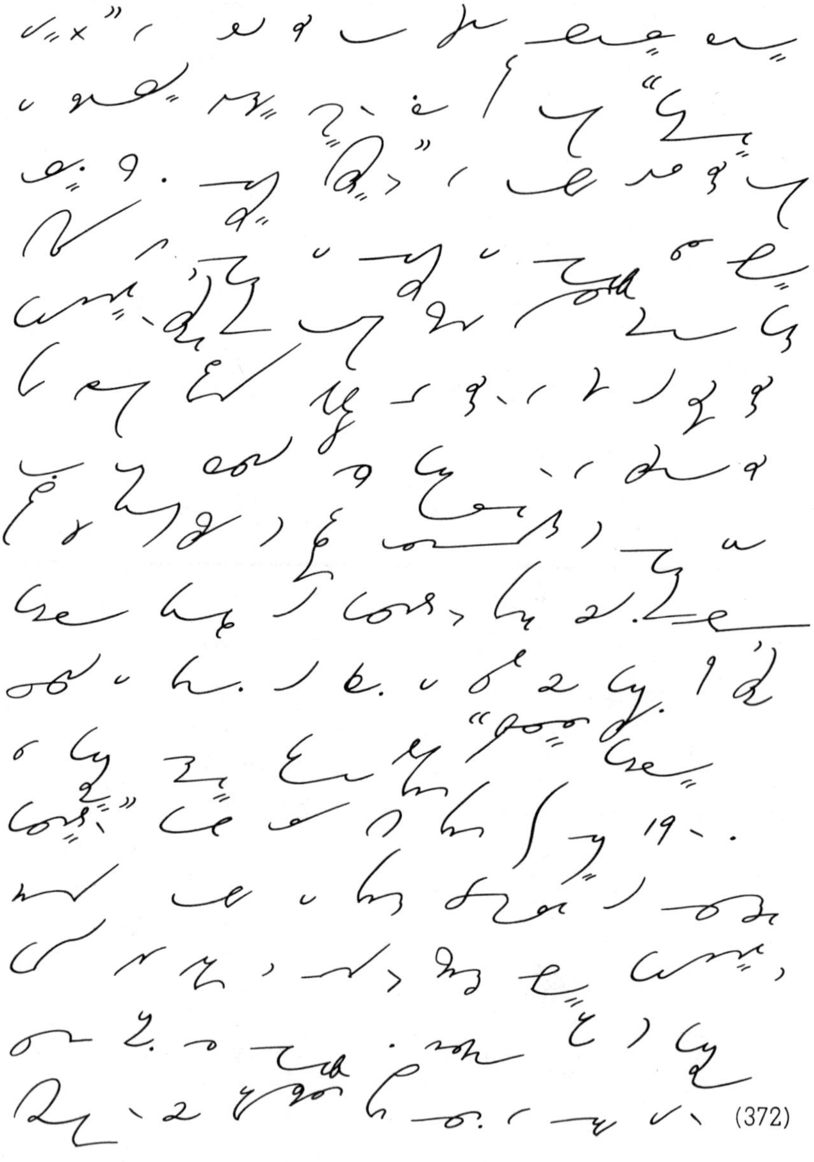

(372)

77 ▸ Miss Marie Fitzgerald, 114 East 177 Street, University City, Missouri 63565.

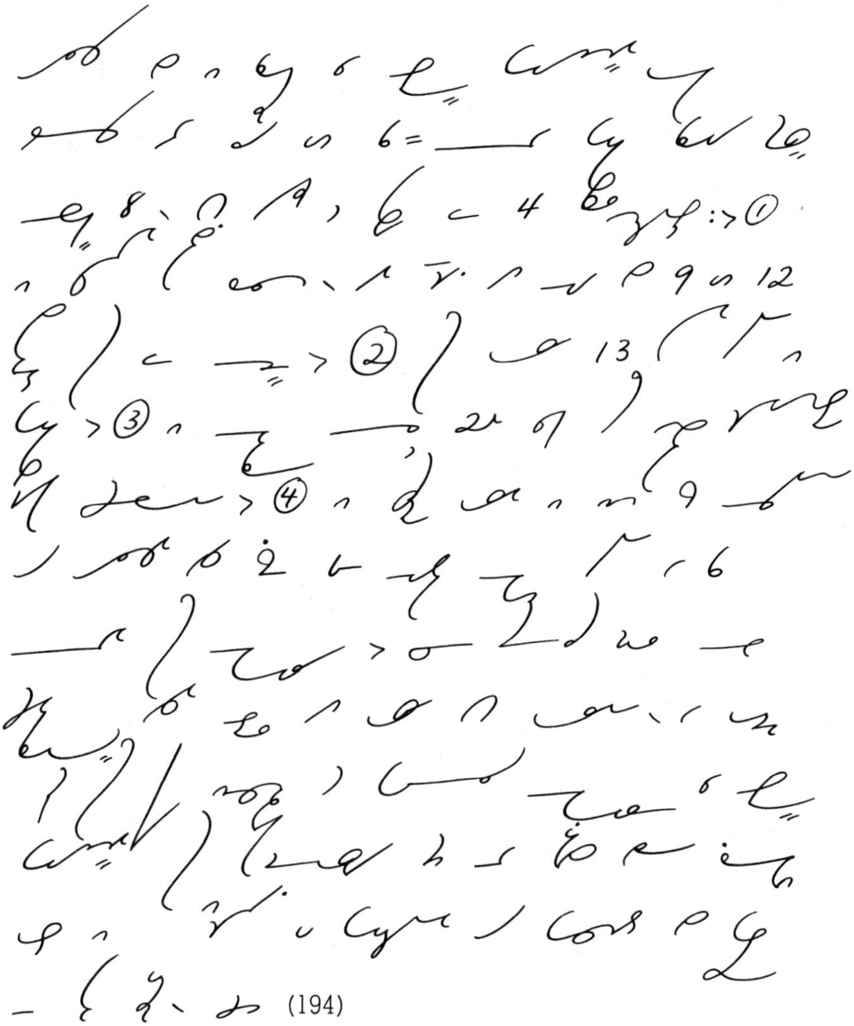

(194)

78 ▸ Professor Nathan Stern, Department of Economics, University of Arizona, Tucson, Arizona 85721.

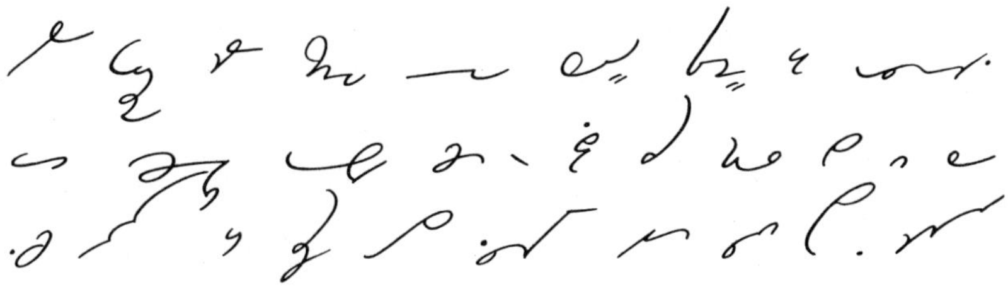

(169)

79▸ Dr. Lawrence Peters, Director of Business Education, Oak Park Public Schools, Oak Park, Illinois 60309.

(89)

lesson

BUILDING PHRASING SKILL 18

PHRASE BUILDER

Drill 1

Drill 2

Drill 3

Drill 4

Drill 5

About it, about its, about my, about that, about the, about them, about these, about this, about those.

Anyone, each one, for one, one thing, one-half, one way, one year, only one.

Does not, does not have, he does, he does not, that does not, this does not, who does not.

Aren't, didn't, don't, hadn't, hasn't, haven't, isn't, won't, doesn't, can't, he didn't, I don't, I haven't, he doesn't, we can't, you don't, they don't.

Be sure, being sure, can be, can be sure, cannot be sure, can't be, he can be, he will be, he would be, I can be, I cannot be, I can't be, I will be, I would be, if it will be, if you can be, if you will be.

TRANSCRIPTION SPEED BUILDER

80 Confidential, To: Harold C. Poling, Credit Manager.

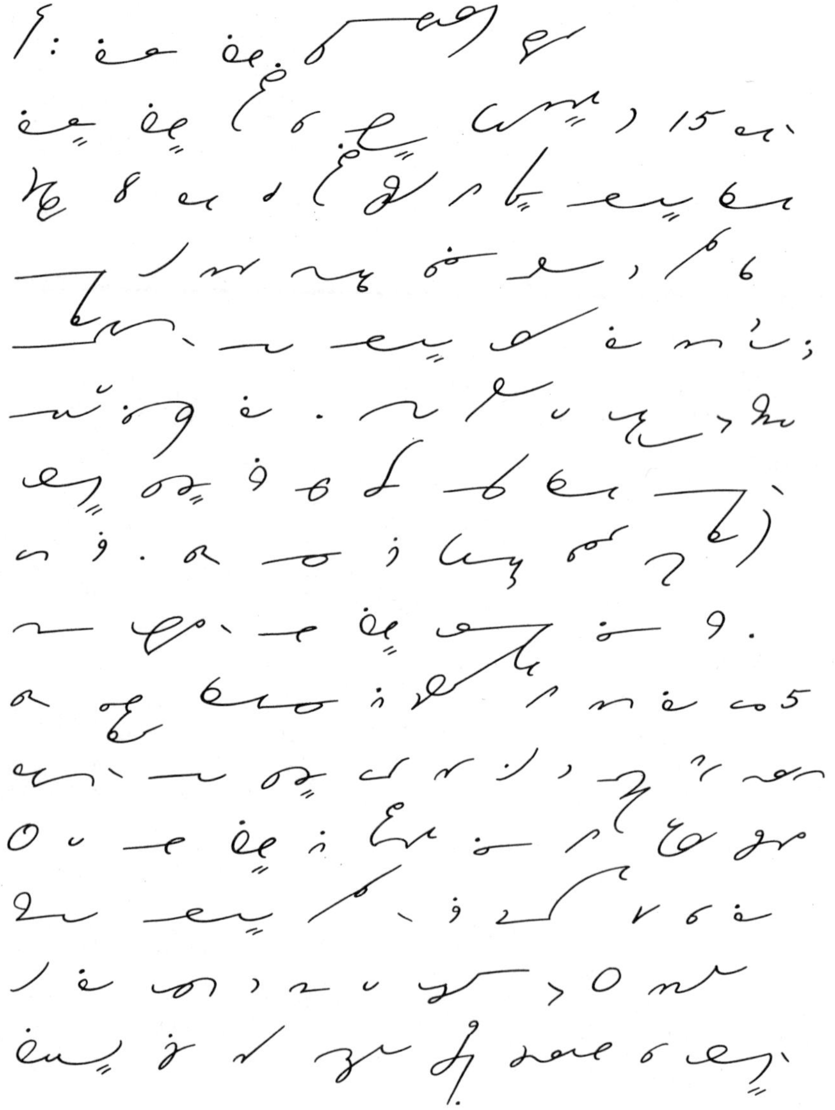

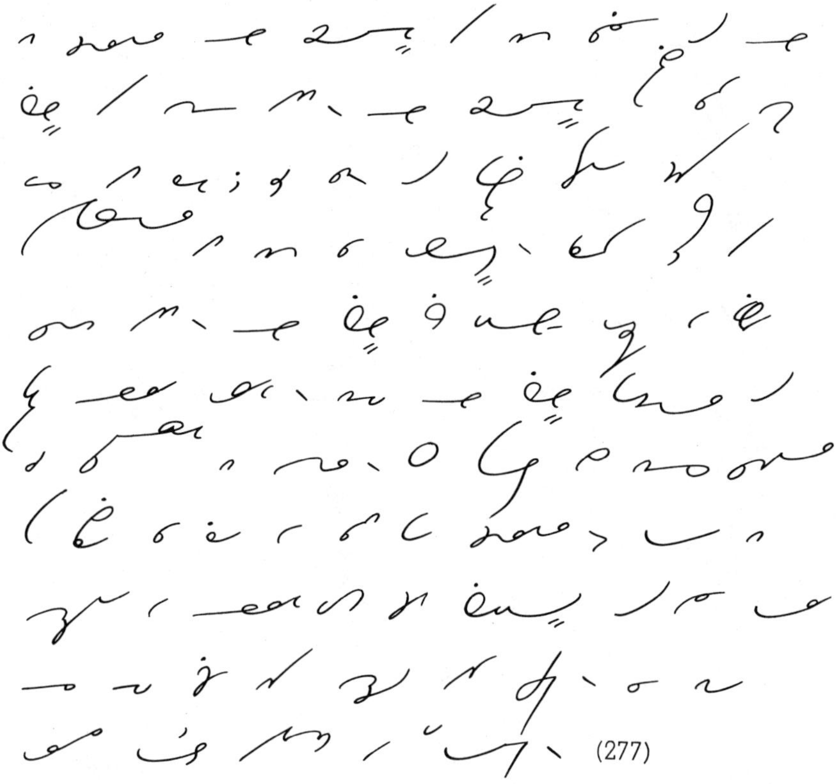

(277)

81▸ To: Section Managers.

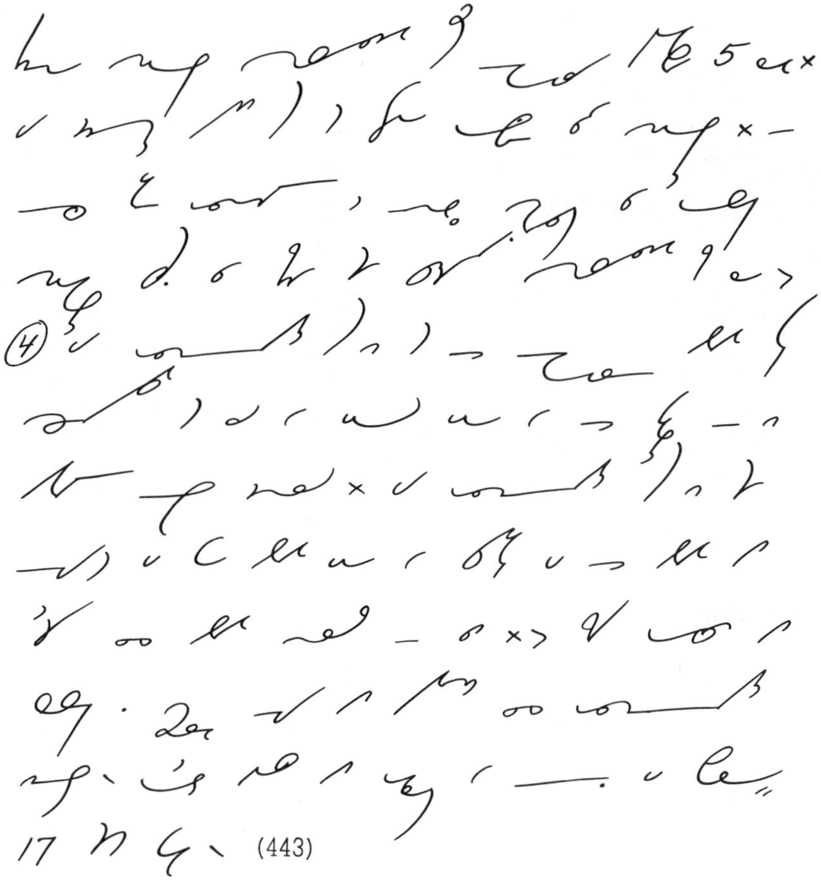

(443)

82 Mr. Peter M. Hall, 4201 Sixteenth Street, Chicago, Illinois 60624.

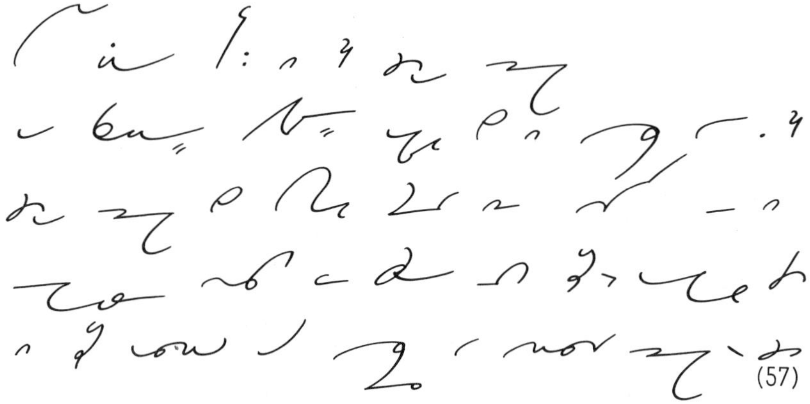

(57)

lesson 19

PROGRESSIVE SPEED BUILDING

In this lesson the one-minute speed-forcing letters are counted progressively at 70, 80, and 90 words a minute; the two-minute reinforcement and control letter is counted at 80 words a minute.

First practice the vocabulary preview that precedes the speed-forcing practice, and then review the specialized vocabulary presented at the beginning of this unit.

SPEED-BUILDING LETTERS

Vocabulary Preview

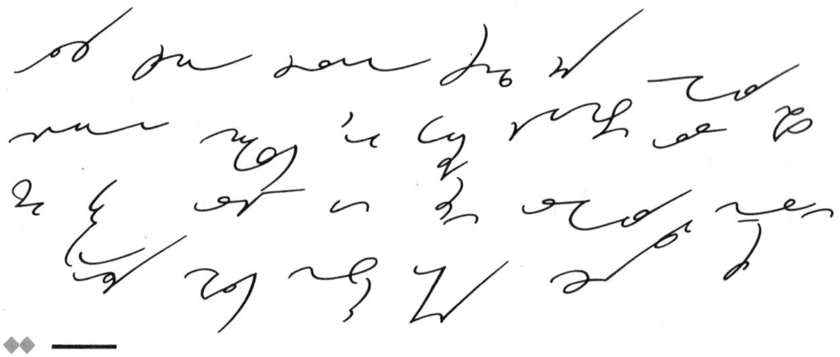

Indicated, psychology, secretarial, vacancy, suited, employed, controller, cooperative, superiors, proficient, stenographic, return, we hope that, as soon as, possibility, reinstatement, of course, physical, reemployed, clerical, requested, competitive, classifications, rejected, candidates, interview.

Speed Forcing

(1 Minute at 70)

83 Dear Miss Williams: You filed an application on April 20 for a position as/secretary in the Personnel Department. You indicated that you have a college major//in psychology and a minor in the secretarial field.

We now have a vacancy///for which we think you may be suited.

If you are still available, please telephone me. Yours truly, (1)

(1 Minute at 80)

84 Dear Mr. Daniels: Phyllis Howard was employed by us from January 11 to August 19 of/this year as secretary to our controller.

Miss Howard was a cooperative, hard-working employee. She//got along very well with superiors and fellow workers. She was highly proficient in stenographic///skills. Her record here was most satisfactory, and we were sorry she resigned. Very cordially yours, (2)

(1 Minute at 90)

85 Dear Mr. Edwards: We are delighted to learn through Mr. Barnes of your return to this city after your long illness.

No/doubt you will soon be available for employment. We hope that you will consider returning to our purchasing department.//Please call on me as soon as you are ready to work, so that we can discuss the possibility of your reinstatement.///

You will, of course, have to have a complete physical examination before you can be reemployed. Very cordially yours, (3)

Reinforcement and Control

(2 Minutes at 80)

86 Dear Mr. Bryan: We have used about 160 of your clerical selection tests. As you requested,/we shall be glad to share the valuable data that we have collected. Through these competitive tests we//have been able to separate our applicants into three classifications: acceptable, mediocre,///and rejected.

During ordinary times we offer positions to all candidates who rate acceptable (1) on the tests and also in the interviews. In especially good times, however, we may be forced to hire/some candidates who rate only mediocre on the tests but have good interview ratings.

We have complete//information on 40 employees who have taken the tests and have been employed by us. After you have///thought it over, please let us know what information you think you want; we shall be glad to give it to you. Yours truly, (2)

TRANSCRIPTION SPEED BUILDER

87 To: Miss Alice Evans, Supervisor of In-Service Training.

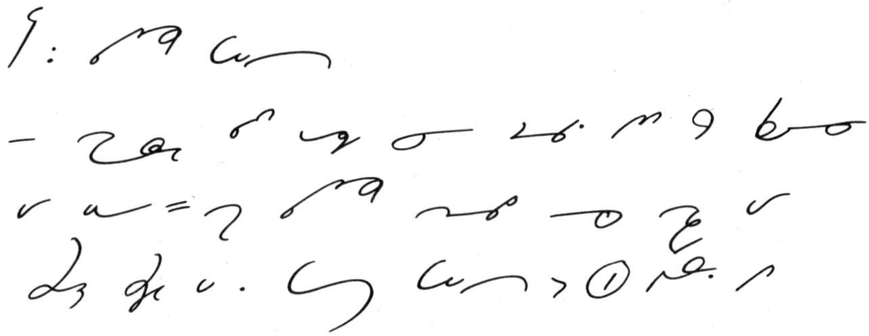

(236)

88 ▸ Mr. Henry Bell, Bell Industries, El Paso, Texas 79906.

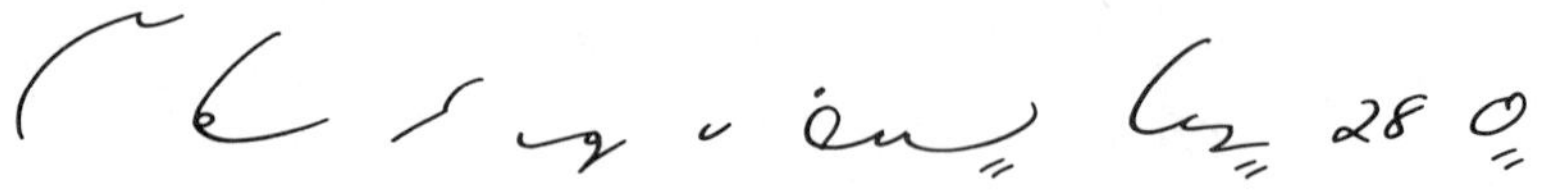

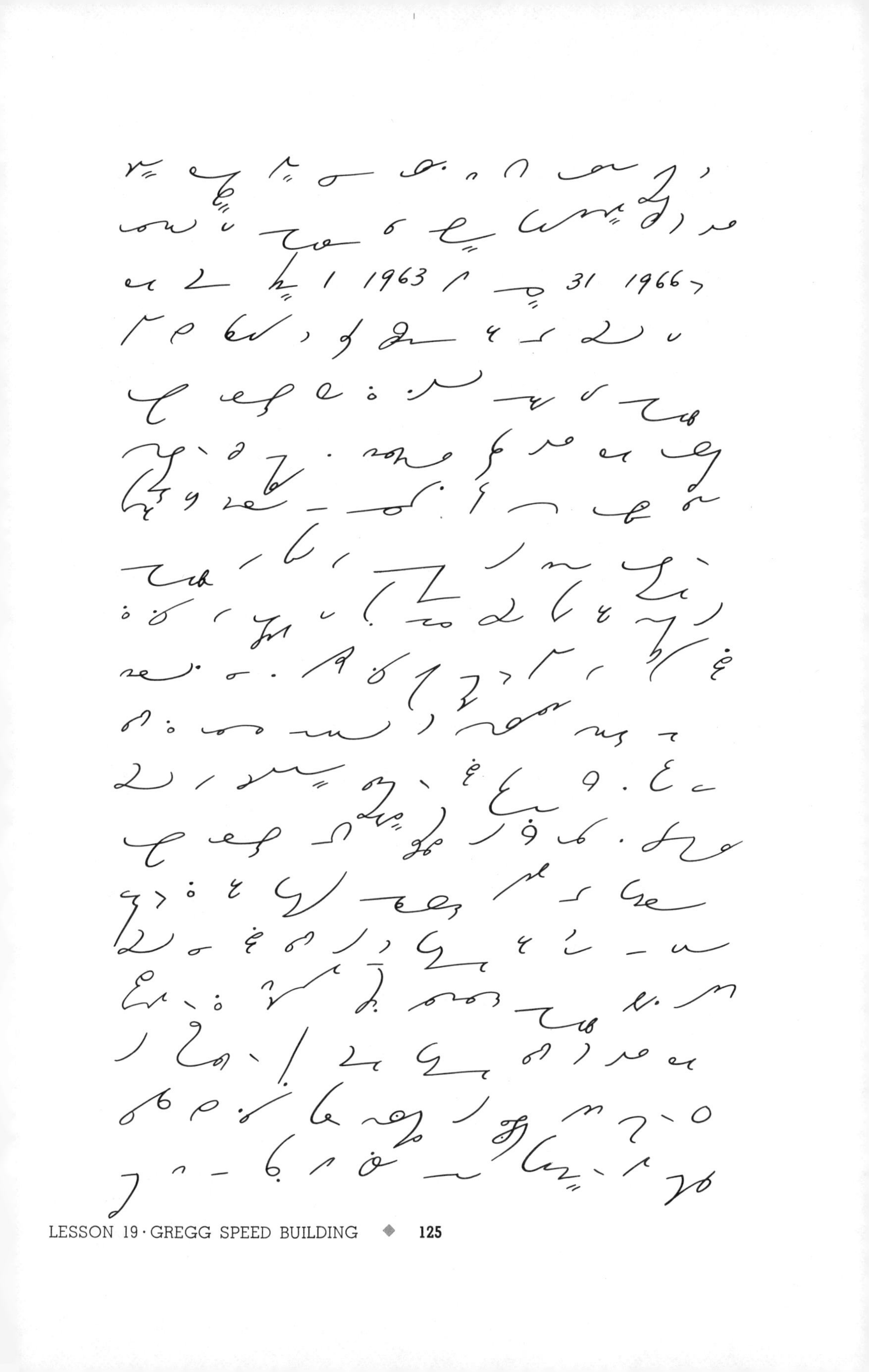

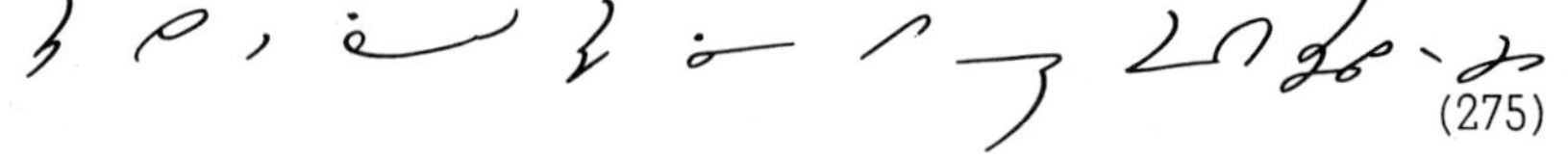

(275)

TRANSCRIPTION PACER

89 To: Miss Nancy Watson, Office Services. 9

15
26
37
51
60
71
82
93
103
114
125
134
148

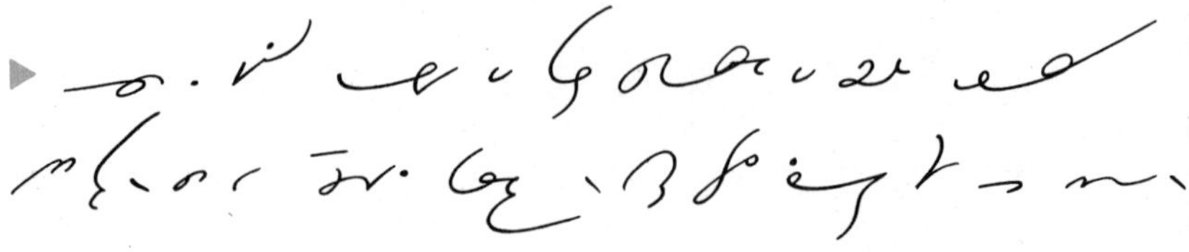

lesson 20

BUILDING TRANSCRIPTION SPEED

SUSTAINED SPEED BUILDER

This sustained speed builder memorandum was dictated by Mr. Harmon for distribution to all section managers.

Practice the following vocabulary preview, and then see how well you can sustain your reinforcement and control speed.

Vocabulary Preview

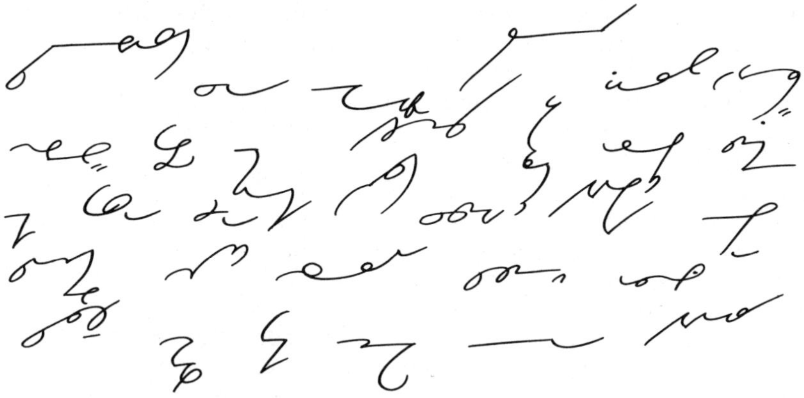

Administrative, annual, employees, determined, holidays, Thanksgiving, Christmas, preferred, involved, designated, observes, religious, uniform, in which the, priority, seniority, tentative, announced, distributed, majority, attractiveness, continuous, calendar, accumulate, recreation, adequate, compensation, punched, numbered, manual, destroyed.

Speed Builder

90 To: Section Managers, Subject: Vacation Schedule.

At a meeting of the Administrative Committee of National Products, the following vacation[1] policies were adopted:

1. Annual vacations with pay are

provided for regular full-time employees[2] with six months or more of service.

2. The amount of vacation time is determined by the length of service on[3] January 1 of the year in which the vacation is to be taken. The following schedule is to[4] be followed:

6 months to 1 year: one day for each month of service.

1 to 5 years: two weeks.

5 to 15 years: three[5] weeks.

15 years and over: four weeks.

3. The following holidays will be given with pay: New Year's Day, May 30, July 4, Election[6] Day, November 11, Thanksgiving, and Christmas. If any of these holidays fall on Sunday, the following[7] Monday will be given. One extra day a year will be given on a Friday if an official holiday[8] falls on Thursday. Employees will choose the preferred Friday by ballot if several holidays are involved. No[9] extra day will be given for holidays occurring on Tuesday. If a designated holiday falls during[10] an employee's vacation, an extra day will be added to his vacation period.

4. Any[11] employee who observes a religious holiday not provided above should discuss taking the holiday with[12] the Personnel Department rather than with his supervisor so that a uniform policy can be[13] adopted.

5. Vacations will be arranged by department heads after employees have expressed their preferences.[14] Priority will be given to employees with seniority. Tentative schedules will be announced by[15] February 1 if possible.

6. Vacations will be distributed throughout the work year, with the majority[16] in the summer. However, advantages of winter vacations, such as reduced travel rates, add to[17] their attractiveness; and we encourage employees to consider them.

7. Vacations are ordinarily[18] to be taken in continuous periods. Vacations for periods of less than one week are discouraged,[19] and long weekends are not interchangeable with single-block vacations.

8. Vacations are to be taken[20] within the calendar year in which they are earned, and they will not accumulate from year to year. Since the primary[21] purpose of a vacation is to provide rest and recreation for the employee, extra pay will not[22] be given for vacation time not used.

9. Salary for the vacation period will be paid in advance[23] when requested.

10. Employees who leave National Products voluntarily and have given adequate[24] advance notice to their department heads will receive in their final paycheck compensation for whatever vacation[25] credit may be due.

This announcement is being distributed to all members of the staff at this time. Please[26] notice that the pages are punched and numbered so that they can be added to your office manual. Insert the[27] announcement in the appropriate position immediately. It supersedes the previous section on[28] vacations, which should be destroyed.

If there is any point in this announcement that is not clear, please feel free to[29] discuss it with me or with a member of my staff. (589)

91 Memo to All Employees.

(163)

TRANSCRIPTION PACER

92 To: All Employees. 4

10

22

35
48
60
71
81
92
104
118
130
145
158
171
181
192
201
211
223
233
245

257
269
279
292
304
316
329
340
351
363
376
387
390
402
413
424
436

Never before have so many businessmen been so busy trying to say so much to the public. Thirty years ago only one out of every 50 of the top 500 companies in the United States had a full-fledged public information department. Today, the proportion is three out of four, with companies starting new departments at the rate of 100 a year.

Maintaining a company image that is attractive to the public is a full-time endeavor. News stories in business magazines introducing new products are used to arouse public endorsement. A report on the financial page of the Wall Street Journal announcing a stock split, a dividend increase, or a new management appointment promotes public confidence. A story in the local newspapers reporting the opening of a new facility, including the speech given by the mayor or other presiding official, builds community goodwill. The an nouncement that a com pany officer has been se lected to head the Com munity Chest drive or tha a company employee ha won a professional awar increases the stature of th company in the eyes o the public. Sometimes no publicizing a story, an an titrust action, for instance is equally beneficial i protecting the company'

unit 5

PUBLIC INFORMATION

image.

Such is the domain of a company's public information service. Its members must be journalistically oriented, with a nose for news and a canny familiarity with the media that will present it. They must understand public attitudes, execute a program of action, and communicate with the public. With these attributes, they project a favorable public image of the company.

Secretarial Assignment

In this unit you will work for Arthur C. Williamson. All letters are signed by him over his title, Public Information Director.

SPECIALIZED TERMINOLOGY

An understanding of the following terms will add to your understanding of the subtle ways in which a publicist works.

Annual Report • A report sent by a corporation to its stockholders at the close of the corporation's fiscal year. It contains the financial statement for the period and usually the company's future plans as well as information about its products. Copies are also sent to the press, community leaders, and financial analysts.

Stockholders' Meeting • Regular annual meeting of stockholders at which directors are elected, financial reports are presented, and general business and other pertinent company business are discussed.

Proxy • Written authorization for someone else to cast a stockholder's vote when he cannot attend a stockholders' meeting.

Clipping Service • An organization or business that scans newspapers and periodicals for news items about subscribers and sends these items to the subscribers at regular intervals.

Earnings Report • Interim financial or comparative statement sent to stockholders. Such a report frequently features the income figures for the current period in one column and the cumulative figures for the year to date in the second column.

House Organ • Internal company publication that attempts to create prestige, goodwill, and understanding among employees, stockholders, and suppliers.

Press Release • A news story sent to news media in the hope that they will give news coverage to it. It includes the date of release and the telephone number at which additional information may be obtained.

Public Relations Firm • A company that specializes in creating an attractive public image of its clients.

Public Service Project • A community event in which a company participates, often at considerable cost to the company, both because the company is interested in community betterment and because it hopes that intangible benefits will accrue.

This list contains 21 words that appear frequently in business letters.

accessible	**catalog**	**phenomenal**
accompanying	**column**	**premiere**
achievement	**criticism**	**sponsor**
adjacent	**extraordinary**	**stockholder**
administrative	**dismantle**	**tentative**
all right	**identifying**	**volume**
biographical	**inevitable**	**warrant**

Transcribe the following sentences, preferably at the typewriter, until you master the spelling of the words that appear in the word list above.

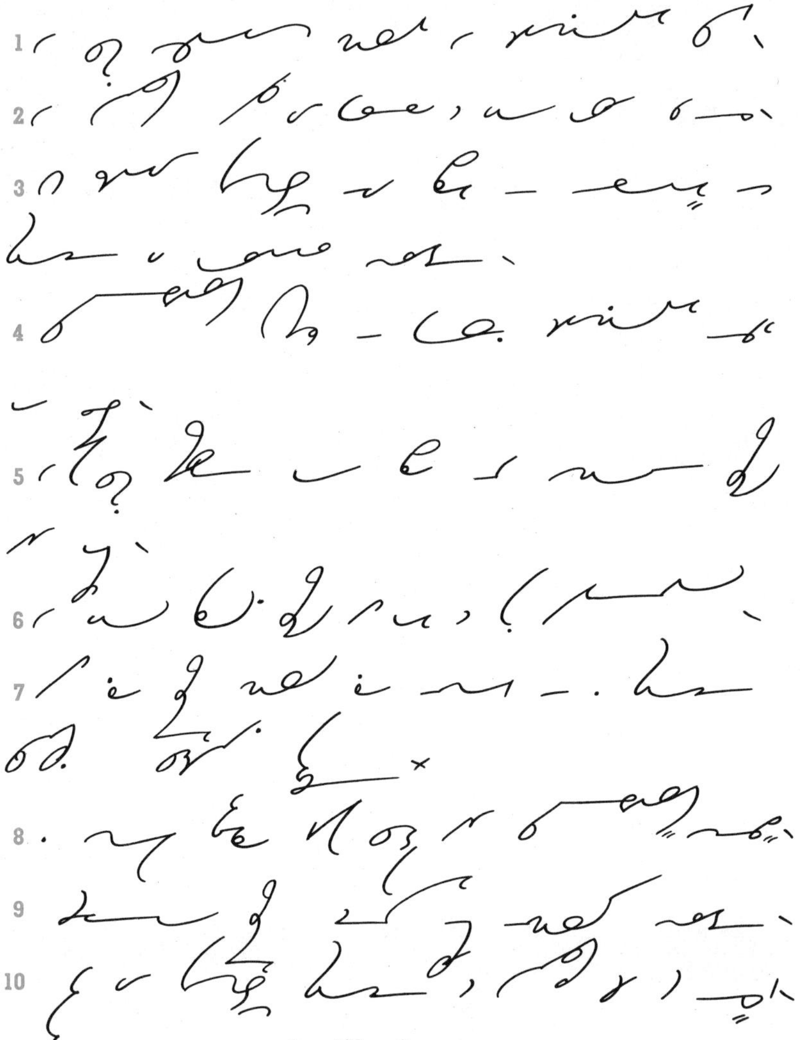

NATIONAL PRODUCTS, inc.

211 FOREST AVENUE
ST. LOUIS, MISSOURI 63100

NPi

PRESS RELEASE

For Release: June 4 after 12 noon

National Products, Inc.
211 Forest Avenue
St. Louis, Missouri 63100

Telephone: 314 432-1781, Arthur C. Williamson

MERGER OF CONTINENTAL AND ABC

At the annual meeting of the stockholders of Continental Products, which recently merged with the ABC Company, a change of company name was approved. Henceforth the corporation will be known as NATIONAL PRODUCTS, INC. The combined assets of the organization total $124,500,000.

At a meeting of the board of directors of the new corporation immediately after the separate meetings of the stockholders of the former companies, Mr. Henry M. Simpson, former president of Continental Products, was elected president of the new organization; and Mr. Henry A. Walters, former president of the ABC Company, was elected vice-president in charge of financial affairs.

Sample press release.

lesson

BUILDING TRANSCRIPTION QUALITY

21

TRANSCRIPTION POINTERS

Uses of the Possessive

Ask yourself whether you know when a possessive should be used. If you can transpose the expression containing the *s* sound and use the word *of*, the possessive form is generally used.

1 To form the possessive of a singular noun not ending in *s*, add an apostrophe and *s* to the noun; add only an apostrophe to form the possessive of a regular plural noun.

employee's record	customers' complaints
salesman's bonus	managers' recommendations

EXCEPTION: To form the possessive of one-syllable singular nouns ending in *s*, add an apostrophe and *s*. However, in nouns of more than one syllable that end in *s*, only the apostrophe needs to be added to form the possessive if the addition of *s* would make the word difficult to pronounce.

Mr. Marks's report	Mr. Watkins' memorandum
My boss's telephone	Miss Reynolds' judgment

2 To form the possessive of compound nouns, add the apostrophe and *s* to the last member of the compound.

secretary-treasurer's note	anybody else's job
runner-up's time	general manager's policy

NOTE: Instead of using the plural possessive of a compound noun, it is sometimes preferable to rephrase the sentence.

3 To show joint ownership, form the possessive on the last noun only; but to show individual ownership, form the possessive on each noun.

Winters and Hunts's store	Winters' and Hunts's stores
buyer and seller's contract	buyer's and seller's contracts

NOTE: A company may omit the apostrophe in its name. Consult the letterhead or the Yellow Pages for correct form.

4 The possessive form is used in many common expressions that refer to time and measurements and in phrases implying personification.

several dollars' worth	a week's delay	for appearance' sake*
a stone's throw	two weeks' vacation	for heaven's sake

*In these idiomatic possessives with the word *sake*, only the apostrophe is used if the word ends in an *s* sound.

Check your understanding of possessive usage by transcribing the following sentences, preferably at the typewriter.

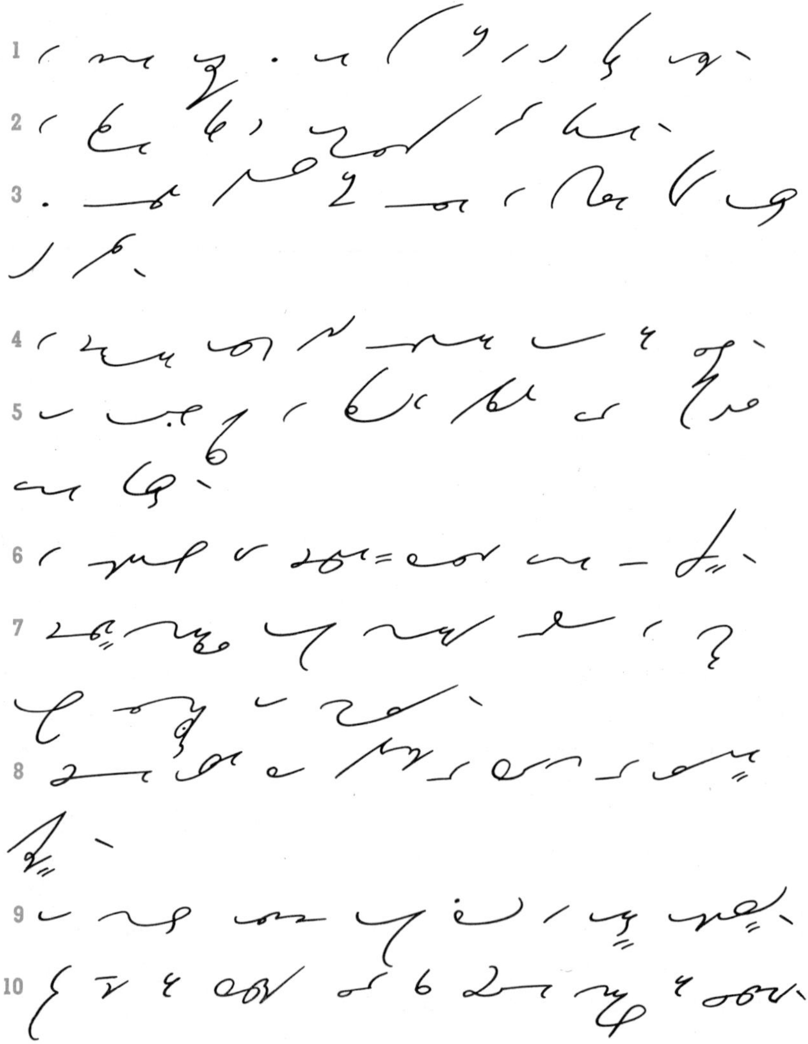

93 Mr. Herbert Miller, Miller's Grocery, Bluefield, West Virginia 24701.

(221)

94 ▸ Reynolds Photographers, 714 South Lewis Street, Charleston, West Virginia 25302.

(221)

95 ▸ The Wall Street Journal, Wall Street, New York, New York 10005.

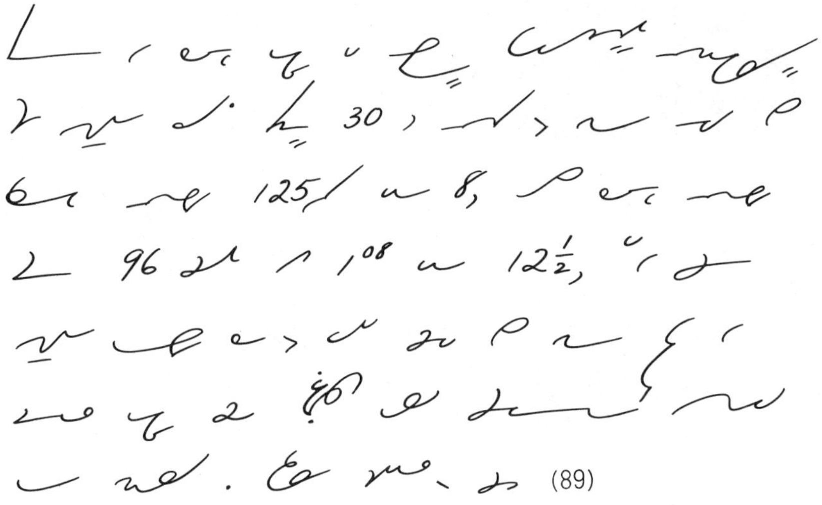

(89)

96 ▸ Professor Mildred Adamson, Northern State Teachers College, Duluth, Minnesota 55805.

(104)

Lesson 22

MASTERING SHORTHAND THEORY

WORD BEGINNINGS

Ex-

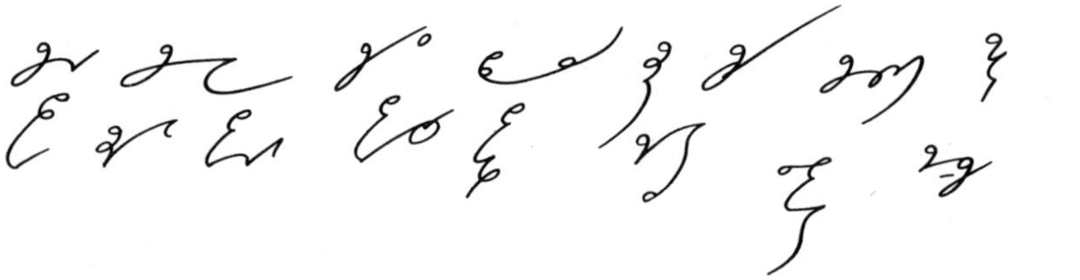

Al-

For-, Fore-, Fur-

Sub-

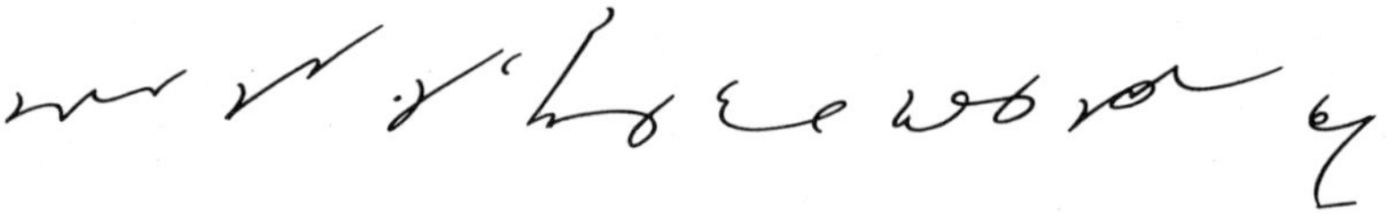

WORD ENDINGS

-ful

-rity

Exact, example, exceedingly, excellent, excessive, excited, executive, exhaustion, exhibit, existence, expectation, expedite, exposition, extensively, inexpensive, exquisite.

Already, alternative, altercation, almanac, almighty, alternate, altered, unaltered.

Forceful, foreclosure, fortunate, misfortune, furlough, furnishings, furthermore, furtive.

Subcontract, subdued, subheadings, subjugate, sublease, subordinate, subtitle, suburban.

Awful, beautiful, carefully, doubtful, faithful, hopeful, powerful, usefulness, helpfully.

Charities, majority, minority, prosperity, securities, verities, asperity.

TRANSCRIPTION SPEED BUILDER

97 Professor Lawrence Wilkins, Department of Business Administration, Business Institute, Sedalia, Missouri 65303.

98 To: Henry M. Simpson, President.

(421)

99▸ Mr. John R. McCann, Editorial Office, Fortune Magazine, Time & Life Building, Avenue of the Americas at 50th Street, New York, New York 10019.

(111)

lesson

BUILDING PHRASING SKILL 23

PHRASE BUILDER

Drill 1

Drill 2

Drill 3

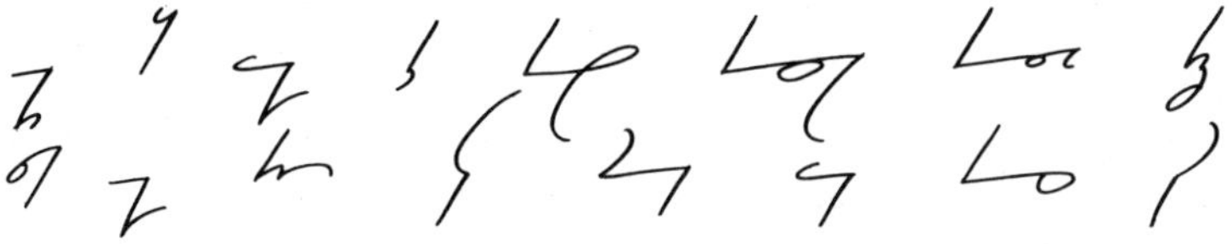

Drill 4

Drill 5

Drill 6

As there is, is there, of their, there may be, there will not be, there would be, to their, if there are, if there will be.

I shall be, I shall have, I shall make, shall not have, you shall have, I shall not have, you shall not, we shall be, we shall mail.

In which you, of which, on which the, which is, which may be, which may not be, which means, which you say, with which, in which the, which you can, by which, from which, on which, which may, for which.

In this, this is not, this date, with this, this would be, hope that this, for this, on this.

Between the, between these, between this, between those, between us, between you, between them.

About that time, any time, at which time, by that time, each time, few times, many times.

TRANSCRIPTION SPEED BUILDER

100 ▸ Press Release, For Release: April 3.

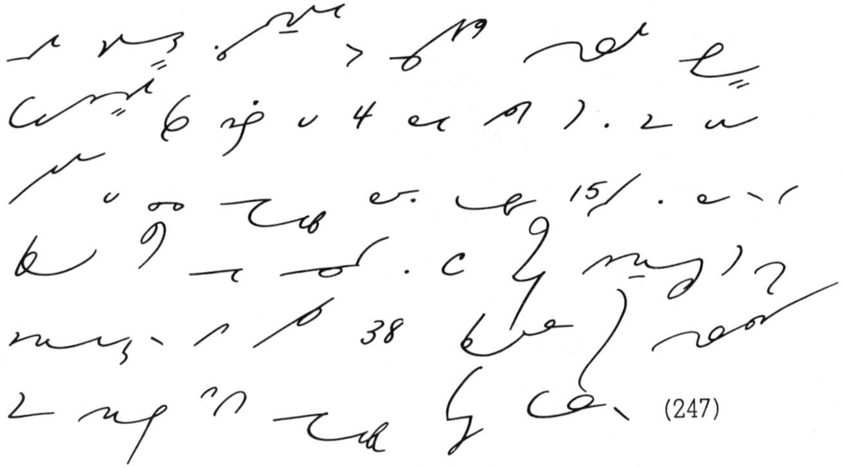

(247)

101 ▸ Press Release to St. Louis Newspapers, For Immediate Release.

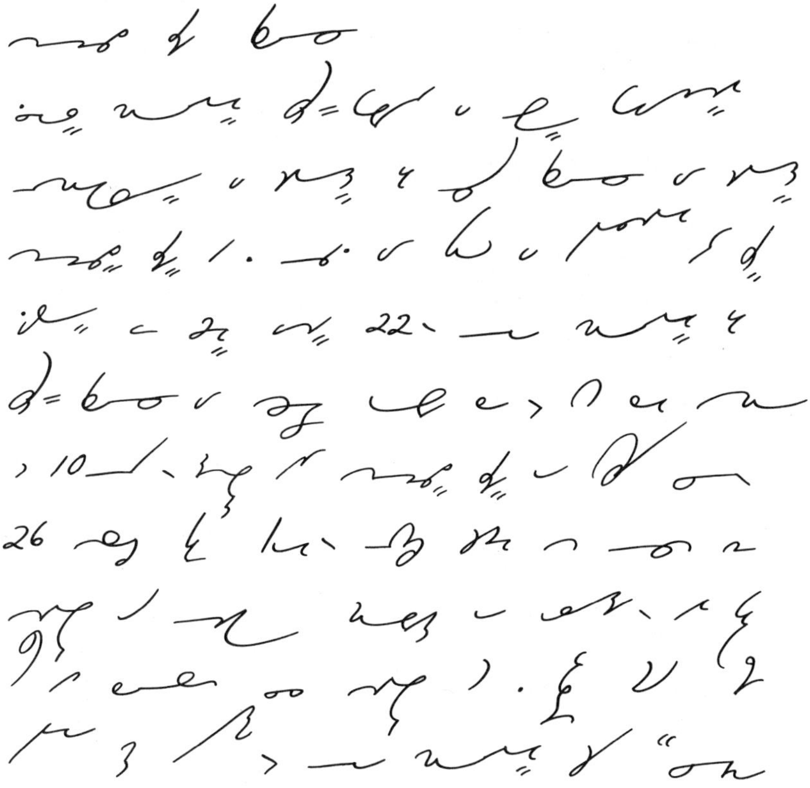

(224)

102 To: Vincent M. Regan, Research and Development.

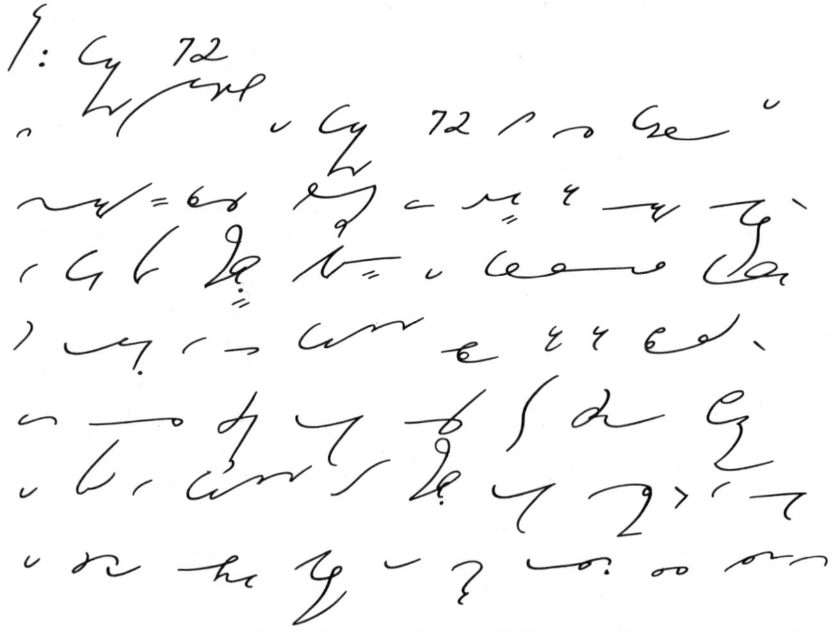

(261)

103 To: Mr. Henry M. Simpson, President.

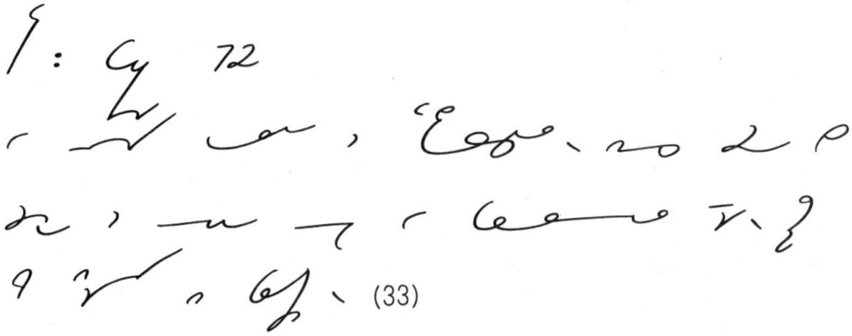

(33)

lesson 24

PROGRESSIVE SPEED BUILDING

In this lesson the one-minute speed-forcing letters are counted progressively at 80, 90, and 100 words a minute; the two-minute reinforcement and control letter is counted at 70 words a minute.

First practice the vocabulary preview that precedes the speed-forcing practice, and then review the specialized vocabulary presented at the beginning of the unit.

SPEED-BUILDING LETTERS

Vocabulary Preview

Weekly, annual, organs, entry, convention, association, employees, competition, photograph, regular, headquarters, prior, vice-president, submit, sponsoring, broadcasts, symphony, consecutive, shareholders, orchestra, extraordinary, up to date, composer, to sponsor, contribution, civic.

Speed Forcing

(1 Minute at 80)

104 Press Release: In the industrial tournament sponsored by Suburban Lanes, the women's team from NATIONAL PRODUCTS,/INC., last night defeated the team from Universal Manufacturing. The winning team scored//220 to Universal Manufacturing's 210. The individual high score was made by Mary/// Smith with 231.

The men's team from Middle States Trucking Company was high with a score of 280. (1)

(1 Minute at 90)

105▸ Gentlemen: Enclosed is a complete file of The National Effort, our weekly corporation newspaper. I should like to/enter this publication in the annual contest for house organs.

The entry blank states that all competing publications//will be displayed at the convention of the Association of Editors of House Organs to be held February///10 to 12 in Dallas. We have 2,000 employees, so our newspaper would be entered in the Class B competition. Sincerely yours, (2)

(1 Minute at 100)

106▸ Gentlemen: We should like to engage you to photograph our executives addressing the board of directors at its next regular/meeting on Thursday, October 4, at 2:30 p.m. in the board room at our St. Louis headquarters.

Plan to provide us with three pictures//that would have wide public interest: (1) the entire board of directors just prior to the meeting; (2) the vice-president in charge of/// finance reporting to the board; and (3) the executives just before their appearances.

Please submit proofs by October 8. Yours very truly, (3)

Reinforcement and Control

(2 Minutes at 90)

107▸ Dear Stockholder: In the public interest, NATIONAL PRODUCTS is sponsoring three broadcasts by the St. Louis Symphony/Orchestra over Radio Station KMOX. These programs will be heard from eight until nine o'clock on three consecutive//Thursday evenings, starting on October 17.

We especially urge our shareholders to invite this orchestra,/// one of the country's finest, into their homes. Ask your friends, too, to listen to these extraordinary programs.

For your added pleasure (1) we are enclosing a special Listeners' Guide, complete with up-to-date biographical notes about each composer./In addition, you will find a guide to music appreciation for each composition to be played.

We hope that you will//note the time of these broadcasts and make plans to listen to these recitals. We hope, too, that you will approve of management's///decision to sponsor such a series as a contribution to the civic life of the community. Very sincerely yours, (2)

TRANSCRIPTION SPEED BUILDER

108▸ To: Helene Marie Potter, Assistant, Public Information Service.

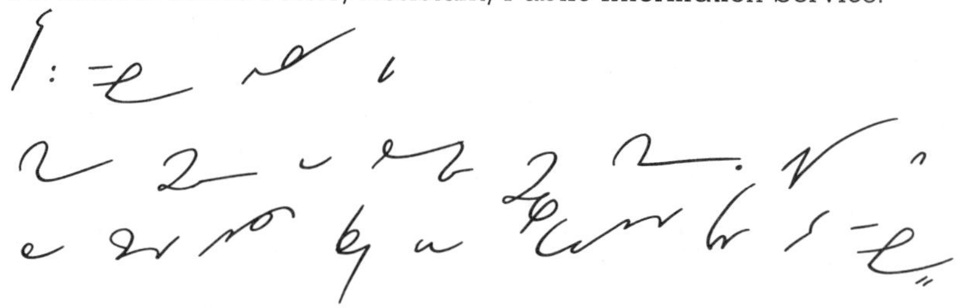

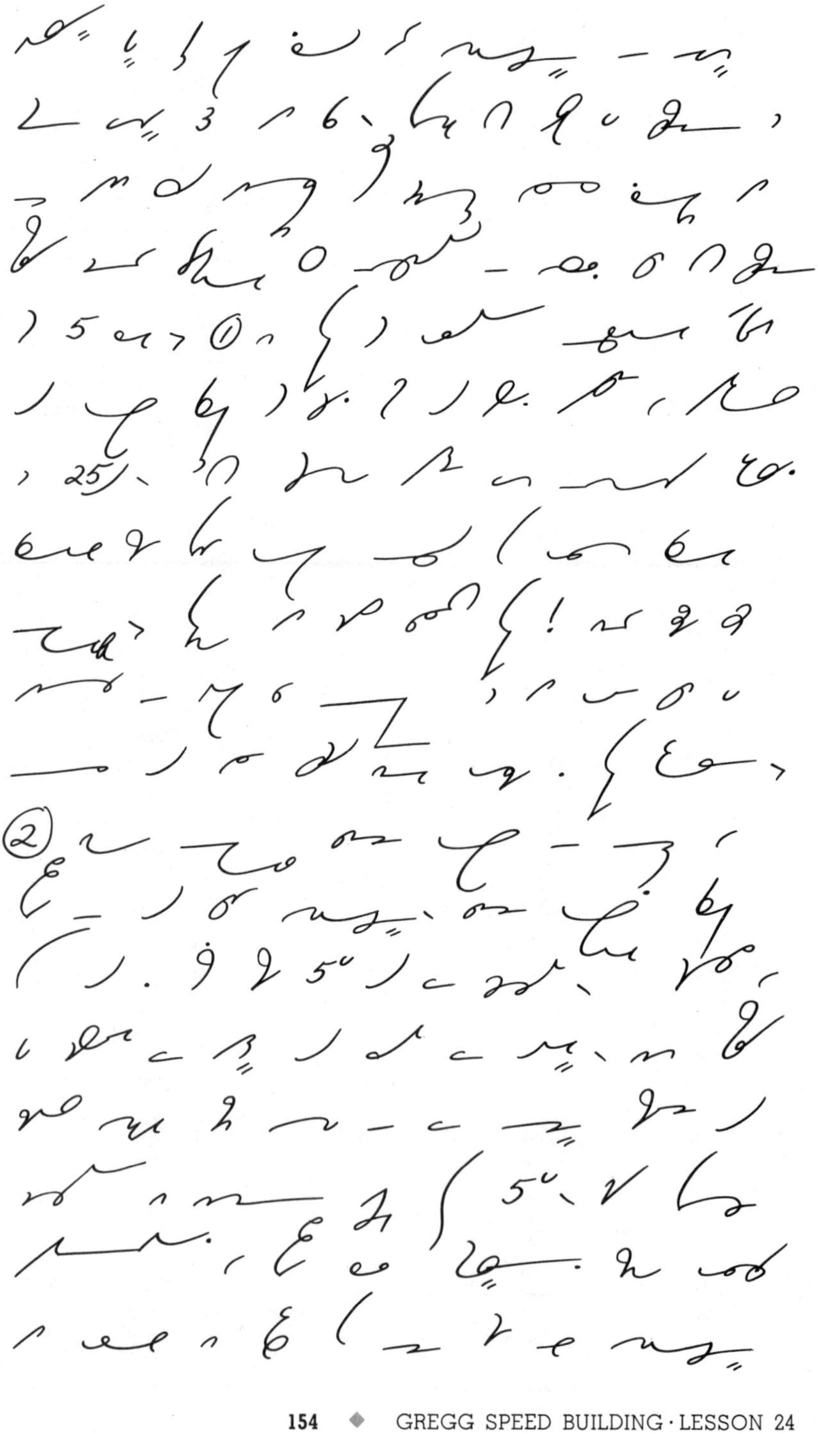

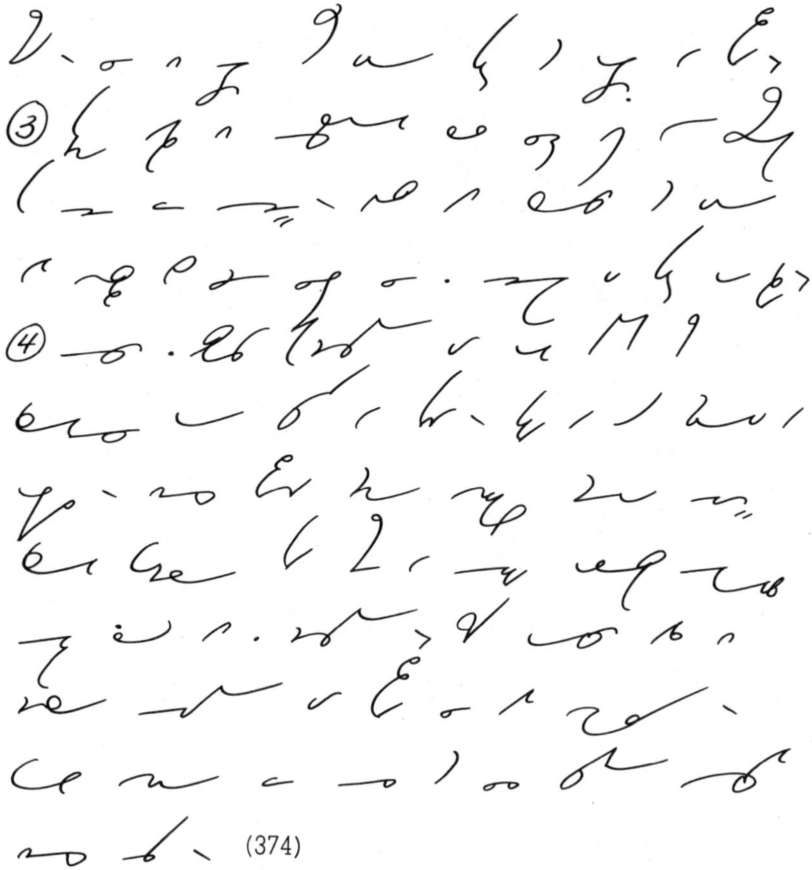

(374)

TRANSCRIPTION PACER

109 ▸ Mr. Phillip L. Stanwood, Midwestern District Manager, National 13
Products, Inc., 2211 Front Street, Houston, Texas 77017. 25

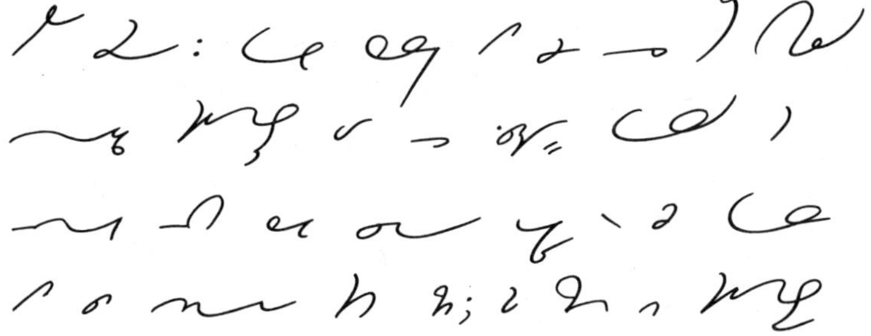

37
46
56
67

79 91 103 115 126 135 149 161 178 189 198 211 219 224

◆◆

Lesson 25

BUILDING TRANSCRIPTION SPEED

SUSTAINED SPEED BUILDER

Mr. Williamson dictated the sustained speed builder letter to be sent to Mr. Henry M. Simpson, President, National Products, Inc.

Practice the following vocabulary preview, and then see how well you can sustain your reinforcement and control speed.

Vocabulary Preview

Memorandum, publicity, exceedingly, adequately, metropolitan, combating, disadvantage, associating, everyday, reporters, infrequently, appointments, editorial, downtown, likely, St. Louis, cultivate, coverage, temporary, headquarters, assignment, crucial, colleague, concentrate, recommend, adoption.

Speed Builder

110 To: Henry M. Simpson, President, Subject: St. Louis Newspaper Coverage.

Thank you for your memorandum questioning me about the small amount of publicity in the St. Louis[1] newspapers on the merger and change of name for our new company.

I, too, am exceedingly concerned that we[2] are not always adequately reported in the metropolitan area. I have given a lot[3] of thought to the reasons behind the problem and to the ways of combating it.

Here are the reasons:

1. As a[4] suburban company, we are at a disadvantage. Maintaining extensive contact with the city press is[5] difficult because we do not associate with reporters every day in the normal course of business.[6] We go into the city on special occasions rather than as a daily routine. We see the key newspaper[7] reporters infrequently, and only when we make the appointments.

2. The majority of the St. Louis[8] newspapers are morning publications. To make the morning editions, we should have our copy on the[9] editorial desk by one o'clock of the previous afternoon. Since it takes an hour and a half to get downtown[10] from our location, any news story we have must leave here by eleven o'clock to allow for traffic[11] delays. Much of our news is made too late to meet the deadline on the day it happens. The result is a day's[12] delay, and by then the story isn't news any longer. The editor may subsequently eliminate the[13] story in favor of a more recent event.

Here are two suggestions for improving the situation:

1.[14] Perhaps a member of the Public Information Service should maintain an office in the city and spend part[15] of each week there. Thus he would have face-to-face contact with the financial reporters, would lunch with them, and would seek[16] them out at every opportunity. He could obtain a membership in the St. Louis Newspapermen's[17] Club and make an extensive effort to cultivate reporters who would give us increased coverage.

We might try[18] this approach for several months or until we have built up the contacts we seem to need. Perhaps this should be only[19] a temporary experiment. Our office at corporate headquarters could telephone the news stories[20] to this representative, who would be able to file for the following morning's coverage.

I am doubtful[21] about the selection of a person for such an experiment. I really feel that the assignment is[22] important enough to warrant my filling it, even though the work here is at such a crucial stage. With two days[23] a week in town, I could probably develop more fruitful connections than an inexperienced colleague. The[24] alternative is, of course, to send a promising subordinate.

2. The second suggestion is that we[25] employ a St. Louis public relations firm to build up our local publicity and concentrate in our[26] national headquarters on national publicity. We could telephone our stories in and thus meet necessary[27] deadlines. The firm would already have all the contacts with the newspapers that we now lack.

I recommend[28] adoption of the first suggestion. When may I discuss the matter with you in detail? (575)

111 To: All Company Officers.

(86)

112 Mr. Richard C. Barry, Central College, Fairfield, Iowa 52556.

TRANSCRIPTION PACER

113▸ Mr. Jack M. Roche, Room 1679Y, State Department, Washington, D. C. 20002. 12 15

25 34 47 60 74 89 100 115 126 136 147

158
172
182
192
207
217
230
240
251
261
272
284
294
305
317
330
342
356
369

At home, in the conduct of personal affairs, and in the world of business, the management of money is a major consideration. Although many people do not keep formal financial records, most think about long-term and short-term goals and attempt to conduct their domestic affairs on a sound financial basis.

In business, financial decisions are made at various levels of management, depending on the nature of the problem and the amount of money involved. The board of directors of a corporation, for instance, usually decides such matters as selling stocks, issuing bonds, borrowing sums, and declaring dividends. A vice-president of finance, on the other hand, carries out the wishes of the board of directors and supervises financial transactions. Most of the financial planning of a business is based on a budget – a plan showing anticipated income and expenses for a given period of time.

The finance section is a top-management team that holds the "purse strings" of a business. In its day-to-day operations, it carefully plans the financial future for the company.

unit 6

FINANCE

Secretarial Assignment

In this unit you will take the dictation of Henry P. Walters, senior vice-president in charge of the financial affairs of National Products, Inc. All letters are signed by him over his title, Senior Vice-President.

SPECIALIZED TERMINOLOGY

In transcribing Mr. Walters' dictation, you will encounter the following terms:

Amortization • The systematic liquidation of the book value of an asset over the period of beneficial or contractual life.

Audit • The examination by public accountants of statements of income and financial condition and the rendering of a professional, independent opinion on these financial statements.

Blanket Contract • A binding agreement to do or to refrain from doing some lawful thing. It covers a group or class of things or conditions rather than a specific item.

Debenture Bonds • Unsecured promises to pay a specified sum of money at a fixed time in the future and at a fixed rate of interest. The bonds rest upon the general credit of the issuing corporation.

Long-Term Credit • Financing by the sale of bonds usually for more than five years.

Short-Term Credit • Financing by borrowing on a negotiable note for a period of one year or less.

Portfolio • The securities held by an investor.

Production Ratio (Operating Ratio) • The relationship of the cost of goods sold plus operating expenses to net sales.

Rate Concessions (Preferential Rates) • Special rates given to large shippers.

Sales Incentive • A plan whereby a salesman receives, in addition to the normal compensation, a percentage of his total sales beyond a specified amount.

Underwriter • One who guarantees the sale of bonds to be offered to the public for subscription.

Voucher • A receipt that substantiates a claimed expenditure.

This list contains words that appear frequently in business letters.

acquisition	**dilemma**	**negotiable**
agenda	**diversification**	**portfolio**
amortize	**equipment**	**ratios**
auditors	**financier**	**foreign**
comparative	**fiscal**	**tariff**
debenture	**intricacies**	**vouchers**
deficit	**municipal**	**withholding**

Transcribe the following sentences, preferably at the typewriter, until you master the spelling of the words that appear in the word list above.

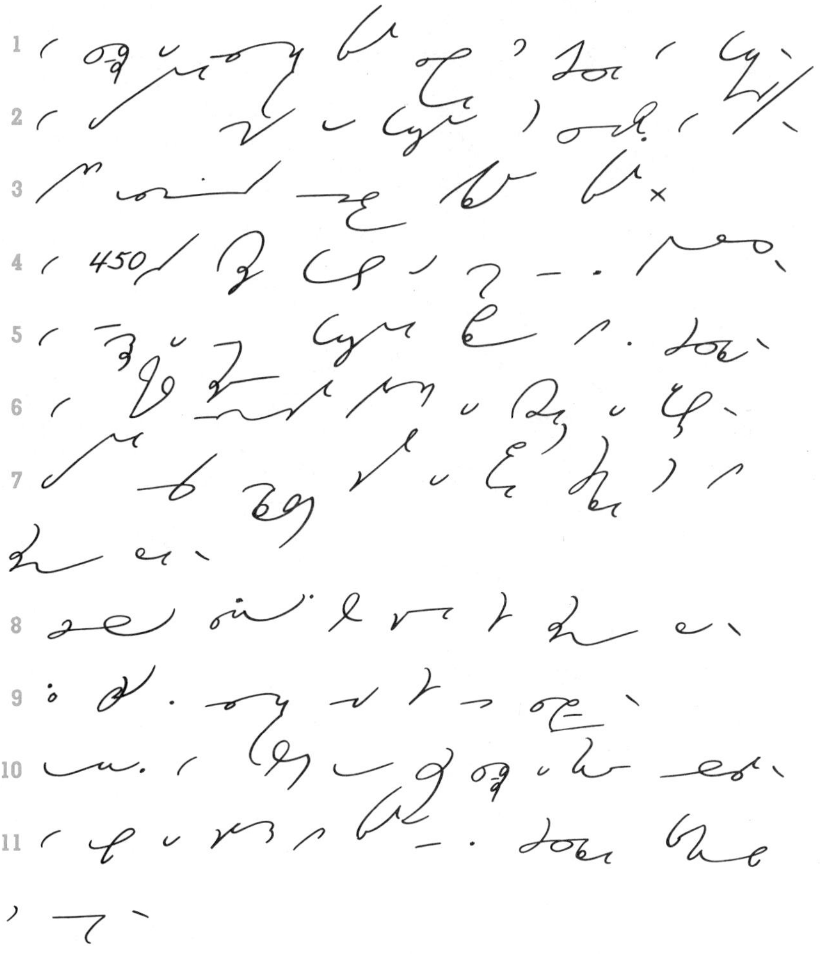

lesson

26 BUILDING TRANSCRIPTION QUALITY

TRANSCRIPTION POINTERS

Expressing Numbers

1 Use figures for exact numbers above ten, for numbers in statistical and tabular work, and for numbers that occur in a connected group within a sentence.

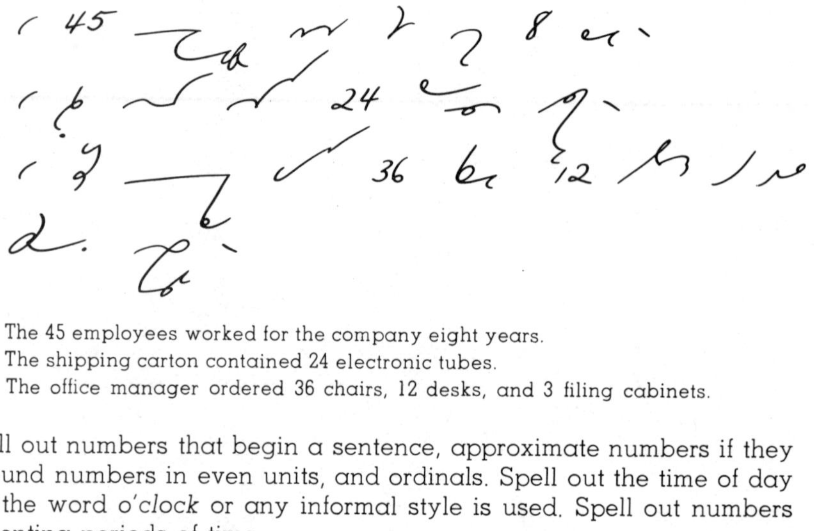

The 45 employees worked for the company eight years.
The shipping carton contained 24 electronic tubes.
The office manager ordered 36 chairs, 12 desks, and 3 filing cabinets.

2 Spell out numbers that begin a sentence, approximate numbers if they are round numbers in even units, and ordinals. Spell out the time of day when the word *o'clock* or any informal style is used. Spell out numbers representing periods of time.

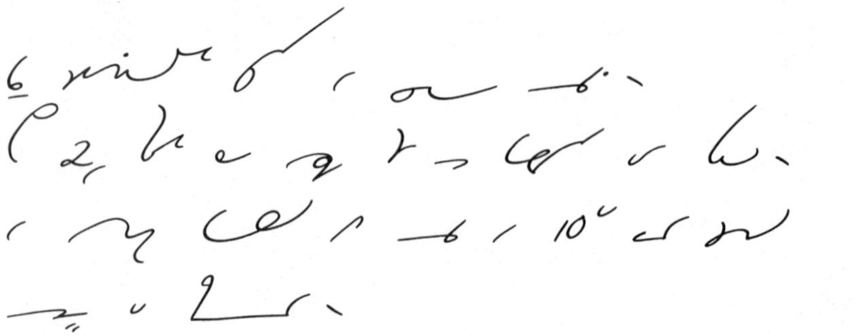

Six hundred stockholders attended the annual meeting.
About two thousand votes were cast for the new president of the board.
The group planned to meet at ten o'clock on the second Monday of each month.

3 Use figures for the day of the month and the year, amounts of money, dimensions, measures, weights, degrees, distances, capacities, percentages, decimals, proportions, and market quotations.

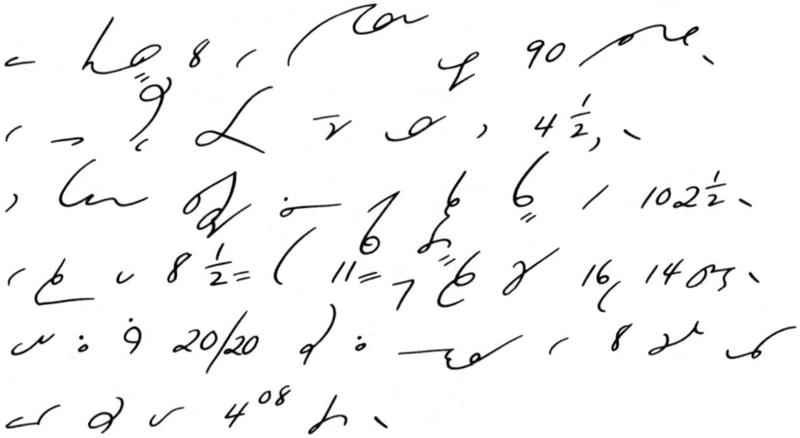

On July 8, the temperature reached 90 degrees.
The new savings bank interest rate is 4½ percent.
His broker advised him to buy Chesapeake Bay at 102½.
The shipment of 8½- by 11-inch paper weighed 16 pounds 14 ounces.
Although he has 20/20 vision, he misread the 8 cents written on the face of the $4.08 check.

Check your understanding of number expression by transcribing the following sentences, preferably at the typewriter.

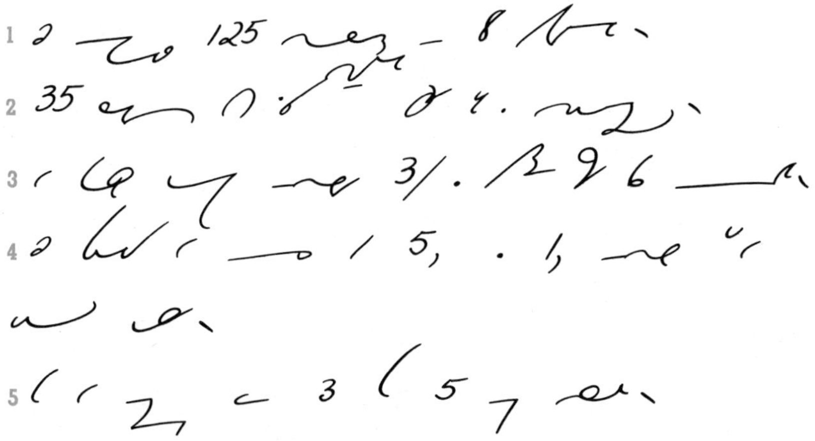

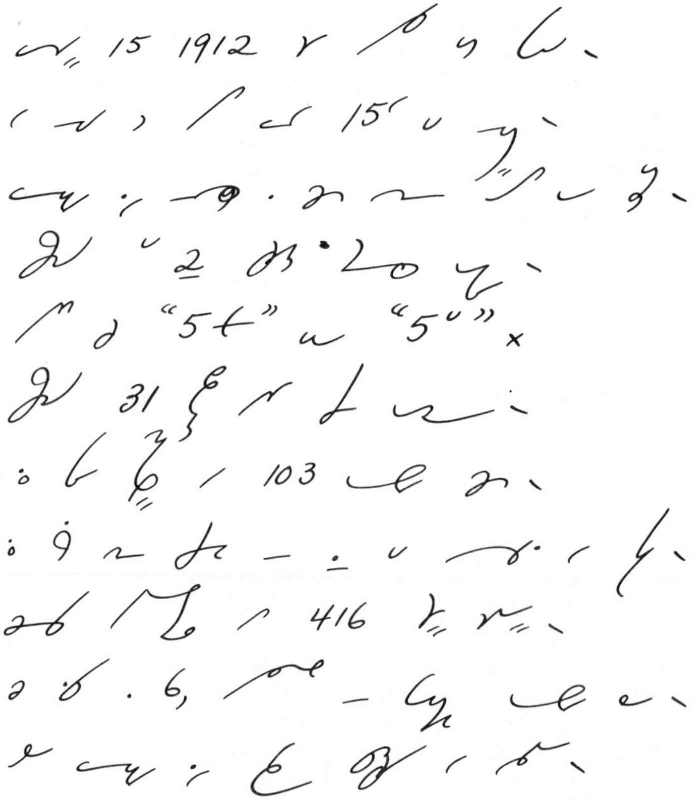

TRANSCRIPTION SPEED BUILDER

114▸ To: Glenn C. Hunter, Chief Auditor.

(202)

115 ▸ To: William A. Scanlon, Payroll.

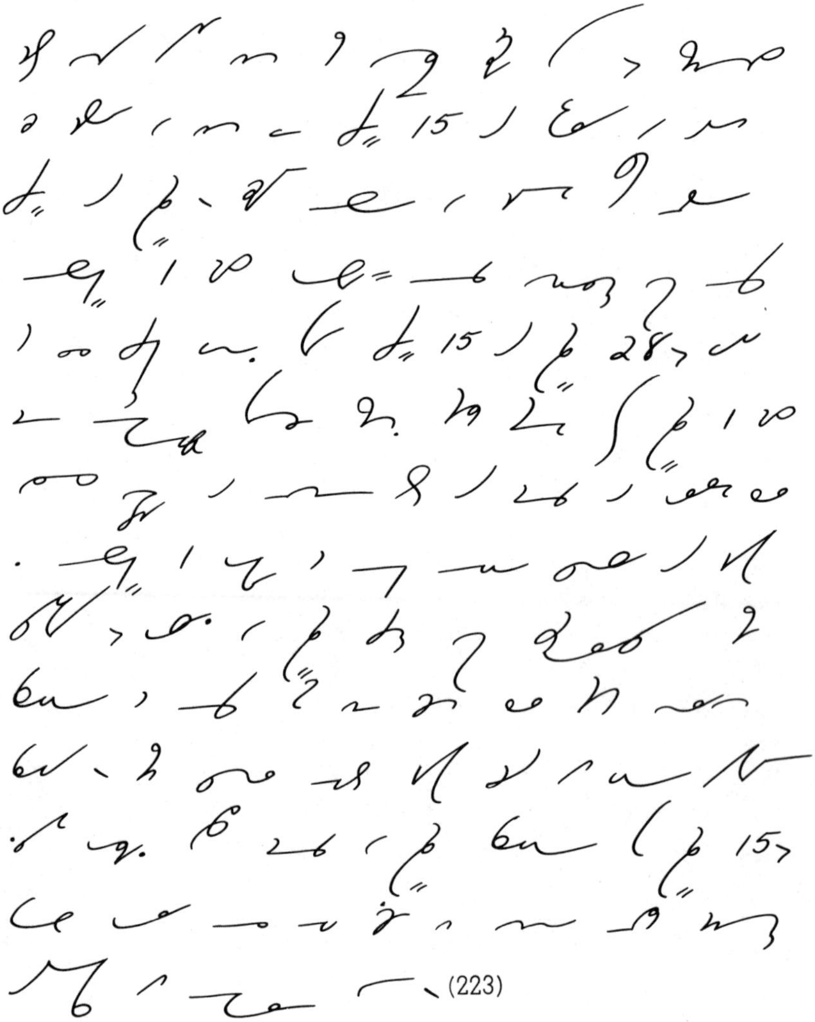

(223)

116▸ To: Mr. Henry M. Simpson, President.

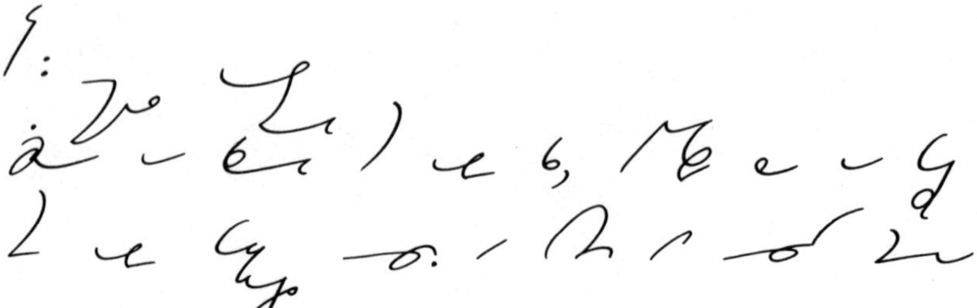

(183)

Lesson 27

MASTERING SHORTHAND THEORY

WORD BEGINNINGS

De-, Di-

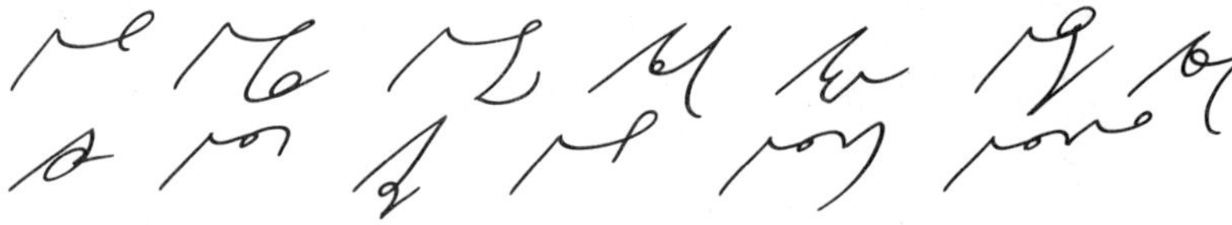

Mis-

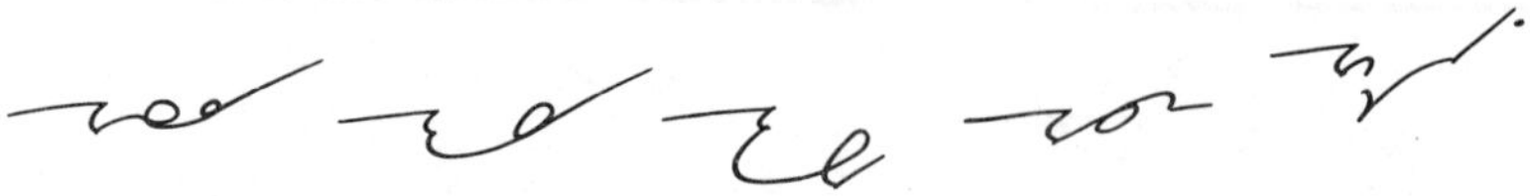

Trans-

WORD ENDINGS

-ble

-hood, -ward

-self, -selves

Delays, deliberate, delivered, dependable, depositor, derived, desirable, design, direction, digest, dilation, directive, directory.

Miscarried, mislaid, misplaced, mistaken, misunderstanding.

Transacted, transcription, transition, transit, transportation, transmitted, transparency.

Adaptable, adjustable, acceptable, agreeable, cable, capable, eligible, feasible, table.

Boyhood, childhood, likelihood, manhood, neighborhood, parenthood, forward, girlhood, awkwardly, onward, backward, outward, afterward.

Herself, himself, oneself, itself, myself, ourselves, yourself, yourselves.

TRANSCRIPTION SPEED BUILDER

117▸ To: Henry M. Simpson, Chairman, Administrative Committee.

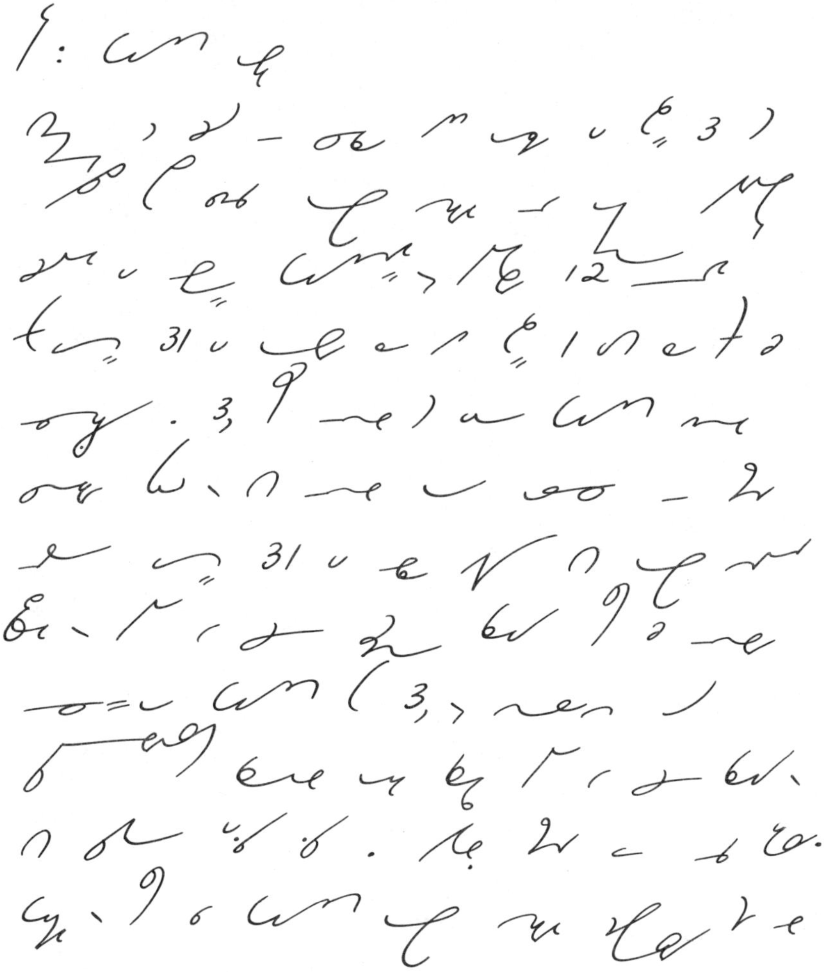

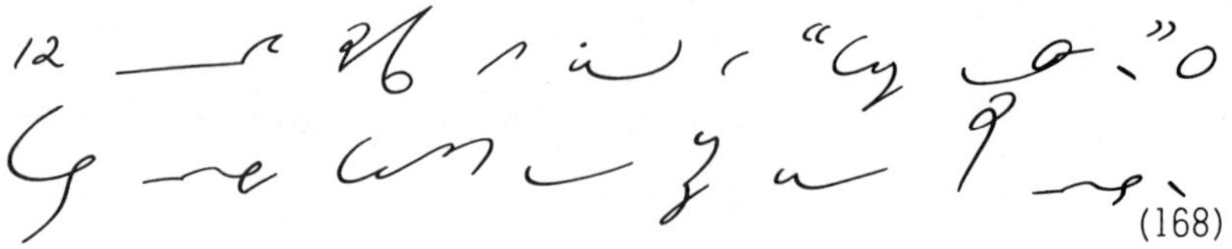

(168)

118▸ To: Lawrence F. Markham, Traffic Manager.

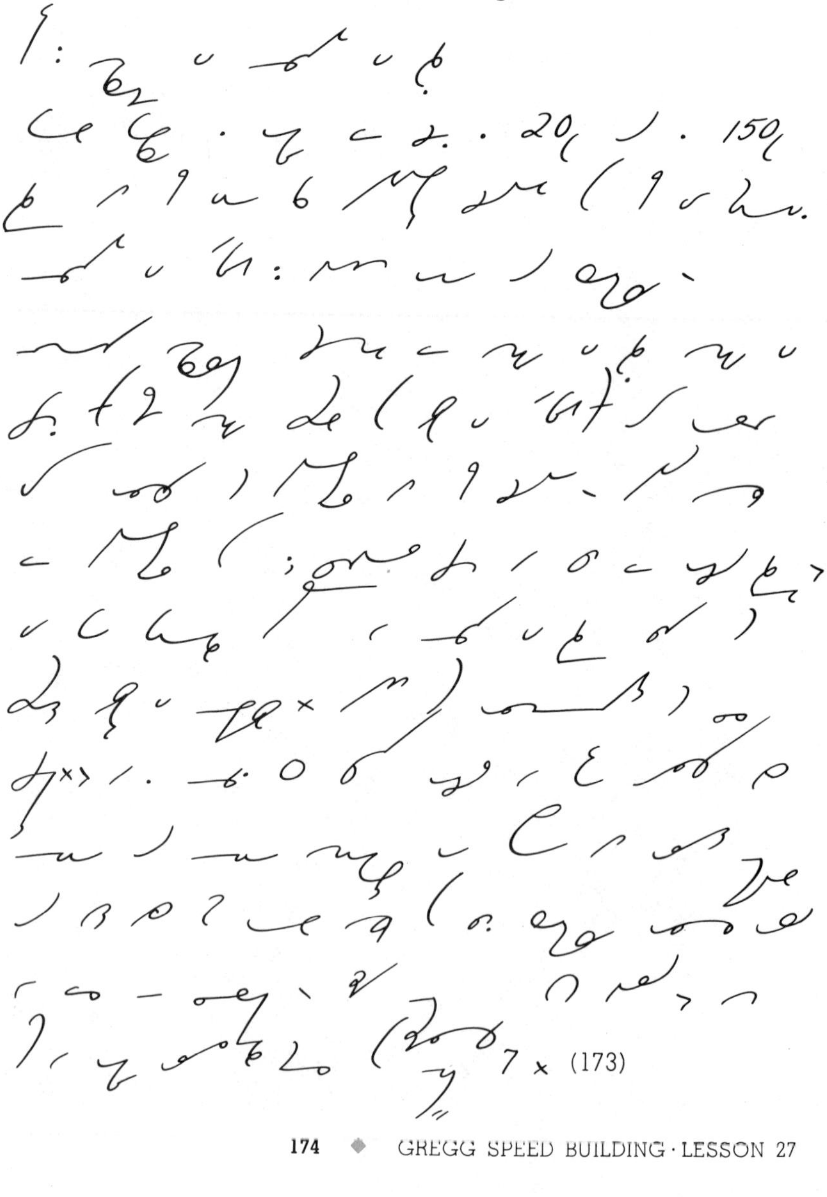

(173)

119 ▸ To: Mr. Henry M. Simpson, President.

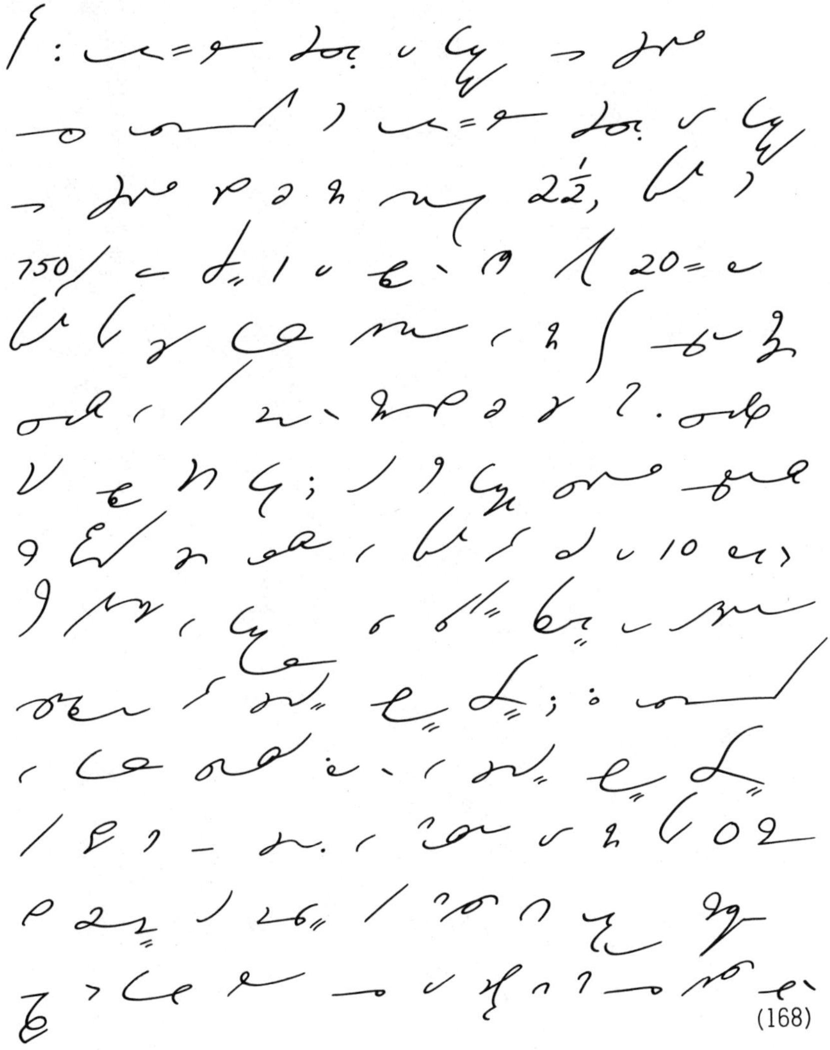

(168)

120 ▸ Bank of Commerce, 410 Lake Avenue, Chicago, Illinois 60612.

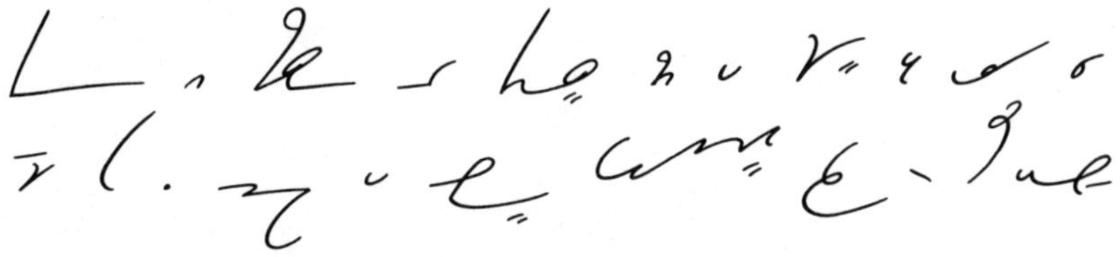

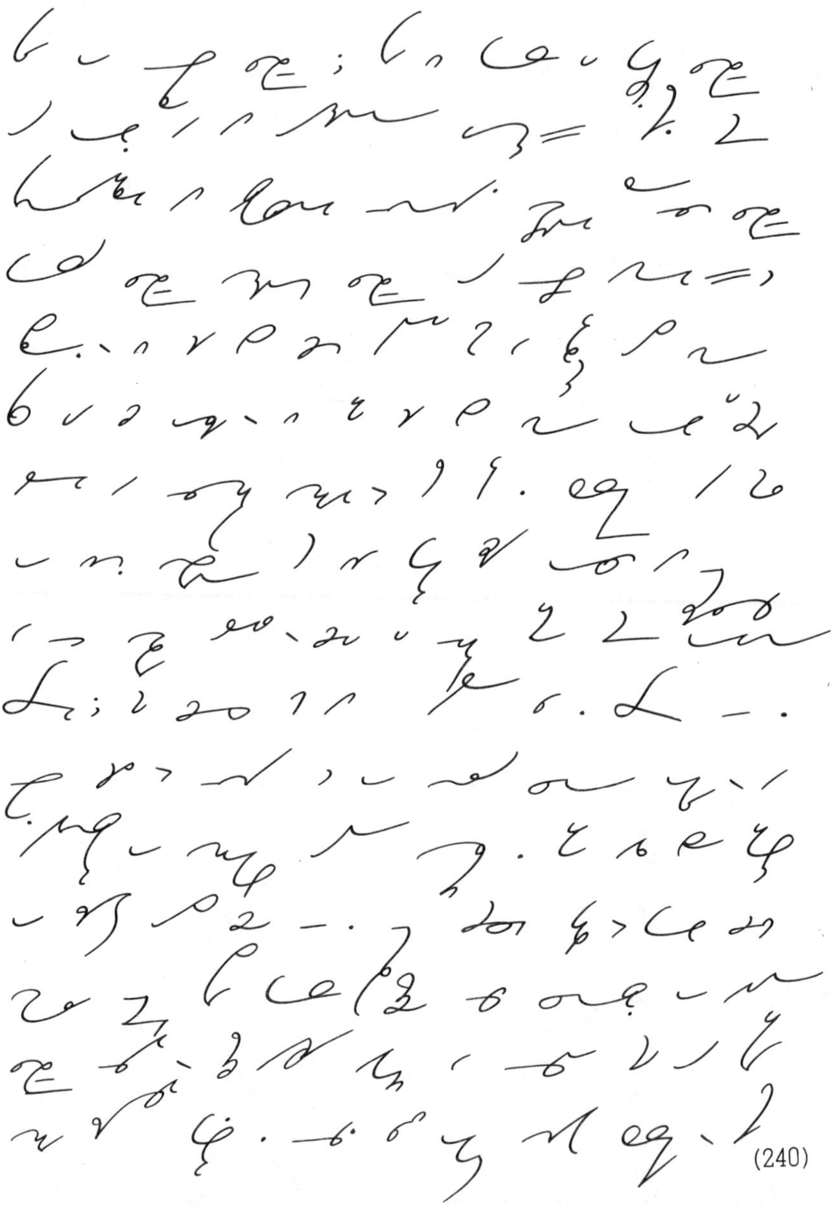

(240)

121▸ Mr. Herbert B. Greenwald, President, First National Bank, Balboa at Sacramento Street, San Diego, California 92116.

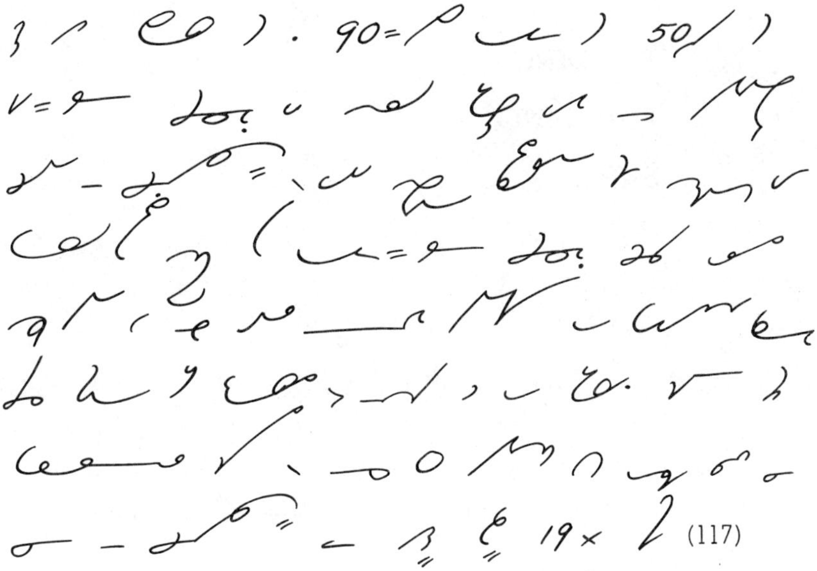

(117)

122 ▸ Wilson and Smith, One Wall Street, New York, New York 10005.

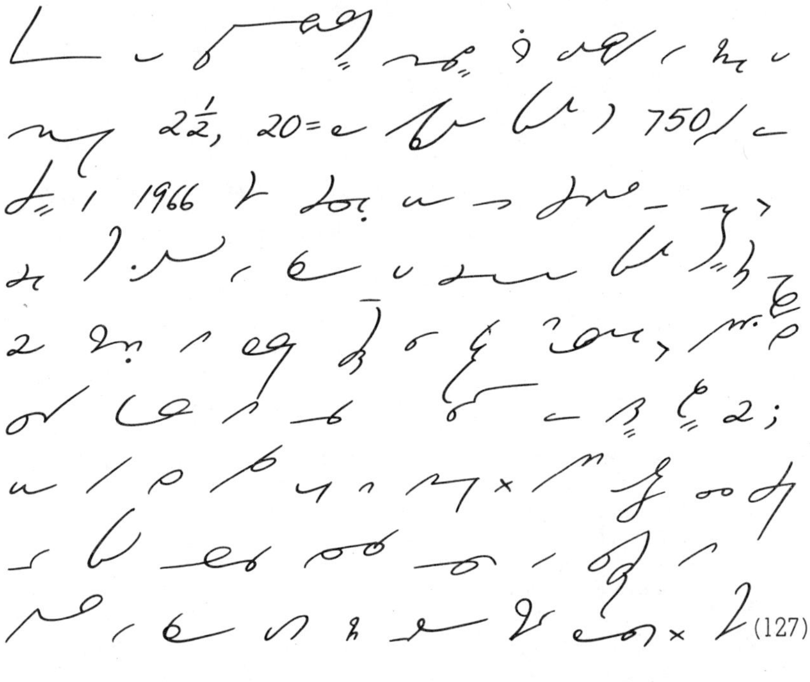

(127)

lesson 28

BUILDING PHRASING SKILL

PHRASE BUILDER

Drill 1

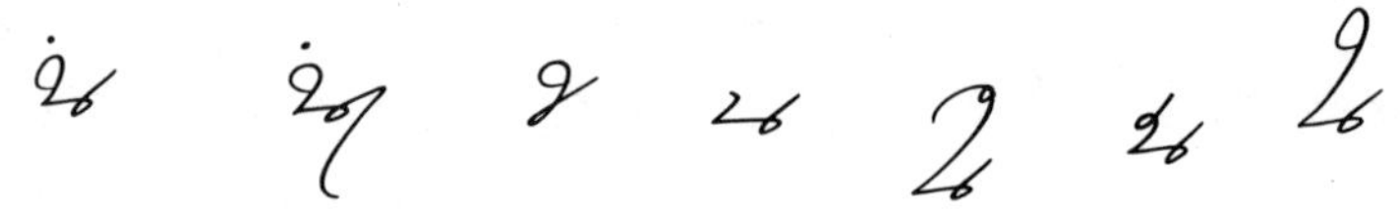

Drill 2

Drill 3

Drill 4

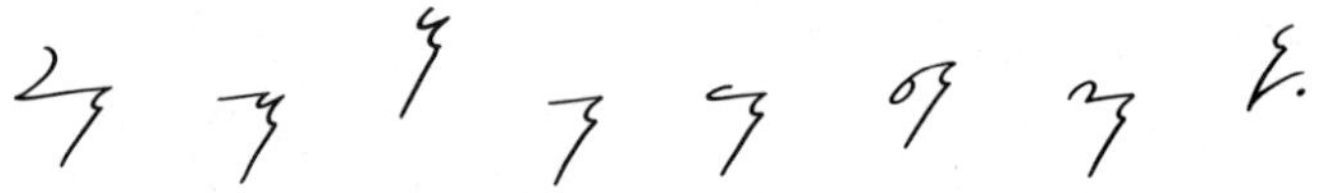

Drill 5

Drill 6

Has not yet, has not yet been, as yet, is not yet, they have not yet, she is not yet, I have not yet.

Several times, several others, several months, several days, several minutes, several moments, several hundred.

Every time, every one, every one of them, every one of the, every other, every month, every day, ever since.

From such, no such, of such, in such, on such, with such, one such, such a thing.

What are, what is, what will, what will be, what has been, what is the, what was.
Very much, very good, very well, very many, very glad, very little.

TRANSCRIPTION SPEED BUILDER

123 To: Ralph C. Akin, Sales Manager.

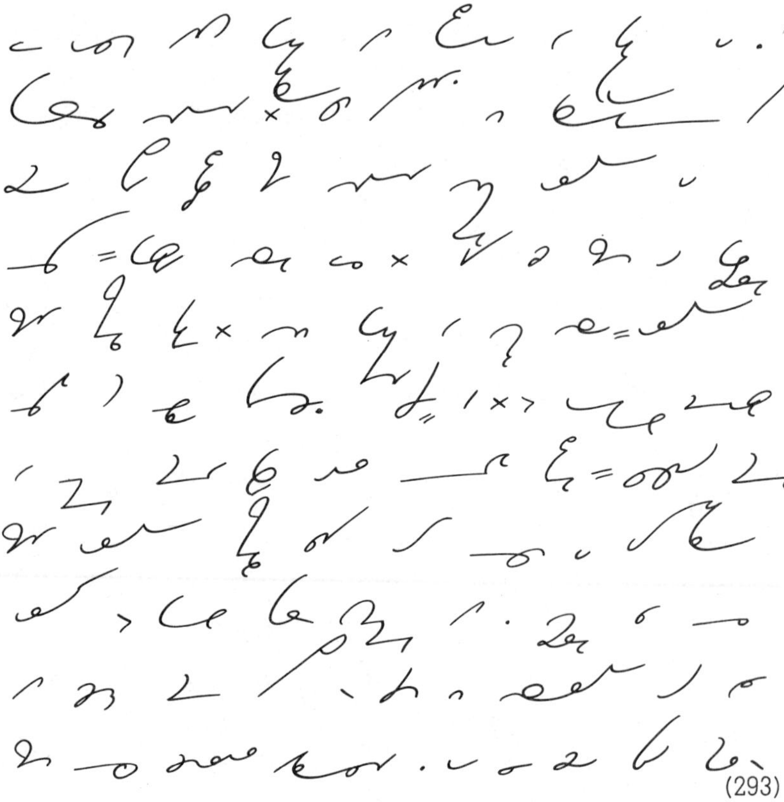

(293)

124 To: Mr. Henry M. Simpson, President.

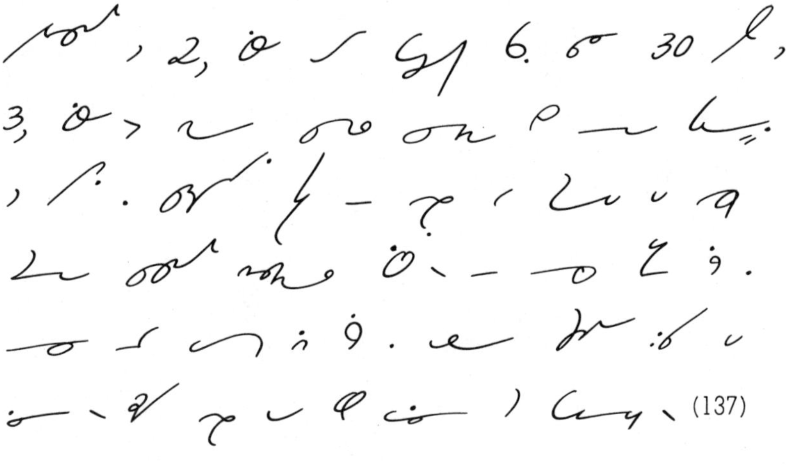

(137)

125 ▶ Mr. J. Alan Franklin, Vice-President, The Martin-Williamson Company, 416 Delaware Road, Baltimore, Maryland 21208.

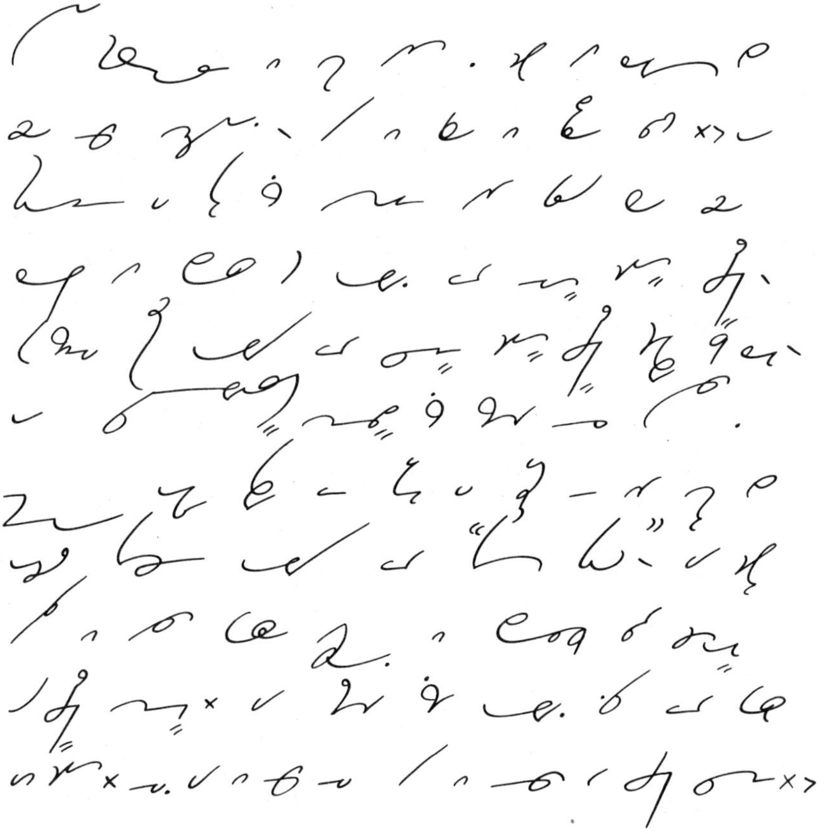

(150)

126▸ To: Harold C. Poling, Credit Manager.

(178)

lesson 29

PROGRESSIVE SPEED BUILDING

In this lesson the one-minute speed-forcing letters are counted progressively at 90, 100, and 110 words a minute; the two-minute reinforcement and control letter is counted at 100 words a minute.

First practice the vocabulary preview that precedes the speed-forcing practice, and then review the specialized vocabulary presented at the beginning of this unit.

SPEED-BUILDING LETTERS

Vocabulary Preview

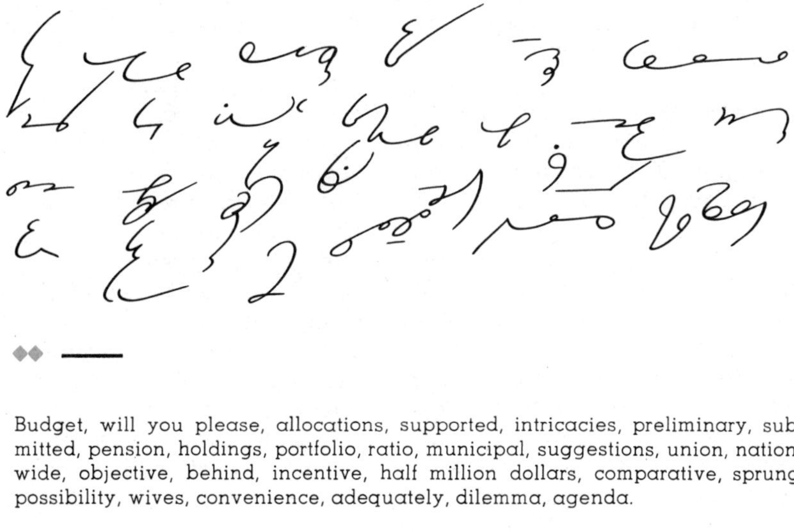

Budget, will you please, allocations, supported, intricacies, preliminary, submitted, pension, holdings, portfolio, ratio, municipal, suggestions, union, nationwide, objective, behind, incentive, half million dollars, comparative, sprung, possibility, wives, convenience, adequately, dilemma, agenda.

Speed Forcing

(1 Minute at 90)

127 Gentlemen: The budget for the next fiscal year is now being planned. Before November 1 will you please estimate the needs/of your department for equipment, supplies, additional personnel, and additional space allocations. Every

//request for additional funds must be supported by definite evidence of the need.

I am sure you understand that/// the intricacies of our budget require that preliminary figures be submitted at this early date. Sincerely yours, (1)

(1 Minute at 100)

128 Dear Mr. Barnes: Our pension funds are at an all-time high, and we have a cash surplus for investment. The enclosed list of current holdings in/our portfolio will enable you to recommend possible purchases.

Our ratio of common stocks to bonds and preferred stocks is//so high that an element of risk is involved. Will you please recommend several high-grade municipal bonds with Moody's AA ratings///and preferred stocks for our consideration.

I should like to discuss your suggestions with you. Would Wednesday morning be convenient? Sincerely yours, (2)

(1 Minute at 110)

129 Dear Mr. Gray: All the information that I have leads me to think that our union will be willing to accept the 3 percent ceiling on increases/recommended by the President in his concern about inflation.

Rather than demand a rise in take-home pay, the union intends to push for a//higher company contribution to pension funds. Its aim is to build up the pension funds so that an employee can retire after twenty years. This///is a nationwide union objective. The reasoning behind it is that automation can be combated only by such early retirements. Yours truly, (3)

Reinforcement and Control

(2 Minutes at 100)

130 Dear Ralph: Thank you for sending me your proposal for a sales-incentive plan that awards a 10-day trip for two to Hawaii to all salesmen/who reach a half million dollars in volume next year.

In general, the plan seems excellent; but I have a few questions that I should like//to raise before it is presented to the Administrative Committee.

1. Have you obtained comparative figures from several///companies? Although you suggest that we adopt the plan submitted by the McDonald Sales Incentive Company, I have the impression that (1) a number of such companies have sprung up recently. We should investigate more than one possibility.

2. Do you propose that all/the salesmen and their wives travel in one group, or should they go at their own convenience? Although group travel would be cheaper, the problem of//covering the sales territory adequately might present a dilemma.

3. How many salesmen did we have on the staff last year who/// would have qualified for such a trip?

When I receive the additional information, I will get the matter on the agenda. Yours cordially, (2)

131▸ Mr. Vincent Jones, Production Manager, National Products, Inc., 271 Mount Washington Boulevard, Louisville, Kentucky 40219.

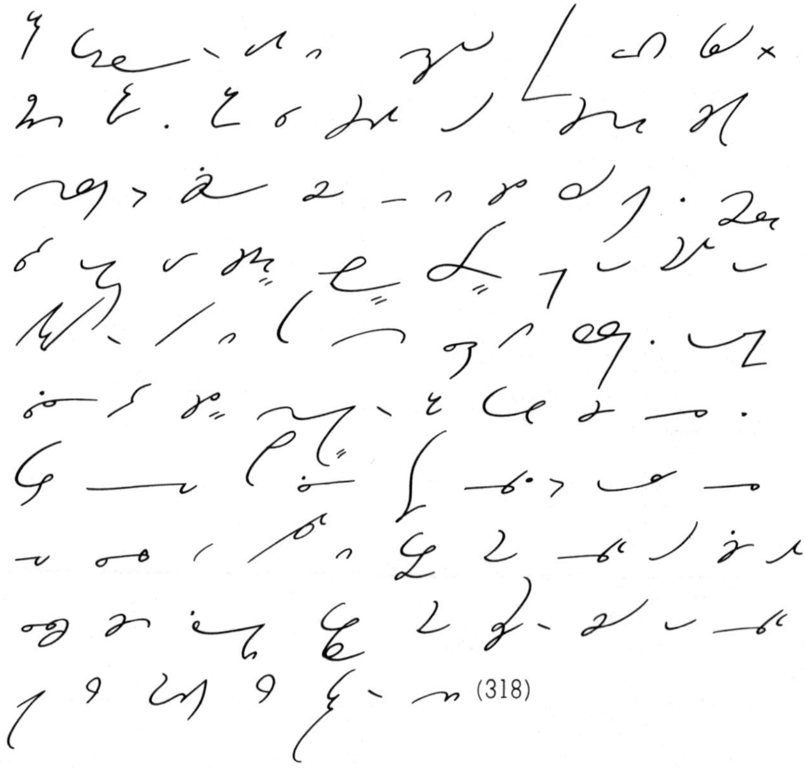

(318)

132▸ Mr. Herbert Ashe, Production Manager, National Products, Inc., 2198 Lafayette Street, New Orleans, Louisiana 70113.

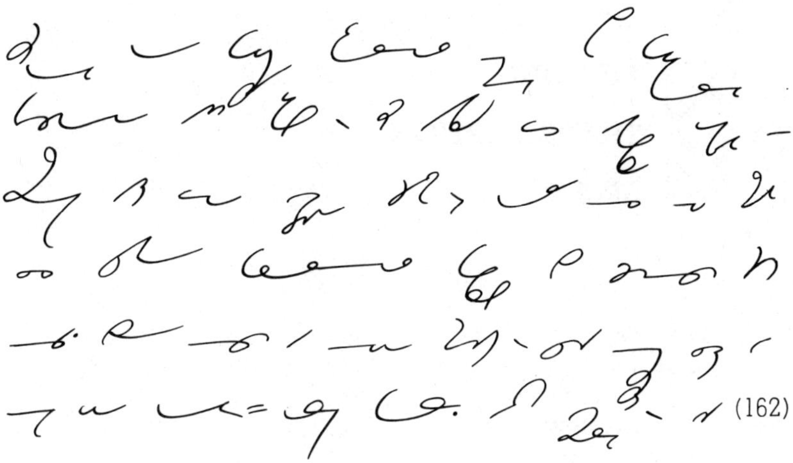

(162)

TRANSCRIPTION PACER

133▸ Brewster & Noble, Public Accountants, 11 Wall Street, New 12
York, New York 10005. 16

29
39
51
65
77
90
101
113
127
139

lesson 30

BUILDING TRANSCRIPTION SPEED

SUSTAINED SPEED BUILDER

Practice the following vocabulary preview, and then see how well you can sustain your reinforcement and control speed.

Vocabulary Preview

Houston, specifically, polyethelene, synthetic, population, Texas, anticipate, statistics, per capita, Galveston, Austin, availability, nearby, concession, authorized, Universal, Elmira, Ontario, containers, plastic, aerosol, Canadian, production, telephone, I shall be, photograph, distribution, periodicals, facilities, locality.

Speed Builder

134 Industrial Development Commission, State of Texas, Austin, Texas 78705.

Gentlemen: We are considering possible sites for the location of a new NATIONAL PRODUCTS plant. Will[1] you please send us any information that your commission has compiled about the industrial advantages[2] of the Houston area.

Specifically, we should like data about the following items:

1.[3] Would we find local sources of polyethylene, synthetic rubber, and plastic materials near Houston?[4] The product that we plan to manufacture requires these raw materials, and we prefer locating our[5] plant close to factories producing them.

2. Would we find a potential labor force in the Houston area?[6] Although we know that Houston is one of the fastest growing areas in the country, we are not sure whether[7] the population is primarily an industrial one. Please tell us the growth rate for the city and also[8] provide an analysis of the types of people comprising this new population.

3. Can you provide[9] information about the going wage rate for factory workers in this city?

4. What market might we[10] anticipate in Texas for our products? I have seen statistics indicating a population of approximately[11] two and a half million people in Houston. I have no information about the purchasing power[12] of these people. What is the per capita income? What is the educational level of the[13] residents of both Houston and the rest of the state?

5. What railroads serve the Houston area? How do freight rates compare[14] with those in other areas?

6. What airlines serve the Houston area? Are preferential rates given on[15] shipments of airfreight?

7. What plans are being made to make the facilities of the port of Galveston more[16] accessible to the factories in the Houston area?

8. Do you know of a site close enough to downtown[17] Houston to make the buyer eligible for an urban-renewal loan?

If your answers to my questions[18] warrant our further consideration of Houston as a plant site, we shall get in touch with you again. Probably[19] a committee from our headquarters in St. Louis would meet with representatives of the Industrial[20] Development Commission in Austin and also travel to Houston to survey possible location for our[21] plant.

We shall appreciate any help you can give us in reaching a decision. Yours very truly, (438)

135▸ Chamber of Commerce, Ashland, Kentucky 41101.

Gentlemen: We are interested in information about the advantages of locating a new[1] NATIONAL PRODUCTS plant in Ashland, Kentucky. Will you please send us any materials your organization[2] has compiled to attract new industry. We should, of course, like to obtain data about potential factory[3] labor supply, transportation facilities, nearby markets for our products, any possible rates[4] concessions by railroads serving the locality, and tax advantages in Kentucky, if any.

We are also[5] interested in the availability of suitable housing for the employees who would move into[6] the area and the kind of schools provided.

We shall appreciate any information you may send us[7] as a basis for further investigation. Sincerely yours, (152)

136 Chamber of Commerce, Houston, Texas 77031.

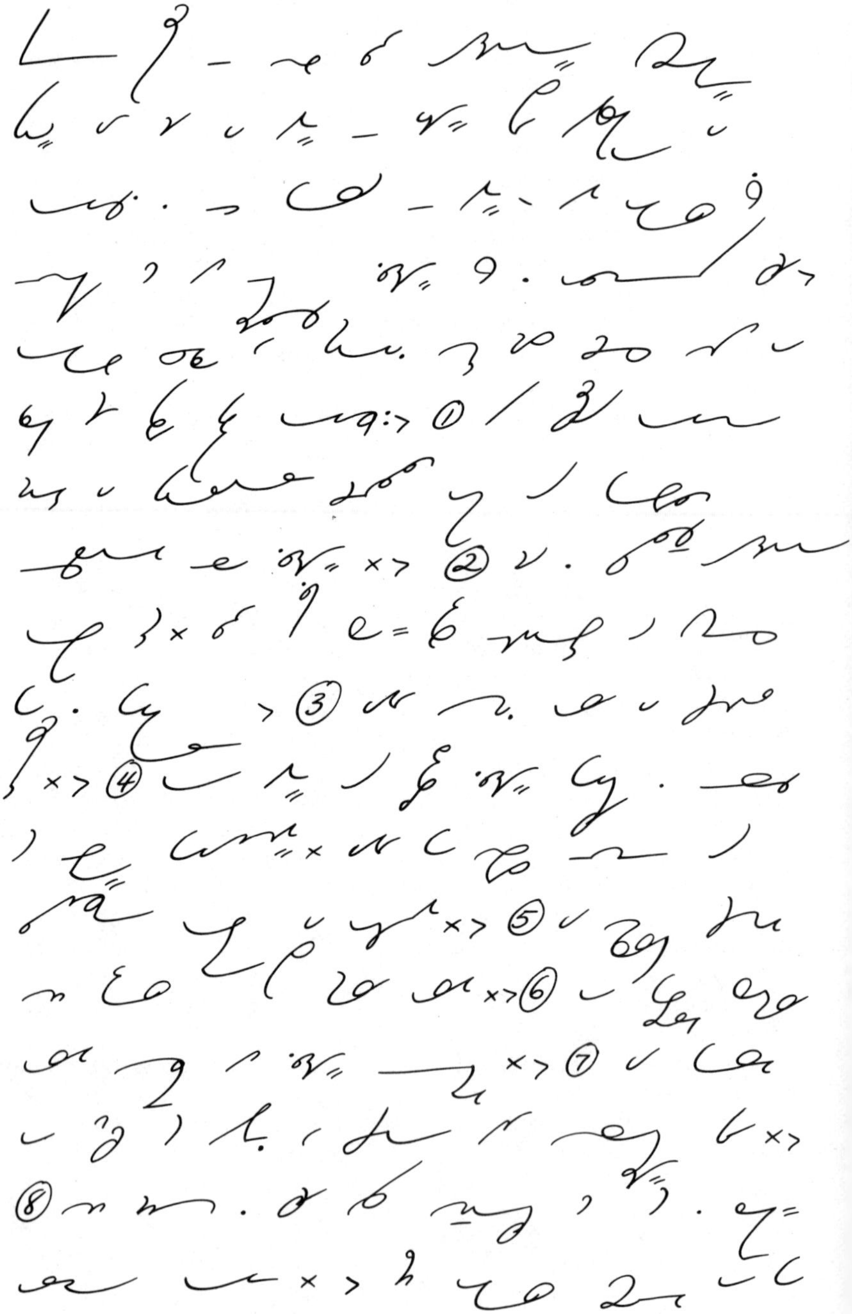

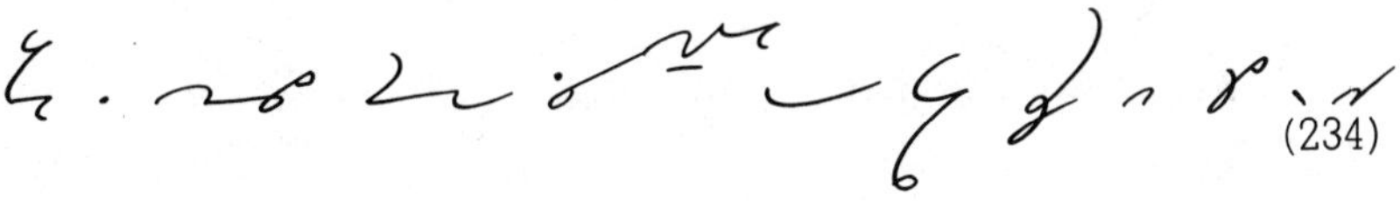

(234)

137▸ Memo to Arthur Williamson, Director of Public Information.

(173)

138 ▸ Chamber of Commerce, Ashland, Kentucky 41101.

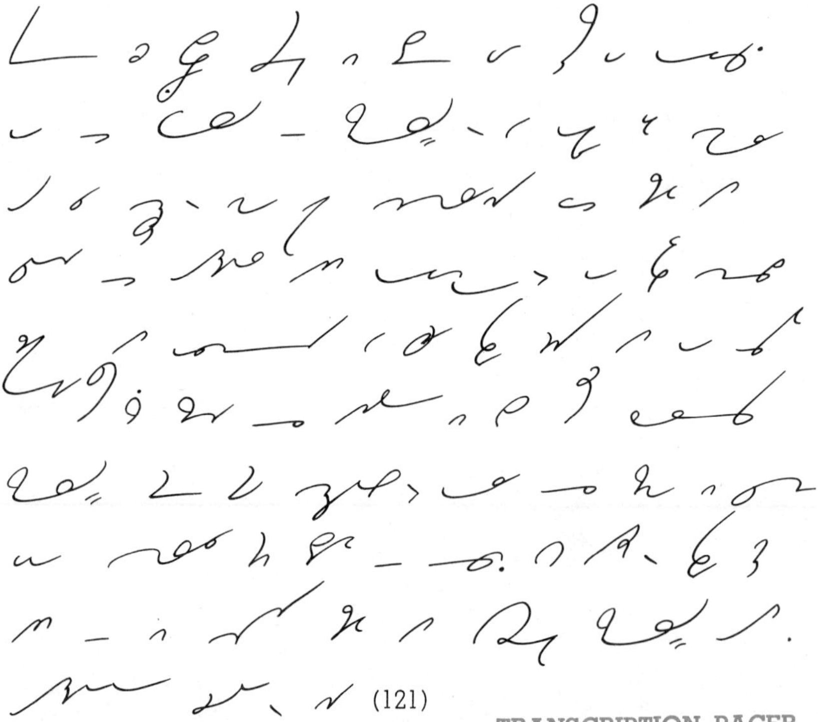

(121)

TRANSCRIPTION PACER

139 ▸ To: Arthur C. Williamson, Public Information Director. 12

19
29
42
53
64
75
86

100
113
123
136
145
156
167
176
187
199
208
223
235
246
256
268
281
294
305

When you purchase an article in a store, do you ever stop to consider that the company that manufactured it probably spent between two cents and twelve cents of every sales dollar to (1) develop new designs and styles for the product, (2) reduce waste by using raw materials more efficiently, and (3) develop new production processes and equipment? In fact, the continued success of many companies, under relentless pressure of competition, can be attributed to the ability of their research and development departments (popularly referred to as "R and D") to discover new products and cheaper ways to produce products already in their lines.

Research and development in business is carried on in production methods, raw materials, products, packaging, marketing and advertising, and most recently, in long-range planning by means of electronic data processing.

unit 7

RESEARCH AND DEVELOPMENT

Secretarial Assignment

In this unit you will take the dictation of Charles C. Haynes, in charge of the research and development for National Products, Inc. All letters are signed by him over his title, Director, Research and Development.

SPECIALIZED TERMINOLOGY

Abstract • Summary of a document, paper, or speech.

Aerosol Package • Method of packaging in which gas under pressure is used to spray a liquid.

Budget • Orderly arrangement of computed cost and revenue estimates that cover all phases of a business operation for a specific period of time.

Flow Diagram (Process Chart) • Brief statements and symbols arranged vertically in chronological order showing the successive steps in a process.

Patent • Government grant giving the inventor the right to exclude all others from making, using, or selling his invention for the term of seventeen years.

Pneumatic • Related to or pertaining to air or, derivately, to other gases.

Royalty • Payment or fee, usually based on a percentage of sales income given to an author or a patent holder by a publisher or producer.

Synthetic • Man-made or artificially prepared material, as opposed to material obtained from natural sources.

Tensile Strength • The degree of stress that a fabric can withstand without being torn when it is pulled in a lengthwise direction.

Toggle Switch • A device used in which a projecting lever is manually pushed through a small arc to open or close an electrical circuit.

Tolerance Test • Measurement of the power of endurance or resistance against pressure, chemical action, or some other force without adverse effect.

SPELLING AND TRANSCRIPTION PRACTICE

If the final consonant of a one-syllable word is preceded by a short vowel, the consonant is doubled when a suffix beginning with a vowel is added.

win	**winning**	**hop**	**hopping**
ship	**shipping**	**slip**	**slipping**

When adding a suffix beginning with a vowel to a word of more than one syllable, do not double the final consonant preceded by a short vowel unless the accent is on the final syllable.

benéfited	**begínners**	**transférred**
díffered	**forbídding**	**inhérited**

Transcribe the following sentences, preferably at the typewriter, until you are thoroughly familiar with the spelling rules presented above.

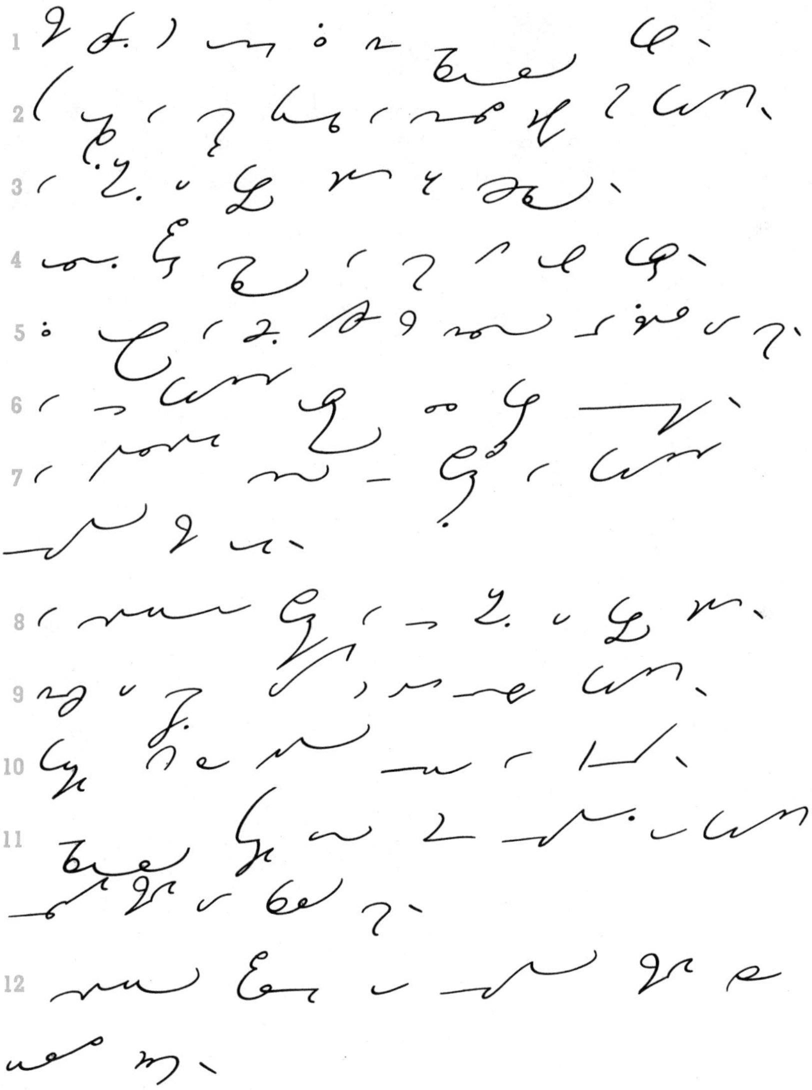

Lesson 31

BUILDING TRANSCRIPTION QUALITY

TRANSCRIPTION POINTERS

Uses of the Comma *(Continued)*

1 Nonrestrictive, or nonessential, words, phrases, and clauses are descriptive or explanatory and can be omitted without changing the meaning of a sentence; they should be set off by commas. Restrictive or essential clauses are necessary to the meaning of a sentence and should not be set off by commas.

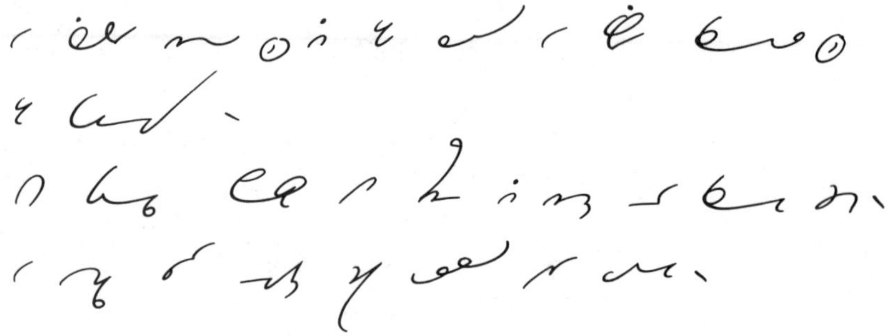

The hardest worker, who also earned the highest salary, was promoted.
This policy applies to everyone who works in the sales section.
The copy with the notations is to be returned to the authors.

2 Names and words used in direct address must be set off by commas.

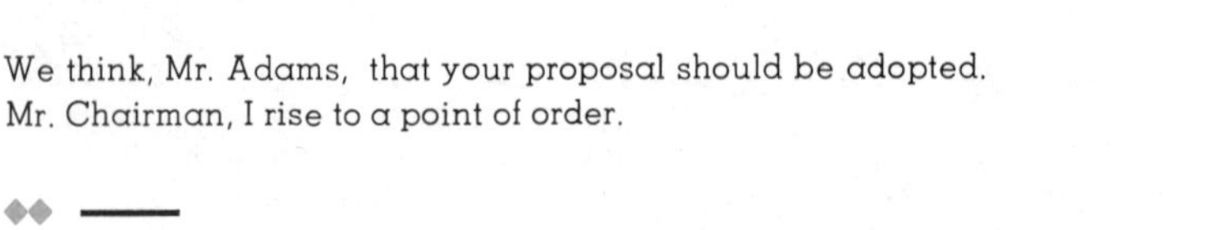

We think, Mr. Adams, that your proposal should be adopted.
Mr. Chairman, I rise to a point of order.

Check your understanding of comma usage by transcribing the following sentences, preferably at the typewriter.

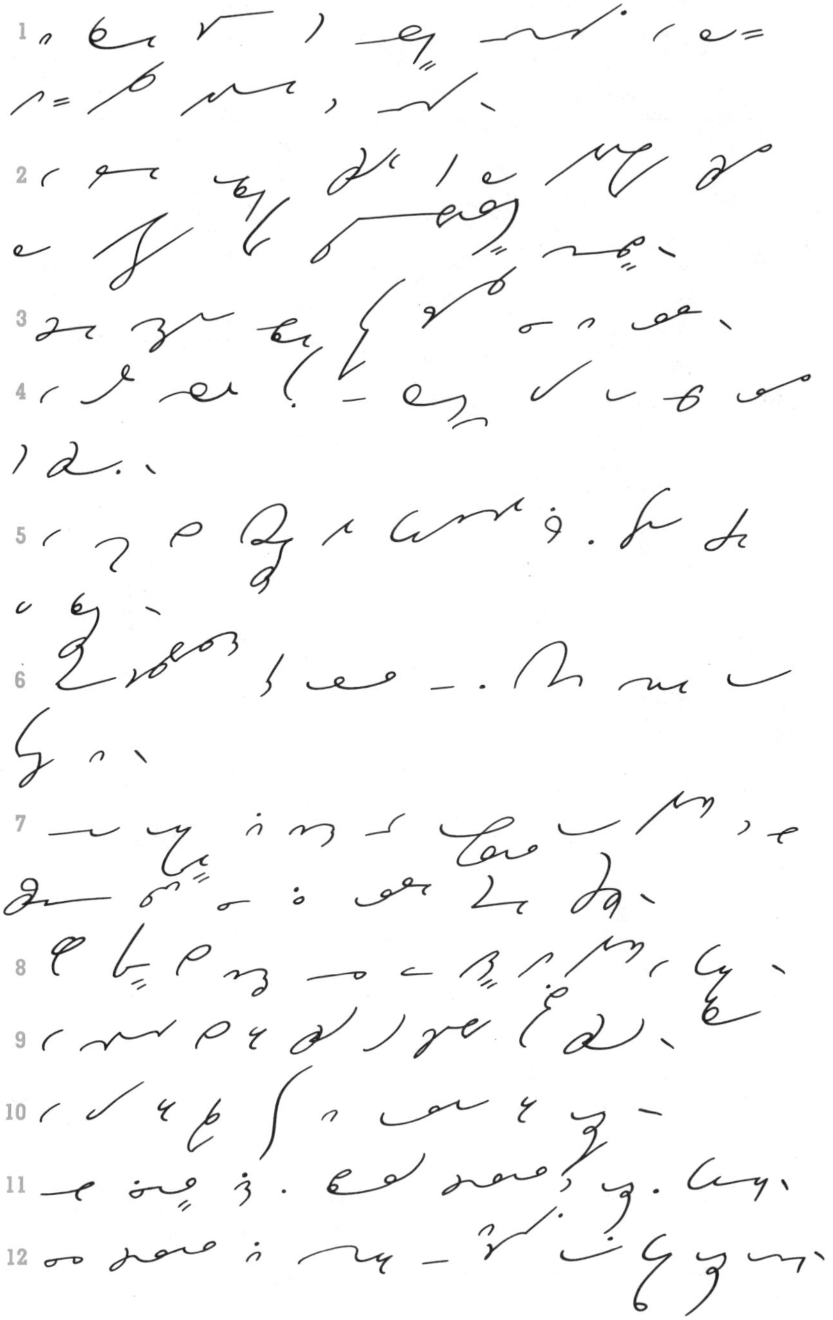

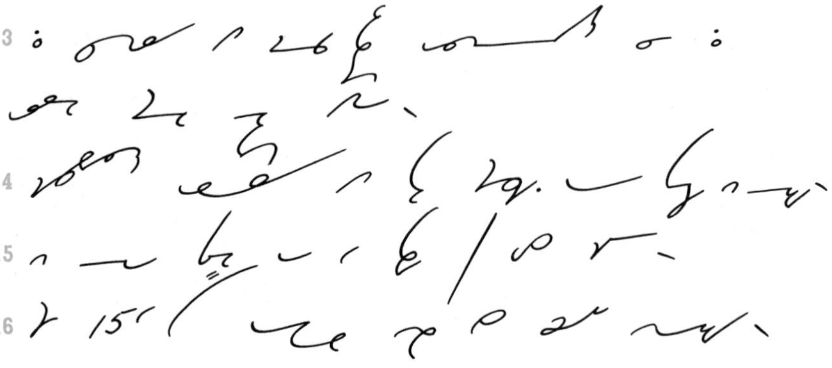

TRANSCRIPTION SPEED BUILDER

140▸ To: All Laboratory Foremen.

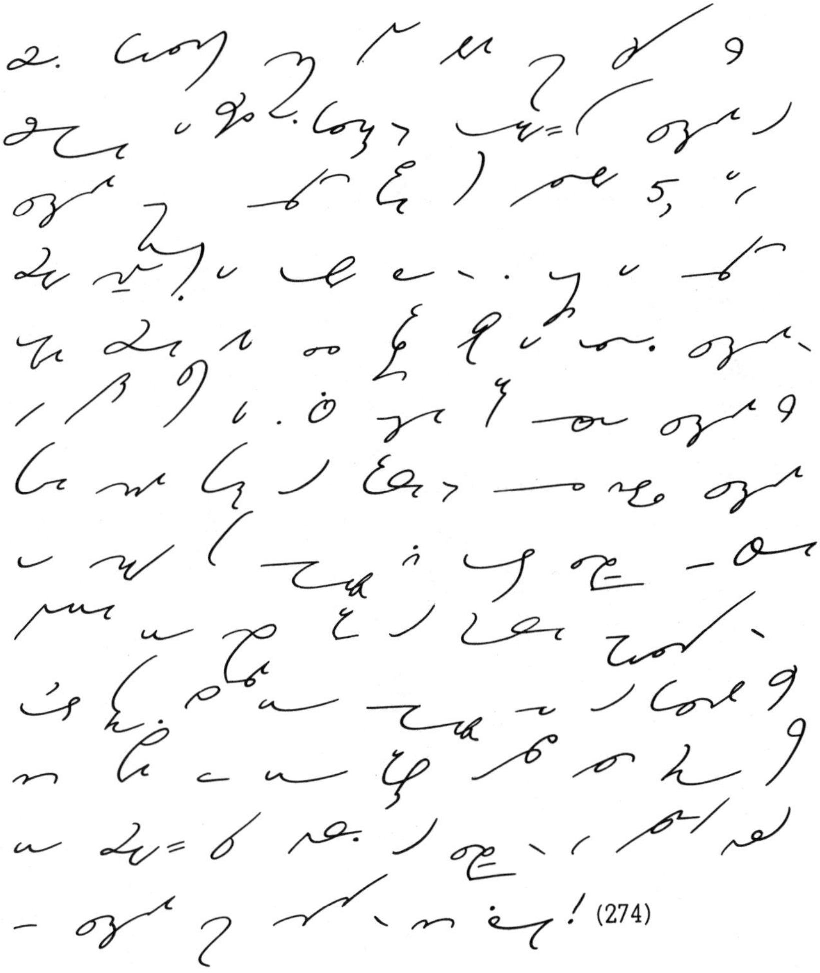

(274)

141 ▸ Dr. Hubert C. Busch, Research and Development Department, National Products, Inc., 211 Forest Avenue, St. Louis, Missouri 63100.

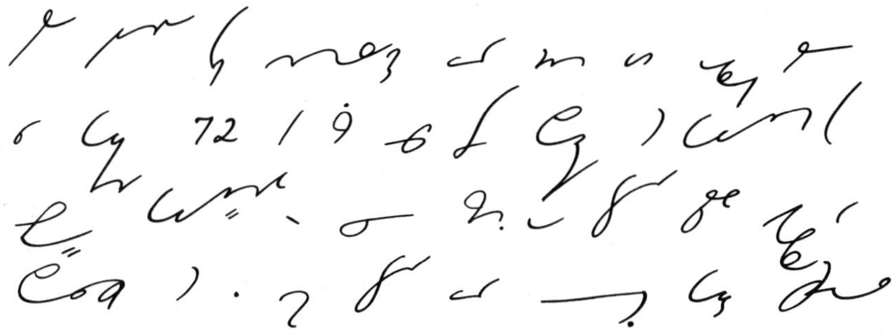

(216)

142▸ Dr. Harvey D. Bentley, The Bentley Research Center, 235 Greentree Road, Columbus, Ohio 43217.

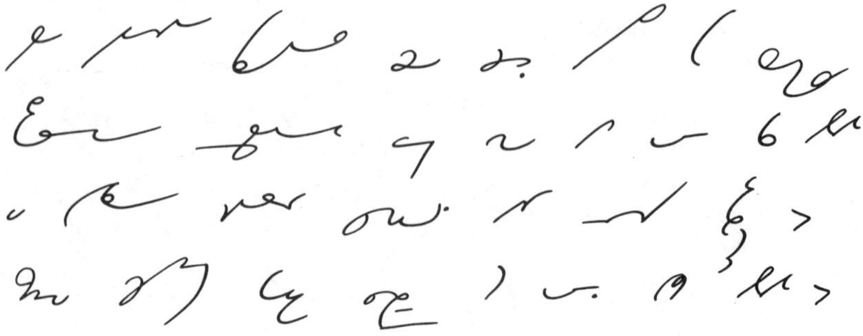

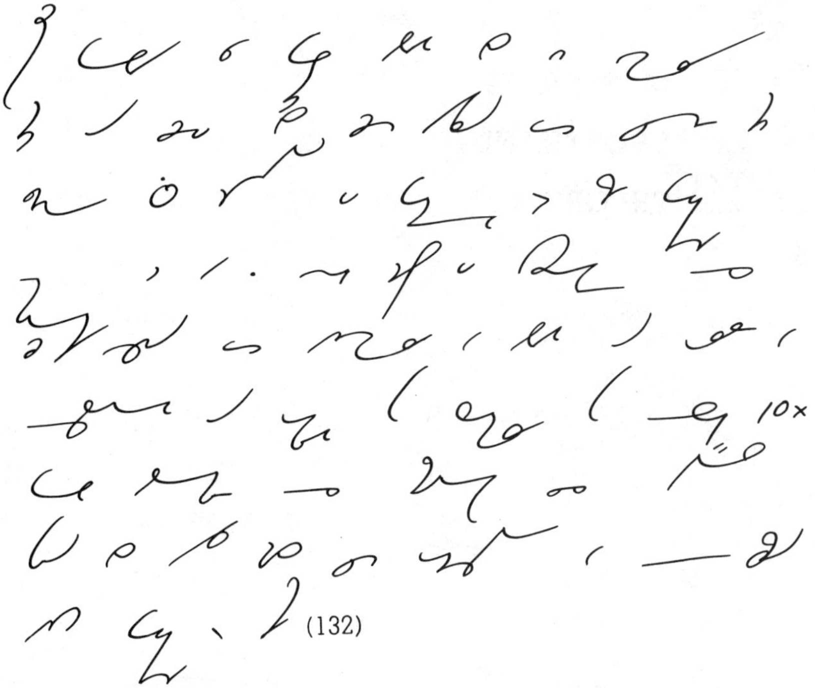

(132)

143▸ Dr. Harvey D. Bentley, The Bentley Research Center, 235 Greentree Road, Columbus, Ohio 43217.

(102)

Lesson

32 MASTERING SHORTHAND THEORY

WORD BEGINNINGS

Con-, Com-

Con-, Com- (followed by a vowel)

Im-, Em-

Im-, Em- (followed by a vowel)

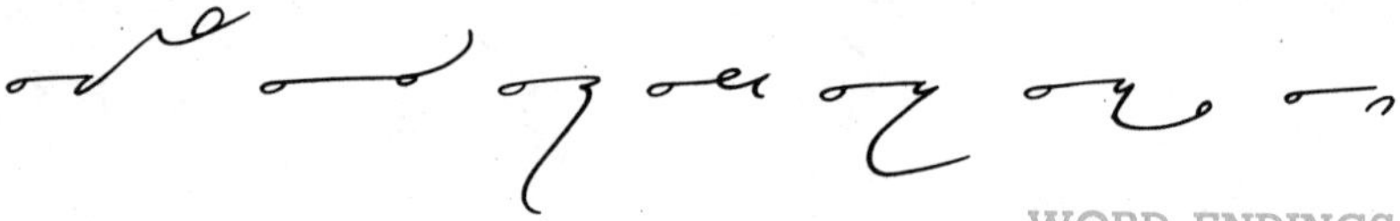

WORD ENDINGS

-ual

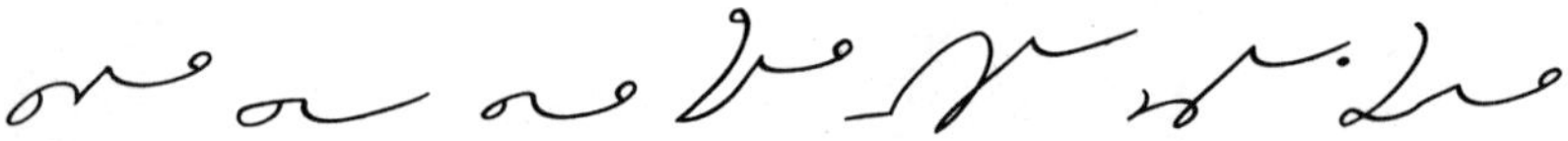

-ure

Confusing, conscientious, conclusion, reconcile, compact, complimentary, conservative.
Connote, committee, commercial, communicate, disconnect, subcommittee.
Impartial, imperative, reimbursed, impracticable, employment, emphasis.

Immoderate, imminent, immovable, immerse, immobile, emotionally, emulate. Actually, annual, equally, eventually, individual, scheduling, virtually. Procure, naturally, secure, mature, signature, structural, fixtures.

TRANSCRIPTION SPEED BUILDER

144 ▸ Wellman Business Machine Company, 211 Bay State Road, Knoxville, Tennessee 37900.

(122)

145 ▸ To: All R and D Employees.

(195)

146▸ Williams, Henderson, and Brown, Attorneys at Law, Crescent Building, 440 Michigan Avenue, Chicago, Illinois 60610.

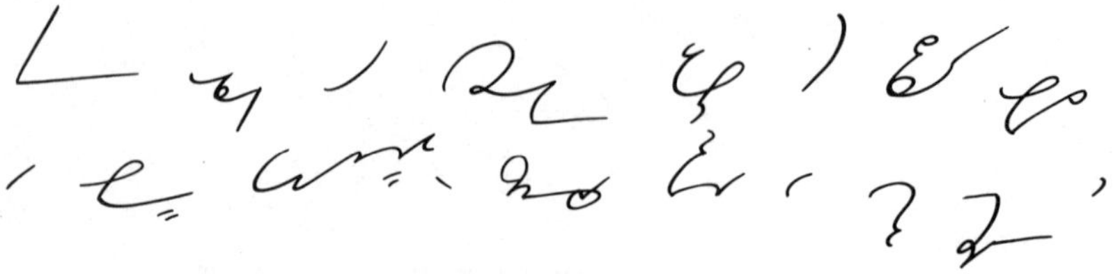

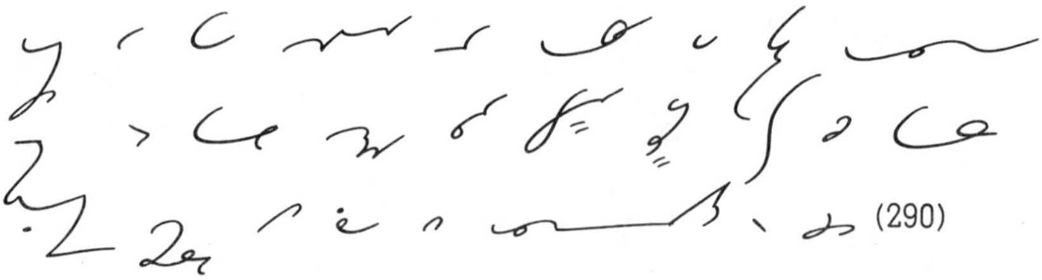

(290)

147 ▸ Dr. Irwin J. Miller, President, American Chemical Society, Massachusetts Technological Institute, 2444 Massachusetts Avenue, Boston, Massachusetts 02215.

(123)

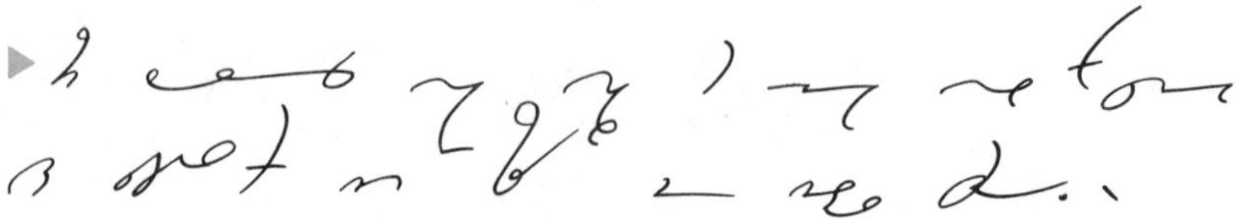

lesson 33

BUILDING PHRASING SKILL

PHRASE BUILDER

Drill 1

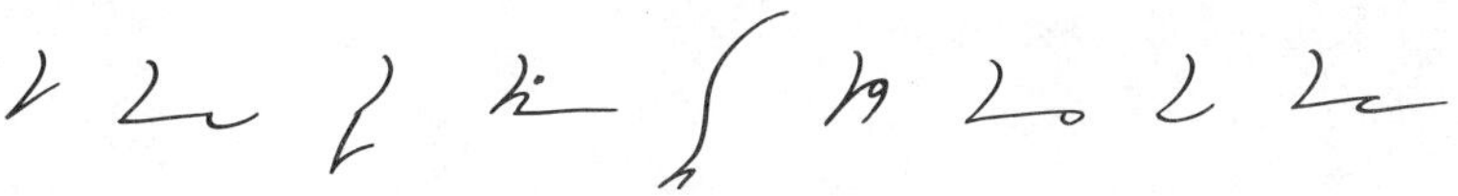

Drill 2

Drill 3

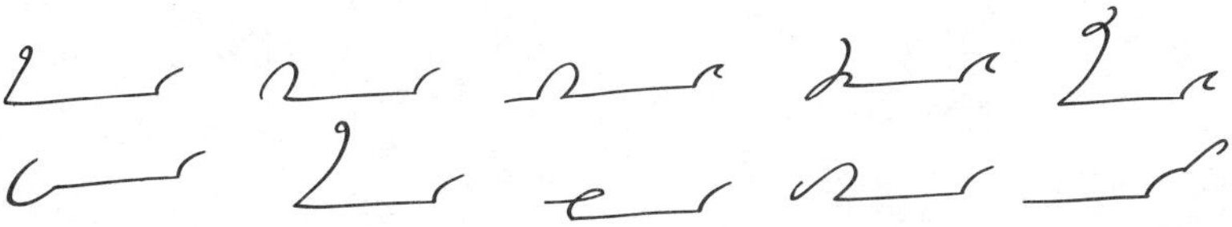

Drill 4

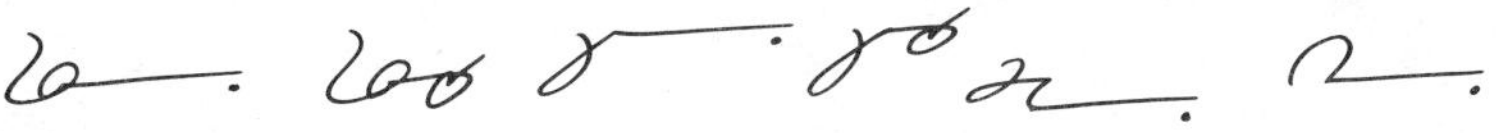

For it, for Mr., for which the, for whom, before your, for these, for me, for our, for a moment.

As this, before this, by this, hope that this, if this is, this can be, with this, this may be, this means, this will be, this would be, of this, since this, in this way, for this.

Each month, this month, in this month's, few months, several months, per month, every month, next month, of this month, month or two.

Friday morning, Friday night, Saturday morning, Saturday night, Wednesday morning, this morning.

148 To: Mr. Henry P. Walters, Vice-President, Finance.

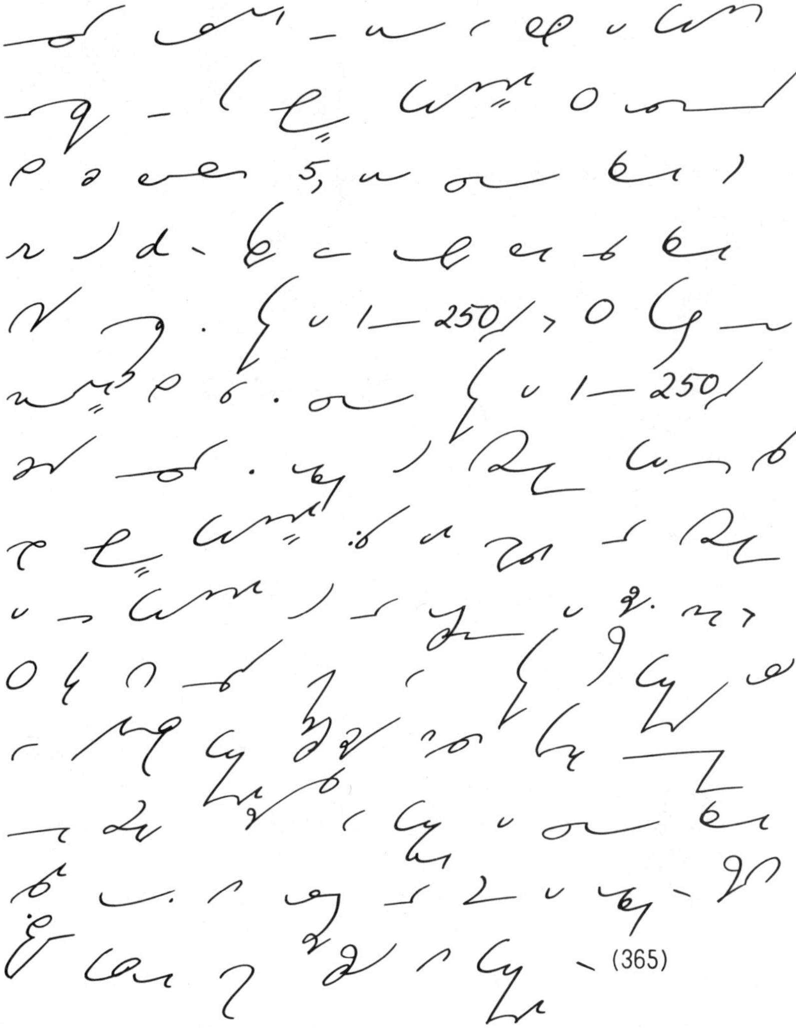

(365)

149▸ To: Mr. Arthur C. Williamson, Director of Public Information.

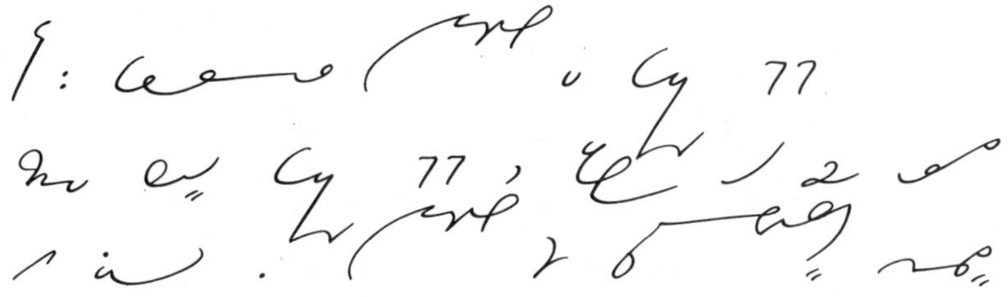

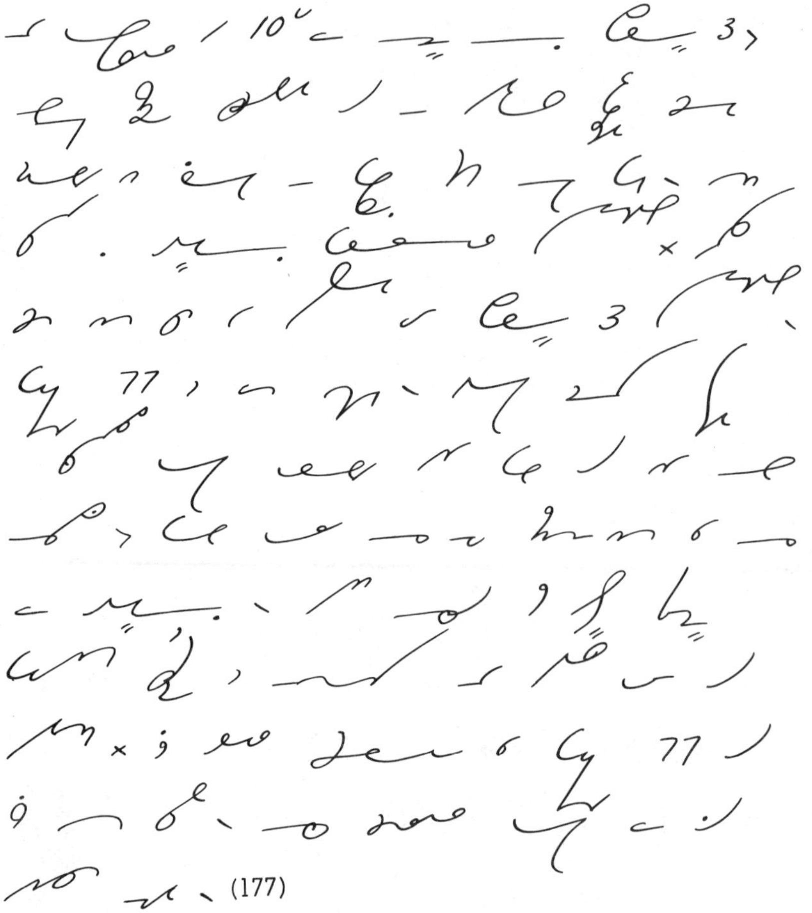

(177)

150 ▸ Memo to Dr. Wilson Atwater, Senior Engineer.

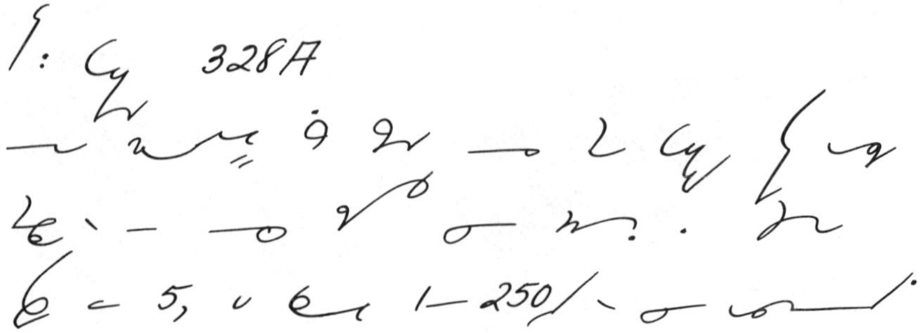

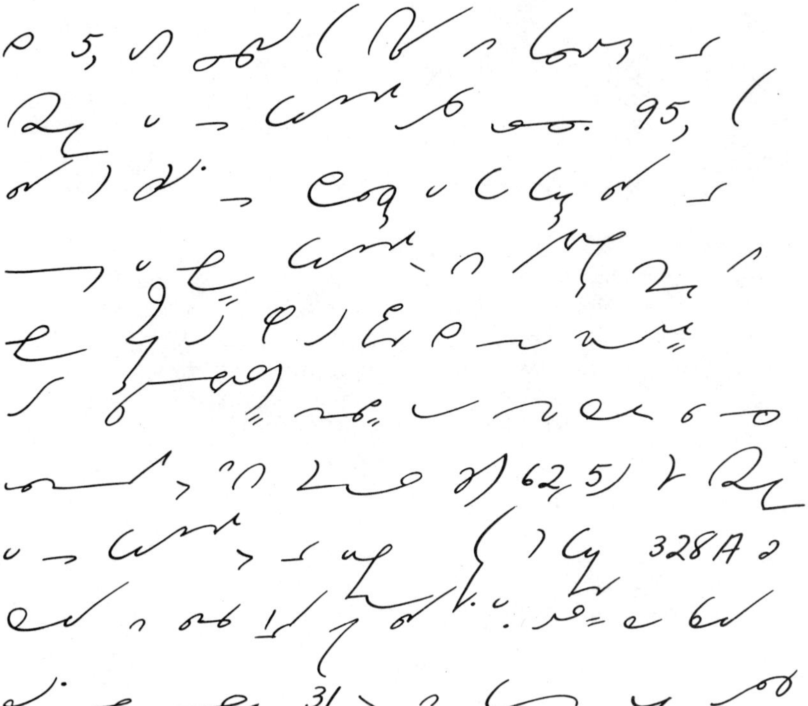

lesson 34

PROGRESSIVE SPEED BUILDING

In this lesson, the one-minute speed-forcing letters will be dictated at 100, 110, and 120 words a minute; the two-minute reinforcement and control letter will be dictated at 110 words a minute.

First, practice writing the vocabulary preview that precedes the speed-forcing practice; then review the specialized vocabulary presented at the beginning of the unit.

SPEED-BUILDING LETTERS

Vocabulary Preview

Microcircuits, transistors, resistors, 80 percent, equipment, literature, pneumatic, laboratory, interfering, bulk, unnecessary, deteriorate, pertinent, drawings, simplifying, diagram, intelligible, crucial, project, blueprint, intricate, dimensions, aluminum, tolerance, precision, suitability, material, specifications, usual, schedule, overtime.

Speed Forcing

(1 Minute at 100)

151 Gentlemen: We are searching for new microcircuits to test in a new process being developed. We understand that you have recently/ put on the market a model that takes the place of 15 transistors, 21 resistors, and almost 4 feet of wiring, yet//requires 80 percent less power. We should like to talk with your engineer about a possible application of your equipment to/// our problem.

Any literature you can send us prior to his visit might help us prepare for a conference with him. Sincerely yours, (1)

(1 Minute at 110)

152▸ Gentlemen: Please send your sales engineer to discuss with us the possibility of our installing a Fuller pneumatic conveying system in/our research laboratory to aid in transferring bulk shipments of chemicals from railroad cars and trucks to storage bins. We are interested in this system//as a means of eliminating the unnecessary handling of shipments, for chemicals deteriorate during moving.

As a///preliminary to your sales engineer's visit, please send us Bulletin G-21 as well as any other pertinent information. Yours very truly, (2)

(1 Minute at 120)

153▸ Dear Mr. Smith: Please prepare flow diagrams of Project 58 for presentation to the Administrative Committee on July 28.

These charts should include the/ revisions in process made on May 8 and May 21. I suggest that you make preliminary drawings immediately so that you and I can discuss possible//ways of simplifying the charts before we present them for final approval.

The problem is to make a rather technical diagram intelligible to laymen,///such as the members of our committee. It is crucial to the success of this project that we obtain full cooperation.

Will the first draft be ready Tuesday? Yours truly, (3)

Reinforcement and Control

(2 Minutes at 110)

154▸ Gentlemen: We are interested in your manufacture of machine parts by the flame-cutting method. I am enclosing with this letter the blueprint/of a rather intricate gear to be used in the manufacture of foil sheets for packaging frozen foods. According to your advertisement, you can//cut the gear without a die or mold from this blueprint showing clearly marked dimensions.

Will you please send us 50 gears cut from alloy steel, 50 from stainless///steel, and 50 from aluminum for our tolerance tests. Also, please include prices for quantity lots cut from each material.

After we have (1) tested the precision of your products and the suitability of each type of raw material, we will consider including the gear of our/choice in the specifications written for the equipment. Another factor that would influence our decision is the speed of delivery that we//may expect.

Please bill us for the trial gears on our usual terms. As these tests are of very great importance in our production schedule, we should/// appreciate it if you could give priority to this order, even if it is necessary to charge us for some overtime. Very sincerely yours, (2)

155 ▸ Mr. Robert Wilkinson, Chairman, School of Engineering, Washington University, Lindell and Skinker Boulevard, St. Louis, Missouri 63130.

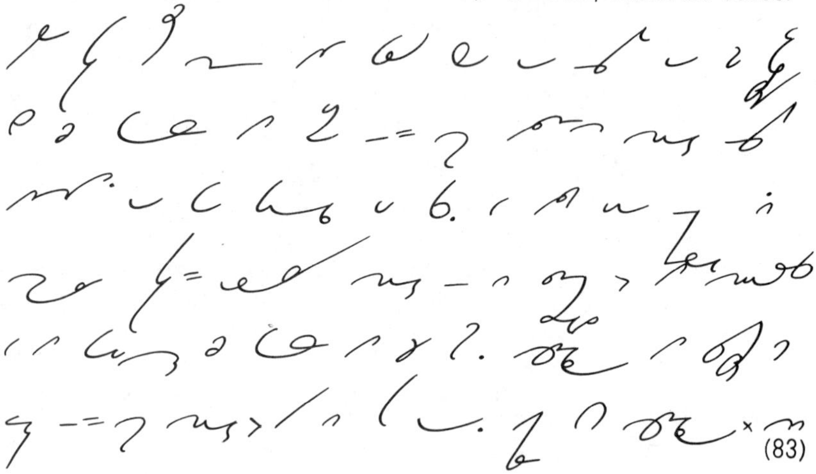

(83)

156 ▸ Mr. Milton G. McGill, Director, Research and Development, McMillan and King, Inc., 1110 Market Street, Duluth, Minnesota 55806.

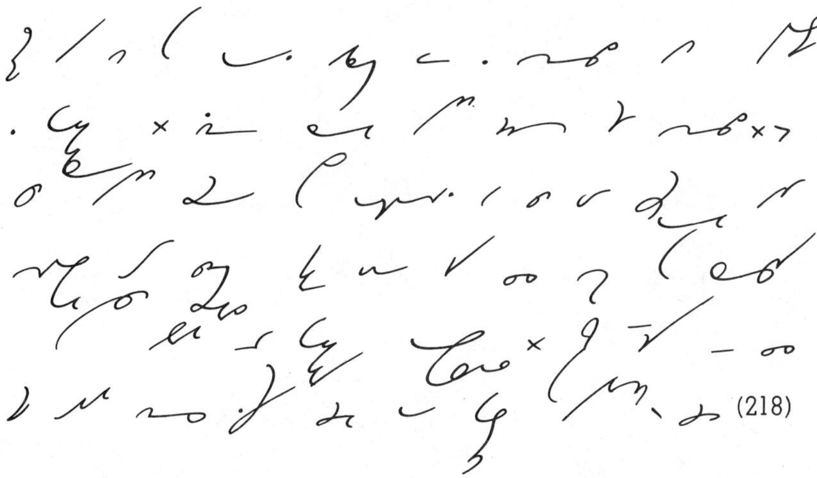

(218)

TRANSCRIPTION PACER

157 ▸ To: Alice E. Evans, Supervisor of In-Service Training. 12

21
34
46
59
71
83
96
109
121
133
144

154
168
179
192
203
214
226
237
248
259
272
282
293
307
319
331
343
352
360

lesson 35

BUILDING TRANSCRIPTION SPEED

SUSTAINED SPEED BUILDER

The Sustained Speed Builder letter is dictated by Mr. Haynes to Mr. Arthur A. Johnson, Personnel Recruitment Specialist, National Products, Inc.

Practice the vocabulary preview, and then see how well you can sustain your reinforcement and control speed.

Vocabulary Preview

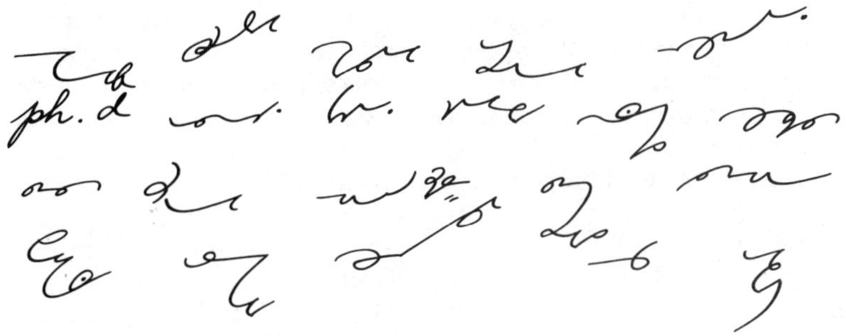

Employees, scientists, competitors, referrals, encountering, Ph.D., recruiting, puttering, strongest, creativity, characteristic, unique, facilities, Northwestern, university, technology, appropriate, reimbursed, candidates, mathematics, receptive.

Speed Builder

158 Mr. Arthur A. Johnson, Personnel Recruiter, Personnel Department.

Dear Arthur: The new R and D budget was finally approved, and we were authorized 25 new employees[1]—7 during the first quarter and 6 additional during each subsequent quarter. In my opinion,[2] at least 20 of these research specialists will have to come directly from college campuses. It is unlikely[3] that we can find more than five experienced scientists with the kind of research experience that would help[4] us in our product development program. Even if we could find additional experienced researchers,[5] we could not pay more than five of them salaries high enough to lure them away from their present assignments.

My[6] major concern at this time is what this year's crop of graduates looks like. So far, I have had only four referrals.[7] Does this mean that you are encountering difficulty in finding qualified candidates for our[8] positions? I do hope that we can stick to the Ph.D. requirement. Even if this means that all 25[9] positions cannot be filled, 10 outstanding employees would help me more than 20 mediocre ones.

Here are a[10] few guideposts that may help you during your recruiting interviews:

1. National Products hires women scientists[11] as well as men. Don't overlook the possibilities in some of the women's colleges.

2. Remind each[12] candidate that at least 15 percent of his time can be spent "puttering" on any project that he wishes.[13] The cornerstone of our R and D program is the firm belief that creativity requires freedom from[14] pressure and precise scheduling, which are characteristic of operations in other areas of[15] the company. Our research personnel have time to experiment and to reflect. You should stress this unique benefit.[16]

3. Our research facilities are located near the center of one of the largest research centers[17] in the United States. In addition to in-company courses, we encourage our scientists to enroll[18] at Washington University, St. Louis University, or Loyola University for graduate[19] study. Upon completion of a company-approved course, the employee is reimbursed for tuition[20] and textbook costs.

Try to keep in touch with me, Arthur, during the time you are visiting campuses. In some[21] instances I may be able to help you to make a contact with key members of the science and mathematics[22] departments. A number of these professors are close friends of mine who are in a position to steer their graduate[23] students in our direction. The injection of a personal note into our recruiting efforts may[24] simplify what might otherwise be a difficult assignment. Sincerely yours, (494)

159 Professor William J. Finley, Chairman, Chemistry Department, University of Illinois, Urbana, Illinois 61801.

Dear Bill: Our personnel recruiter, Arthur A. Johnson, will be on your campus on Thursday, March 5. He has been[1] in touch with your placement officer and has sent him our recruitment brochures. I don't want to bypass a placement[2] office, especially one that does as fine a job as yours; however, you may know of one or two Ph.D.[3] candidates who you think would be interested in the kind of research we are conducting.

Herb Wilson, whom you[4] referred to NATIONAL PRODUCTS just a year ago, is doing a fine job on his first project. He is a very[5] competent physical chemist and has contributed a great deal to our synthetic container project.[6] Sincerely yours, (122)

TRANSCRIPTION CHECKPOINT

160 Memo to Mary Hendrix, Research Librarian.

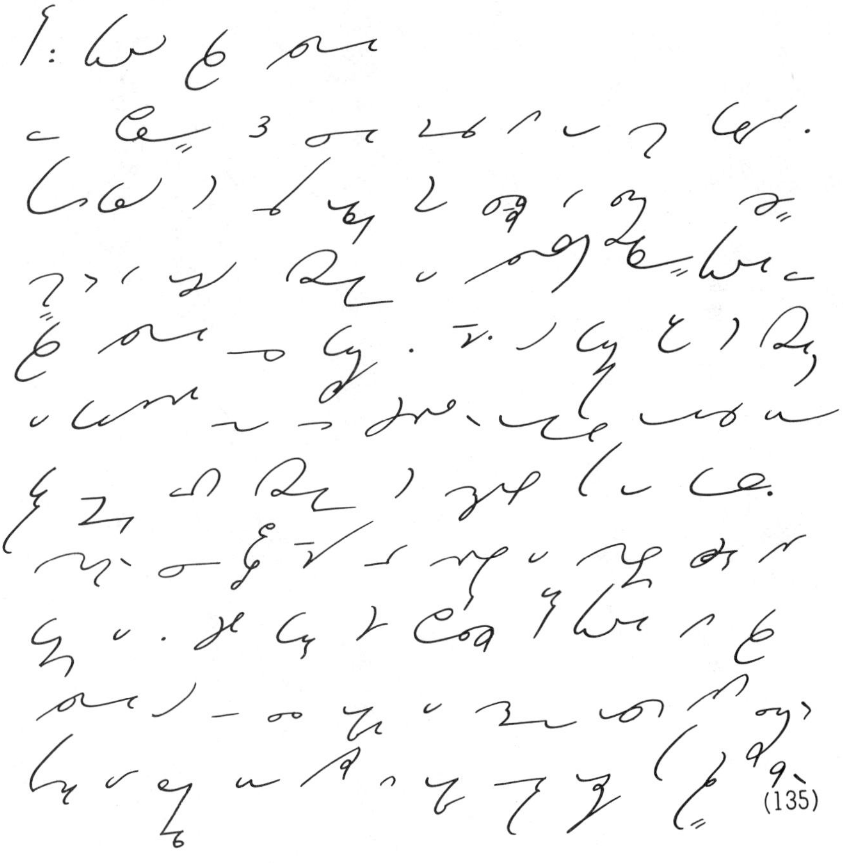

(135)

TRANSCRIPTION PACER

Practice reading and writing the memo to Mr. Simpson. Review the spelling and punctuation pointers. Your instructor will either dictate the letter and ask you to transcribe from your shorthand notes or instruct you to transcribe directly from the text. Your efforts will be judged for correctness of transcript and for rate of transcription.

161 ▸ To: Mr. Henry M. Simpson, President. 8

16
26
39
49
57
69
80
92
106
116
132
143
152
161
172
182
192
202

212
224
238
249
258
269
281
292
303
313
324
335
347
357
367
377
387
398

What should you buy, Brand X or Brand Y? You probably ask yourself this question many times a week when purchasing items for personal use. Purchasing for a business is also buying, but it usually includes much more. A number of important considerations arise in connection with purchasing. Someone must decide what to buy, how much to buy, when and where to buy, how much to pay, on what terms, and so on.

In most businesses the responsibility for making purchases is delegated to a purchasing agent or to a director of purchases who has several assistants or buyers working with him, as well as stenographers and clerks who take care of purchase orders and requisitions. The director of purchases is the specialist who knows the needs of the business and is acquainted with market and price trends. He coordinates the procurement of materials with capital and sales requirements so that production will be in harmony with consumer demands.

unit 8

PURCHASING

Secretarial Assignment

In this unit you will take the dictation of David R. Monroe, who is responsible for obtaining goods that will meet the requirements of both the production and the selling departments of National Products, Inc. All letters are signed by him over his title, Director of Purchases.

SPECIALIZED TERMINOLOGY

C. O. D. • Collect on delivery service whereby an ordered item is paid for when it is delivered.

Cockle Finish • Puckered or wrinkled finish.

Custom-Built • Made or done to order of the customer.

Formica • Chemical-proof and heatproof plastic coating.

Purchase Order • Form on which purchase information, such as quantity, description, and specifications, is outlined by a purchasing agent and sent to a supplier.

Quality Control • The process of determining average and/or minimum quality needed to satisfy customer needs and expectations and of rejecting products that fall below the standards set.

Ream • Quantity of paper, usually twenty quires, or 480 sheets, but sometimes 500 sheets.

Purchase Requisition • Form that sets forth the details and specifications required to guide the purchasing agent in buying.

Sight Draft • A written order on the buyer to pay the amount of the purchase price of the goods to the seller on demand.

Substance • In paper identification, the weight in pounds of 500 sheets of 17- by 22-inch paper. A ream of 20-pound paper would weigh one-fourth of 20 pounds, or 5 pounds.

Telex • Direct transmission of telegrams from one business concern to another for concerns that subscribe to the service. Connections are made by dialing the subscriber's number.

Watermark • Figure or design in paper produced by pressure of a projecting design, and visible when the paper is held up to the light.

SPELLING AND TRANSCRIPTION PRACTICE

Words ending in *y* preceded by a consonant usually change the *y* to *i* on the addition of any suffix except the suffix *-ing*.

necessary	**necessar*ily***	**vary**	**var*ied***	**var*ying***
century	**centur*ies***	**copy**	**cop*ies***	**cop*ying***

Words ending in *y* preceded by a vowel usually retain the *y* before suffixes.

valley	valley*s*	delay	delay*ed*	delay*ing*
attorney	attorney*s*	buy	buy*er*	buy*ing*

Transcribe the following sentences, preferably at the typewriter, until you can accurately apply the spelling rules that appear above.

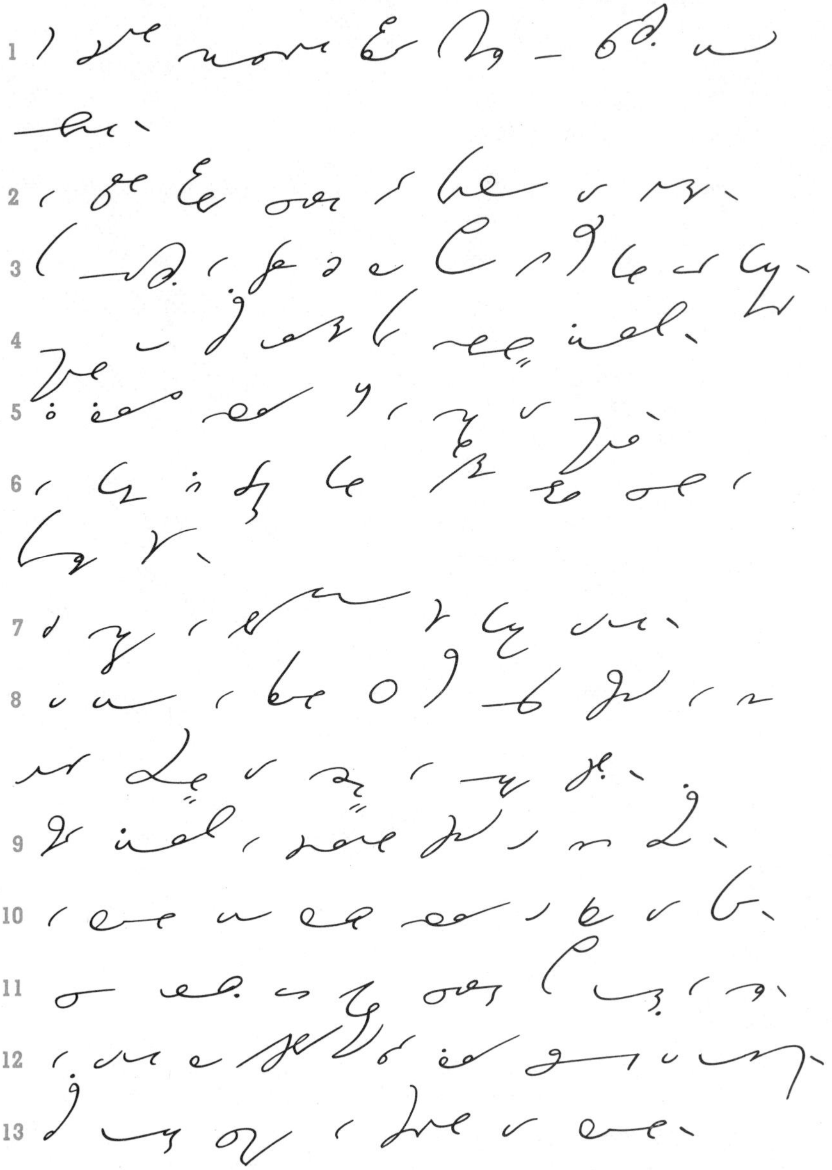

lesson

36 BUILDING TRANSCRIPTION QUALITY

TRANSCRIPTION POINTERS

Uses of the Comma *(Continued)*

1 Use commas to set off a phrase, a name, or a number that makes a preceding reference more specific.

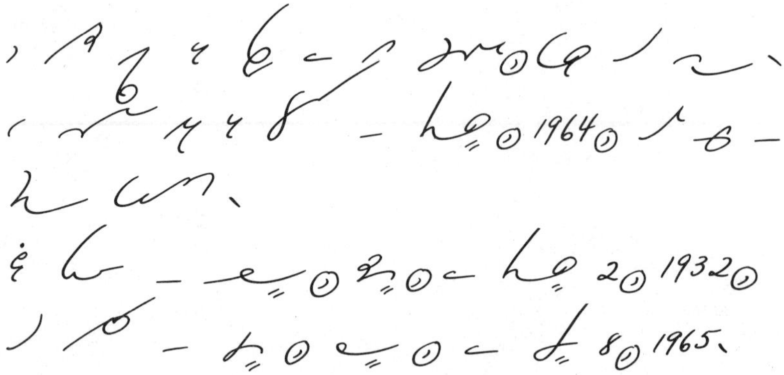

His decision to buy was based on two factors, price and quality.
The container top was patented in July, 1964, and is now in full production.
He was born in Milwaukee, Wisconsin, on July 2, 1932, and died in Chicago, Illinois, on January 8, 1965.

2 Use commas to set off an appositive from the rest of the sentence.
EXCEPTION: Do not set off restrictive appositions.

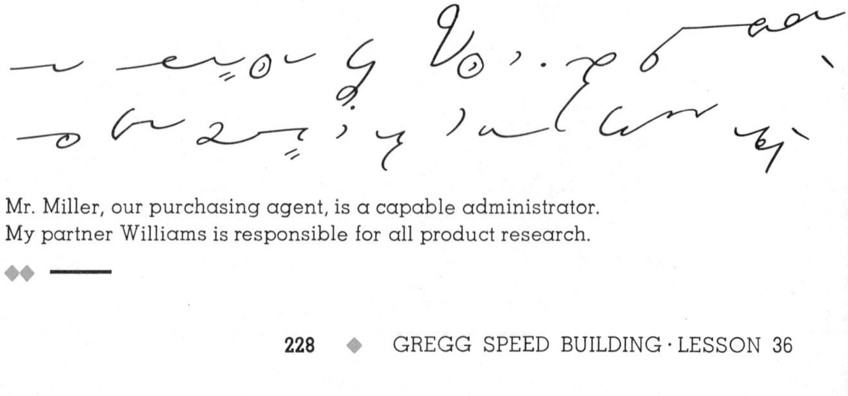

Mr. Miller, our purchasing agent, is a capable administrator.
My partner Williams is responsible for all product research.

Check your understanding of comma usage by transcribing the following sentences, preferably at the typewriter.

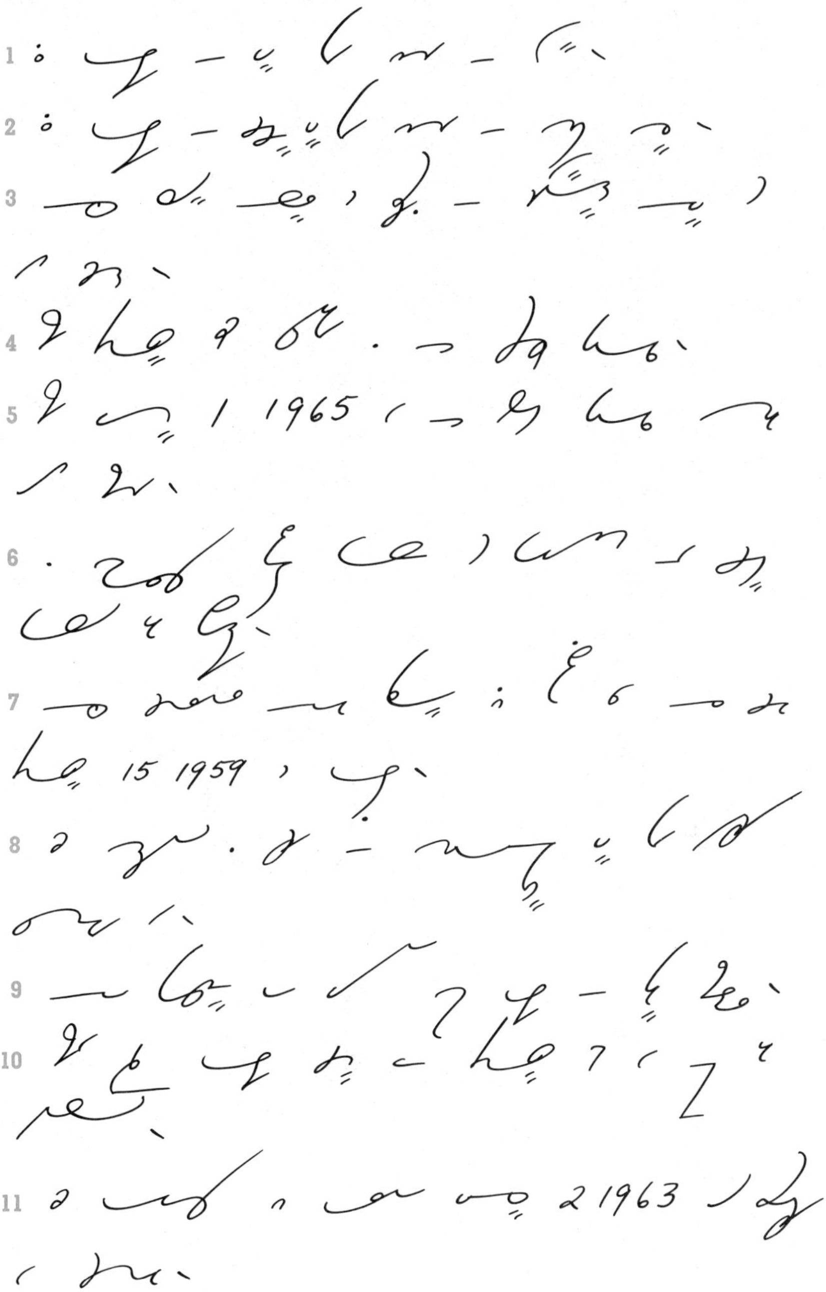

12 

13 

14 

15 

16 

TRANSCRIPTION SPEED BUILDER

162 ▸ Lake Erie Steel Company, 200 Richmont Avenue, Toledo, Ohio 43637.

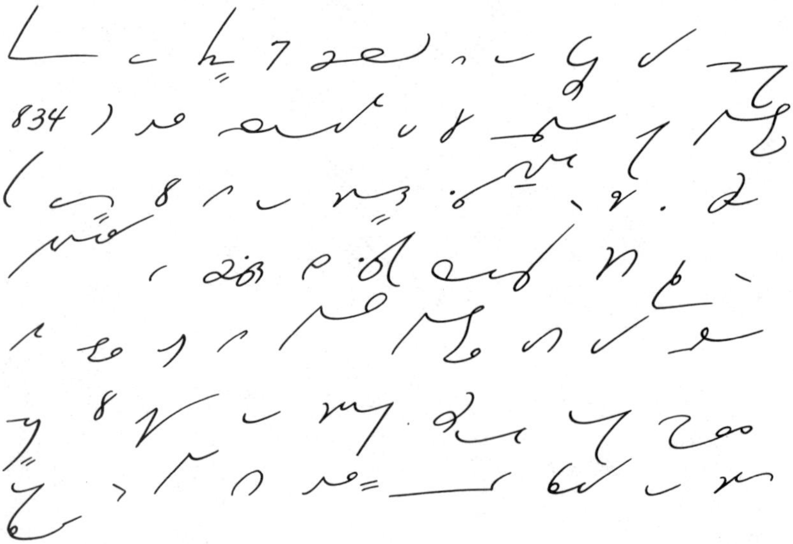

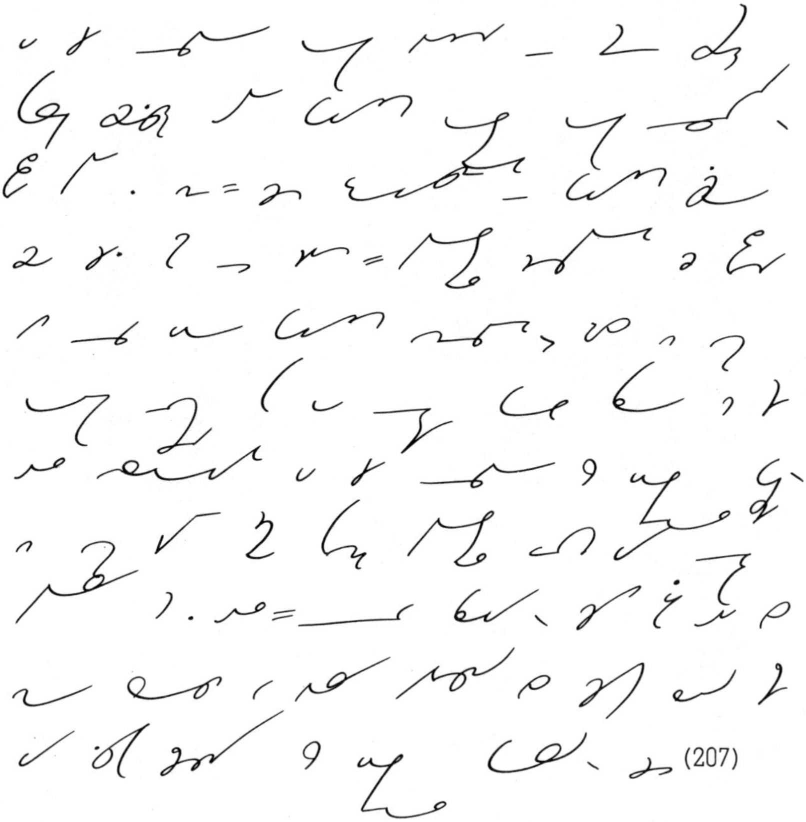

(207)

163 ▸ Mr. Harman J. Cooper, Cooper Office Furniture Company, 2511 Belltown Road, Jamestown, New York 14701.

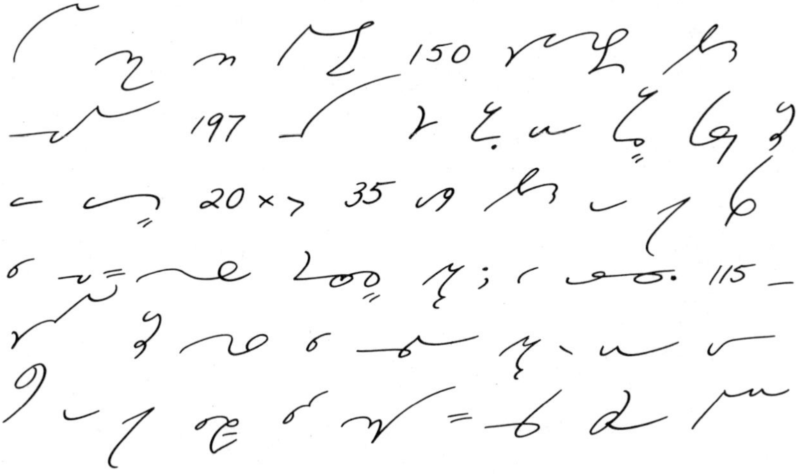

(174)

164▸ Almark Metal Products, Inc., 722 Division Street, Mansfield, Ohio 44902.

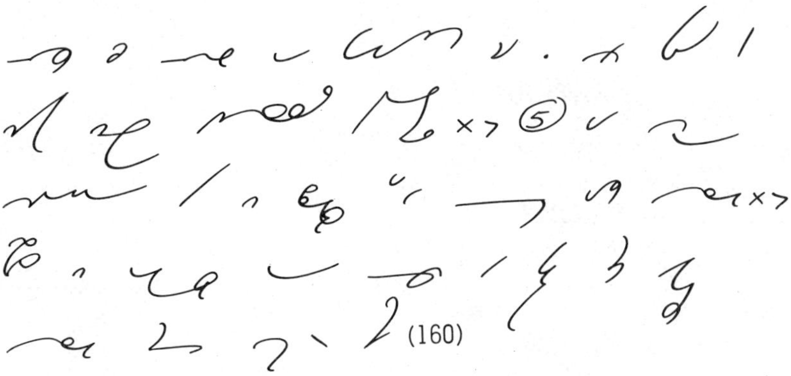

165 ▸ Williamson Chemical Company, Berea Road, Lexington, Kentucky 40505.

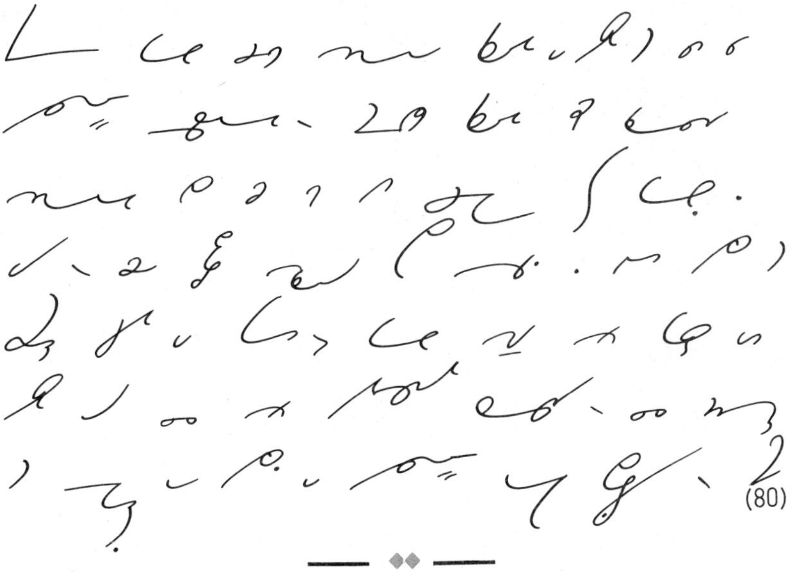

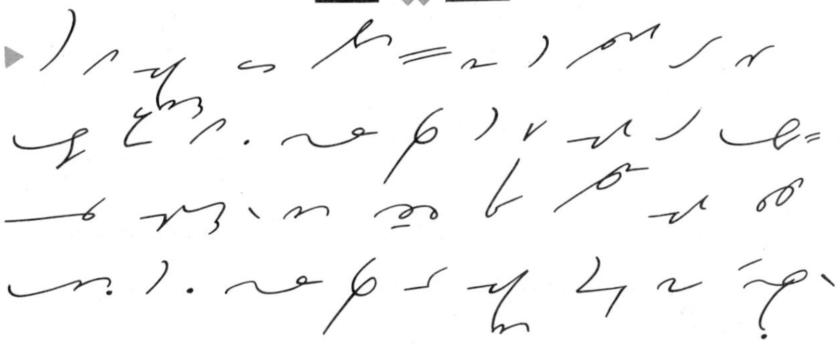

lesson

37 MASTERING SHORTHAND THEORY

WORD BEGINNINGS

Post-

Self-, Circum-

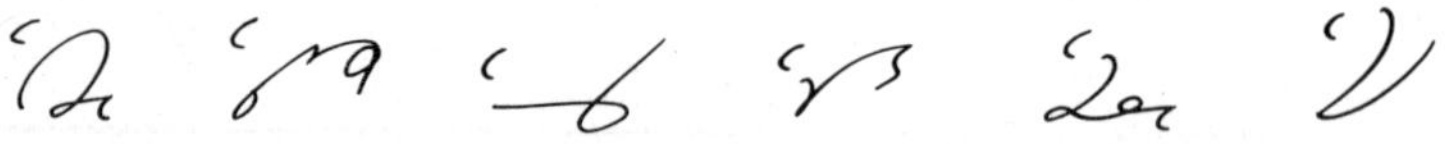

Super-

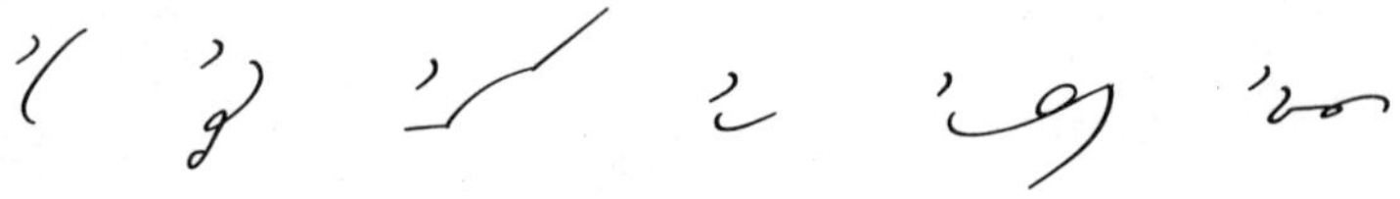

WORD ENDINGS

-ily

-ther

Postage, postal, postscript, post office, postmaster, postponed, postpaid.
Self-defense, self-education, self-made, circumstances, circumference, circumvent.
Superb, superficially, superintend, superiority, superlative, supersonic.
Easily, families, heartily, heavily, necessarily, readily, steadily, temporarily.
Another, brother, farther, father, feather, gathering, otherwise, whether.

166 To: Mr. Henry P. Walters, Senior Vice-President.

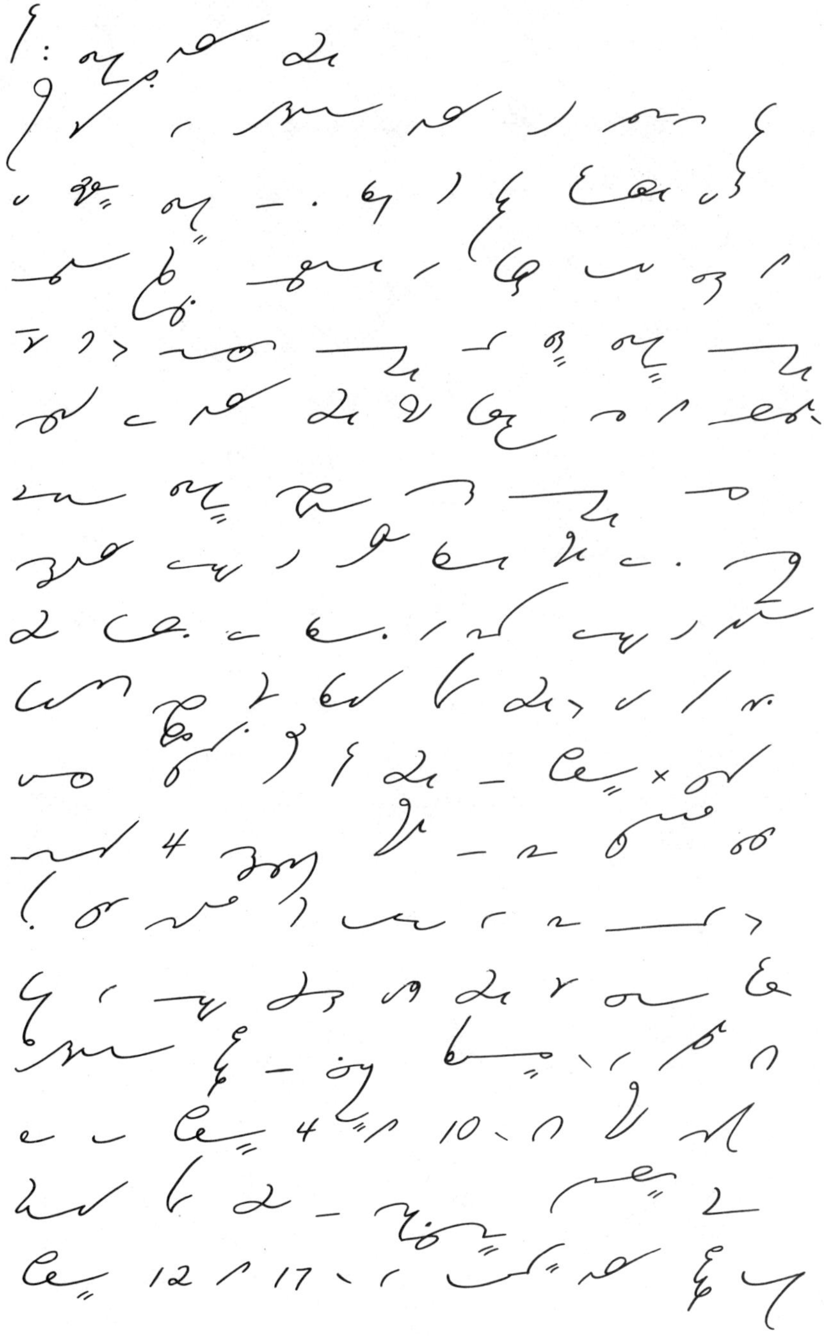

(321)

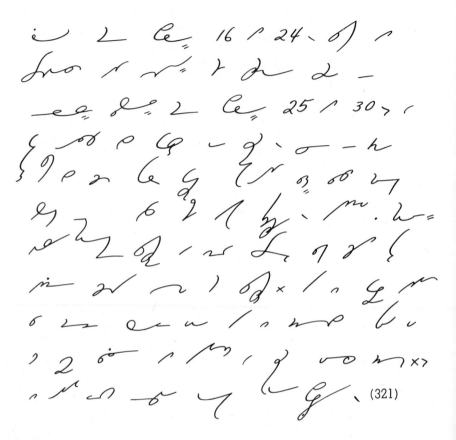

167 ▸ BBB Manufacturing Company, 216 Broad Street, Indianapolis, Indiana 46241.

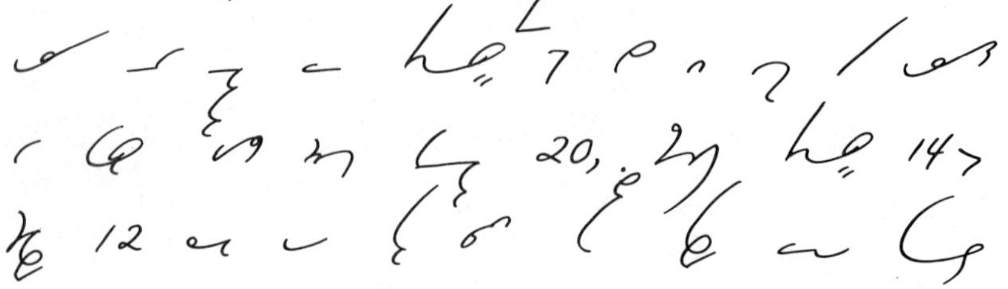

(176)

168 To: All Section Heads.

(194)

169 ▸ Watterson Electronics, 29 Waters View Drive, Bridgeport, Connecticut 06614, Attention of James R. Mitchell.

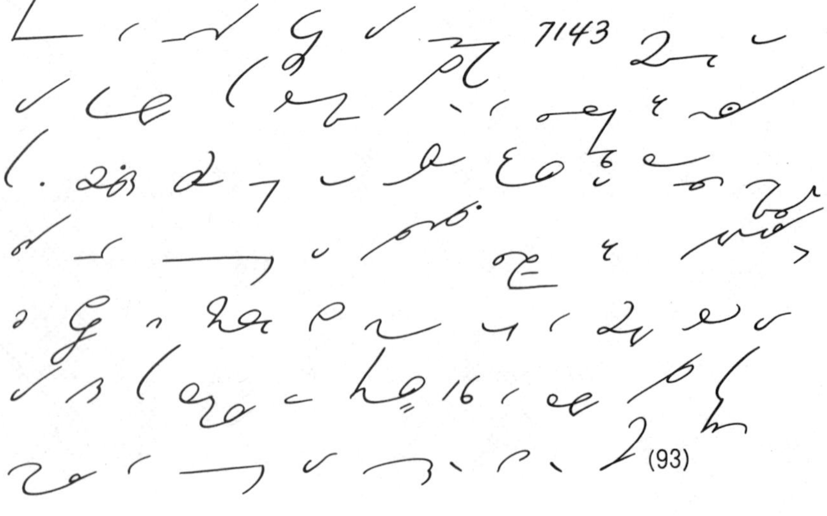

(93)

lesson

38 BUILDING PHRASING SKILL

PHRASE BUILDER

Drill 1

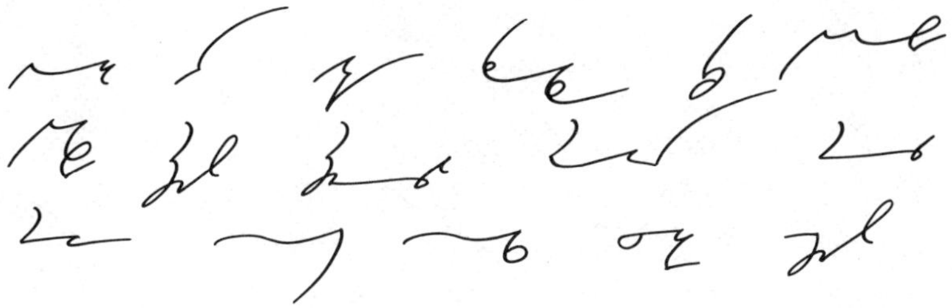

Drill 2

Drill 3

At a loss, at a time, at such a time, bill of sale, by the way, during the last, during the past, for a few days, for a few minutes, for a long time, for a minute, for a moment, glad to have, glad to say, I am of the opinion, in a few days.

In a position, in addition to this, in order to be, in order to become, in the past, in relation to the, in such a manner, in the future, in the world, line of business, many of them, men and women, none of the, none of them, on the subject, one of the best.

One of the most, one of these, one or two, ought to have, out of date, out of that, out of the question, out of them, out of this, some of our, some of this, such a thing, two or three, up and down, up to date, week or two, will you please, able to say, here and there.

TRANSCRIPTION SPEED BUILDER

170 Griswold Manufacturing Company, 448 Spring Hill Road, Wheeling, West Virginia 26001.

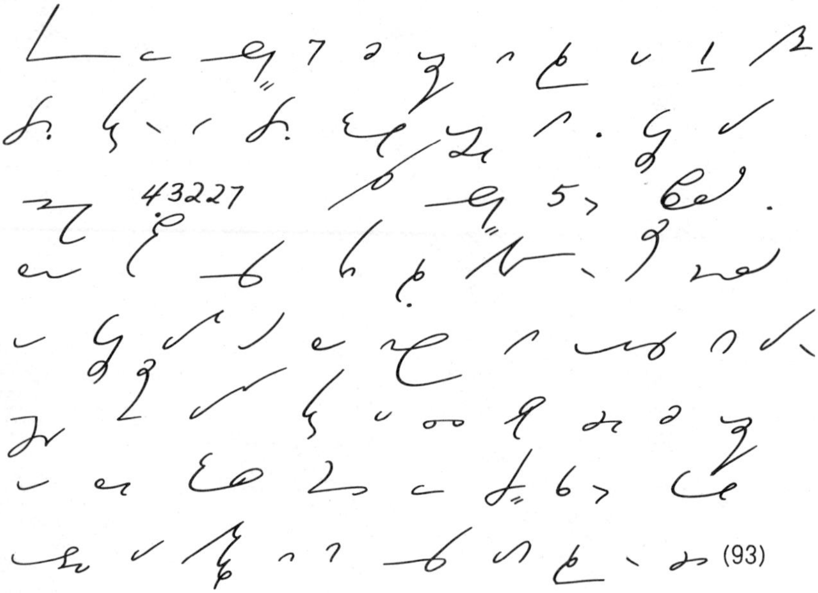

(93)

171 M & L Steel Company, 245 Second Avenue, Pittsburgh, Pennsylvania 15212.

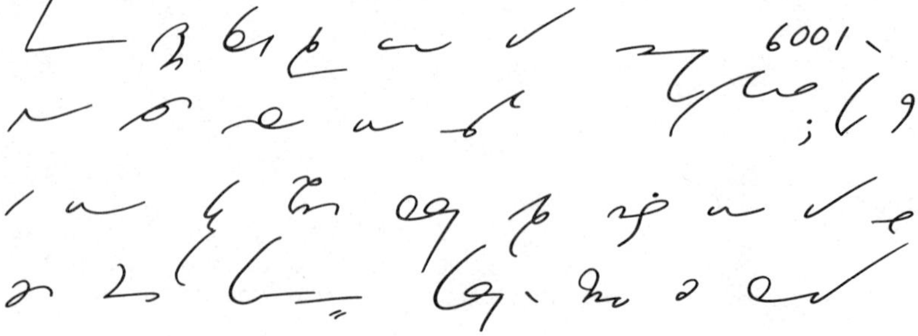

(209)

172 ▸ The Bradshaw Chemical Company, 900 Plains Boulevard, Houston, Texas 77021.

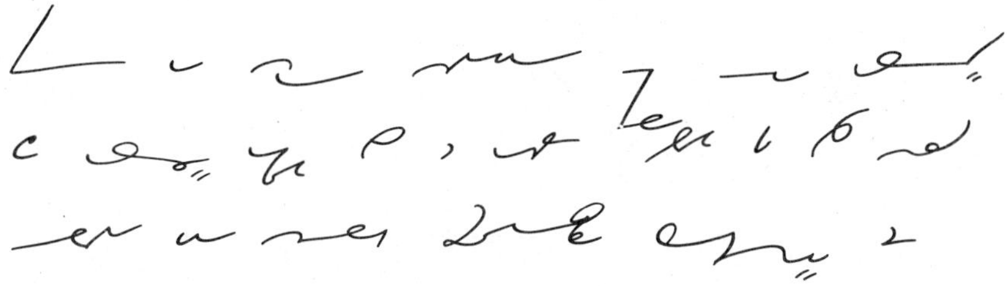

(183)

173 ▸ Hammer Paint & Building Supplies, Inc., 5734 North Pacific Avenue, San Diego, California 92111.

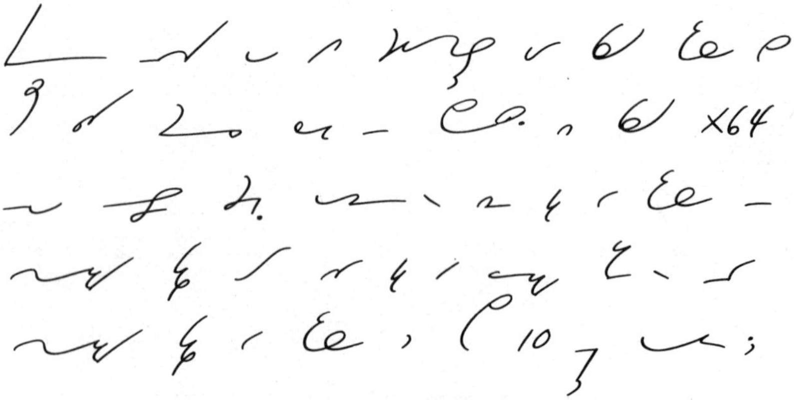

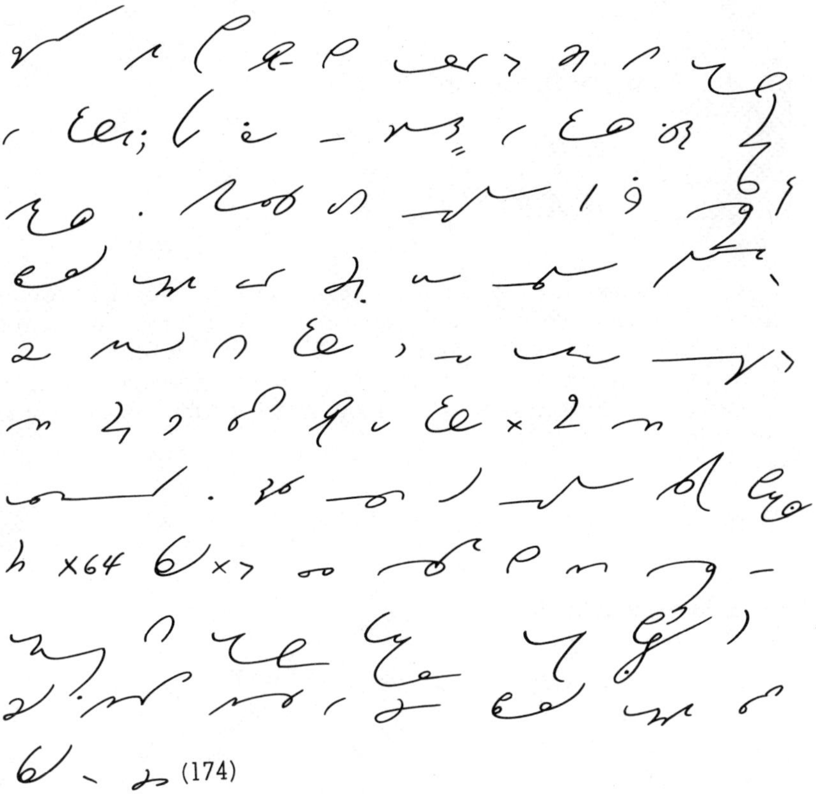

(174)

174▸ Harmon and Bowman Steel Corporation, 231 Beacon Drive, Cleveland, Ohio 44122.

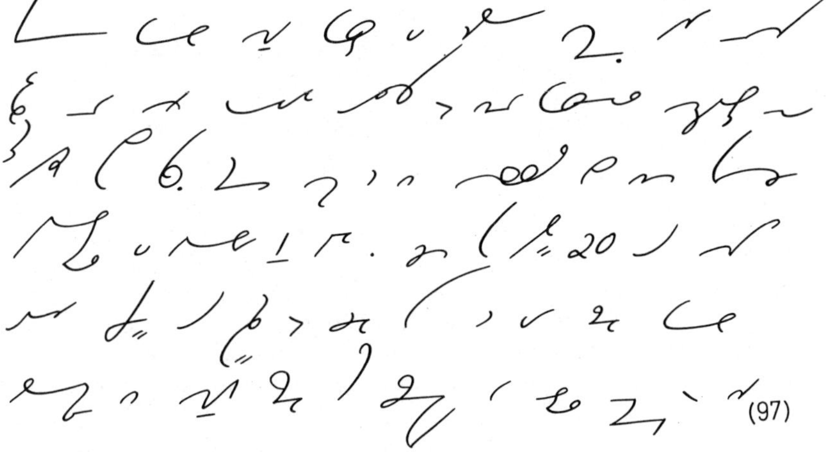

(97)

lesson

39 PROGRESSIVE SPEED BUILDING

In this lesson the one-minute speed-forcing letters are counted progressively at 110, 120, and 130 words a minute; the two-minute reinforcement and control letter is counted at 120 words a minute.

First practice the vocabulary preview that precedes the speed-forcing practice, and then review the specialized vocabulary presented at the beginning of this unit.

SPEED-BUILDING LETTERS

Vocabulary Preview

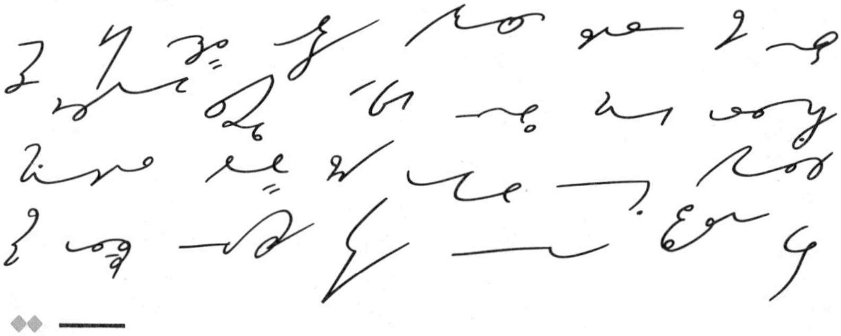

Unforeseen, shortage, Kansas City, anticipated, dislike, extreme, effort, crisis, schedules, adversely, transportation, increasingly, solution, renegotiate, upholstery, Telex, issued, will you please, manufacturing, duplicate, if so, requisition, modified, budgeted, manual, expenditure, privilege.

Speed Forcing

(1 Minute at 110)

175 Gentlemen: An unforeseen shortage has just developed in our plant in Kansas City, and we must obtain larger quantities than we anticipated/of the chemicals that you have been supplying.

Can you possibly make delivery of our last order by the 15th of the month instead of by//the 30th?

We know the pressures under which your company operates, and we dislike to request special favors. We know, however, that you will ///understand that this is an extreme emergency.

We shall make every effort to see that such a crisis does not arise again. Yours very truly, (1)

(1 Minute at 120)

176 Gentlemen: Unfortunately, delays in delivery of materials ordered from your company are affecting our production schedules adversely. Our/deliveries are taking an average of a week longer than they did a year ago. Apparently, the great distance between our plants makes railroad transportation//increasingly unsatisfactory.

The solution may lie in changing to airfreight for shipment of all our orders from your company. On what terms would you renegotiate ///our contract with you to cover this mode of transportation? A renegotiated contract would cover the five months beginning November 1. Sincerely yours, (2)

(1 Minute at 130)

177 Gentlemen: On June 4 we ordered 6,000 yards of upholstery material from your company for delivery to our Kansas City plant. On June 10 we received/your Invoice No. 198899, but our Kansas City Receiving Department tells me by Telex that we have not received the order, although it is now fifteen days since//the invoice was issued.

Will you please start a tracer on the order at once. In the meantime, we need the material very badly, as we are scheduled to start manufacturing///the product involved within ten days. Would it be possible for you to send a duplicate order by airfreight? If so, we should appreciate it very much. Yours very truly, (3)

Reinforcement and Control

(2 Minutes at 120)

178 Dear Mr. Jones: Your requisition for 5 electric typewriters for use in your department is being processed. Before it can be authorized, however, it must/be modified.

Your department budgeted $7,000 for typewriters during the fiscal year. To date, you have purchased 15 new electric typewriters//at $335 net and 5 manual typewriters at $185 net. This leaves only $1,050 of your budgeted///total unspent, and your requisition calls for an expenditure of $1,675.

Perhaps you can reduce your requisition (1) to 3 electric or 5 manual machines, depending on your needs. Only in cases of extreme urgency may a department exceed its budget. If you feel/that you have a satisfactory reason for exceeding the $7,000 total that has been allotted, it is your privilege to outline your needs to//the Budget Committee, explaining any unforeseen circumstances that warrant your request for funds in excess of your allowance.

As you know, budget requests for///the coming year are due on April 15. The new budget will be adopted in time to permit the purchase of approved items on July 1. Very truly yours, (2)

179 Hadley Machine Tooling Company, 275 Euclid Avenue, Erie, Pennsylvania 16518.

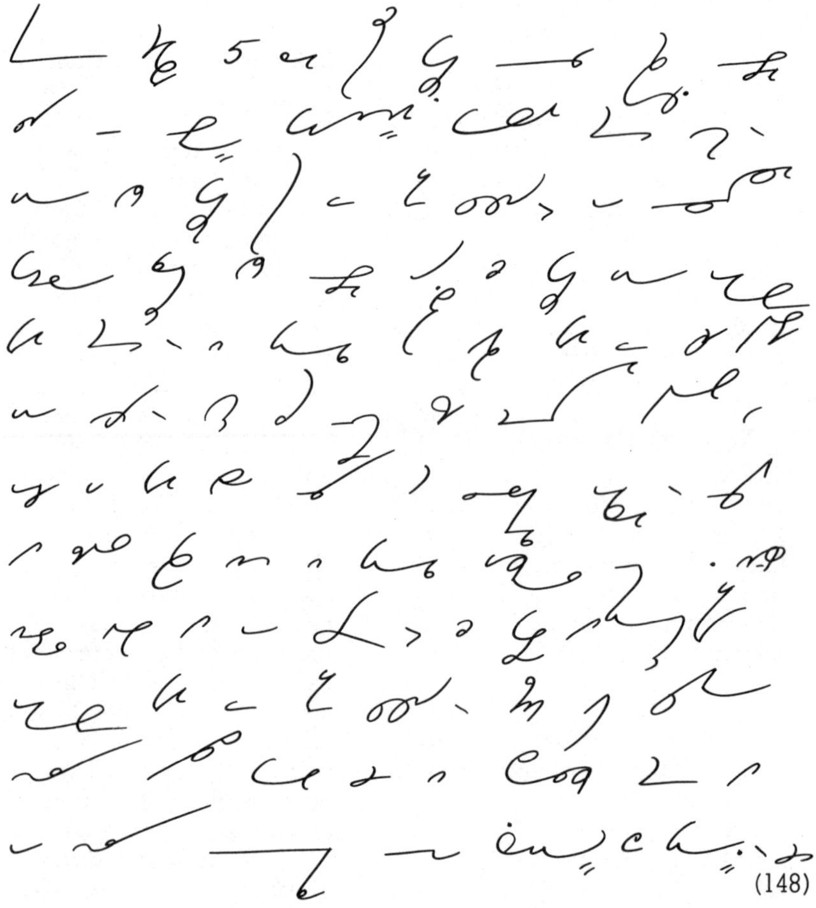

(148)

180 Larkin Engineers, 422 Second Street, Eau Claire, Wisconsin 54701.

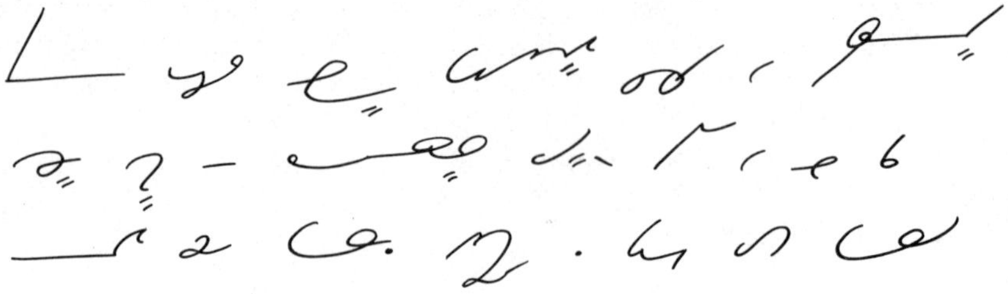

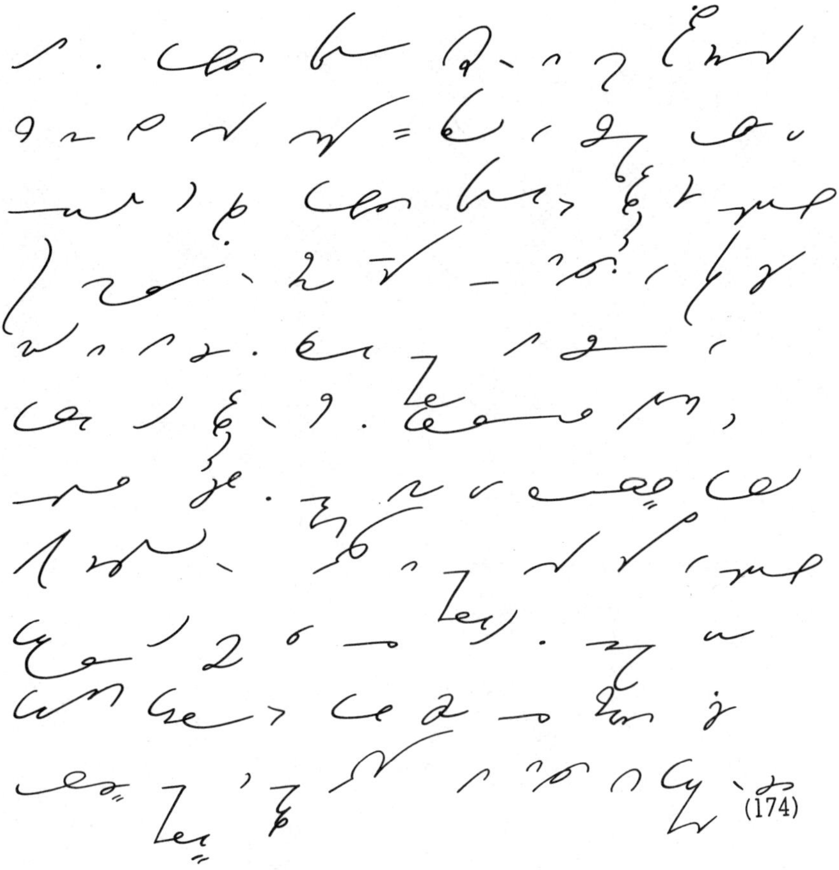

(174)

181 ▸ Memo to Stuart P. Henderson, Advertising Manager.

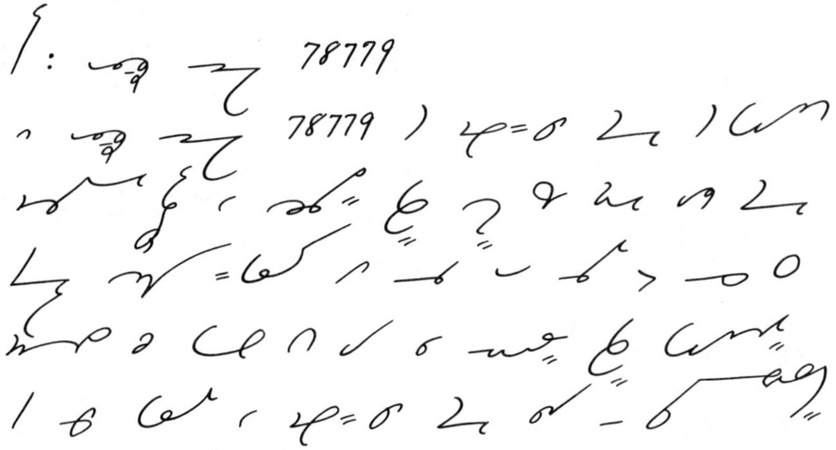

(154)

182 Memo to John Parker, Administrative Services.

(177)

TRANSCRIPTION PACER

183 The McBride Corporation, 4100 Gulf Street, Baytown, Texas 12
77520. 14

Lesson 40

BUILDING TRANSCRIPTION SPEED

SUSTAINED SPEED BUILDER

Practice the following vocabulary preview, and then see how well you can sustain your reinforcement and control speed.

Vocabulary Preview

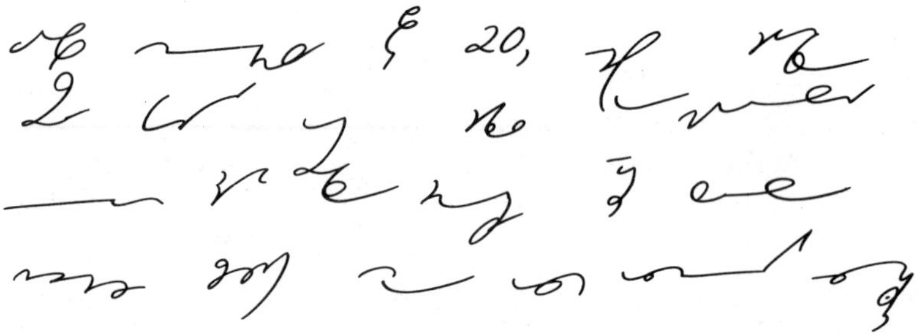

Authorization, commensurate, exception, 20 percent, instability, stockpile, avert, prudent, reversal, stationery, watermarked, monarch, substance, sulphite, interoffice, airmail, onionskin, executive, quality, reaction, recommendation, negotiations.

Speed Builder

184 To: Mr. Henry P. Walters, Senior Vice-President, Subject: Increases in Steel Inventory.

As you know, on August 15 the Administrative Committee budgeted an 8 percent increase in[1] production in all departments of our Kansas City plant during the months of October and November.

On August[2] 21 your authorization to increase our purchases of raw materials by 8 percent during[3] September and October to build up inventories commensurate with new production levels was[4] received and studied. The increases indicated for most raw materials seem adequate.

In the case of steel[5] plate, however, I recommend that we make an exception and increase our purchases by 20 percent during[6] the two-month period. Although we are striving for a reduction in ratio of inventory of[7] raw materials to finished goods, recent labor-management negotiations in the steel industry may[8] make a temporary reversal of inventory policy advantageous. Price instability and[9] the possibility of an industry-wide strike indicate that we should stockpile a supply of steel plate[10] large enough to avert any threat to our operations. Of course, buying now is something of a gamble; but[11] I doubt that the price is going any lower than it has been this week. We might save a few dollars by waiting;[12] but the more prudent course, it seems to me, would be to buy now and thus be sure later that we can keep the plant[13] going in case strikes do occur.

Please let me have your reactions to this recommendation. If this policy[14] exception is approved, we shall need $350,000 for steel plate immediately and[15] $150,000 in October. (308)

185▸ Dean Paper Manufacturers, 211 Pilgrim Road, Holyoke, Massachusetts 01040.

Gentlemen: We should like to have your bid on the following stationery, all watermarked with the NATIONAL[1] PRODUCTS seal:

Monarch-sized executive stationery imprinted with the name and title of the specified[2] executive, 1,000 reams. Substance 20, 50 percent rag content bond.

Monarch-sized executive[3] envelopes to match executive stationery in quality, 500,000.

Company letterheads[4] imprinted with the headquarters or branch address and the name of appropriate departments, 100,000 reams.[5] Substance 20, 25 percent rag content bond.

No. 6¼ envelopes to match company[6] letterheads in quality, 5,000,000.

No. 10 envelopes to match company letterheads in quality,[7] 5,000,000.

Plain onionskin, 300,000. Substance 9, cockle finish.

Onionskin imprinted with COPY in[8] red ink and the headquarters or branch address and appropriate department, 1,000 reams. Substance 9, cockle[9] finish.

Airmail letterheads imprinted with company name and name of appropriate administrator,[10] 5,000 reams. Substance 9.

No. 6¼ airmail envelopes to match airmail letterheads in quality,[11] 5,000,000.

No. 10 airmail envelopes to match airmail letterheads in quality, 5,000,000.

Interoffice[12] memorandum forms imprinted with appropriate headings (To, From, Subject, and Date), 50,000 reams.[13] Substance 16, sulphite.

We shall place the order for an entire year's needs at one time, but you may deliver one[14]-half of the order within one month after receiving it and the other half the first of November. For your[15] guidance, we are enclosing samples of each type of stationery to be purchased.

Please send your bid to our senior[16] vice-president, Mr. Henry P. Walters. Cordially yours, (330)

186 To: William C. Wilson, Foreman, Shipping Department.

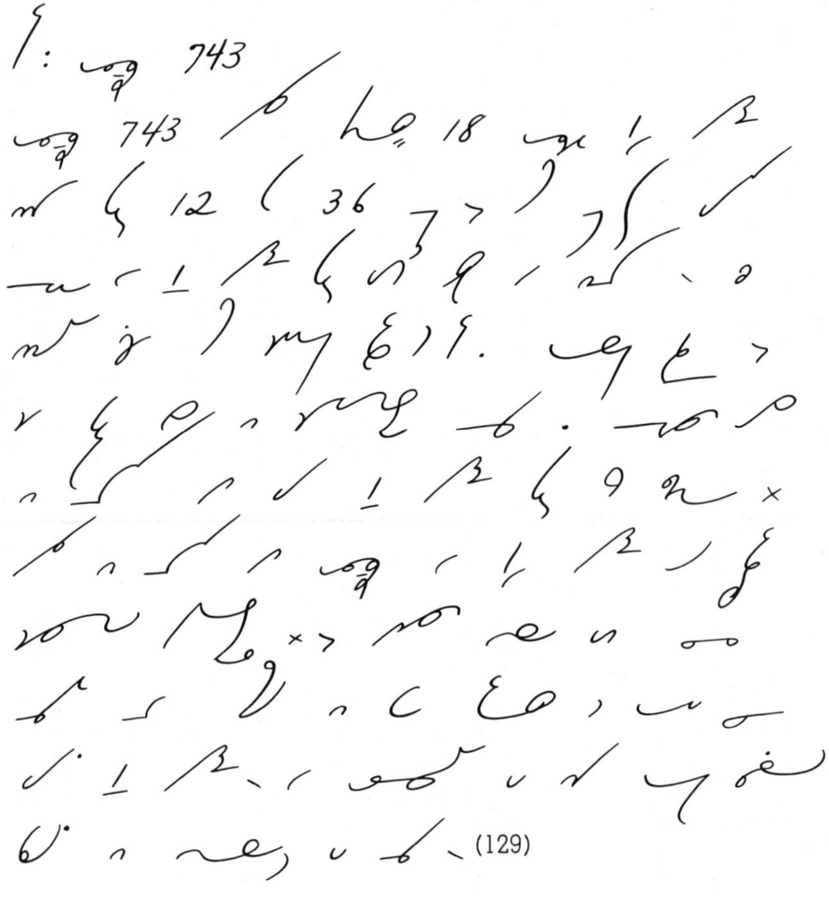

(129)

187 To: Charles C. Haynes, Director, Research and Development.

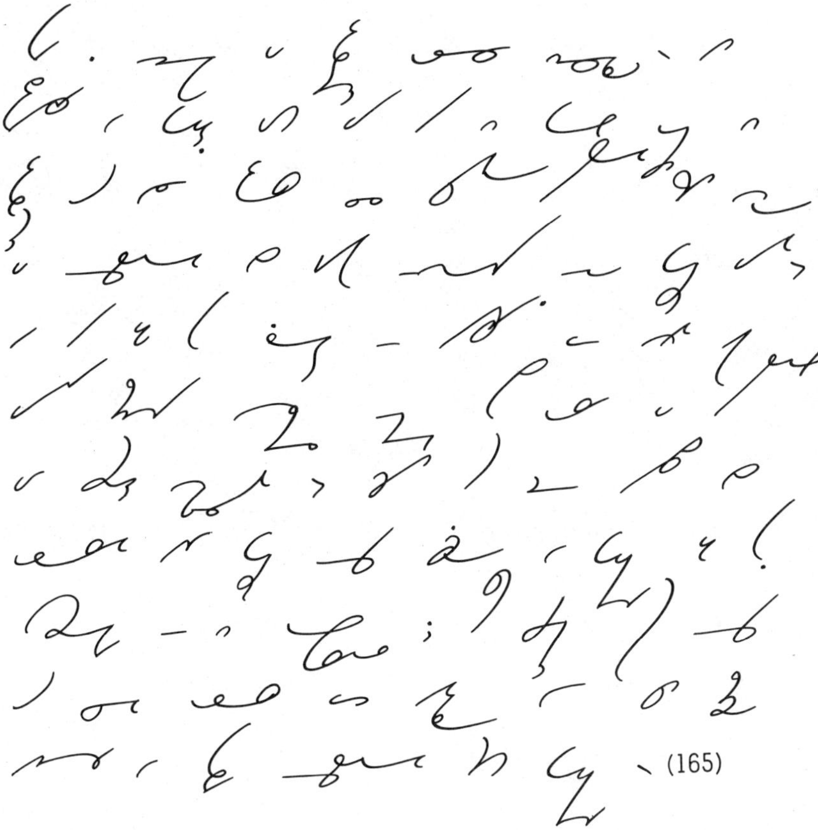

(165)

188 ▸ Office Furnishings Inc., 410 Olive Street, St. Louis, Missouri 63102.

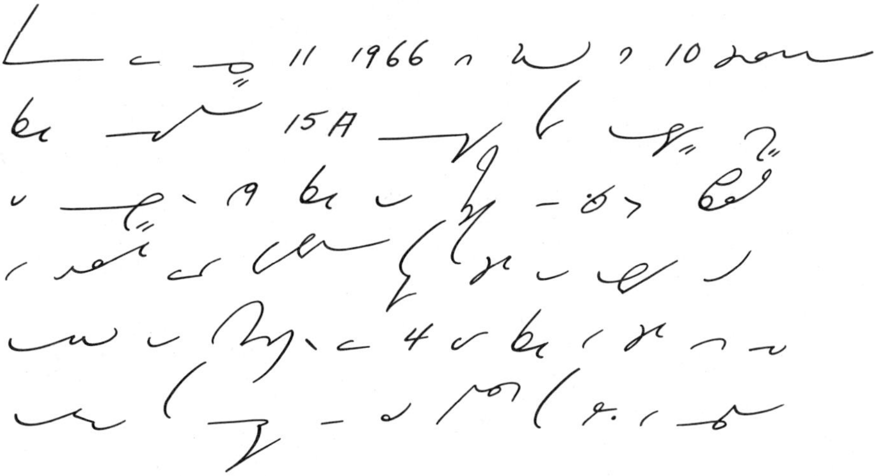

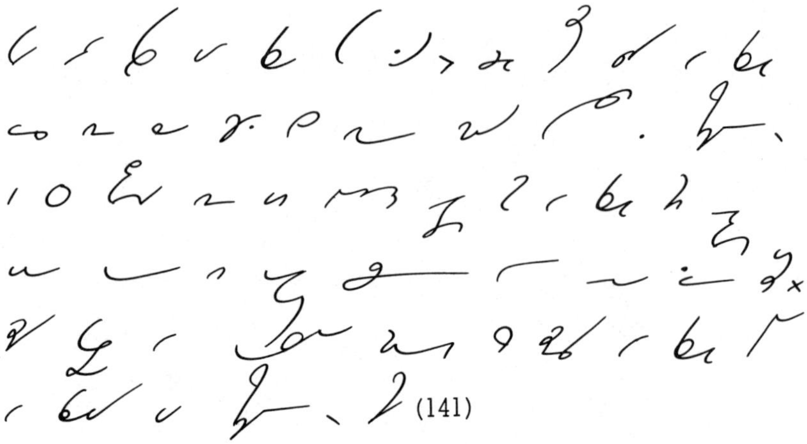

(141)

189▸ Lifton Company, 816 Second Avenue, Minneapolis, Minnesota 55405.

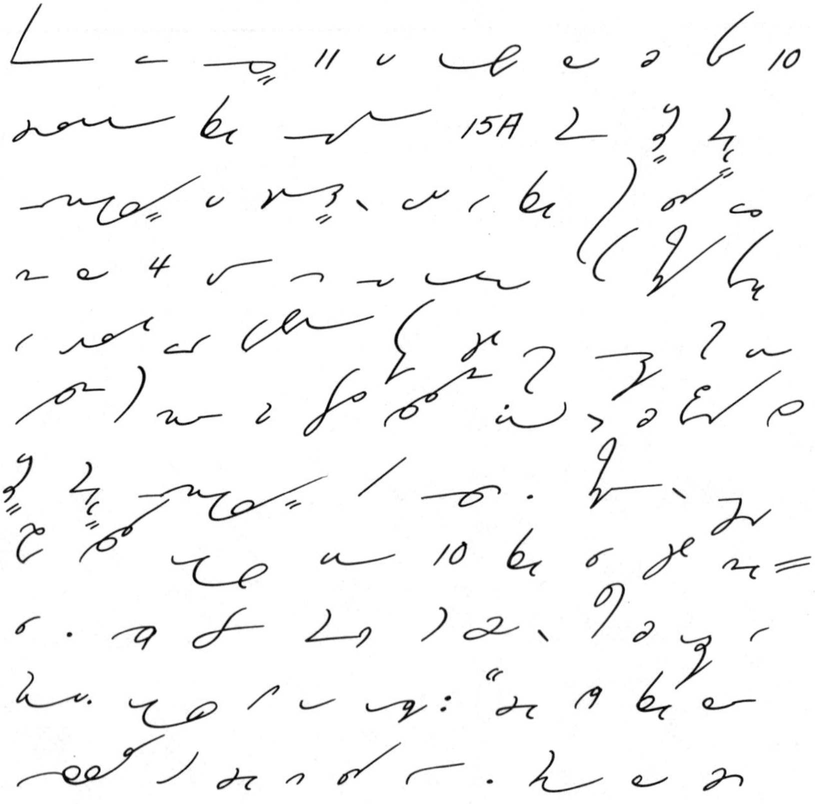

(205)

TRANSCRIPTION PACER

190 Truxton Products, 299 Dearborn Avenue, Detroit, Michigan 12
48252. 13

27 40 51 63 76 86 97 109 124 136 144

A business organization produces what the customer wants, not what it has always turned out or would like to turn out. To this end, production is a delicate mixture of men and machines and raw materials. The goods and services fashioned are in a form, at a price, and available at a time that is acceptable to consumers.

You might conclude that production is the cornerstone of American business, for it directly supports more than 25 percent of all gainfully employed workers. Without production there would be little need for semiskilled and skilled workers or for other types of business activity, such as transportation, warehousing, wholesaling, and retailing.

The production process requires advance planning, coordination with other functions of a business, and careful control. Those responsible for producing goods and services direct the activities of specialists, such as engineers and foremen, and work closely with purchasing, marketing, and finance personnel.

unit 9

PRODUCTION

Secretarial Assignment

In this unit you will take the dictation of James W. Walsh, who is responsible for the coordination of National Products' production personnel, machines, processes, and materials, so that the right quantity of goods of the right kind and quality are produced at the right time and place and cost. All letters are signed by him over his title, Production Manager.

SPECIALIZED TERMINOLOGY

Continuous Process • Manufacturing process in which there is a sufficient volume of production to keep the production process in operation for long periods of time.

Impulse Goods • Merchandise that the customer buys without prior intention because he is stimulated by attractive displays.

Industrial Engineer • Production specialist responsible for layout, standards, methods, scheduling, and other means of product improvement and cost reduction.

Job Lot • Amount of product produced under similar conditions and with similar materials.

Plant Engineer • Production specialist concerned with power, building maintenance, machine maintenance, and other factors concerned with maintaining the functions of the plant.

Plant Service Manager • Production specialist in charge of receiving and storing raw materials and tools.

Route Cards (Schedules) • Production instructions that show the sequence of operations and schedule for each part that passes through a department.

Subcontracting • Contracting with another manufacturer to produce certain components required in the manufacture of a product.

Wastage • Scraps of raw material remaining as processed products move to the subassemblies and to final assembly and finally emerge as finished units.

SPELLING AND TRANSCRIPTION PRACTICE

In words that end in *ce* or *ge*, the e is retained before suffixes beginning with *a* or o, such as *-able* and *-ous*.

notice	notice*able*	cour*age*	cour*age*ous
peace	peace*able*	outr*age*	outr*age*ous

Most words ending in c add *k* before endings that start with e, *i*, or *y*.

picnic **picnic*ker*** **mimic** **mimic*king***

Transcribe the following sentences, preferably at the typewriter, until you can accurately apply the spelling rules that appear above.

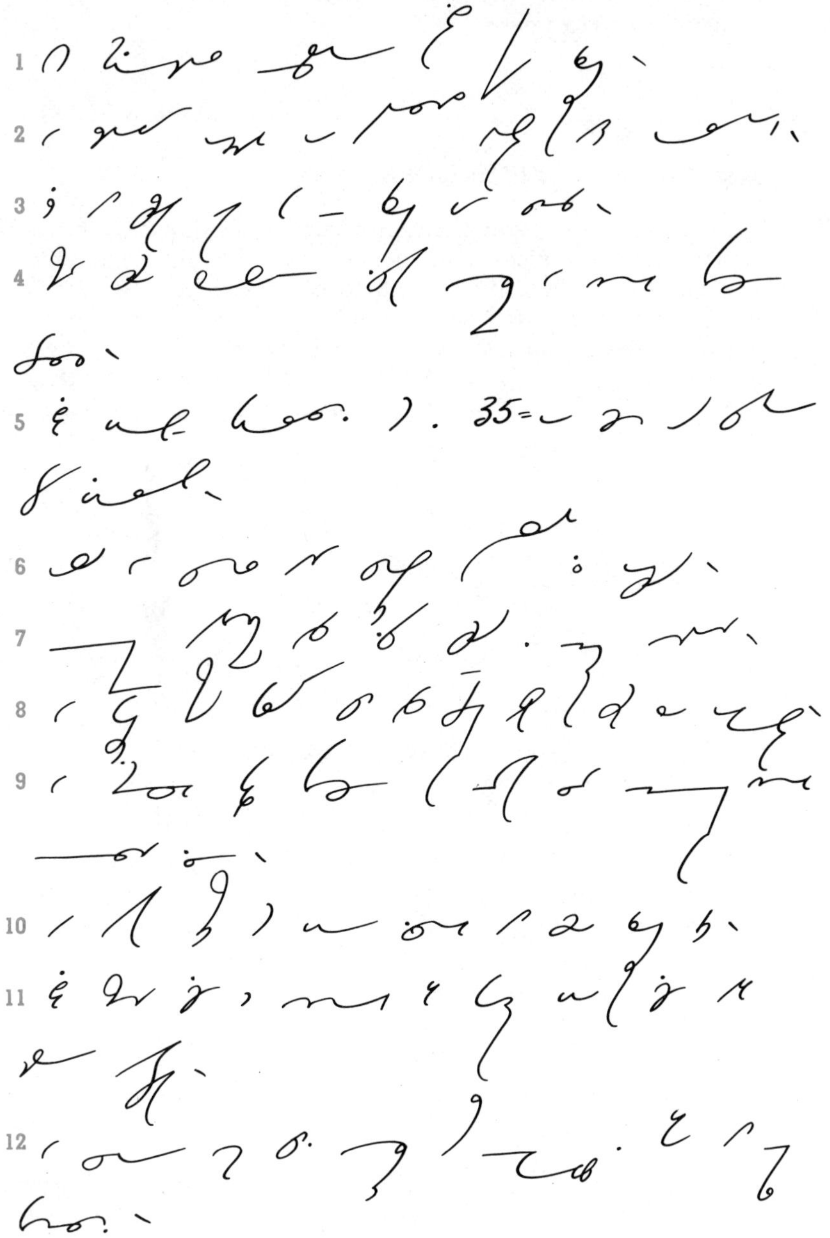

lesson

41 BUILDING TRANSCRIPTION QUALITY

TRANSCRIPTION POINTERS

Uses of the Comma *(Concluded)*

1 An introductory, parenthetic, or transitional expression that is not necessary to the grammatical completeness of the thought of the sentence should be set off by commas. If a parenthetical word or phrase does not interrupt the thought of the sentence, the commas may be omitted. Some of the words, phrases, and clauses frequently used in this way are as follows: *accordingly, as you know, evidently, for instance, fortunately, however, in any case, in the first place, obviously, perhaps, personally,* and *therefore.*

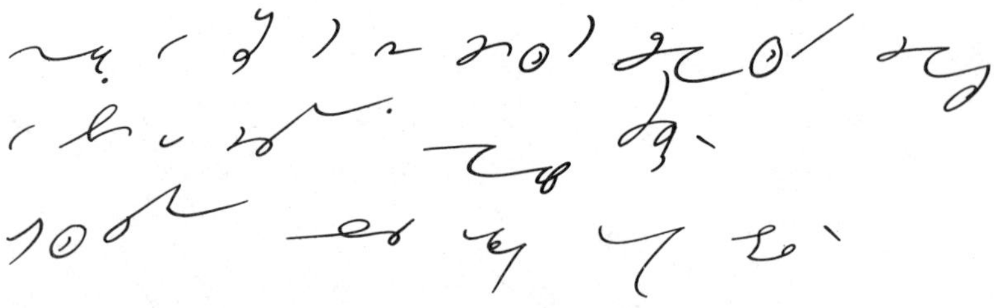

Closing the office for one week, for example, would simplify the task of scheduling employee vacations.
Therefore, additional market research will be necessary.

2 When such introductory words or parenthetical terms are used as plain adverbs (modifying a verb, adjective, adverb, or verbal in the clause or phrase of which they are a part), no commas should be used.

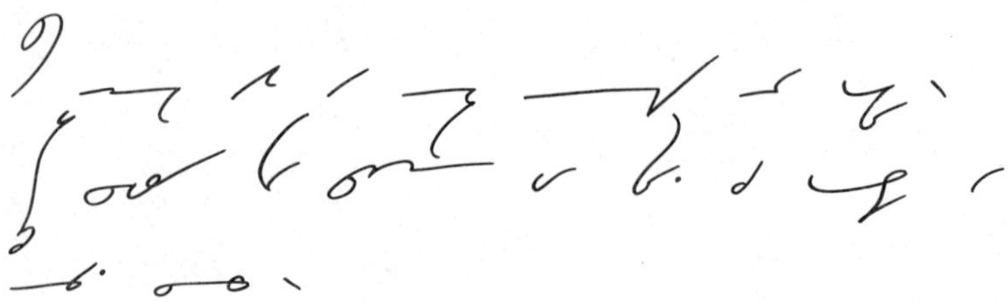

However unimportant it is, it must be mentioned in the report.
Obviously annoyed by the outcome of the voting, she left the meeting immediately.

Check your understanding of comma usage by transcribing the following sentences, preferably at the typewriter.

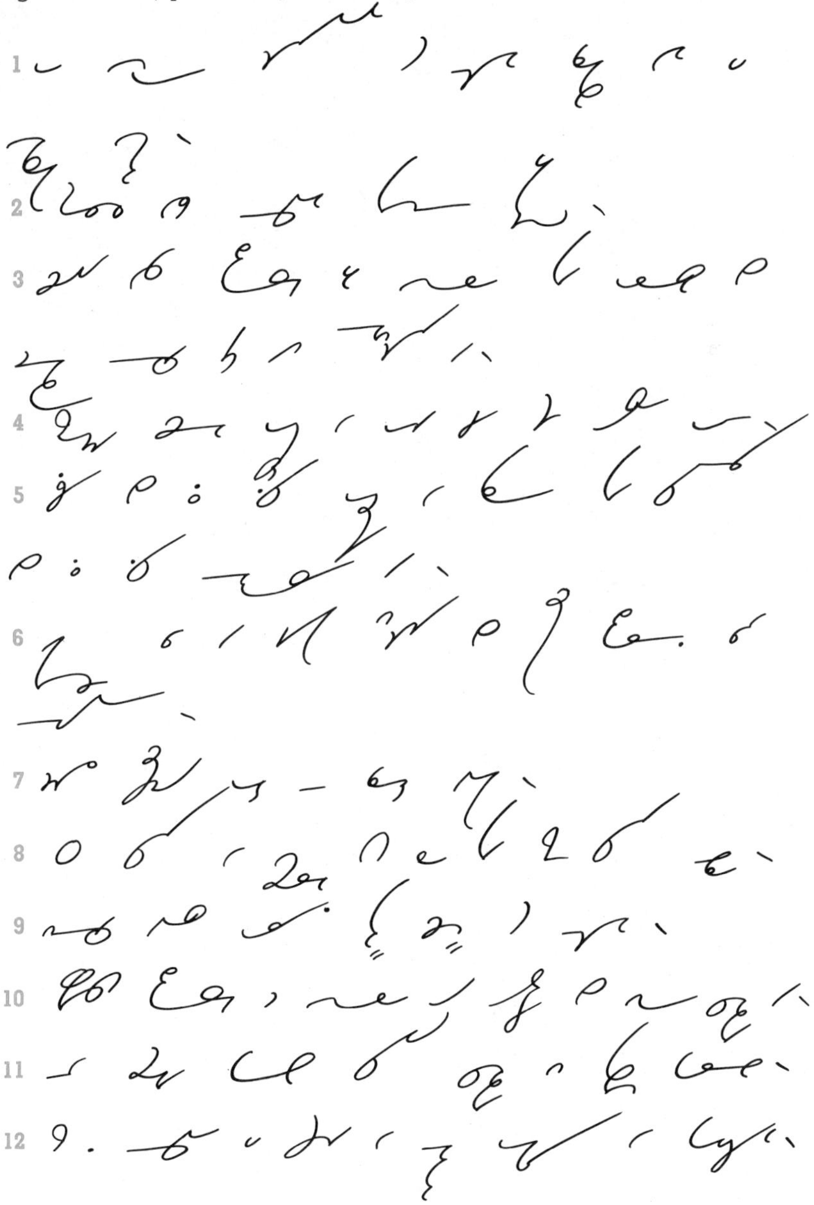

13 

14 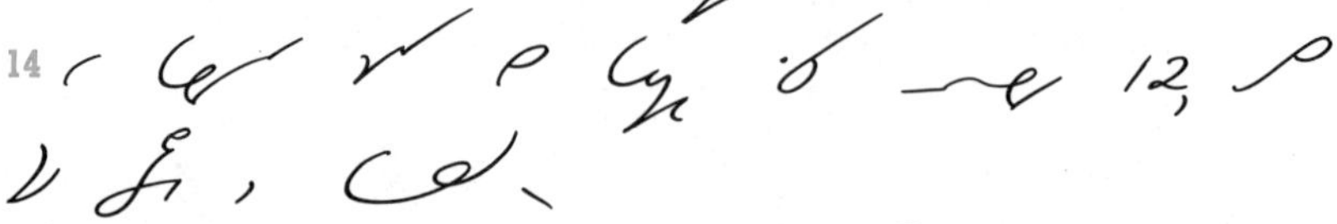

15 

16 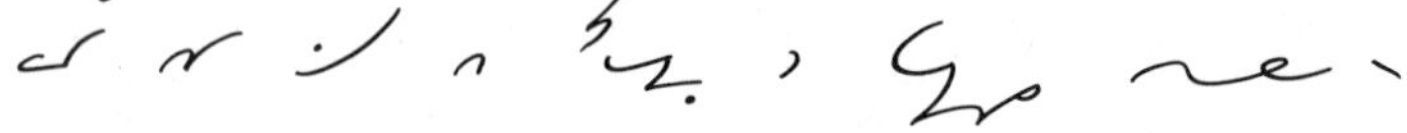

TRANSCRIPTION SPEED BUILDER

191 To: Ralph C. Akin, Sales Manager.

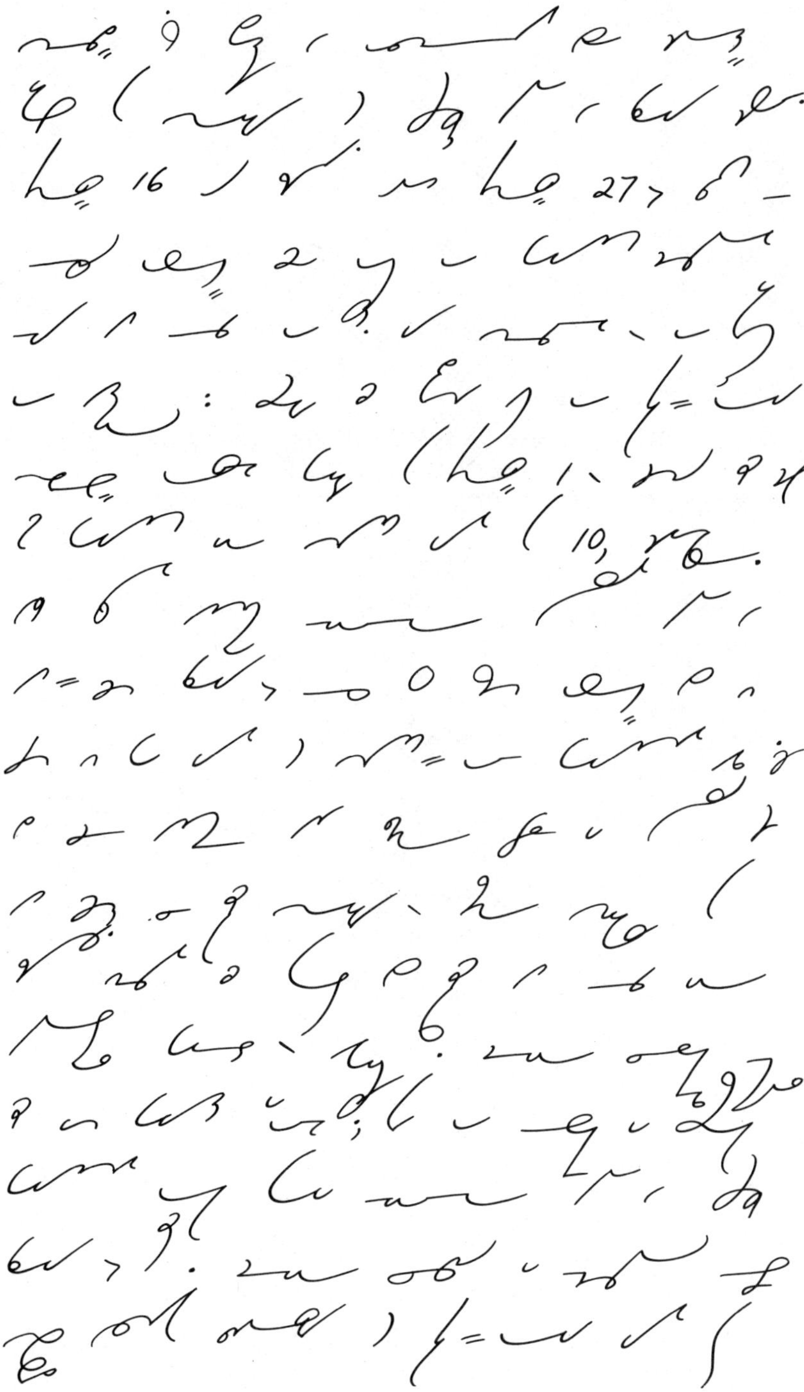

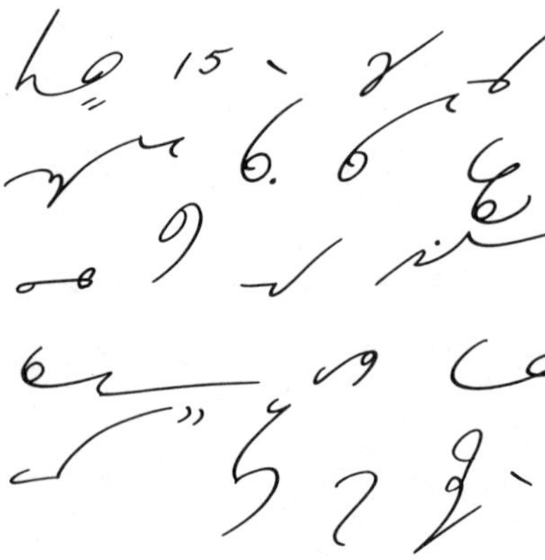

(372)

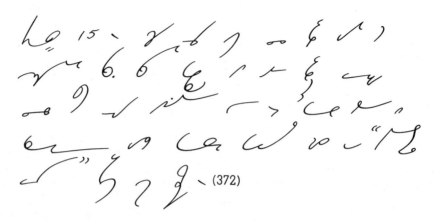

192 Mr. Byron J. Brown, New York Hilton Hotel, Avenue of the Americas at 53rd Street, New York, New York 10019.

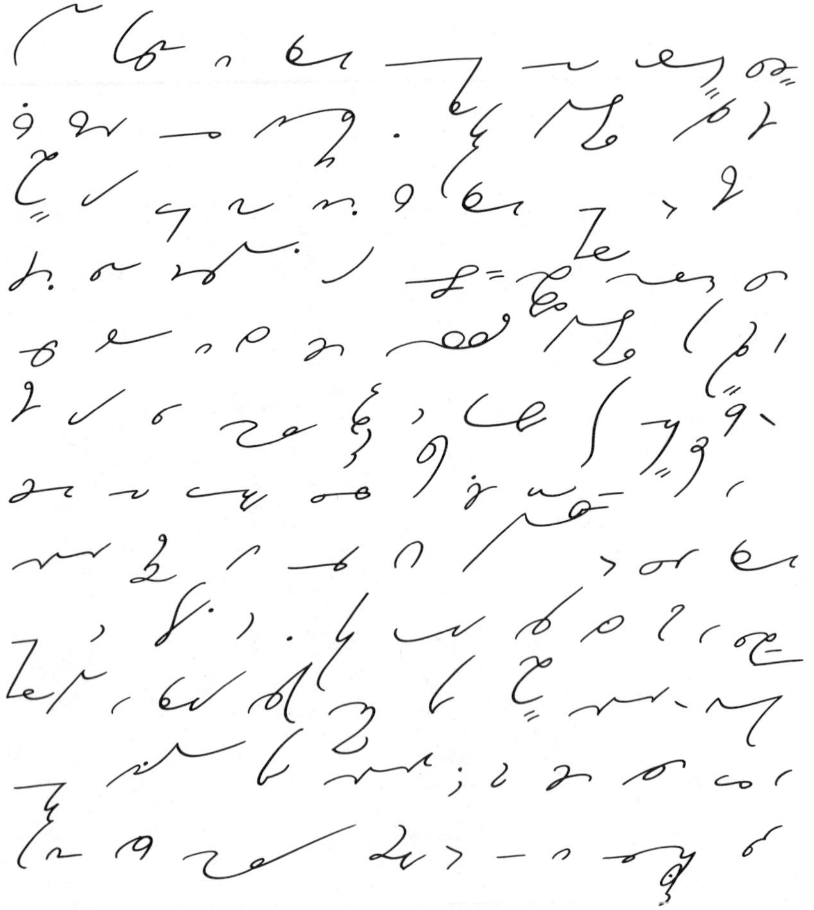

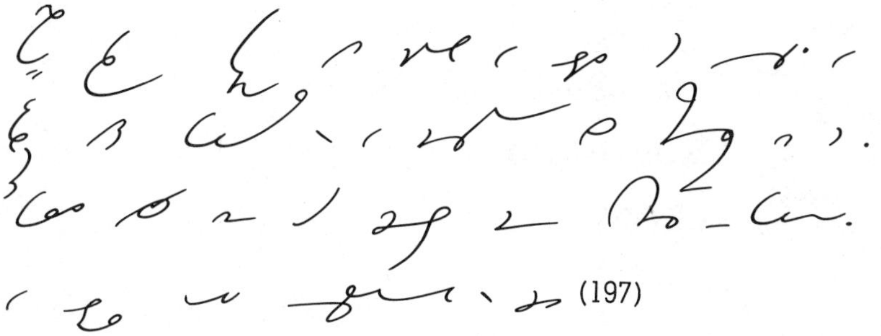

(197)

193 ▸ Mr. Elmer Weeks, Lenox Motor Inn, 1811 London Road, Duluth, Minnesota 55812.

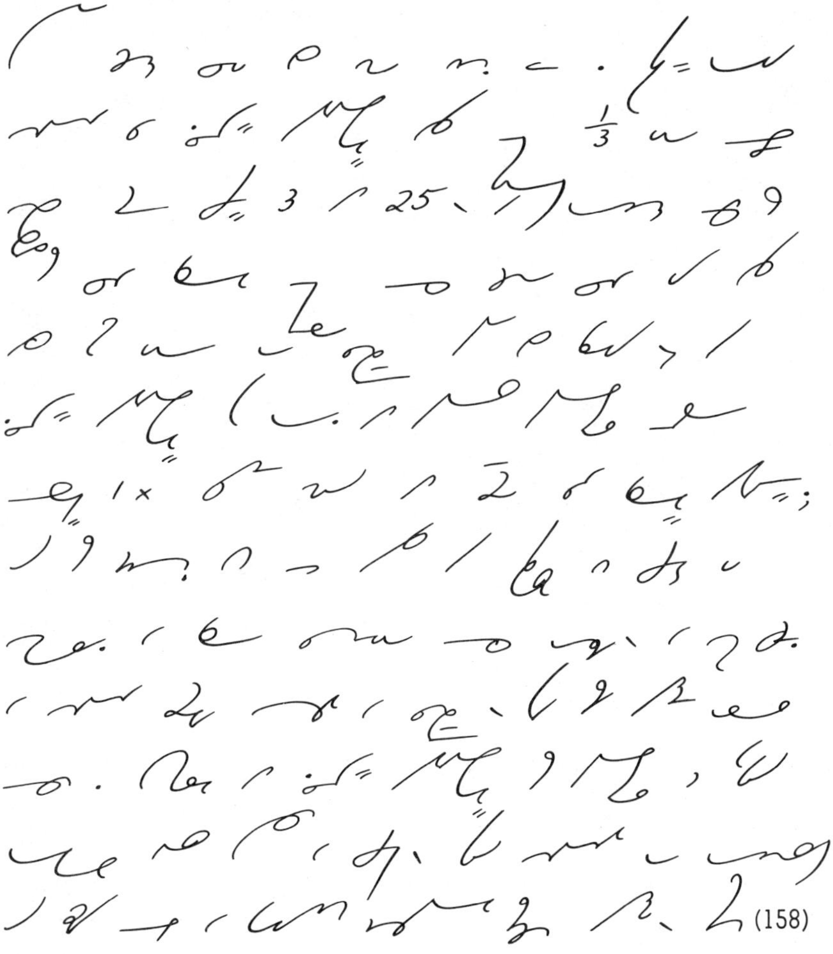

(158)

lesson

42 MASTERING SHORTHAND THEORY

WORD BEGINNINGS

Ort-

Ul-

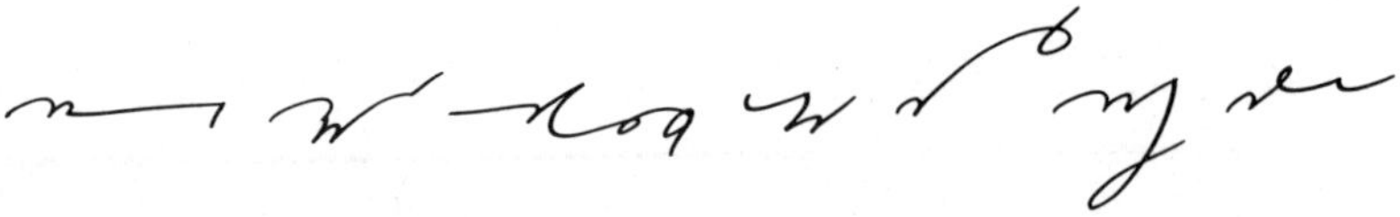

Be-

WORD ENDINGS

-ment

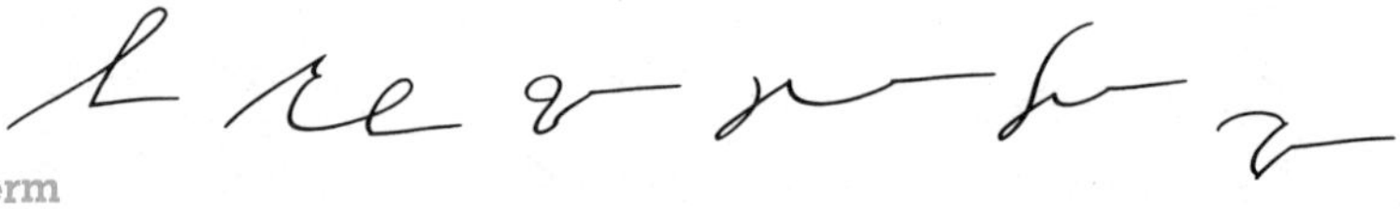

-ern, -erm

-tion, -tial

Assorted, court, export, headquarters, portable, quarterly, supports, reported. Culmination, consultant, multiplication, result, ultimate, cultivate, ulterior.

Belated, believe, behold, because, belongings, below, beyond.
Detachment, displacement, assortment, settlement, betterment, compartment.
Determine, modern, terminate, attorney, thermostat, terminology, eastern.
Connotation, credentials, confrontation, regulation, motivational, emission, commercial, musician.

TRANSCRIPTION SPEED BUILDER

194 ▸ To: Henry E. Wilson, Plant Engineer.

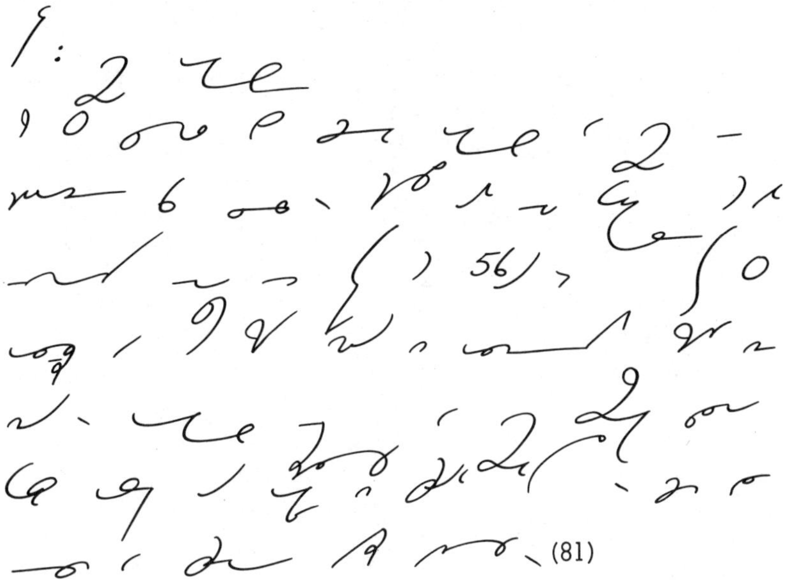

195 ▸ To: Walter L. Hayes, Factory Superintendent.

(160)

196 ▸ To: Henry P. Walters, Senior Vice-President.

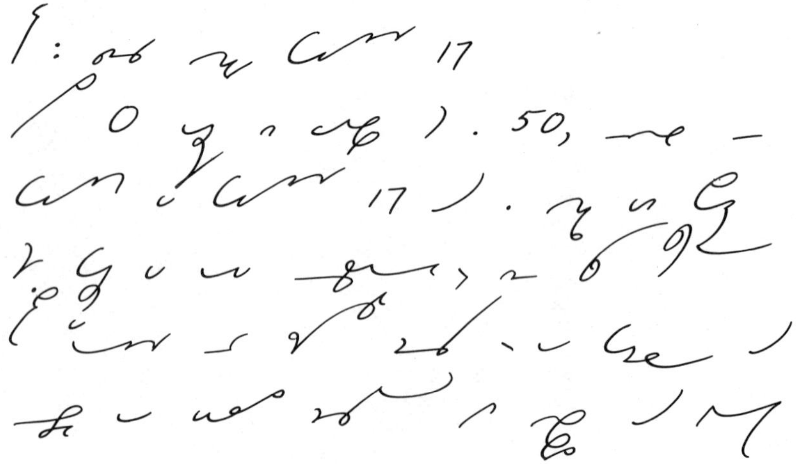

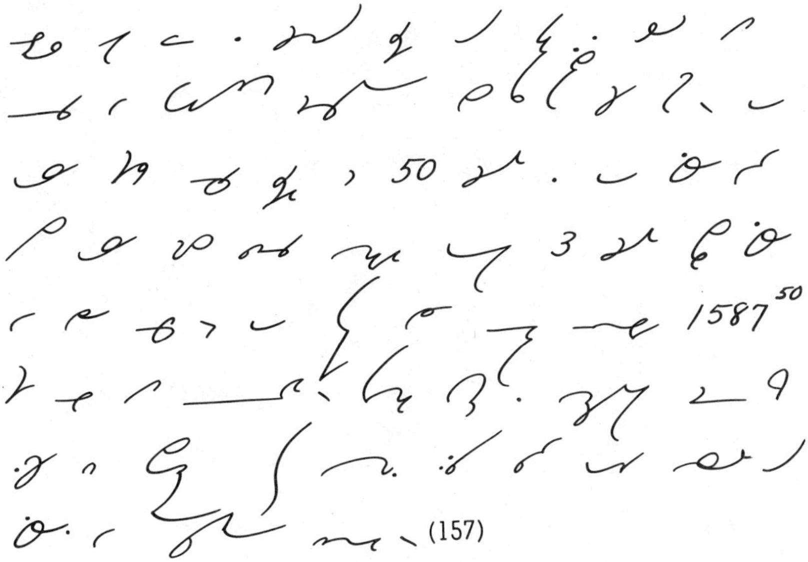

(157)

197 ▸ McCormick Machinery Corporation, 411 West Lake Drive, Milwaukee, Wisconsin 53217 (Teletype Message).

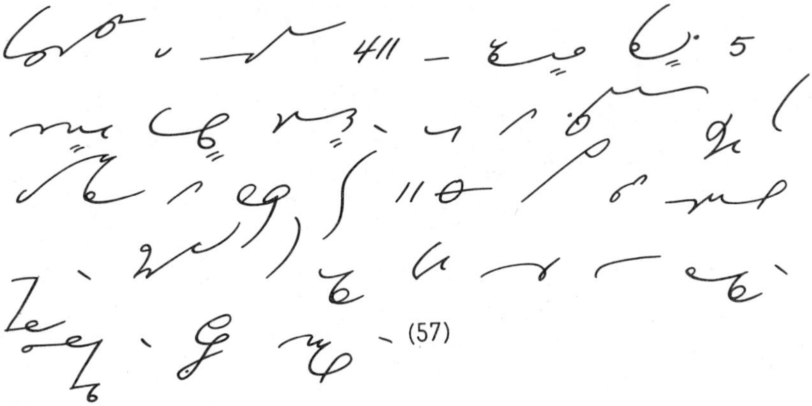

(57)

198 ▸ To: Frederick C. Willis, Supervisor, Paint Shop.

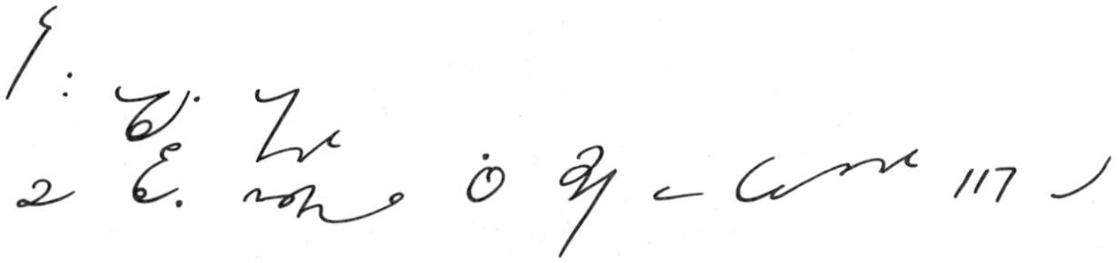

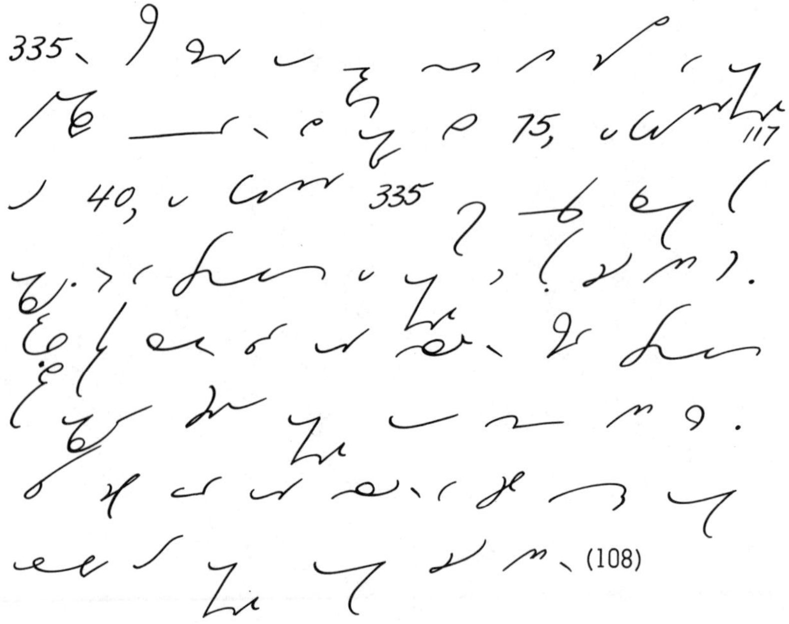

(108)

199 To: William S. King, Plant Service Manager.

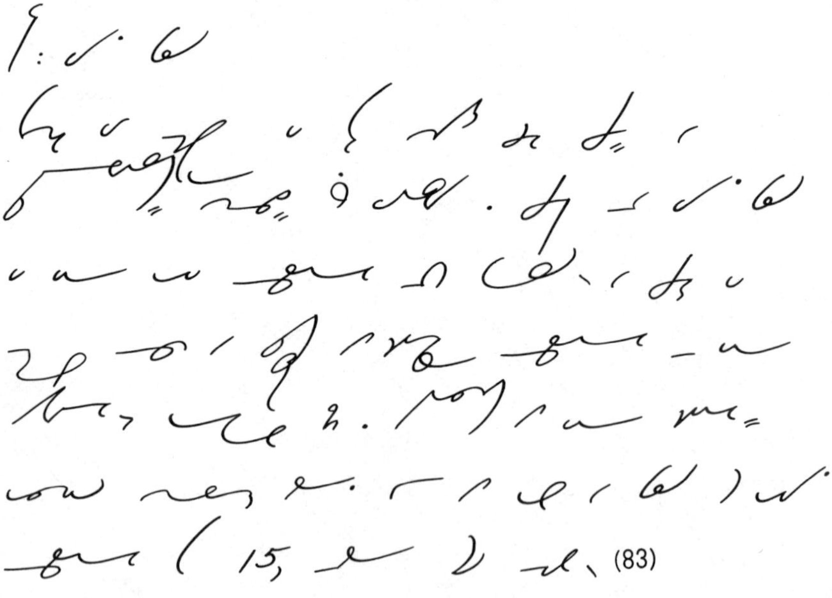

(83)

lesson

BUILDING PHRASING SKILL 43

PHRASE BUILDER

Drill 1

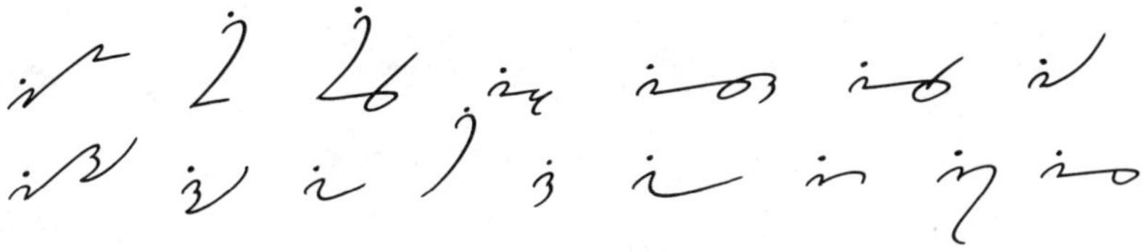

Drill 2

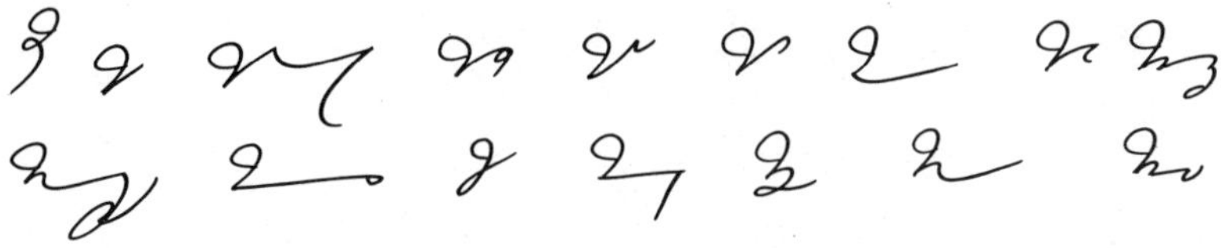

Drill 3

Drill 4

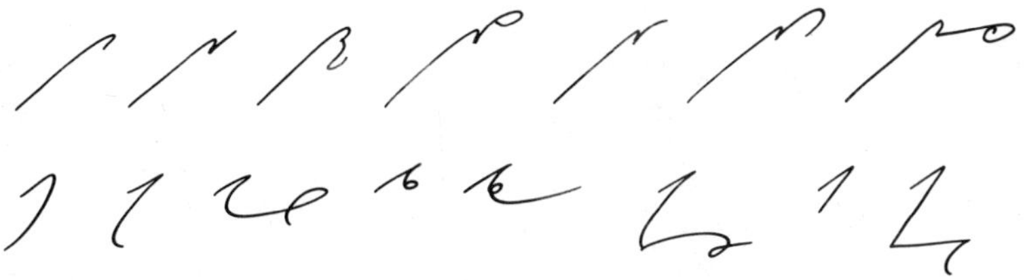

Who do not, who have not, who have made, who knows, who makes, who might, who want, who doesn't, who isn't, who are, who have, who is, who will, who can, who can be, who may.

As if, as it, as it will be, as these, as though, as to, as well, as those, as you can see, as you will find, as many, as yet, as much, as we are, as you will, as you know.

I knew, he knew, I wish, he wishes, I doubt, he doubts, he considered, I considered, I remember, I turned, he turned, I want, he wants, I was, he was.

To do, to do it, to do so, to do that, to do the, to do this, to do my, to have, to be, to place, to see, to sell, to begin, to which, to jump.

TRANSCRIPTION SPEED BUILDER

200 ▸ To: All Department Foremen.

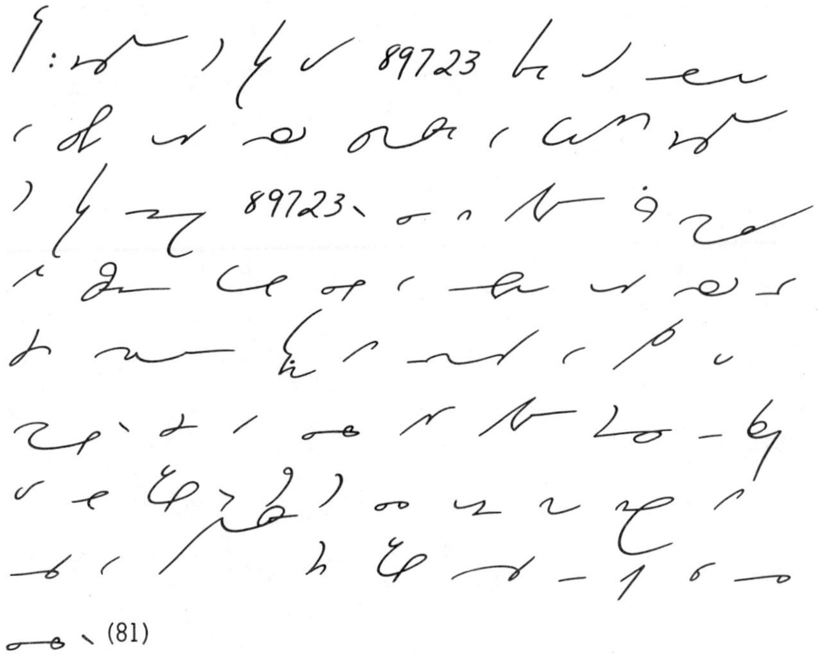

(81)

201 ▸ To: Department Heads.

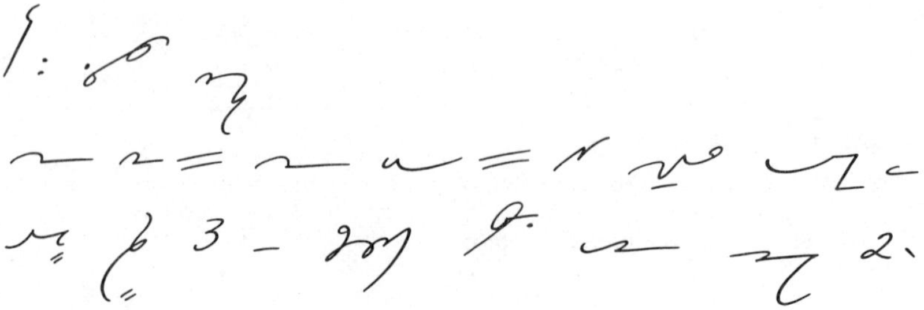

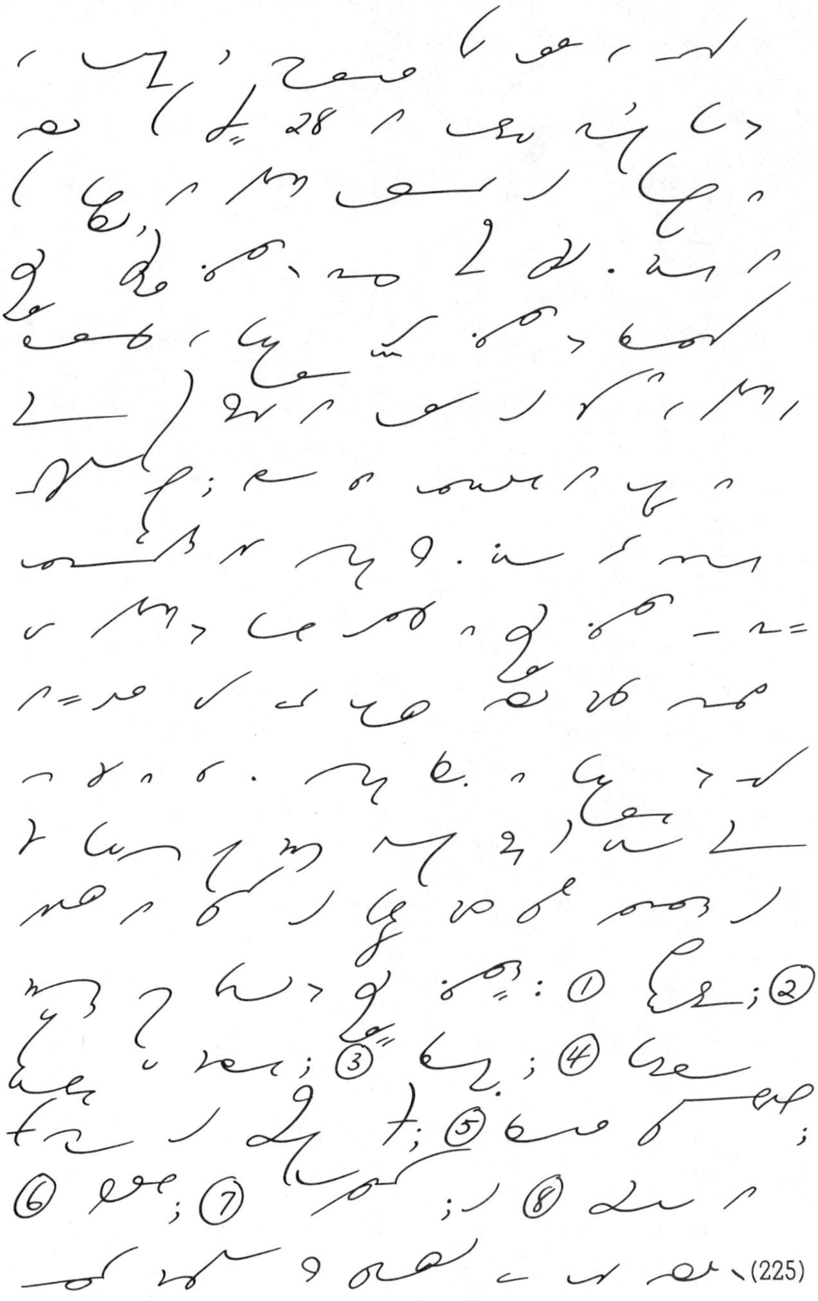

(225)

202 ▸ Mr. Charles C. Metchell, Production Manager, Atlas Manufacturing Company, Galveston, Texas 77552.

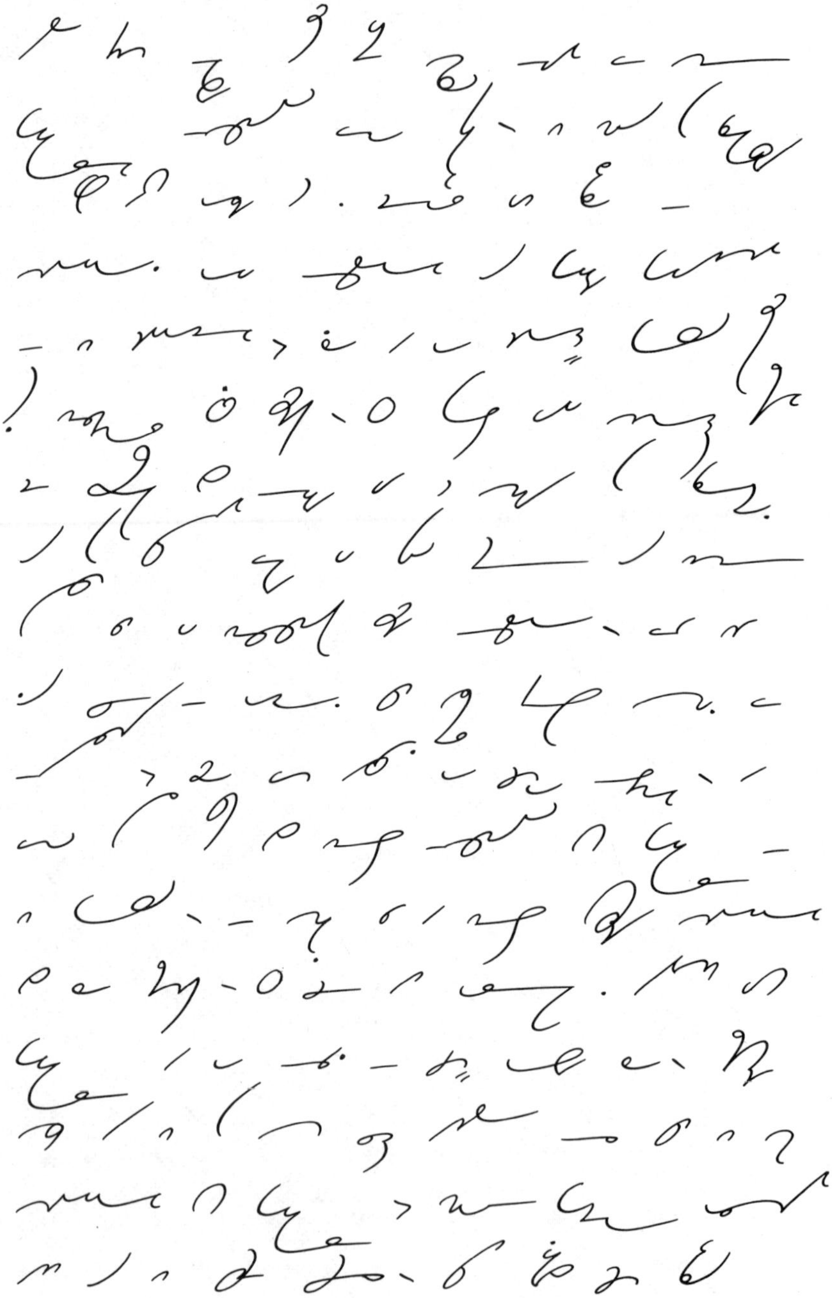

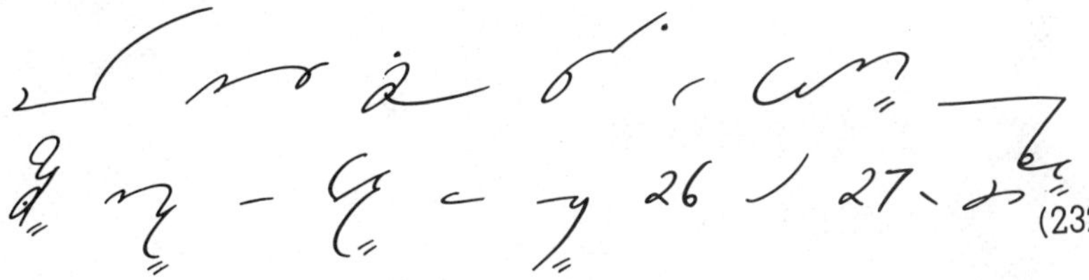

(232)

203 ▸ Memo to Arthur Fleece, Training Department.

(170)

lesson 44 PROGRESSIVE SPEED BUILDING

In this lesson the one-minute speed-forcing letters are counted progressively at 120, 130, and 140 words a minute; the two-minute reinforcement and control letter is counted at 130 words a minute.

First practice the vocabulary preview that precedes the speed-forcing practice, and then review the specialized vocabulary presented at the beginning of this unit.

SPEED-BUILDING LETTERS

Vocabulary Preview

Article, management, necessity, preventive, maintenance, downtime, terms, calendar, heavily, concept, realistically, reaction, renewed, electric mixers, sufficient, continuous, sequence, scheduling, minor, identical, appreciated, impulse, enthusiasm, 50 percent, phenomenal, usually, decoration, engineers, consumer, extensive, popular, recognized, appointment.

Speed Forcing

(1 Minute at 120)

204 Mr. Smith: An article in this month's Production Management discussed the necessity for improving preventive maintenance of plant equipment in order to/reduce downtime.

The author suggested that all

service contracts be written in terms of the number of units produced rather than in terms of the calendar. It stands//to reason that some of our equipment is used more heavily than other equipment, and this new concept of servicing takes use into consideration more///realistically than our present policy does.

What is your reaction to this suggestion? I should like to discuss it with you before the present contracts are renewed. (1)

(1 Minute at 130)

205▸ Gentlemen: Our sales manager, Mr. Ralph Akin, told me of your interest in having us manufacture for you our Kitchen Helper electric mixers during our slack/season. You would merchandise these mixers through your catalog.

He asked me to tell you what month our machines could be made available to you for this production. If we have sufficient//advance notice, we could arrange for a continuous run during the month of August. As no change of sequence in operations would be necessary, there need be no time wasted///in machine scheduling.

No doubt Mr. Akin told you that you must make some minor change in the product so that it is not identical with our Kitchen Helper. Sincerely, (2)

(1 Minute at 140)

206▸ Mr. Henry: Your request for my opinion about production quotas for Product 17 is appreciated very much.

Frankly, I think that Product 17 is an impulse item/and that the fad for it will soon have passed.

I can understand Mr. Akin's enthusiasm for increasing production to meet the demand that is so high today, and I agree with him//that we should raise our production figures 50 percent for each of the next two months. It is my suggestion, however, that we start to phase out production about 10 percent a month starting May 1.///

Perhaps it is a bit early to make a final judgment about such a phenomenal item, but the sale of impulse goods usually drops even more rapidly than it rises. (3)

Reinforcement and Control

(2 Minutes at 130)

207▸ Gentlemen: We are turning to your company for help in researching a color problem for lawn furniture. Our policy is to make major changes in design of our/regular lines every ten years. During the other nine years we rely on color changes or changes in decoration to attract additional customers to our basic//products.

Our product engineers usually conduct all market research for our plants in all locations. Right now we are in such a period of expansion that they cannot///schedule this piece of needed research within the next four months. We shall have to go outside our own organization for data about changes in consumer preferences.

We should (1) appreciate your consideration of the following questions:

How long would it take your organization to analyze consumer preferences in the color of lawn/furniture?

How extensive should a market

survey be to get answers to our problem?

Should we market three colors only, or should we expand our colors?

Would the cost of//additional colors be offset by increased sales?

What new colors are popular?

Have you made any studies that are comparable to the one we want?

You are recognized leaders in market///research, and we hope it will be possible to work with you. If you can undertake a survey for us, may I make an appointment with you in Chicago next week? Sincerely yours, (2)

TRANSCRIPTION SPEED BUILDER

208 ▸ KMC Communications Corporation, 211 Randolph Avenue, St. Paul, Minnesota 55131.

(172)

209 ▸ Memo to Mr. Henry Simpson.

(117)

TRANSCRIPTION PACER

210 ▸ Wells and Sawyer, 66 Bridge Street, Bridgeport, Connecticut 13
06630. 14

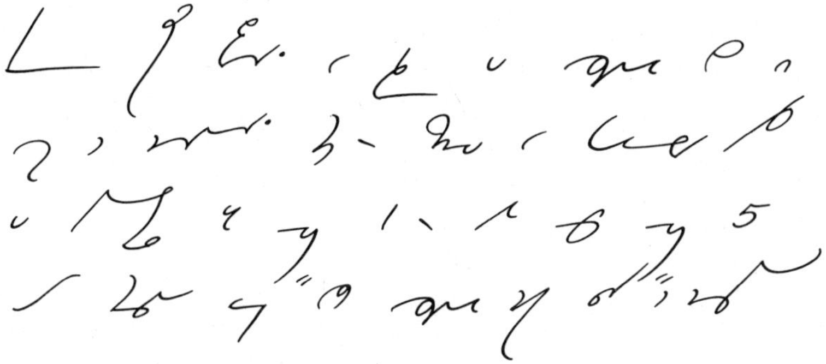

28 41 51 65

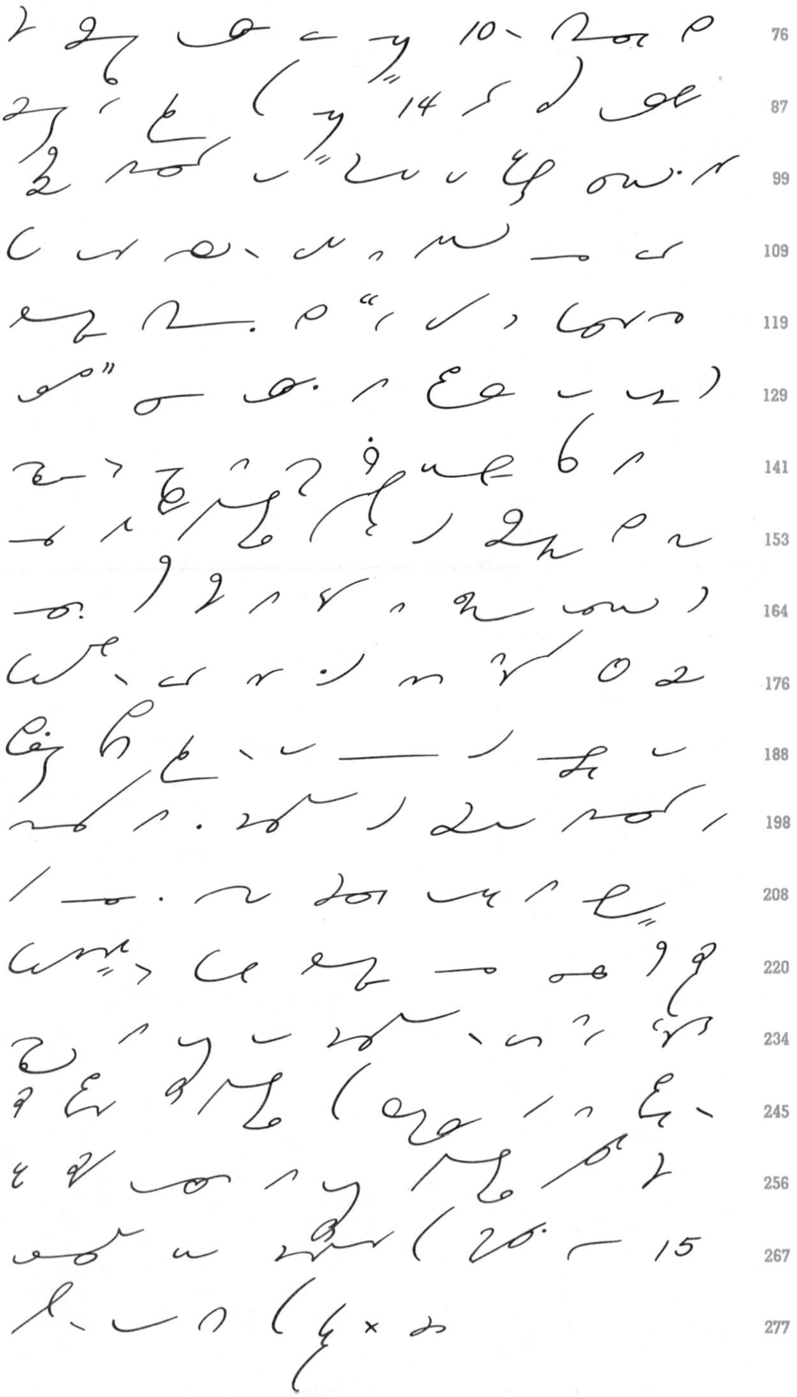

76
87
99
109
119
129
141
153
164
176
188
198
208
220
234
245
256
267
277

lesson 45

BUILDING TRANSCRIPTION SPEED

SUSTAINED SPEED BUILDER

Practice the following vocabulary preview, and then see how well you can sustain your reinforcement and control speed.

Vocabulary Preview

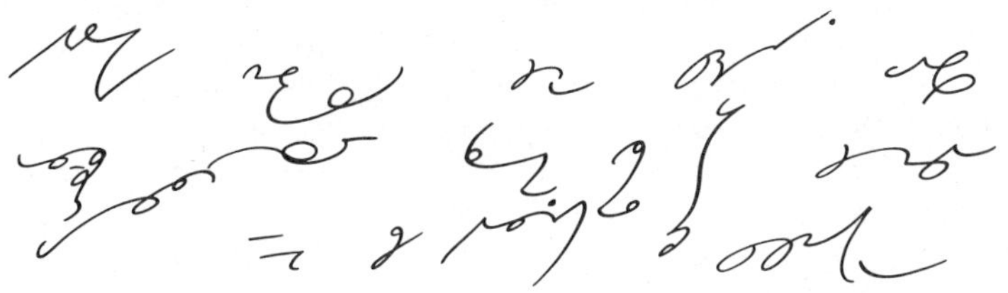

Disturbed, unexplained, security, outstanding, authorization, requisitions, garden, pilfering, thievery, obviously, signature, automatic, entrance, exit, directive, accountability.

Speed Builder

211▸ To: Henry E. Wilson, Plant Engineer, Subject: Losses from Wastage and Misappropriation.

I am very much disturbed about an unexplained and sudden rise in losses of both materials and tools.[1] I have always thought that our inventory control and security measures were outstanding. Our stores-record[2] clerks issue materials from the storerooms only on the written authorization of certain designated[3] persons. These requisitions are checked against actual stores inventory annually. The stores ledger,[4] showing flow of materials into the plant and storeroom and out to the production floor, as well as any[5] returns from the production floor to the storeroom, is kept in a location different from the stores-record[6] clerk's station. The two records are constantly checked against each other. Inventories of finished goods are similarly[7] controlled.

From here on, however, the security system seems to have broken down. Completed garden[8] tools ready for shipment to our customers have been disappearing at an alarming rate, indicating that[9] our employees are probably pilfering not only the tools with which they work but also finished goods for their[10] own home use. In addition, inventories of raw materials show unaccounted-for shortages. We may[11] be plagued not only by petty larceny but also by organized thievery.

In addition, plant foremen[12] are apparently lax about issuing new materials to workmen who want to disguise substandard work[13] by replacing it with new products from materials for which their operation has not been charged.

Obviously,[14] the security system must be tightened. I recommend that the following new precautions be[15] instituted immediately:

1. All locks on storerooms should be changed.
2. New keys should be issued only to authorized[16] personnel.
3. Two signatures rather than one should be required for the removal of raw materials[17] and finished goods.
4. Present security guards for all storerooms should be transferred to new assignments[18] unrelated to the storage areas—possibly to the plant entrances and exits. This step would not affect[19] their employment status, for we can merely exchange present assignments of the entire force.
5. An[20] automatic camera should be placed at the entrance to every storeroom so that every person's entrance[21] and exit is photographed.
6. A directive should be issued to all foremen stressing their accountability[22] for materials issued to cover up wastage.
7. Workmen should be checked at all exits when they leave work.[23]
8. A directive should be issued to all workmen on the subject of pilfering.

Until further notice, please[24] report to me weekly on the situation. (489)

TRANSCRIPTION CHECKPOINT

212▸ To: All Foremen.

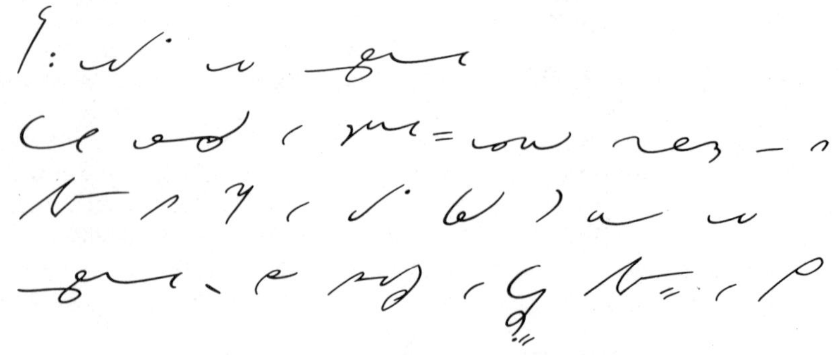

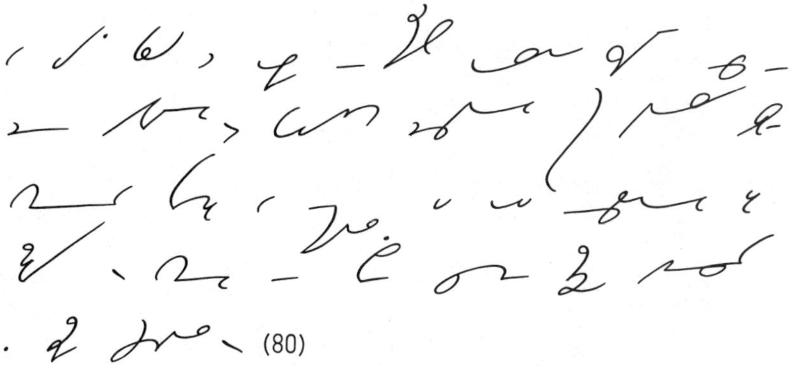

(80)

213 Mr. John P. Hopkins, Missouri Power and Light Company, 2341 Davis Boulevard, St. Louis, Missouri 63125.

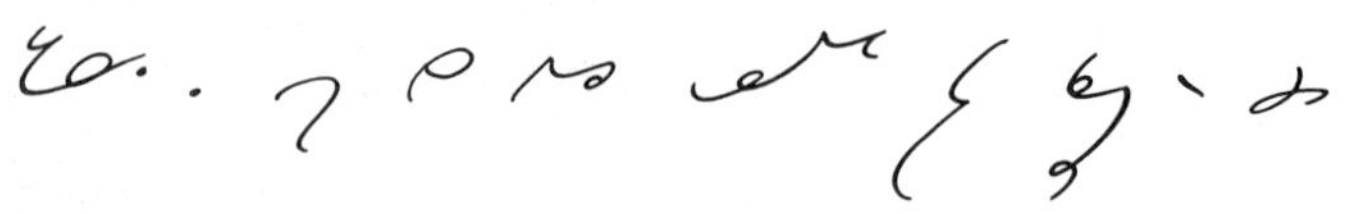 (142)

214 Memo to Herbert Schultz, Factory Personnel.

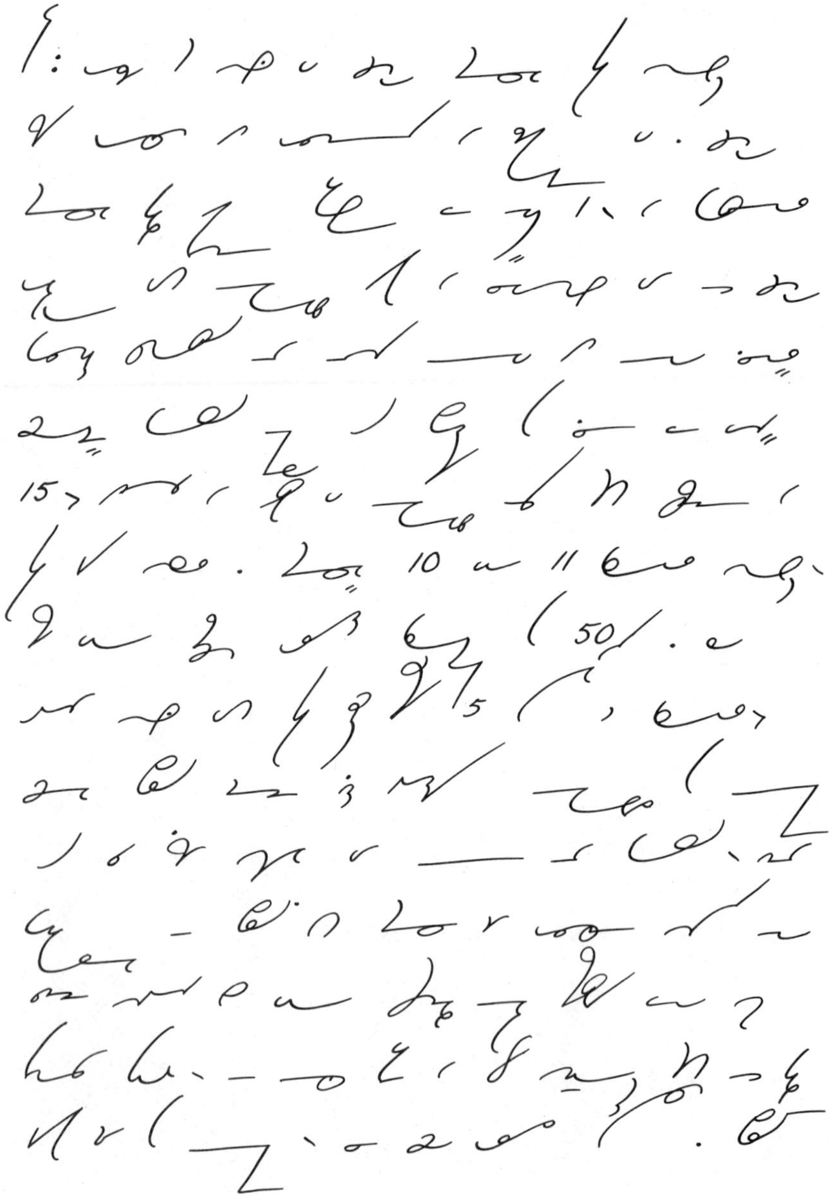

(234)

TRANSCRIPTION PACER

215 ▸ All-State Mail Order Company, 711 Bay Bridge Drive, San 12
Francisco, California 94133. 18

29
41
51
64
74
88
97
105
116
128
141
154
168
180
188

Under the free enterprise system, those who have goods or services to sell rely on advertising (in addition to personal selling) to locate consumers, to communicate the nature and advantages of their wares, and to persuade consumers to buy. As such, advertising — a paid form of impersonal presentation and promotion of goods or services — performs an important part in the flow of goods from production to consumption.

Various media — newspapers, magazines, television, radio, direct mail, trade publications, and outdoor displays — are used in advertising to reach groups of consumers. Although mixed feelings surround the question of the overall success of advertising in serving the consumer, most support the argument that advertising is vital to economic and social growth and that it increases competition,

unit 10

ADVERTISING

creates markets, and reduces unit costs and prices.

The advertising manager is responsible for the preparation and insertion of advertising copy. Where an advertising agency is used, he interprets company objectives to the agency.

Secretarial Assignment

In this unit, you are secretary to Stuart P. Henderson, manager of advertising. All letters are signed by him over his title, Advertising Manager.

SPECIALIZED TERMINOLOGY

You will transcribe Mr. Henderson's dictation more efficiently after you have become familiar with the specialized terms he uses.

Media (Medium, singular) • Types of devices or vehicles by which advertising reaches its audience.

Institutional Advertising • Announcements of general interest to consumers, usually not closely related to the sale of any particular good or service.

Account Executive • Advertising agency employee responsible for the advertising for which a company contracts.

Conference Report • Standard report on every client-agency conference, which includes date, report number, names of those present, identity of product under discussion, and summary of decisions.

Bleed • Effect achieved when a photograph or piece of artwork extends to the very edge of the printed page.

Credit Lines • Due recognition to artist, photographer, publisher, or agency. A credit line is usually placed immediately below a published illustration.

Layout • Designer's blueprint of an advertisement that the printer is to follow.

Dummy • Page-by-page layout of a publication made up to show the size, shape, form, sequence, and general style.

Galley Proof • Proofs that are pulled from type that has been set and placed in a shallow metal tray. The type will be divided later into pages.

Leading • Spacing between type lines and paragraphs.

Mat (Stereotype) • Paper matrix that is forced down over type or cuts to take an impression. The mat then serves as a mold, duplicating the old surface when melted metal is poured into it.

Size (Sizing) • Gelatin and resin treatment of paper in order to modify its surface qualities.

Tear Sheets • Extra unbound sheets of a published article that may be sent to those requesting additional copies.

Vandyke • A photographic print similar to a blueprint, made so that any mistakes can be corrected before printing plates are made.

CONFUSED WORDS AND TRANSCRIPTION PRACTICE

Study the following pairs of similar-sounding and similar-looking words that are often confused:

affect (verb) to change; to influence

effect (noun) outcome; result
(verb) to bring about

respectively in the order given

respectfully in a courteous manner

advice (noun) counsel

advise (verb) to recommend

principal chief; leading

principle general truth; rule

lead (noun) metal
(verb) to guide or direct

led (verb) guided — past tense of ***lead***

choose to select

chose did choose — past tense of ***choose***

biannual occurring twice a year

biennial occurring every two years

council an assembly

counsel an attorney; advice

Transcribe the following sentences, preferably at the typewriter. These sentences contain the words that appear in the list above. Some of the sentences contain two words in parenthesis — one of them right, the other wrong. When you transcribe, be sure to select the correct word.

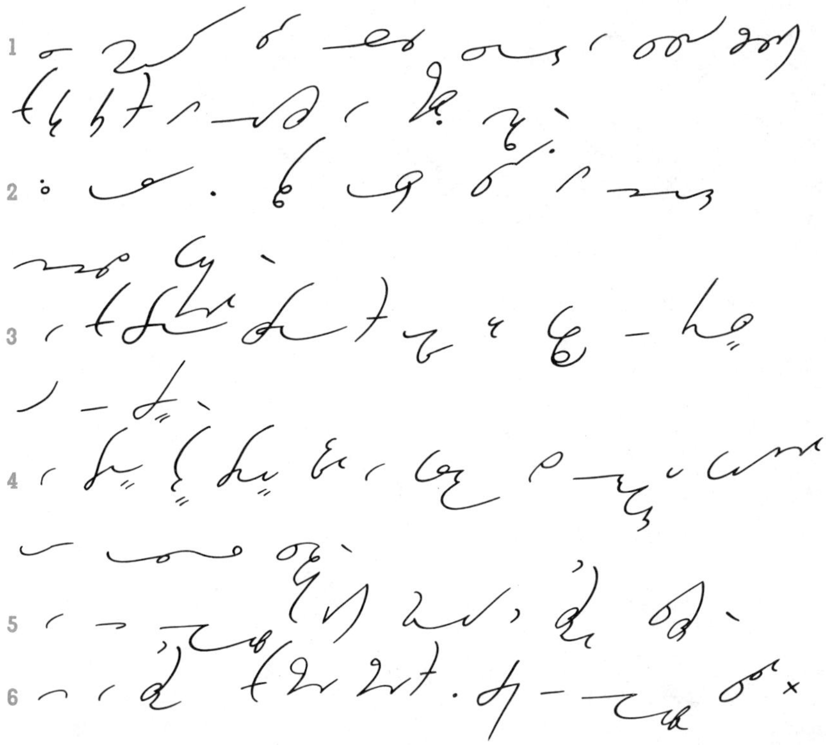

lesson

BUILDING TRANSCRIPTION QUALITY 46

TRANSCRIPTION POINTERS

Uses of the Semicolon

1 When a conjunction (*and, but, or, nor*) is omitted between two independent clauses, separate the clauses by a semicolon.

The arbitrators were willing to compromise the issues; the management representatives were not.
The function of the broker is to bring together buyers and sellers; he receives a commission or fee for this.

2 A semicolon is often used to separate two independent clauses joined by a coordinate conjunction when either or both of the clauses contain internal punctuation.

NOTE: The growing trend is to use a comma between such clauses—even though commas are also used within the clauses—as long as no confusion or misreading occurs. In light of this standpoint, therefore, the examples below, as well as sentences 6 and 11, would be acceptable with a comma between the independent clauses.

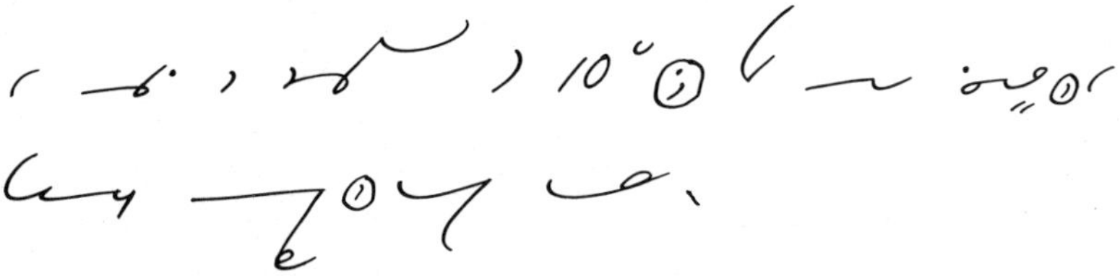

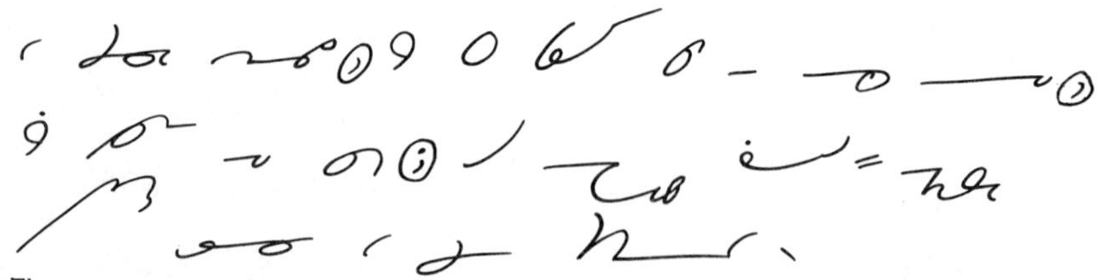

The meeting is scheduled for ten o'clock; but Mr. Henry, the promotion manager, will be late.

The finance committee, as I pointed out in my memorandum, has taken no action; and employee health-insurance deductions remain the same for this month.

3 When independent clauses are joined by an adverbial connective (*accordingly, consequently, however, nevertheless, otherwise, therefore*), place a semicolon before the connective and a comma after it.

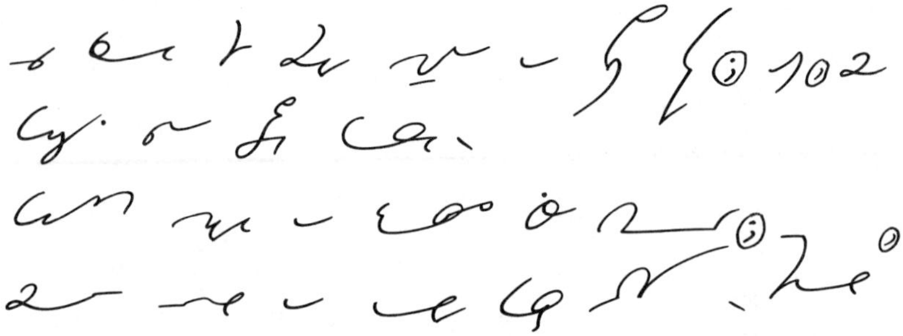

Net sales for the first quarter are above budget; therefore, we are proceeding with our expansion plans.

Production costs are slightly higher this month; nevertheless, we will not increase our list prices at this time.

Check your understanding of the uses of the semicolon by transcribing the following sentences, preferably at the typewriter.

1 

2 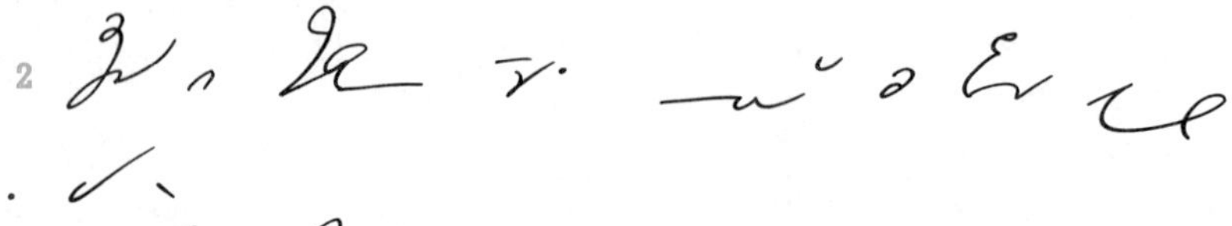

3 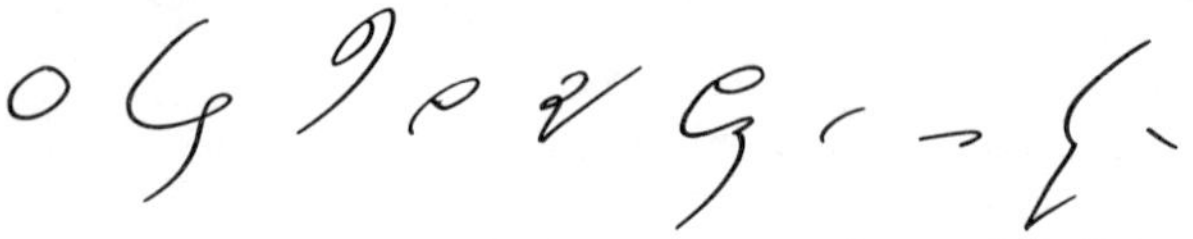

4 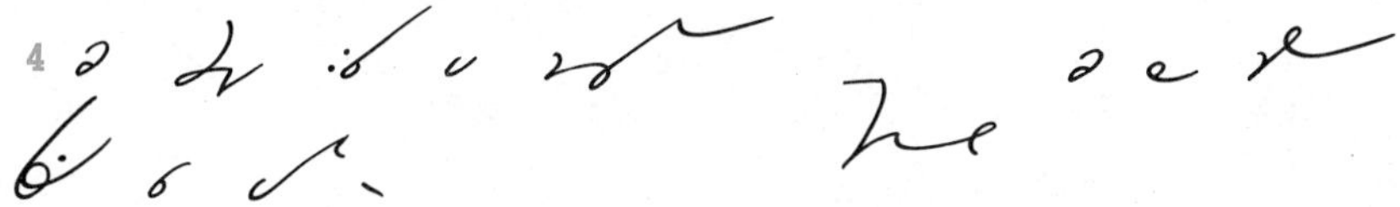

5 

6 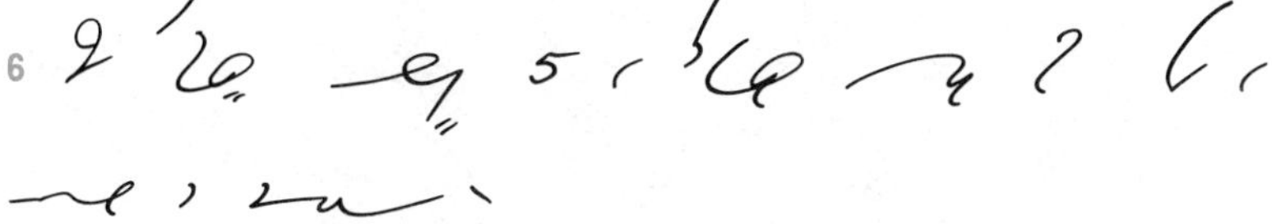

7 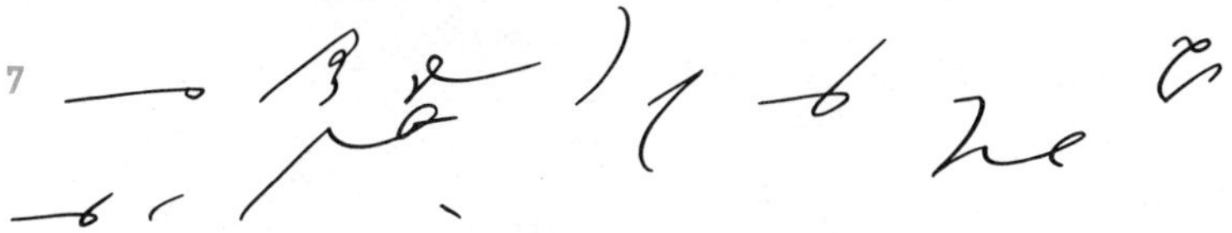

8 

9 

10 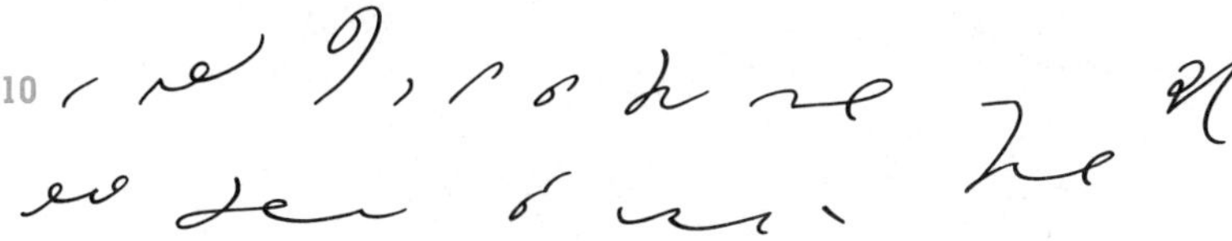

11 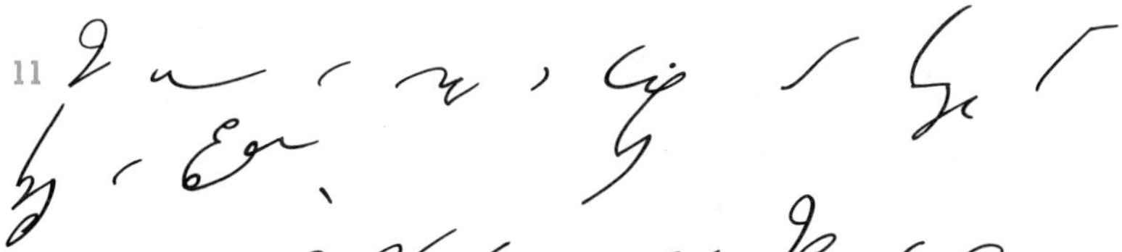

12 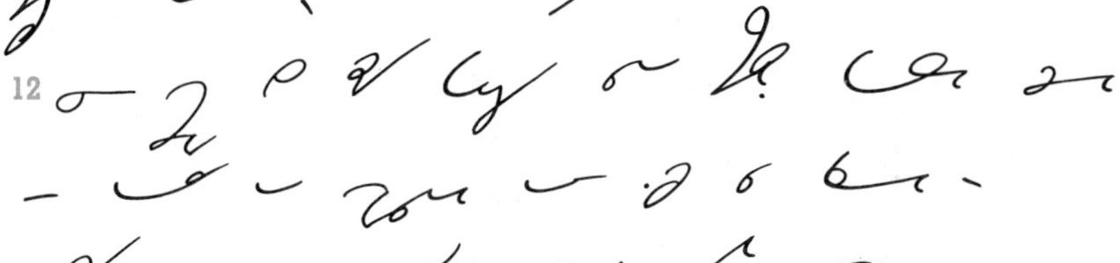

13 

216 ▸ Mr. Willis P. Hall, Customer Consultant, Rice Hotel, Houston, Texas 77017.

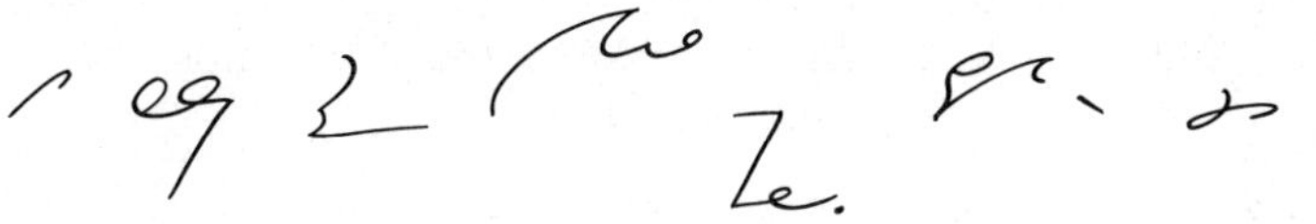
(223)

217 ▸ Mr. Henry M. Simpson, President, National Products, Inc., 211 Forest Avenue, St. Louis, Missouri 63100.

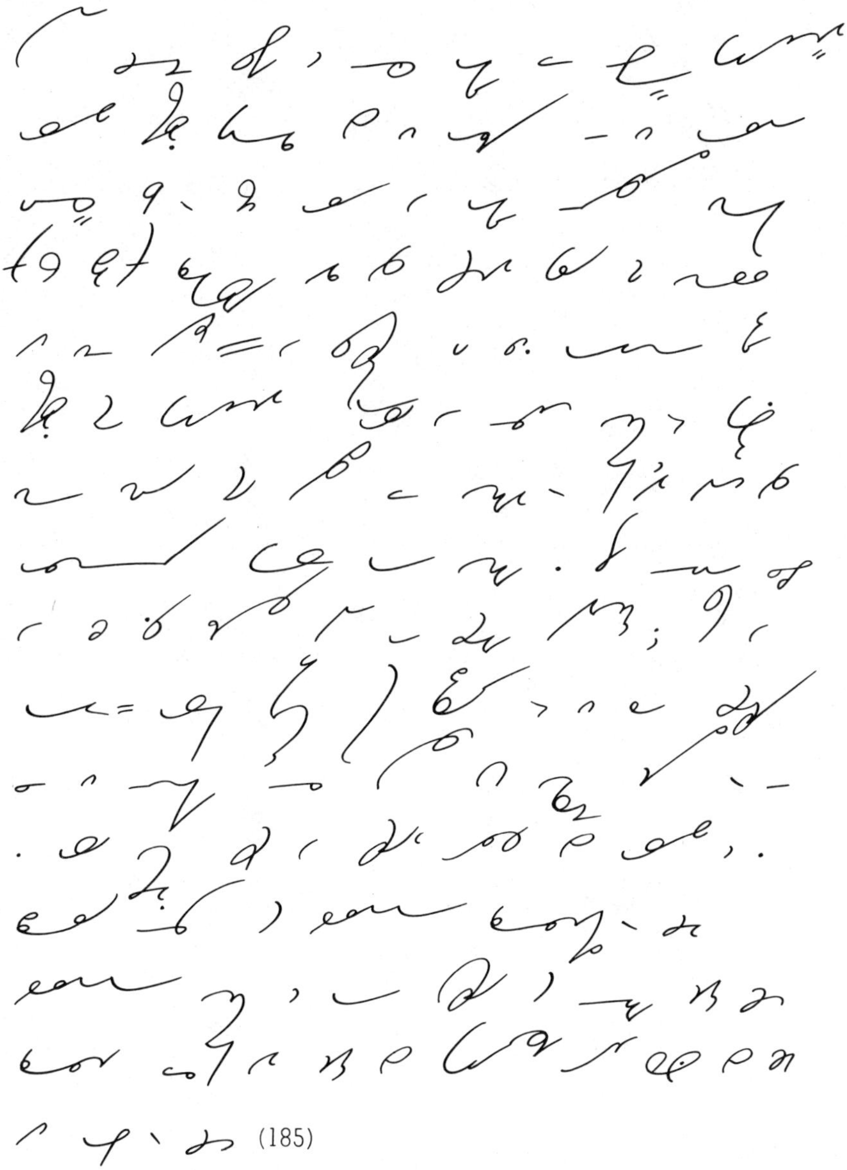
(185)

218▸ Burton and Dodson Advertising Agency, 3244 Sutter Avenue, San Francisco, California 94144, Attention Mr. Kent C. Thomas.

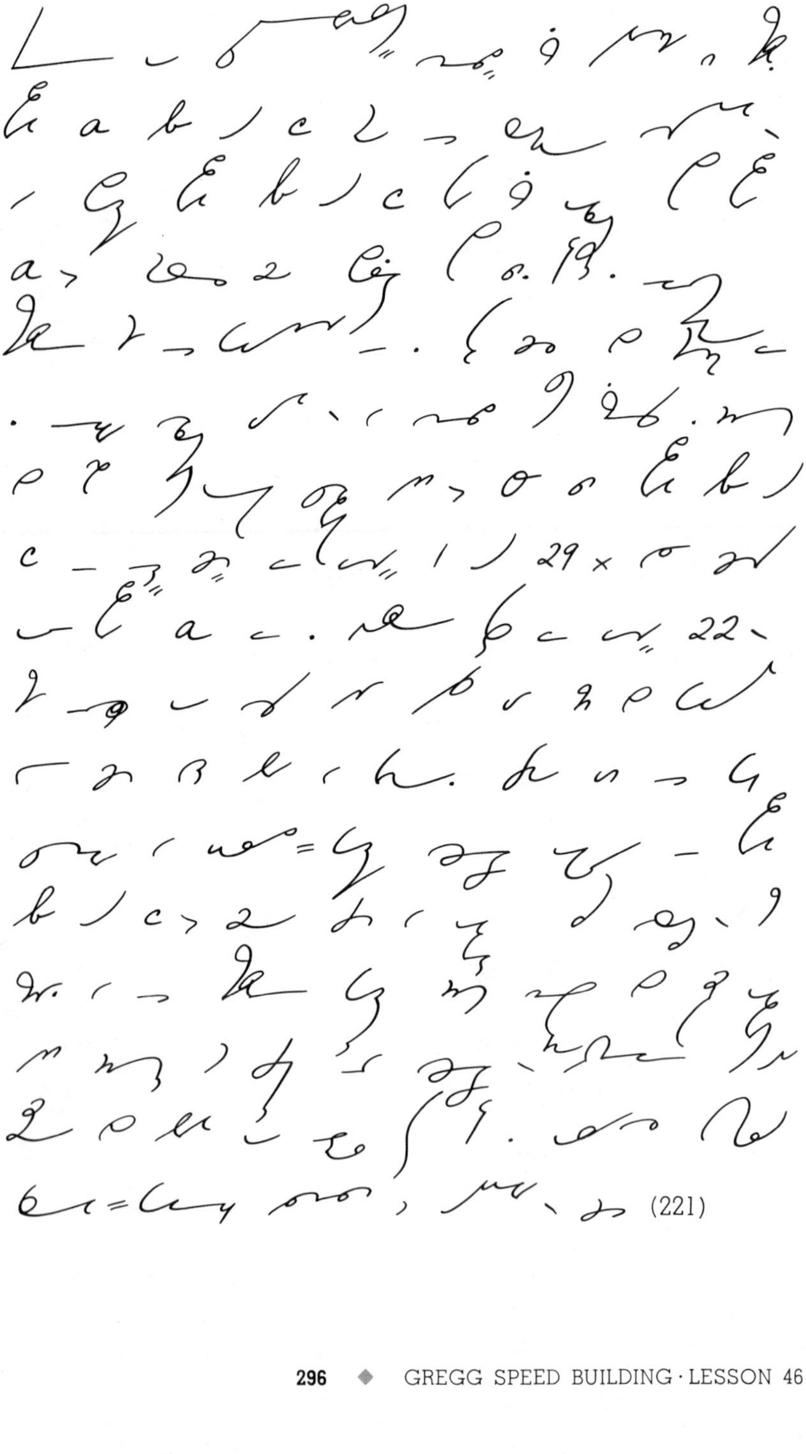

(221)

lesson 47

MASTERING SHORTHAND THEORY

WORD BEGINNINGS

Electr-, Electric

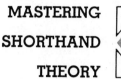

Over-, Under-

WORD ENDINGS

-ification

-ship

-ward

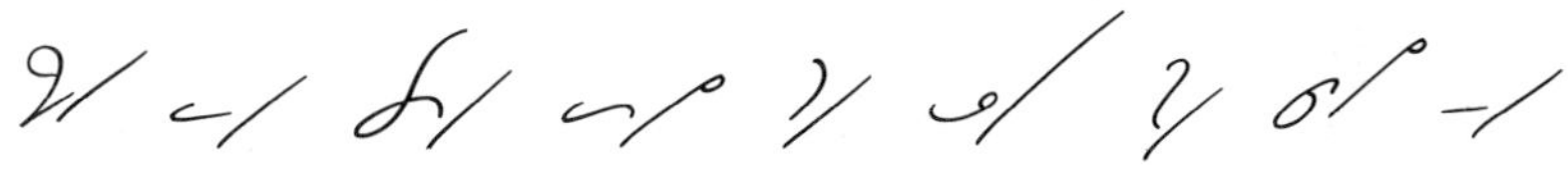

-sume, -sumption

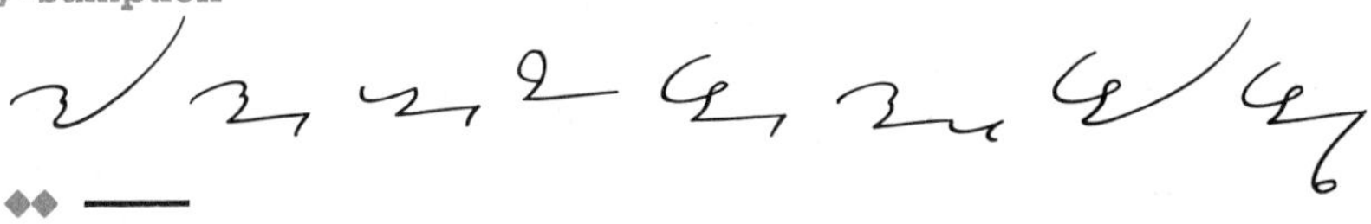

Electronic, electric typewriter, electrotype, electroplated, electrons, electrically, electric furnace, electrician, electrify, electrolysis, electroscope, electrode, electric shock.

Overawed, overtones, overdone, overwrought, undertaken, undersell, underwriters, underlying.

Intensification, nullification, ratification, rectification, stultification, ramification, classification.

Ownership, stewardship, hardship, kinship, friendship, relationship, township, scholarship.

Afterward, onward, backward, awkwardly, forward, rewarded, upward, outwardly, inward.

Consumed, consumption, resumption, assume, presumption, consumers, presumed, presumably.

TRANSCRIPTION SPEED BUILDER

219 Dependable Mailing Lists, Inc., 380 Park Avenue South, New York, New York 10021.

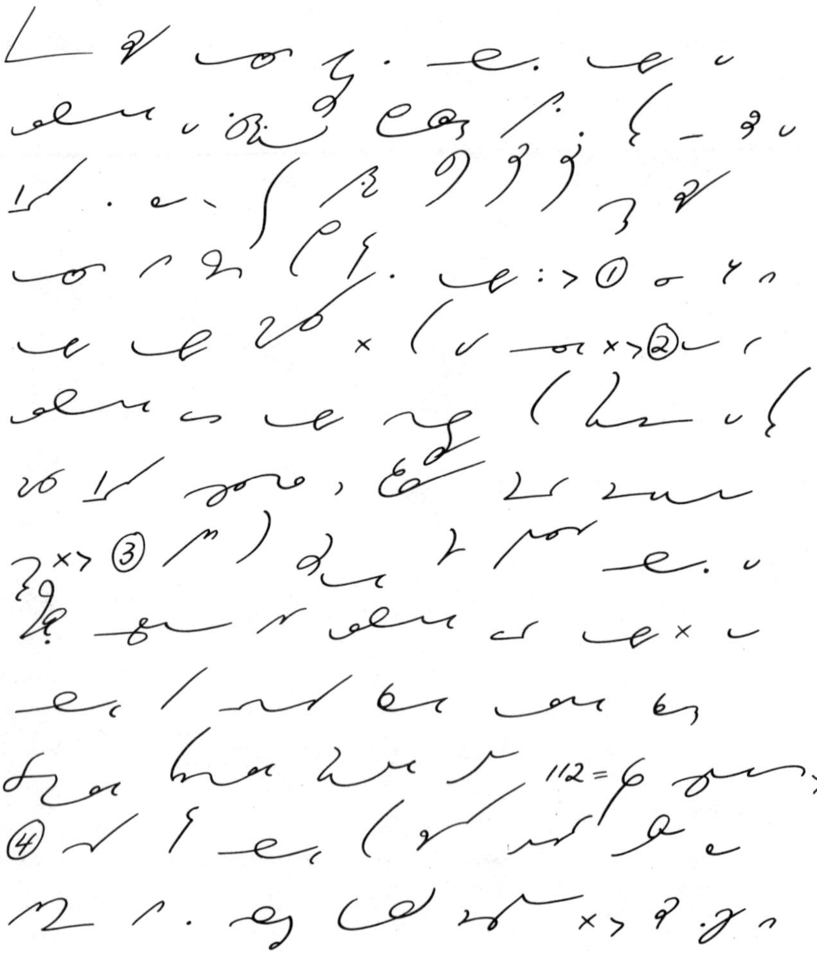

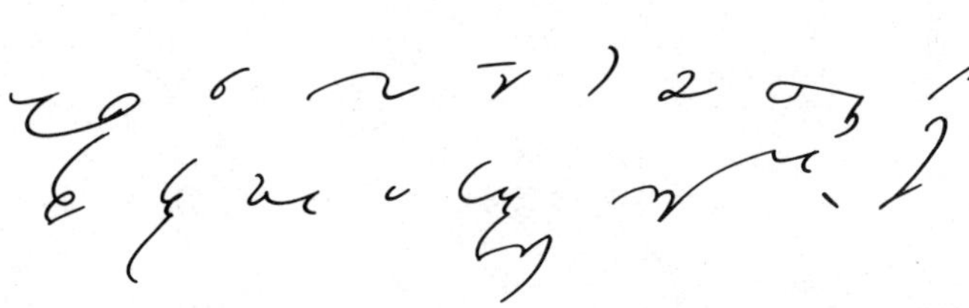

(174)

220 ▸ Fortune Magazine, 540 North Michigan Avenue, Chicago, Illinois 60611.

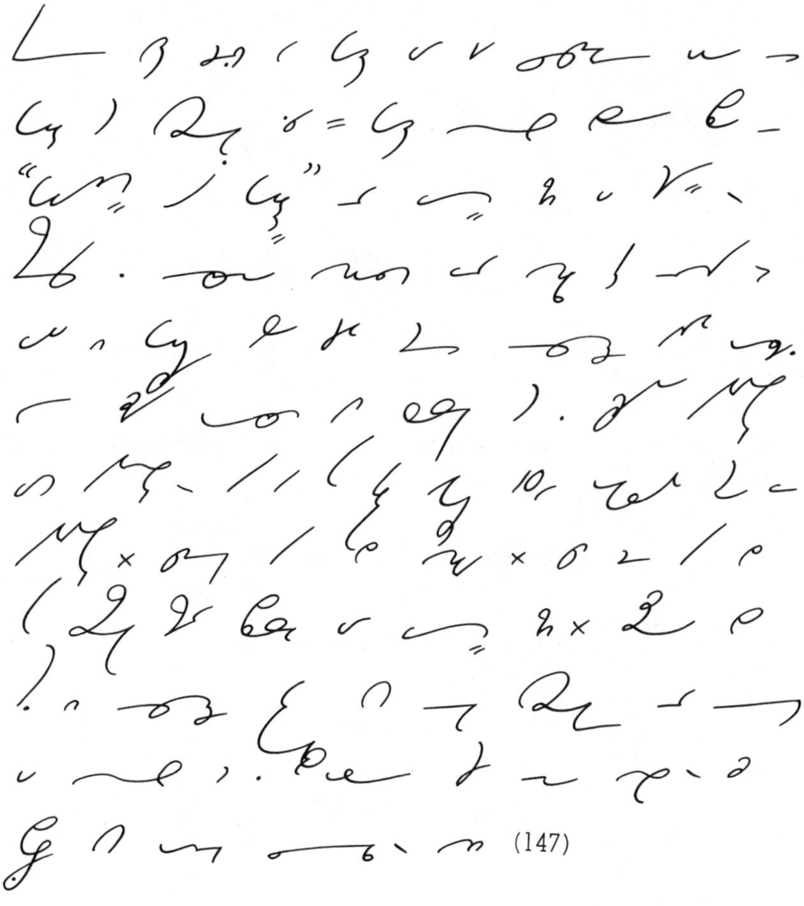

(147)

221 ▸ To: Arthur C. Williamson, Public Information Director.

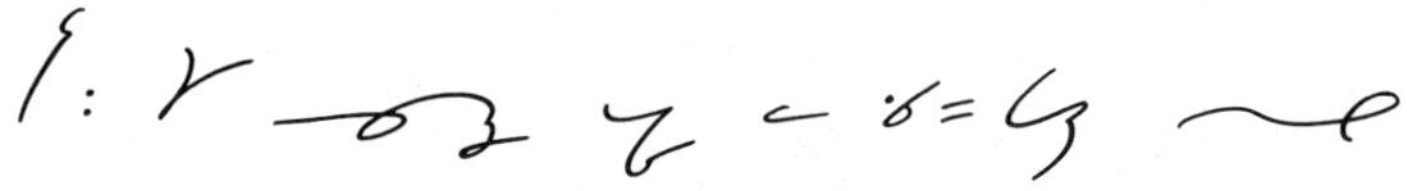

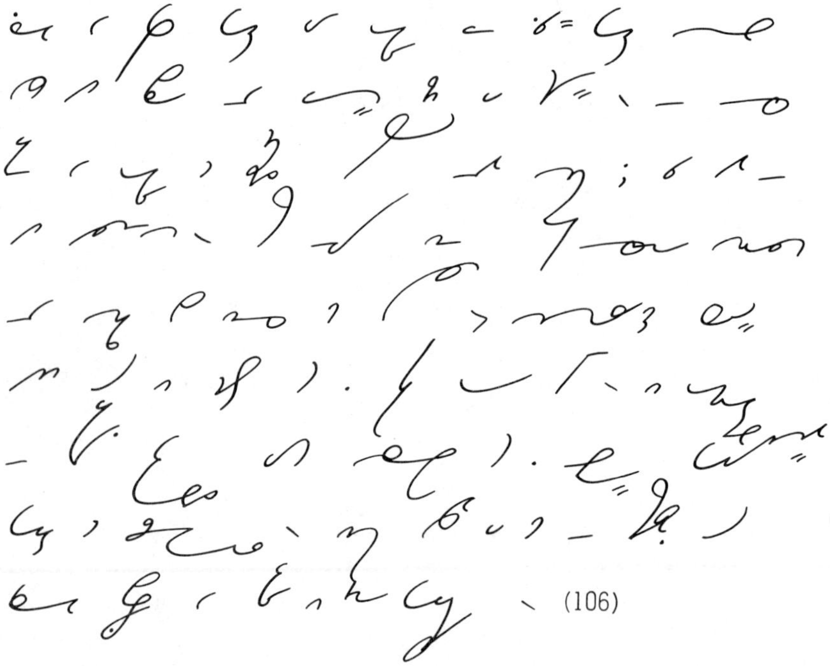

(106)

222 ▸ The Acme Printing Company, 345 Hudson Street, Champaign, Illinois 61820.

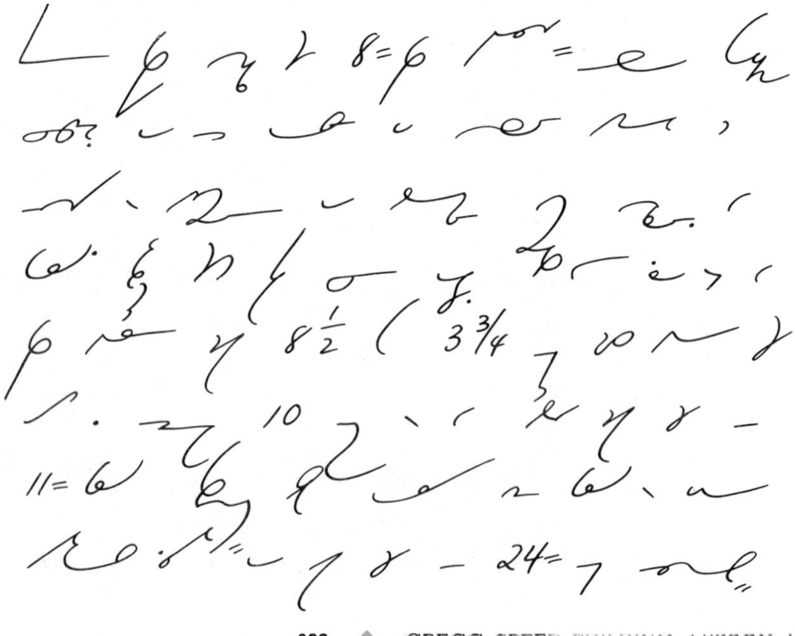

15
572-3244
267
(220)

lesson 48 OFFICE-STYLE DICTATION

YOUR SHORTHAND NOTES

The businessman's dictation is not always smooth. It may be choppy—sometimes fast and at other times slow and uncertain. As a rule, the businessman's dictation is paced by his mind as it grapples with the thought he is trying to express. In the process, he occasionally deletes or inserts a word or a phrase, even a sentence or a paragraph. At various points during dictation, sometimes in the middle of a sentence, he may stop to give an instruction or a suggestion.

In the following lessons in Part Two you will encounter some of the note-taking problems met by practicing secretaries. Learn to handle these dictation problems by applying the office-style dictation suggestions presented in this lesson and in subsequent lessons.

1 To indicate a deletion in your notes, use a heavy backward stroke; if several words are to be taken out, a wavy line is preferable.

For example, the dictator may say:

We shall take excellent care of the material. (Take out **excellent.**)

This would appear in your notes thus:

Or he may say:

Because of the demand for these kits, we are asking users to whom we send them to return them when they have served their purpose. (Scratch out **to whom we send them.**)

This would appear in your notes thus:

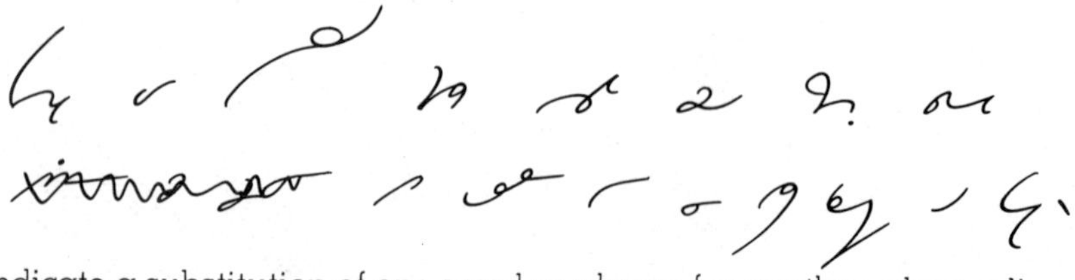

2 To indicate a substitution of one word or phrase for another, place a line through the word or a wavy line through the deleted phrase and write the substituted word or phrase right next to it or above it.

For example, the dictator says:

You are hereby authorized to proceed with final production. (No, **to release this copy immediately.**)

You would record this in your notes thus:

Or he may say:

This will, of course, immediately support (make that **quickly support**) the marketing concentration in the suburban area.

Your shorthand notes will look like this:

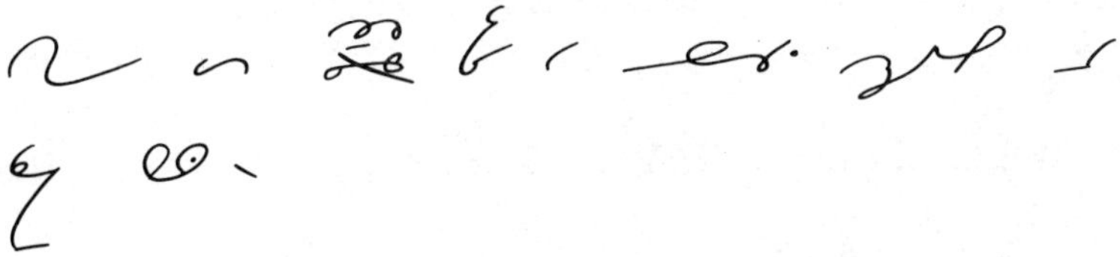

3 To restore an original outline after it has been struck out and changed, rewrite the word or phrase as though it were a completely new form.

The dictator may say:

Our sales specialist will visit your plant (no, **telephone you;** oh, leave it **visit your plant**) early next week.

Your notes should look like this:

4 To provide sufficient space to record special instructions during or after the dictation of a letter, always separate each piece of dictation from the next by several blank lines. Examples of special instructions are:

Send as a day letter   bcc to Mr. Johnson   cc to Sales Manager

Such instructions should stand out prominently in your notebook. Some secretaries prefer to use a colored pencil to record special instructions.

NOTE: Your instructor may dictate some letters to you that simulate untimed office dictation and that contain the office-style problems you have just studied.

223 Burton and Dodson Advertising Agency, 3244 Sutter Avenue, San Francisco, California 94144.

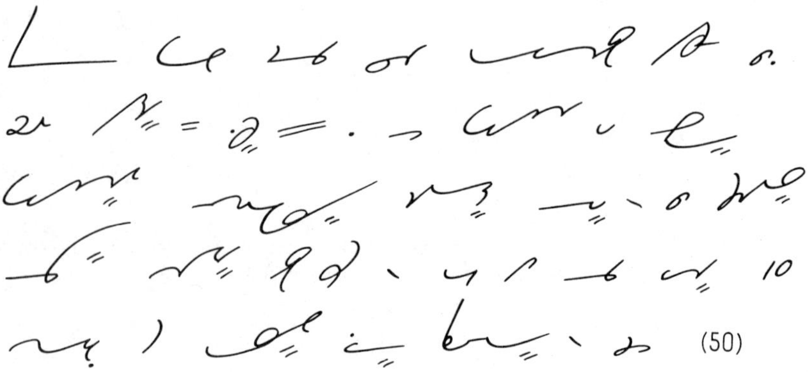

(50)

224 Girl Scouts of the USA, 830 Third Avenue, New York, New York 10022.

(181)

225 ▸ The Reuben H. Donnelly Company, 420 LaSalle Street, Chicago, Illinois 60610.

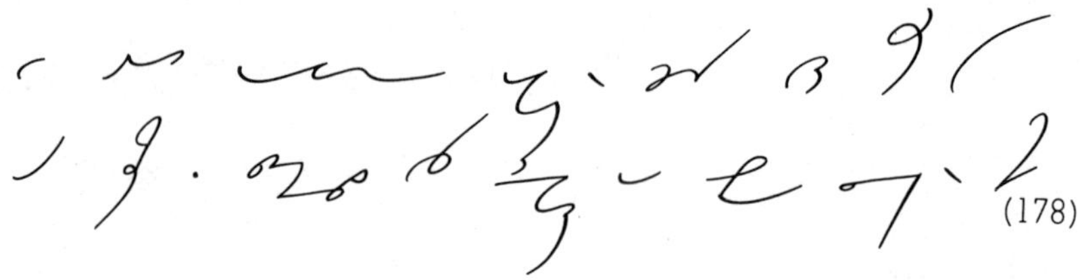

(178)

226 ▸ To: Mr. Henry M. Simpson, President.

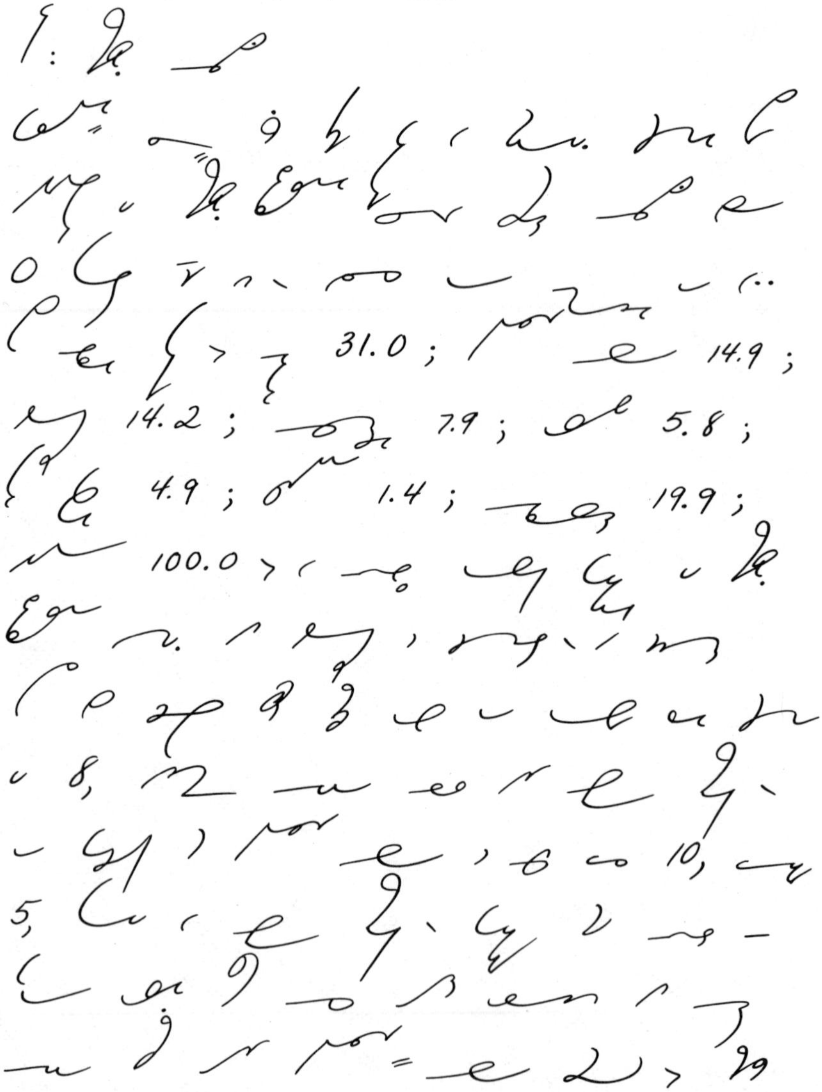

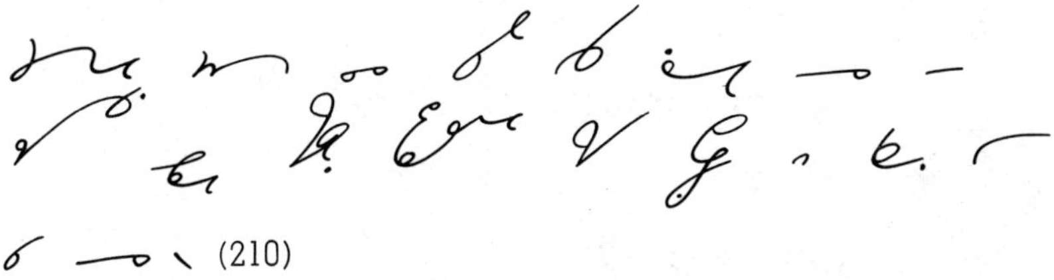

(210)

227 ▸ McGill Advertising Company, 416 South Wabash Avenue, Chicago, Illinois 60605.

(178)

lesson

49 PROGRESSIVE SPEED BUILDING

In this lesson the one-minute speed-forcing letters will be dictated at 110, 120, and 130 words a minute; the two-minute reinforcement and control letter will be dictated at 120 words a minute.

First practice writing the vocabulary preview that precedes the speed-forcing practice, and then review the specialized vocabulary presented at the beginning of the unit.

SPEED-BUILDING LETTERS

Vocabulary Preview

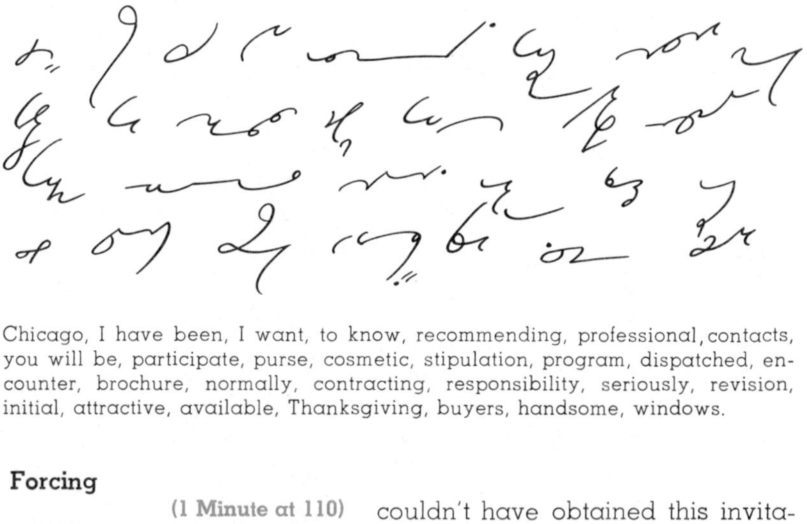

Chicago, I have been, I want, to know, recommending, professional, contacts, you will be, participate, purse, cosmetic, stipulation, program, dispatched, encounter, brochure, normally, contracting, responsibility, seriously, revision, initial, attractive, available, Thanksgiving, buyers, handsome, windows.

Speed Forcing

(1 Minute at 110)

228▸ Dear Harry: Today I was notified by the Chicago Advertising Club that I have been accepted for membership. This is wonderful news, and/I want you to know how much I appreciate your recommending me. Without your help, Harry, I couldn't have obtained this invitation, which will give me//many professional contacts so necessary in this job.

I'll try to carry my share of committee assignments and help with club activities///in all possible ways. If I can participate in any of the projects now under way, just let me know. It will give me great pleasure. Cordially yours, (1)

(1 Minute at 120)

229▸ Dear Miss Lewis: NATIONAL PRODUCTS will be glad to supply 500 purse cosmetic kits for distribution at your national forum for secretaries on July/14 and 15. Our only stipulation is that you give us a credit line in the convention program and send us a copy.

The kits will be sent by express// to the same address used on this letter. They will be dispatched in plenty of time to arrive by July 14; but in case you encounter any difficulty///in receiving them, please telephone Miss Mary Byrd, my administrative assistant. I shall be on vacation in California that week. Yours very truly, (2)

(1 Minute at 130)

230▸ Dear Ralph: Your suggestion that we revise Brochure 32 is a good one. I have just checked our inventory, and we have on hand 9,000 brochures. This supply could normally/be expected to last two months.

This means that we must design and produce the new material within the short period of sixty days. As you know, I prepared this brochure myself//rather than contract with an advertising agency for it. In the interest of economy, I believe that I should also assume responsibility for the new///one. Do you agree?

Please make a critical examination of our present brochure and let me have any suggestions before I get down seriously to my revision. (3)

Reinforcement and Control

(2 Minutes at 120)

231▸ Gentlemen: Our salesman in New Haven has told me that you have just placed an initial order for 50 sets of our stainless steel carving sets with electric cutting/blades. He has asked me to suggest sales-promotion ideas so that this new product will become one of your Christmas sales leaders.

I am sending you today 1,500// copies of a four-page brochure in color, which can be mailed either with your monthly bills or to a special mailing list. If you wish to order additional///copies of this attractive brochure, just let me know how many you need.

We have available three mats for newspaper advertising of these carving sets: one to be (1) run about a week before Thanksgiving, one to be run about ten days before Christmas, and the third to be used several times during the pre-Christmas buying season./The first two mats are designed to attract buyers who will use the sets at their own holiday parties. The other one recommends the carving sets for Christmas giving. The//name of your store can be inserted on each mat.

With your initial order you will receive a handsome display case for either your store windows or counter promotion.///

All sales-promotion material is, of course, sent to you without charge. It's our way of saying thank you for doing business with NATIONAL PRODUCTS. Cordially yours, (2)

232 ▸ Chicago Rapid Transit System, 403 State Street, Chicago, Illinois 60610.

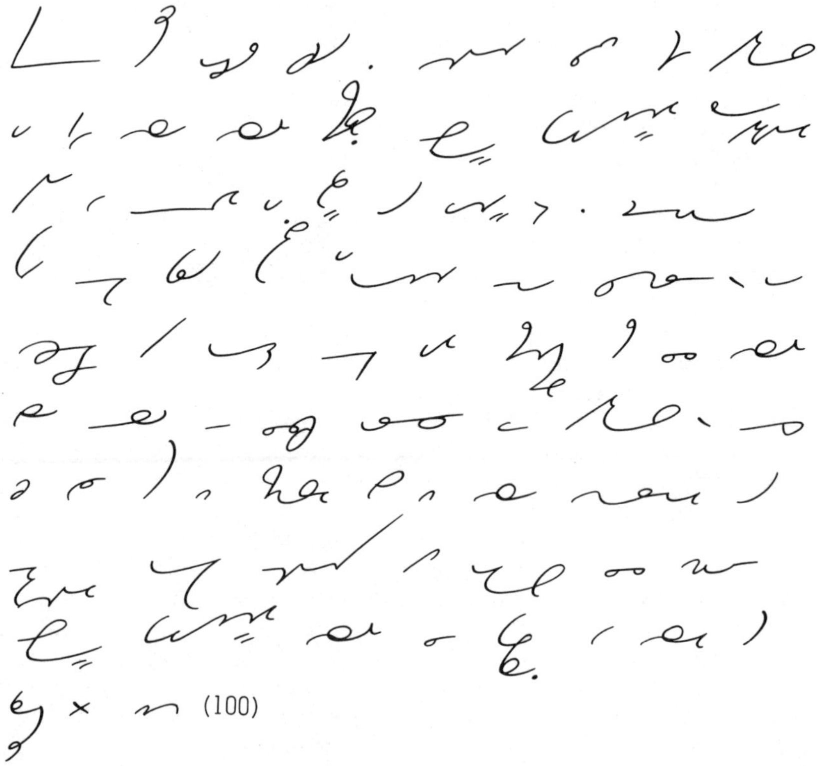

(100)

233 ▸ Middle-Western Printers, 514 Oak Street, Bloomington, Indiana 47401.

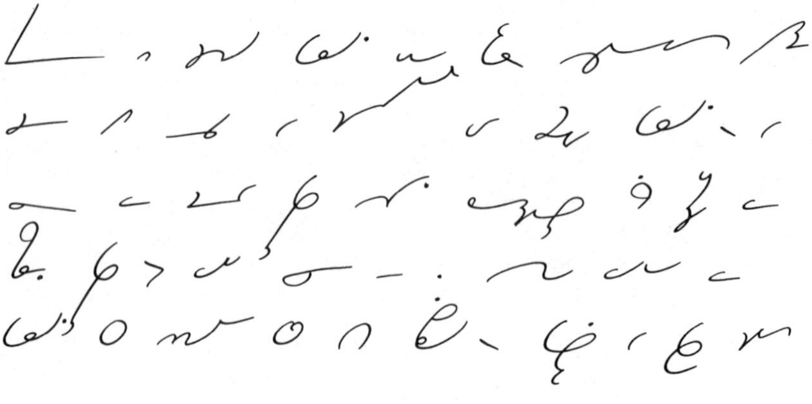

(160)

234 ▸ To: Fred R. Hart.

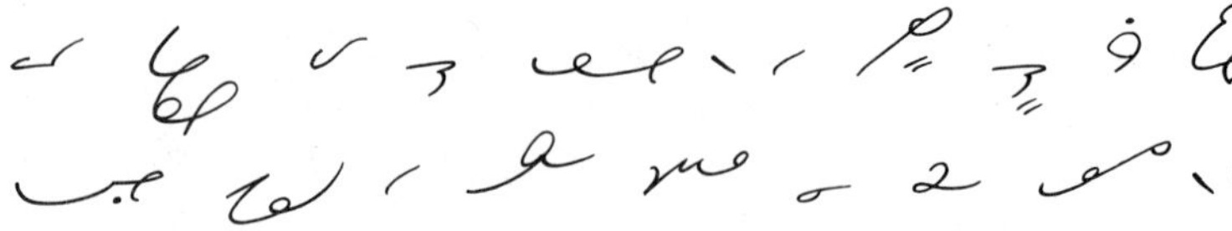 (118)

TRANSCRIPTION PACER

235 To: Ralph C. Akin, Sales Manager. 8

19
29
39
52
62
75
87
102
114
123
134
145
154
159

lesson

BUILDING TRANSCRIPTION SPEED 50

SUSTAINED SPEED BUILDER

Practice the following vocabulary preview, and then see how well you can sustain your reinforcement and control speed.

Vocabulary Preview

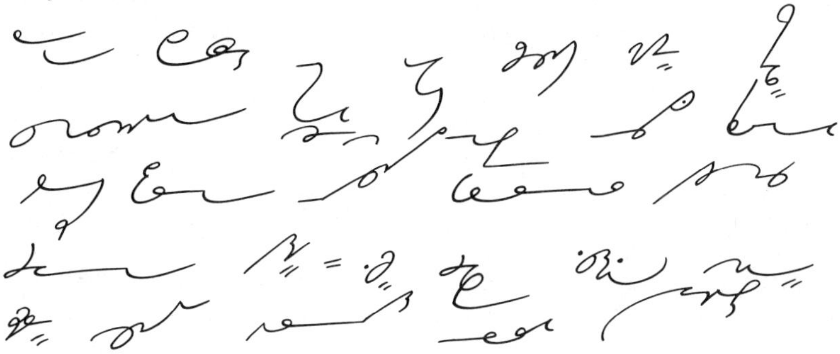

Electrical, appliances, envelopes, representative, executive, Watson, Agency, agricultural, chemical, enrichment, media, journals, television, experimental, undoubtedly, preliminary, designate, phenomenal, Dust-Away, sensational, household, Colorado, Western, counter, tremendous, merits, demonstrations.

Speed Builder

236 The Davenport Press, 265 Lake Shore Drive, North, Chicago, Illinois 60611.

Gentlemen: We plan to publish a promotion piece covering all electrical appliances manufactured[1] by the NATIONAL PRODUCTS, INC. This six-page brochure in three colors would fit our regular[2] billing envelopes.

Each page except the cover and the back page would feature two appliances. Included would[3] be toasters and grills, percolators and frying pans, can openers and hair dryers, and blankets and room heaters.[4] While back cover would feature irons, the bottom part of the page would be left blank so that the store distributing[5] the brochure can imprint its name in this space.

We should like to set up the brochure with two possible cover[6] pages. For the first printing we want a holiday motif that would encourage gift buying. Subsequent printings would[7] have a more general appeal to purchasers for their own home use.

If your company would care to bid for this[8] contract, will you please send a representative to discuss design and production plans with us? Sincerely yours,[9] (180)

237▸ Mr. John C. MacCarthy, Watson Advertising Agency, 411 Madison Avenue, New York, New York 10017.

Dear Mr. MacCarthy: We are happy that you have been appointed account executive on our contract with[1] the Watson Advertising Agency for advertising our new agricultural chemical for soil[2] enrichment. You may be sure that we plan to cooperate in every possible way in developing[3] advertising for all media covered by the contract: newspapers, farm journals, business magazines, radio,[4] and television.

We are enclosing basic product information provided by our Research and[5] Development Division. After you have studied this material, we shall arrange the details of your visit[6] to our headquarters, our experimental farms, our laboratories, and the factory in which this product will[7] be manufactured. After you have made this study of the product, you will undoubtedly have some preliminary[8] ideas for the advertising campaign and will be ready to discuss the relationship of your[9] agency to our advertising staff and to designate the types of services you want us to provide.

Thank[10] you again for your many courtesies to Mr. Johnson and me when we were in New York discussing the[11] possibility of a contract. All of us are looking forward to working with you in developing an[12] outstanding presentation of our product that will lead to phenomenal sales. Yours cordially, (257)

238▸ Mr. Herbert E. Hall, Hall Brothers, 324 Cheyenne Street, Denver, Colorado 80230.

Dear Mr. Hall: Enclosed is a series of five mats that you requested for newspaper advertising of[1] Dust-Away. You will notice that on each mat there is space for listing the local stores in which Dust-Away may be[2] purchased.

This sensational new household product is already being sold in 11 states in the East and is[3] now to be distributed by your company, which serves retailers throughout the state of Colorado. Sales in[4] the eastern states have increased 200 percent over the past year; and the product now has a substantial part[5] of the potential market, although it was introduced only three years ago. You may expect similar[6] results in your area.

Mr. John O. Timmons, NATIONAL PRODUCTS' regional sales manager, would like to call[7] on you to discuss the promotion of Dust-Away in Colorado and possibly in neighboring states. Would[8] 2 p.m. on

February 10 be a convenient time? He will stress the buyer's point of view, an approach that,[9] we think, will be helpful in planning any newspaper advertising to supplement these mats. He will have with[10] him some television spot advertisements that you may want to introduce on local stations. He will also[11] have suggestions for demonstrations of Dust-Away in local stores and for counter advertising suitable[12] for use by retailers who stock the product. Please let us know immediately whether that appointment time[13] will be suitable.

Either Mr. Timmons or I shall be glad to work with you on further sales promotion. Both[14] of us want to help you achieve the tremendous sales success that Dust-Away's performance merits. Yours very truly,[15] (300)

TRANSCRIPTION CHECKPOINT

239▸ Burton and Dodson Advertising Agency, 3244 Sutter Avenue, San Francisco, California 94144.

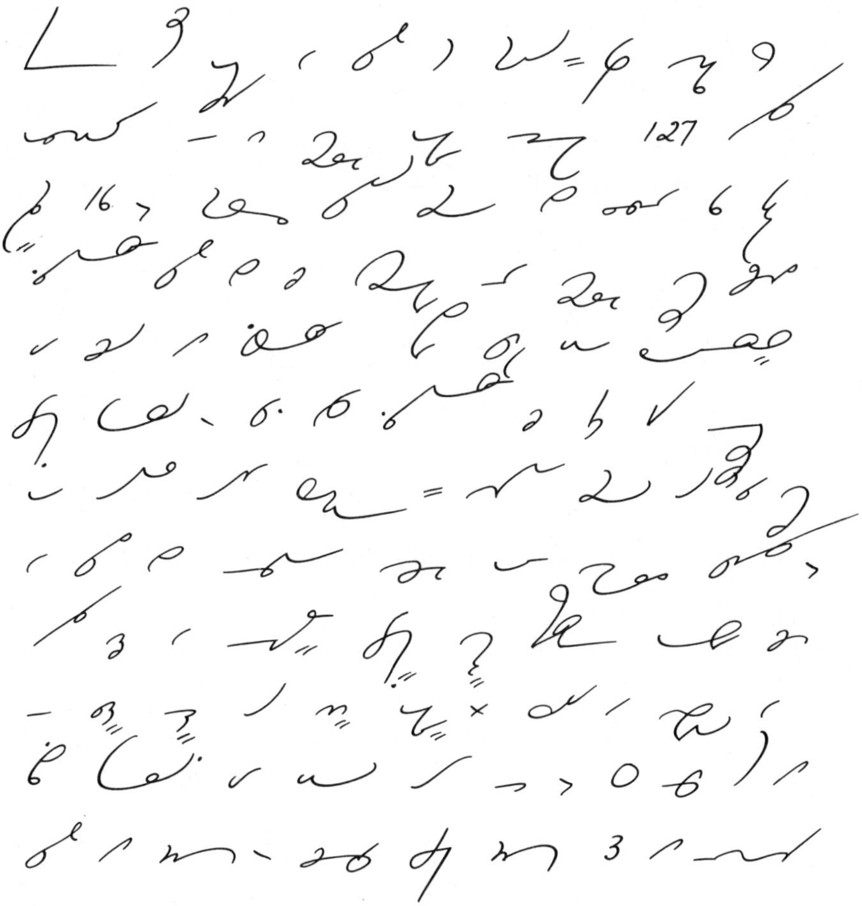

(230)

240 ▸ Mr. Kent C. Thomas, Burton and Dodson Advertising Agency, 3244 Sutter Avenue, San Francisco, California 94144.

(108)

241 ▸ Atlantic Printers, 430 Olive Street, St. Louis, Missouri 63166. 13

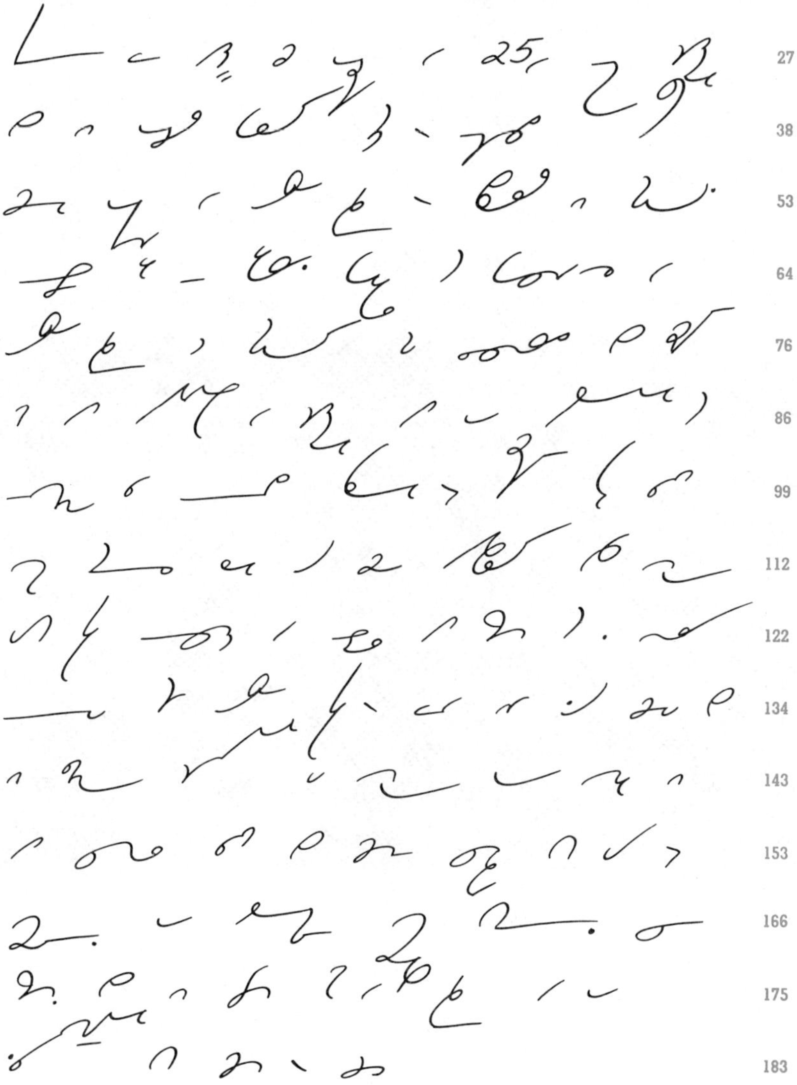

Today, in our highly competitive economy, the selling function lies at the very heart of a business enterprise. Only when the minds of customers are influenced favorably can a company sell its goods or services and prosper. In fact, everyone in and out of business must practice in one way or another the fundamental principles of selling. In practically every face-to-face encounter, one is called upon to gain another's attention, arouse interest, support a point of view, and induce a desired action or reaction.

The modern trend in selling is toward helping customers to buy rather than forcing them to accept a product. Sales organizations stress the value of fair competition and the qualities of dependability, integrity, and honesty. Low-pressure selling, with emphasis on dependable, satisfactory, and prompt service to the customer, is the emerging cardinal rule.

The sales manager is re-

unit

11

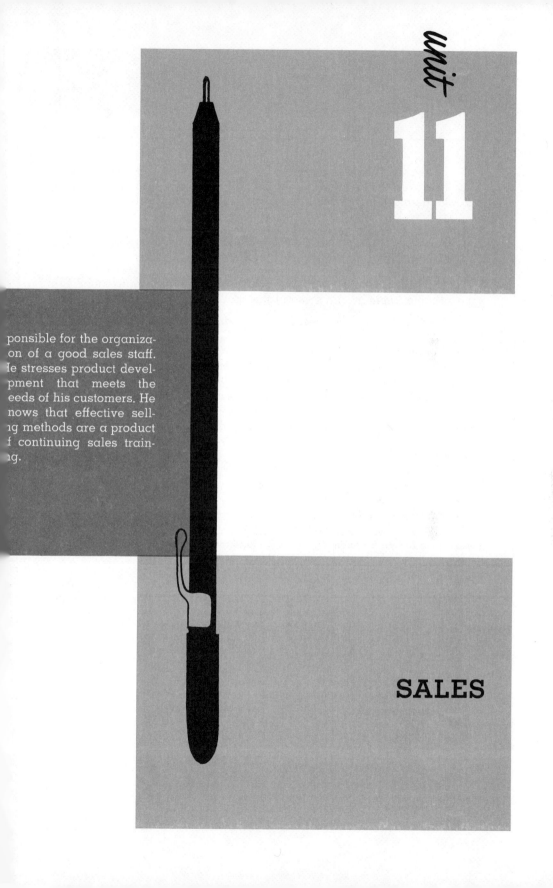

ponsible for the organiza-
on of a good sales staff.
le stresses product devel-
pment that meets the
eeds of his customers. He
nows that effective sell-
ıg methods are a product
f continuing sales train-
ıg.

SALES

Secretarial Assignment

In this unit you are secretary to Ralph C. Akin, who is responsible for carrying out the selling and marketing functions of National Products, Inc. All letters are signed by him over his title, Marketing Director.

SPECIALIZED TERMINOLOGY

You will transcribe Mr. Akin's dictation more efficiently after you have become familiar with some of the specialized terms he uses.

Briefing Session • A meeting during which a summary of details or a review of procedures is presented.

Prospects • Potential buyers or customers.

Counter Handout • Free promotion material that is displayed on a store counter.

Coup (koo) • An unexpected and successful accomplishment.

Dictation Belt • A flexible plastic belt on which dictation is recorded. Salesmen sometimes report their sales calls immediately after they have made them, using a portable dictation unit, and mail the belts to their office, where they are transcribed.

Pliofilm • A transparent synthetic used in packaging material.

Template • A pattern, sometimes made of a cardboard or plastic, that serves as a guide to the form of a piece being made.

Tie-in • The advertising of two related goods or services simultaneously.

WATS (Wide Area Toll Service) • Unlimited long distance telephone service sold in broad bands across the United States, so that companies pay a flat rate rather than tolls for individual long distance calls.

CONFUSED WORDS AND TRANSCRIPTION PRACTICE

Study the following pairs of similar-sounding and similar-looking words that are often confused.

sometime at an indefinite time
some time a period of time
sometimes now and then

all ready all prepared
already previously

eminent important
imminent impending

compliment to praise; a flattering remark
complement to provide something felt to be lacking

therefore consequently
therefor for or in return for that

Transcribe the following sentences, preferably at the typewriter, until you can distinguish between the expressions that appear in the list.

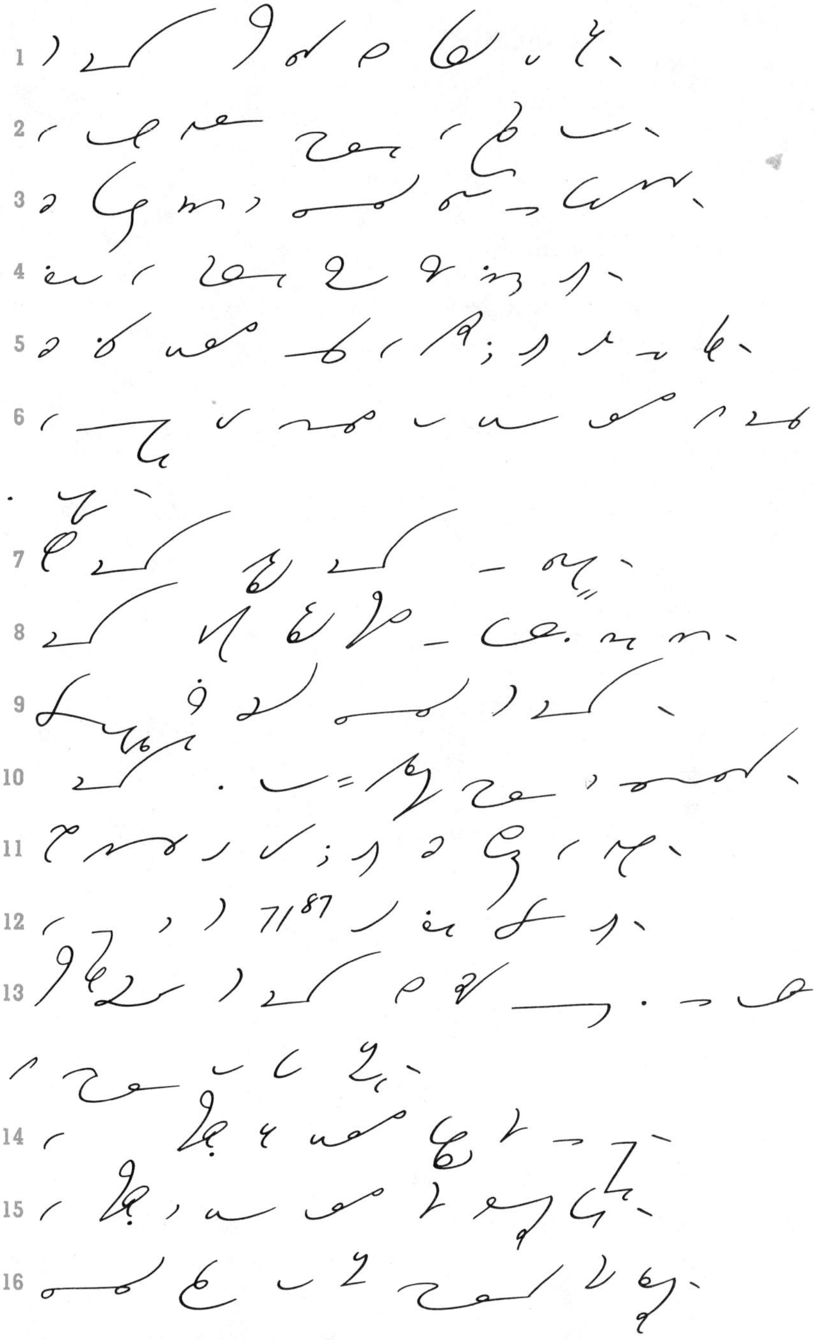

lesson 51

BUILDING TRANSCRIPTION QUALITY

TRANSCRIPTION POINTERS

Uses of the Hyphen

1 A hyphen follows a prefix that is added to a word that begins with a capital.

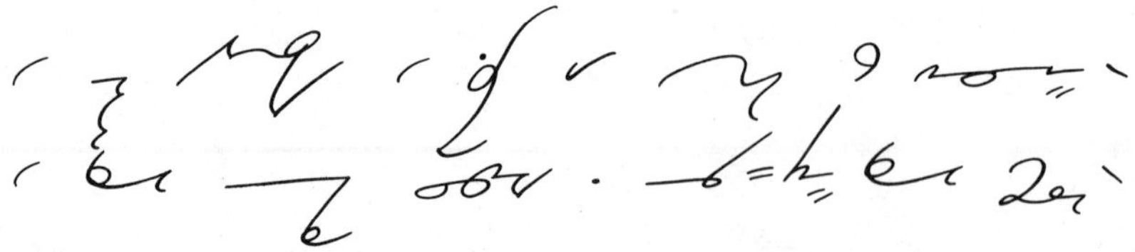

The newspapers described the behavior of the group as un-American.
The sales manager announced a mid-June sales conference.

2 When the last letter of a prefix is the same as the first letter of the word to which it is joined, a hyphen is sometimes used between the two vowels but usually the form is solid. It is advisable to check such words in the dictionary.

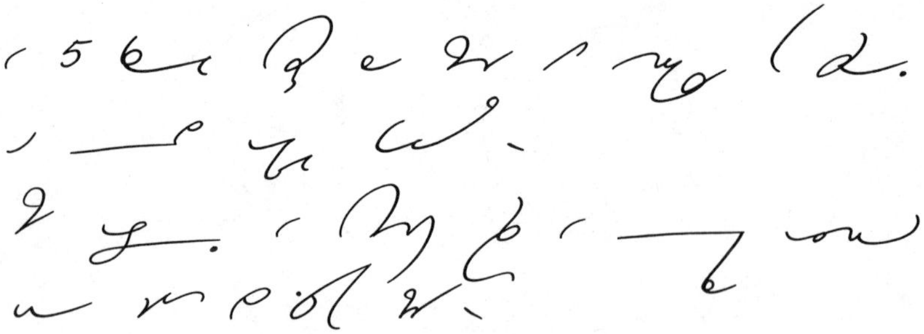

The five sales divisions were asked to cooperate by filing their monthly reports promptly.
After reexamining the defective fabric, the manager recalled all stock that had been issued.

3 If the addition of a suffix results in three identical consonants coming together, a hyphen is used before the suffix.

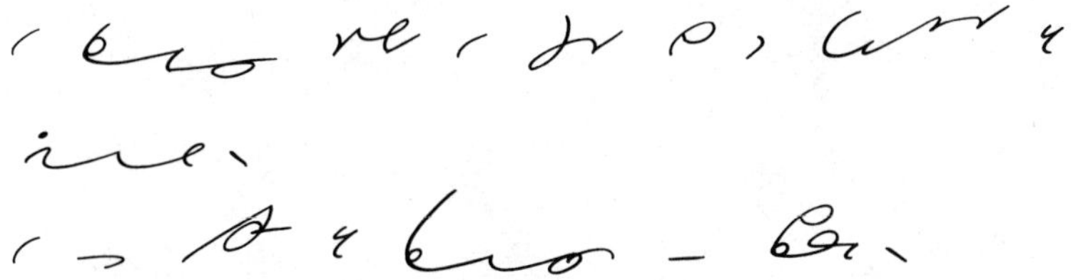

The salesman stressed the fact that his product was hull-less.
The new design was bell-like in appearance.

4 Compound numerals below 100 are hyphenated when spelled out. When spelling out numbers over 100, do not insert a hyphen between *hundred* and *thousand* and the rest of the number.

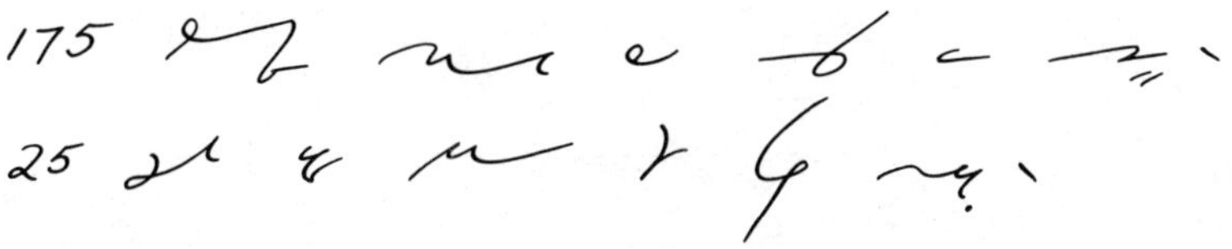

One hundred seventy-five telephone calls were made on Monday.
Twenty-five cents was the toll for the bridge crossing.

Check your understanding of hyphen usage by transcribing the following sentences, preferably at the typewriter.

7

8

9

10

11

12

13

14

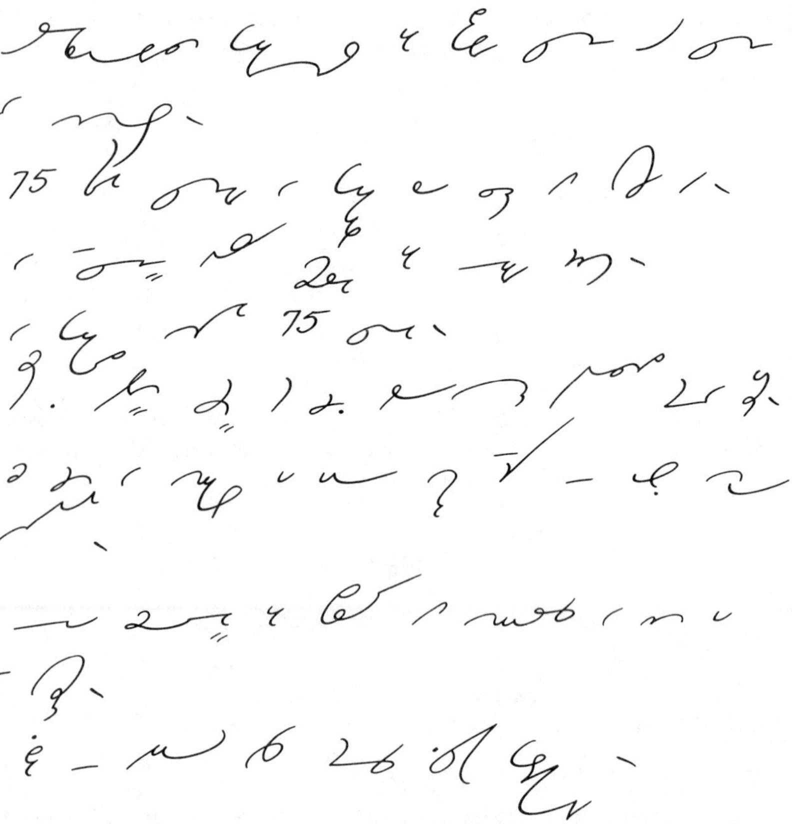

TRANSCRIPTION SPEED BUILDER

242 ▸ Mr. Mark M. Gibson, Rice Hotel, Houston, Texas 77004, Hold for Arrival on May 27.

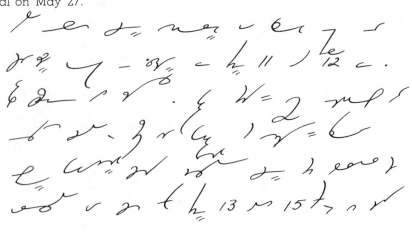

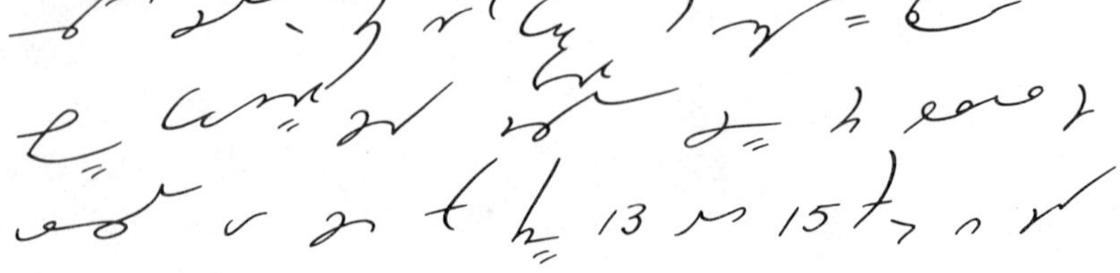

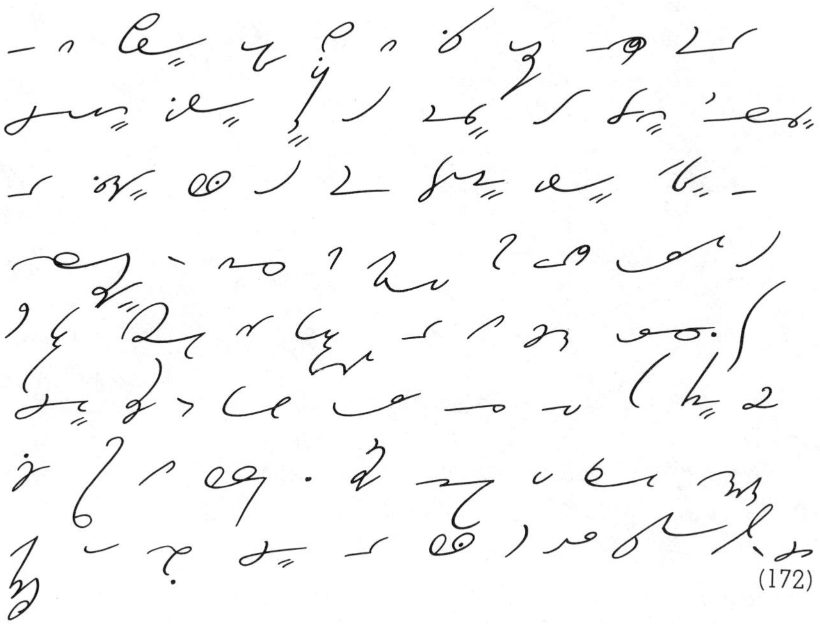

(172)

243 To: All Salesmen.

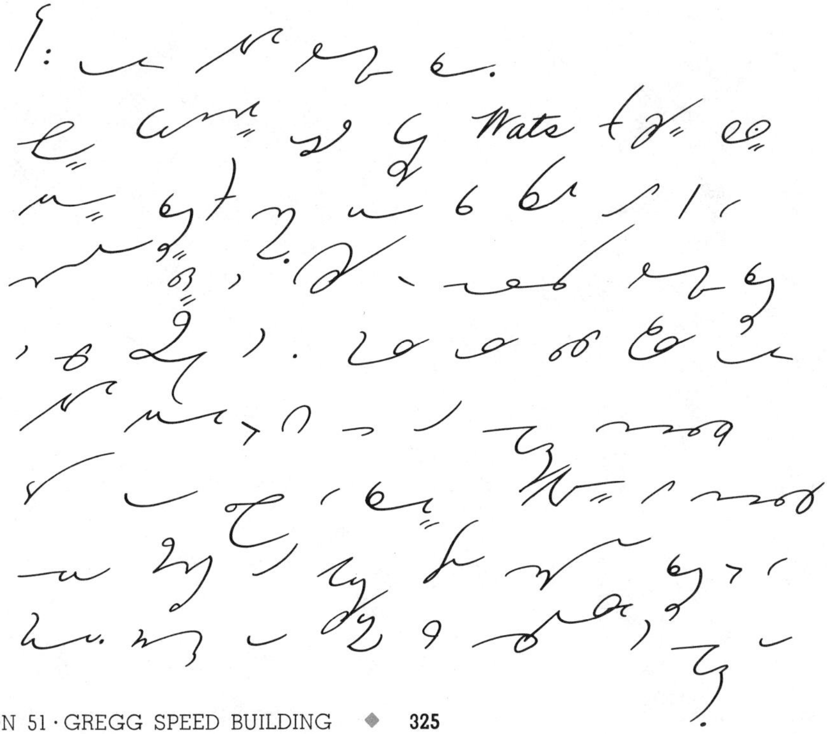

(403)

244▸ Mr. Walter C. Forbes, Regional Sales Manager, National Products, Inc., 725 Buena Vista Drive, Raleigh, North Carolina 27638.

(98)

lesson

52 MASTERING SHORTHAND THEORY

GEOGRAPHIC AND PROPER NAMES

-burg

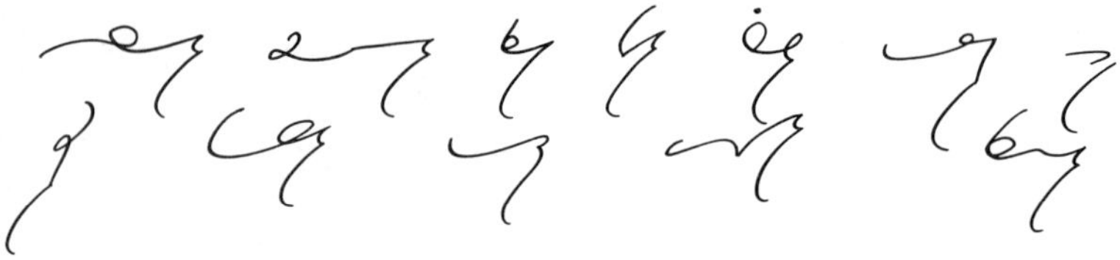

-ingham

-ington

-ville

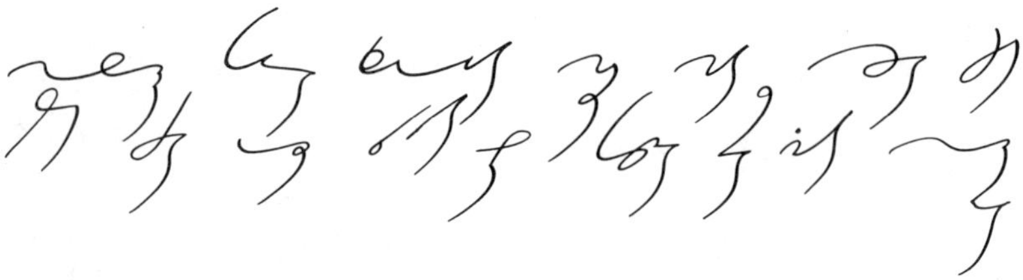

Galesburg, Williamsburg, Cherbourg, Pittsburgh, Harrisburg, Lynchburg, Newburgh, Fitchburg, Plattsburgh, Lewisburg, Ogdensburg, Parkersburg.

Effingham, Framingham, Buckingham, Cunningham, Nottingham, Warringham.

Covington, Harrington, Lexington, Ludington, Worthington, Wilmington, Washington, Bloomington, Burlington, Huntington, Irvington, Arlington.

Clarksville, Bronxville, Charlottesville, Coffeyville, Coatsville, Gainesville, Fayetteville, Danville, Janesville, Louisville, Edwardsville, Nashville, Brownsville, Evansville, Huntsville, Gloversville.

TRANSCRIPTION SPEED BUILDER

245 To: Stuart P. Henderson, Manager of Advertising Department.

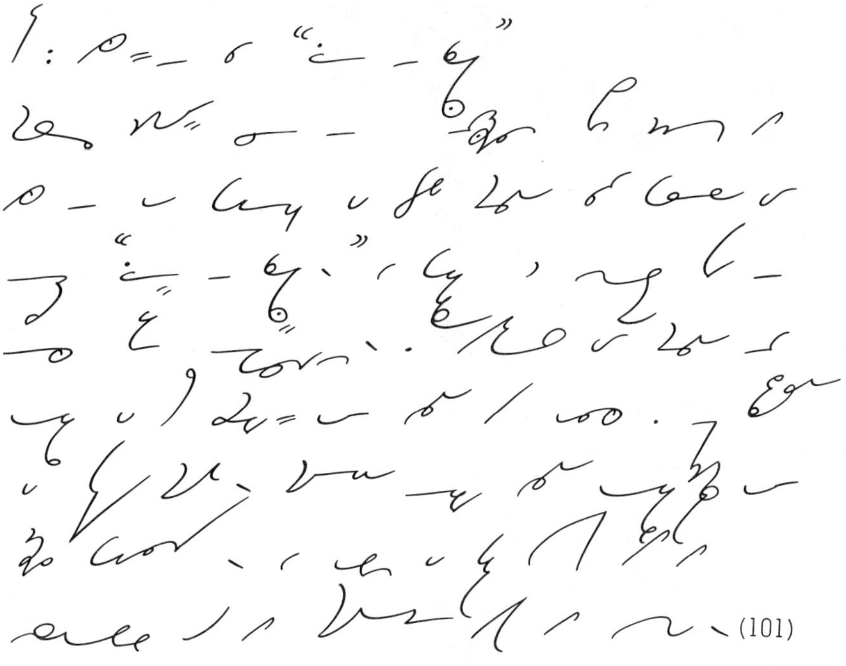

(101)

246 Mr. Benjamin J. Carter, 4123 Euclid Avenue, Cleveland, Ohio 44125.

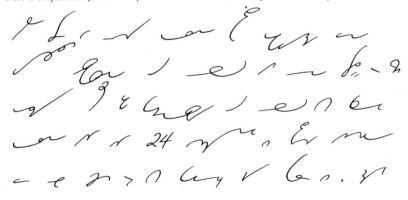

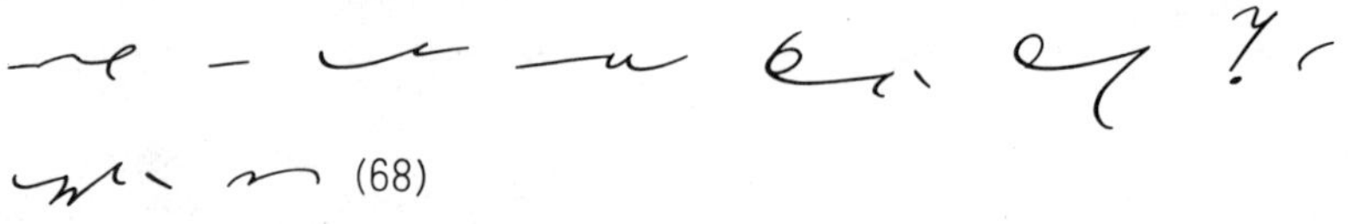

(68)

247 ▸ Mr. Harmon R. Beatty, Beatty Hardware Store, 222 Davis Boulevard, Bowling Green, Ohio 43402.

(312)

248▶ To: Henry P. Walters, Vice-President.

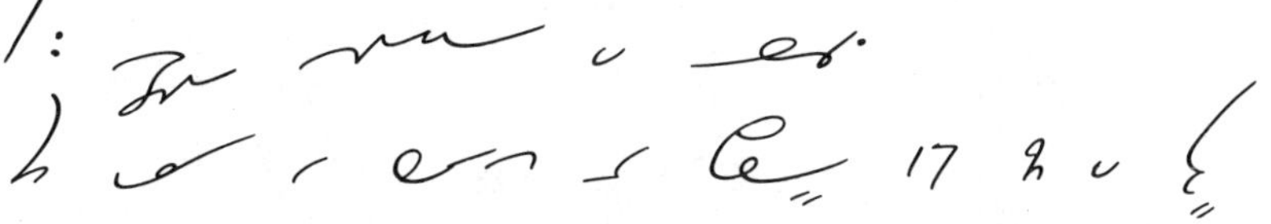

(105)

249 ▸ Plattsburgh Retail Center, 390 North Margaret Street, Plattsburgh, New York 12902.

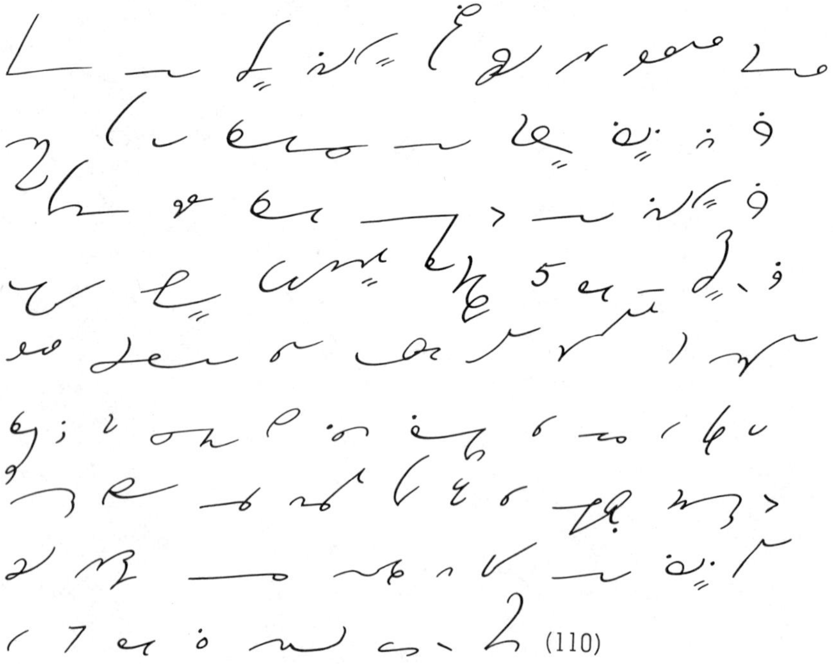

(110)

lesson

OFFICE-STYLE DICTATION 53

YOUR SHORTHAND NOTES

Learn to handle dictation problems by applying the office-style dictation suggestions presented in this lesson.

1 To transpose words or phrases for emphasis or for some other reason, indicate the transposition in your notes and then subsequently transcribe the marked notes in correct order.

The businessman may say:

> We had, in addition, extra expenses amounting to $30,000 (make that **in addition, we had**...).

In your notes this would appear thus:

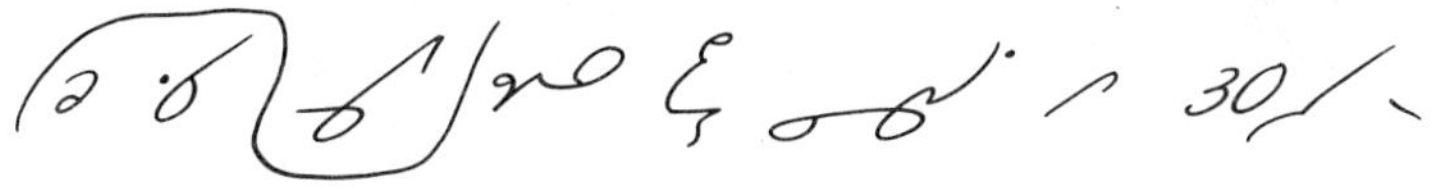

2 To transpose an entire sentence or even a paragraph to another part of a letter, encircle the material to be transposed and indicate the new position by an arrow.

The businessman may say:

> On Wednesday, May 6, you will see in all local papers a notice of stock clearance. Prices will be drastically cut. Obviously, the time for action is near. (Let's put this last sentence at the head of the paragraph.)

In your notebook, this would appear thus:

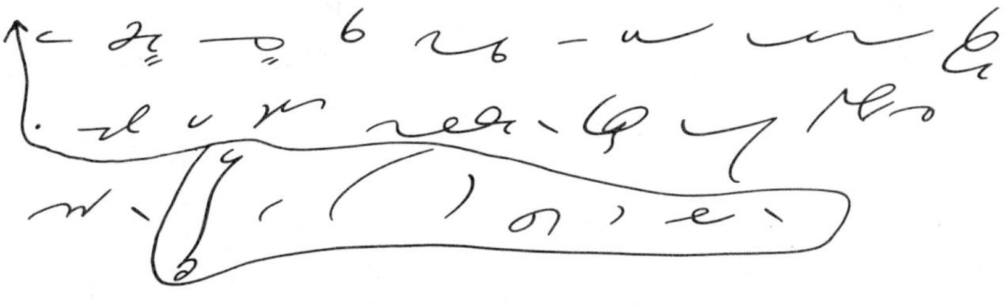

3 To indicate a long insertion, first write a large "A" in a circle at the point where the new material is to be inserted; draw two heavy lines after the

last sentence taken from dictation to separate the insert from the rest of your dictation; write and encircle "Insert A" under the two heavy lines. Write the insert. Finally, draw two heavy lines to indicate the end of the insert.

The businessman may say:

We are happy to supply you with the forms you requested. The family plan is a new idea in health coverage, and we are confident that it will be of interest to many of your patients. (After the word **requested,** add this sentence: **These forms and a descriptive booklet are enclosed.**)

In your notebook, this would appear thus:

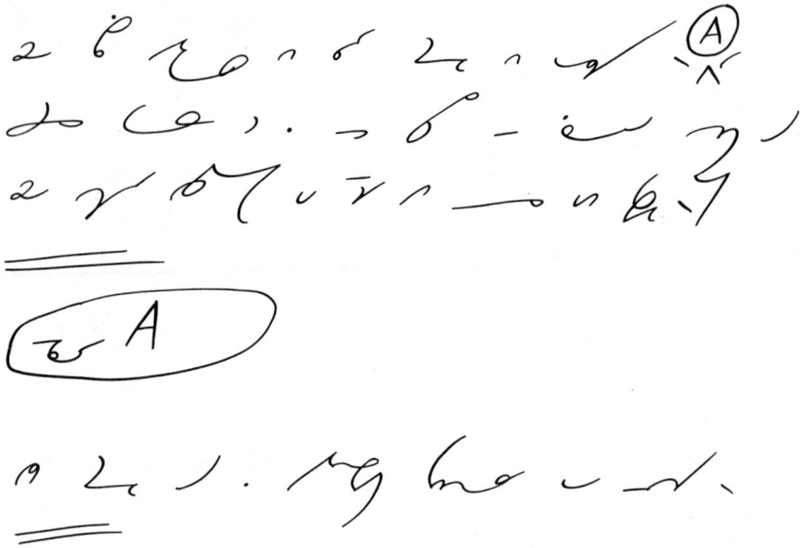

TRANSCRIPTION SPEED BUILDER

250▸ To: Henry Miller, Sales Engineer; Harry Nelson, Sales Engineer; Abe Olsten, Sales Engineer; Ben Phillips, Sales Engineer; Walter Reston, Sales Engineer; Jim Summers, Sales Engineer.

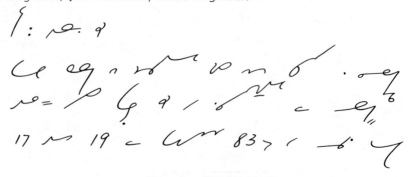

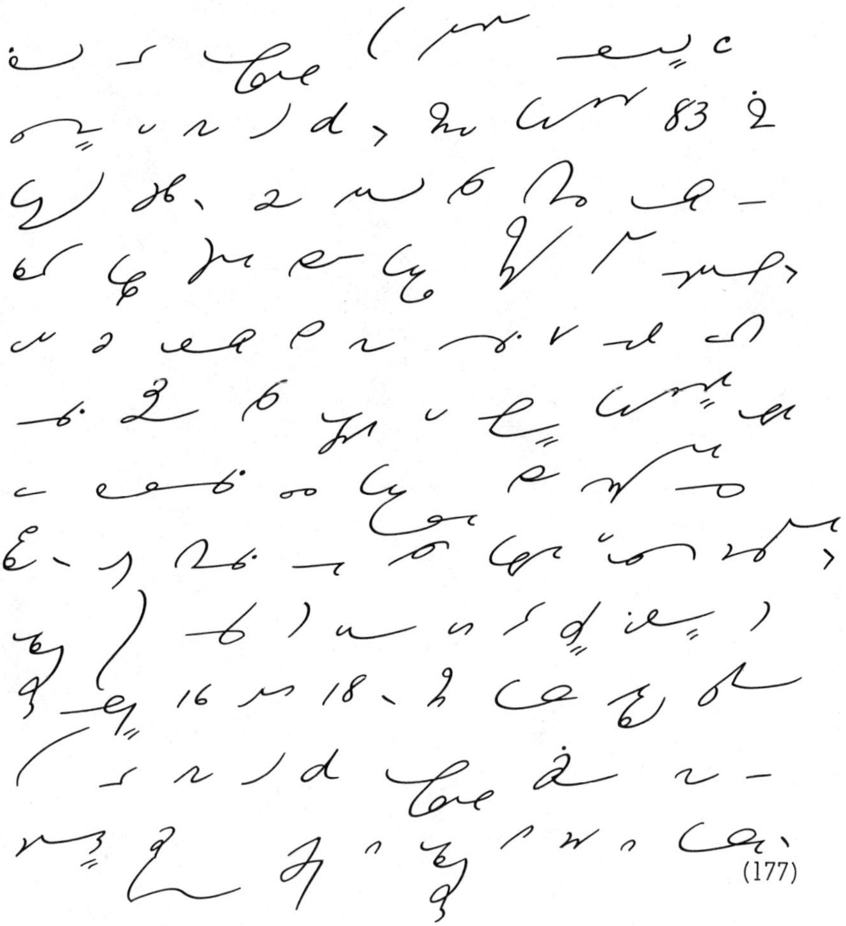

(177)

251 ▸ To: Regional Sales Managers.

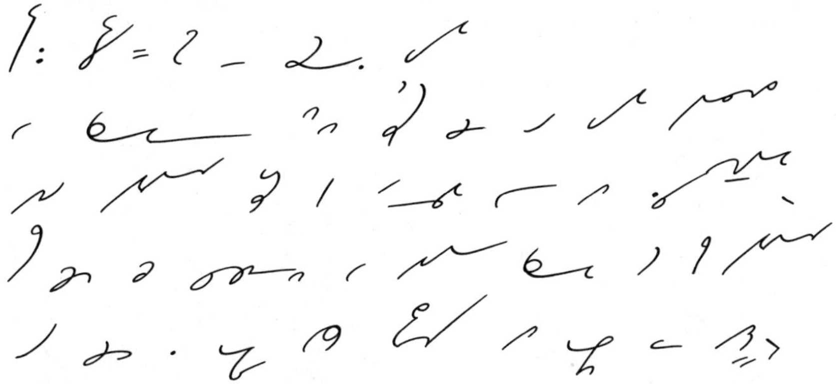

(151)

252 ▸ To: All Salesmen.

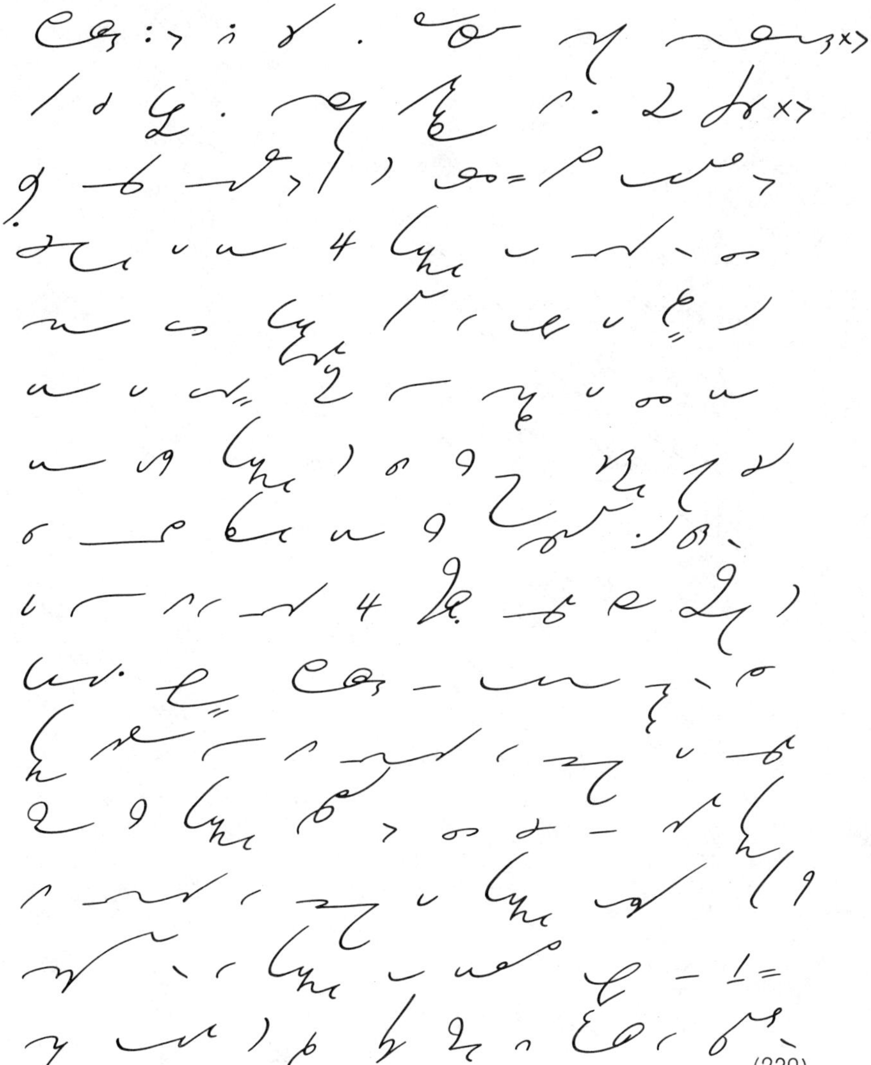

(230)

253▸ Dr. Franklin Miller, Chairman of the Accounting Department, Miller College, Front Street at Brown Boulevard, Denver, Colorado 80205.

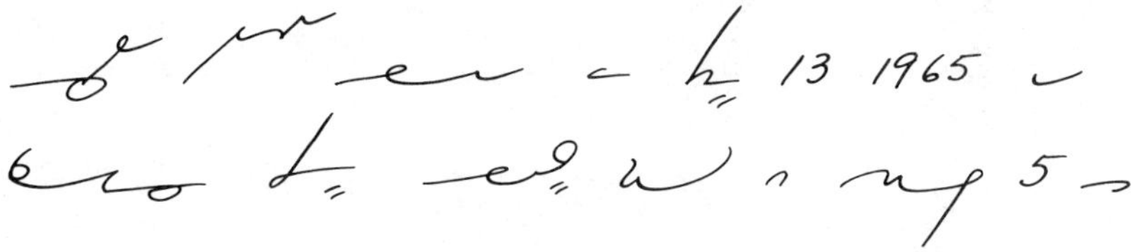

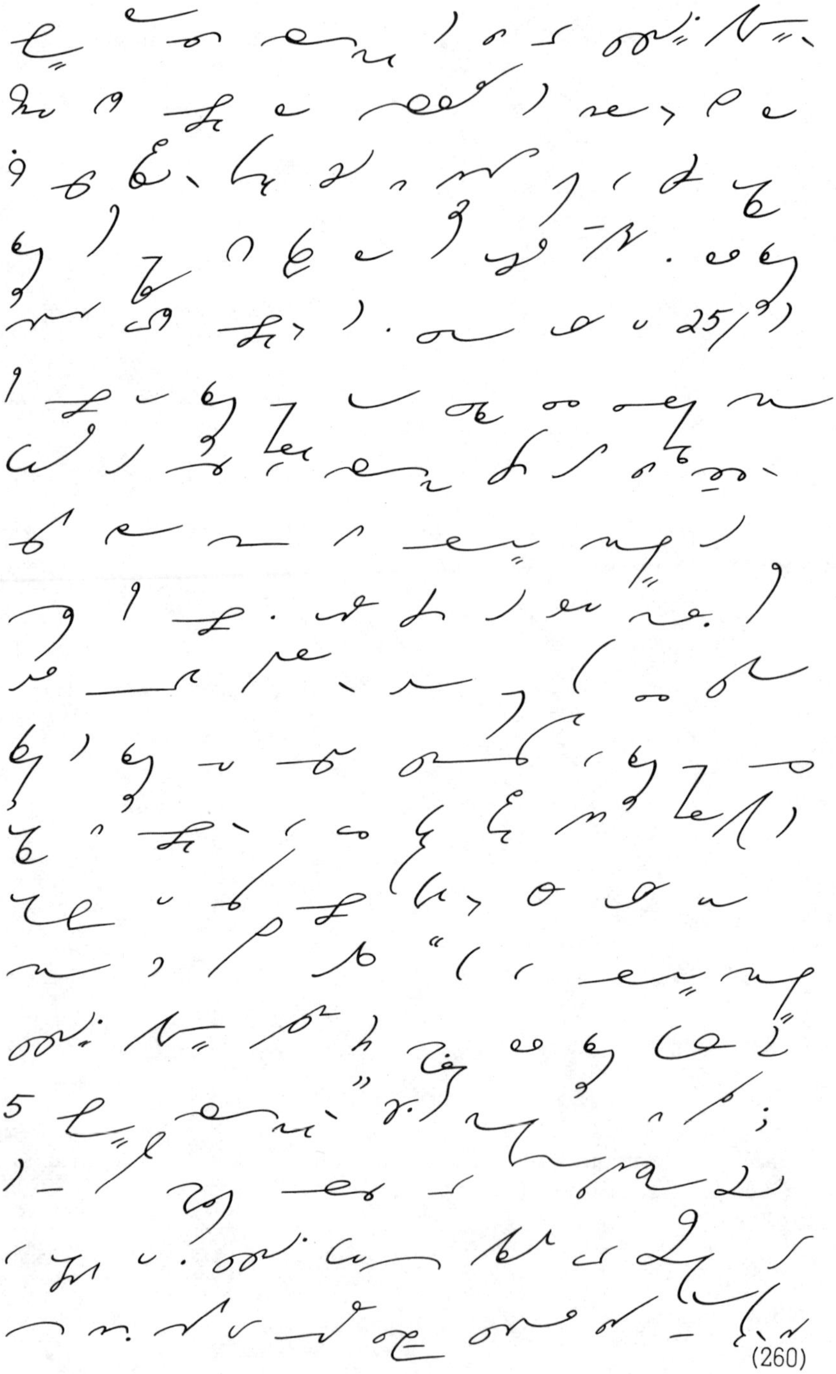

(260)

Lesson 54

PROGRESSIVE SPEED BUILDING

In this lesson the one-minute speed-forcing letters will be dictated at 120, 130, and 140 words a minute; the two-minute reinforcement and control letter will be dictated at 130 words a minute.

Preview the vocabulary before attempting the dictation.

SPEED-BUILDING LETTERS

Vocabulary Preview

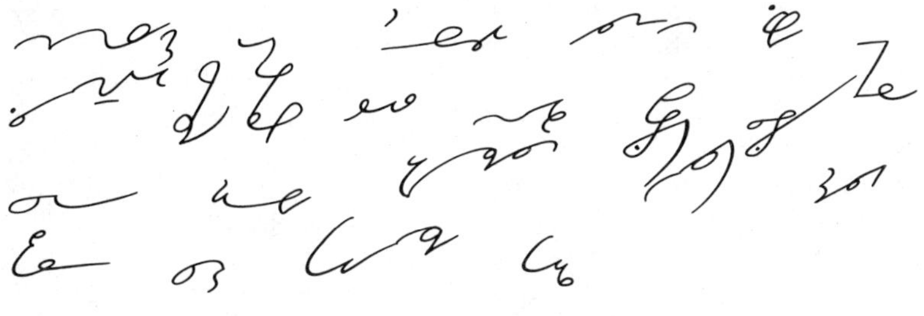

Congratulations, refrigeration, supermarkets, technical, highest, engineer, headquarters, adjacent, thoroughly, courtesies, appreciative, initiated, annual, solicit, optimistic, tentative, substitution, experiment, access, broadcast, proxy.

Speed Forcing

(1 Minute at 120)

254 Dear Bob: Congratulations on getting the contract for refrigeration in 300 Scott Supermarkets. The combination of sales know-how and technical background/has paid off again. This contract means a lot to National Products as well as to you personally. Incidentally, this coup will bring you the highest commission//ever paid to a sales engineer.

When you are at the St. Louis headquarters next week, I should like to discuss the possibility of your leaving your regional///territory and working out of the National offices on special assignment. Your work would be restricted to refrigeration installations. Yours truly, (1)

(1 Minute at 130)

255▸ Gentlemen: We are pleased to announce that Mr. Ralph M. Kennedy has joined NATIONAL PRODUCTS as sales representative in your territory. Mr. Kennedy had been a/salesman for another company in an adjacent state for many years and understands the food-processing industry so thoroughly that he can not only supply packaging//to meet your every need but can also give technical advice on frozen-food problems.

We are sure that you will enjoy working with Mr. Kennedy, who will soon call on///you.

If you show Mr. Kennedy the same courtesies that you extended to Mr. Smith during all the years he called on you, we shall be most appreciative. Cordially yours, (2)

(1 Minute at 140)

256▸ Mr. Henry: Two months ago we initiated a new policy of reducing sales calls on customers whose annual orders total less than $500. Instead of calling/on these accounts every month, we shall call once a year and use WATS for a once-a-month telephone call to solicit orders.

The enclosed figures indicate that last month we reduced//the number of salesmen's visits by 47 percent and we reduced travel expenses by 53 percent.

Reports on salesmen's use of WATS show that telephone calls increased///78 percent. The cost of a telephone call, however, is only one-tenth the cost of a personal call.

Of course, we must not be too optimistic on the basis of one month's figures. (3)

Reinforcement and Control

(2 Minutes at 130)

257▸ To all Regional Sales Managers: Thank you for sending in so promptly your tentative programs for sales conferences on Monday and Tuesday, August 23 and 24./ They look most interesting.

Although the substitution of regional conferences for a national sales meeting is an experiment, I think that two advantages will// accrue: economy and greater attention to local problems. Travel expense will be reduced by 35 percent. The second advantage may be even more important,///as we find that local business conditions and consumer needs vary from location to location so much that regional approaches may be effective.

So that you may still (1) have access to product information from headquarters, we shall broadcast to the five local conferences, via closed-circuit television. This broadcast, consisting of a sales/presentation on aerosol containers, will be given on Monday morning, August 23, from ten to eleven. You may want to provide time on your program following//this broadcast for an analysis of the presentation and a discussion of ways to adapt it locally.

Mr. Henry M. Simpson, our president, and I shall attend///your closing banquets by proxy from nine to ten on Tuesday evening, August 24, for that is when we shall address you by closed-circuit television.

You have my best wishes. (2)

258▸ Mr. Edwin C. Leighton, Brown Palace Hotel, Denver, Colorado 80202.

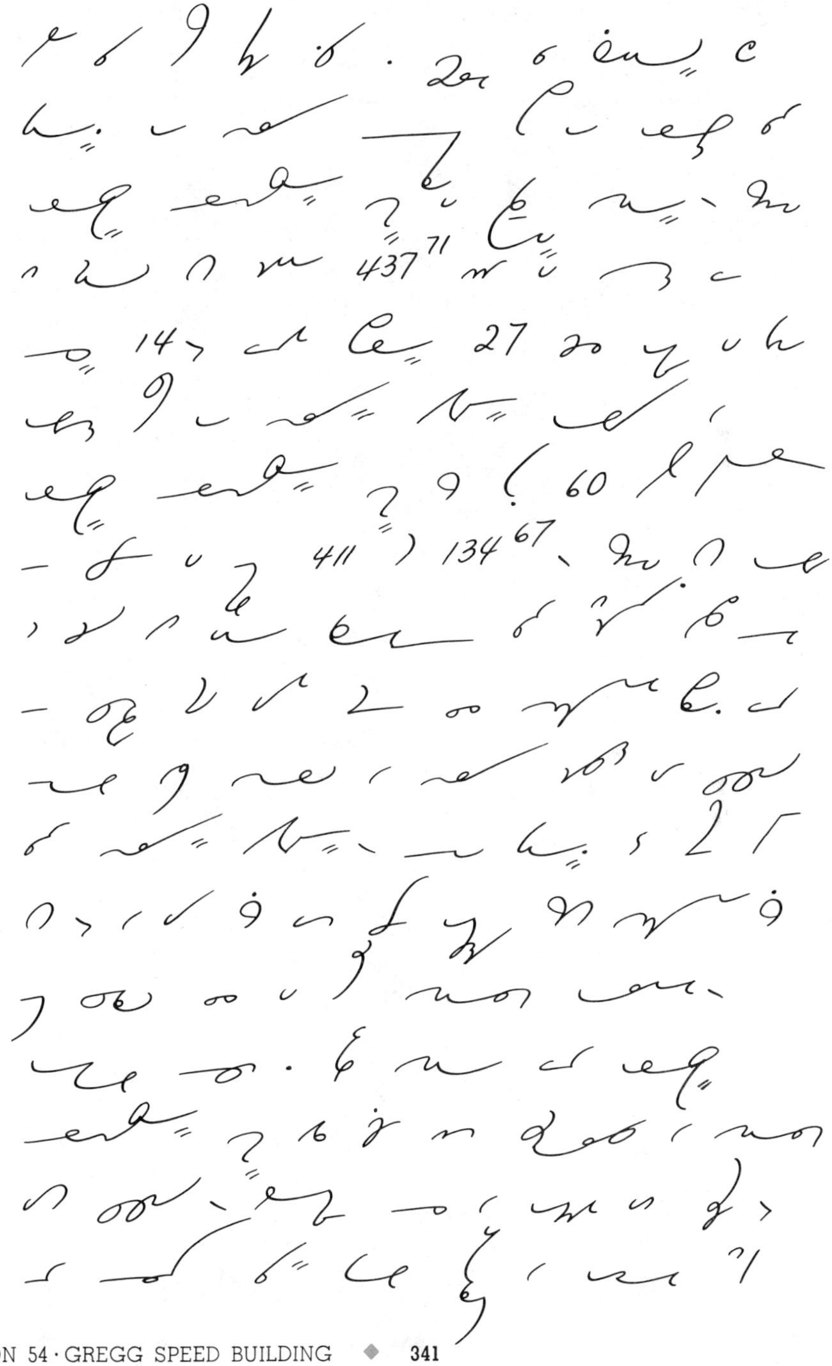

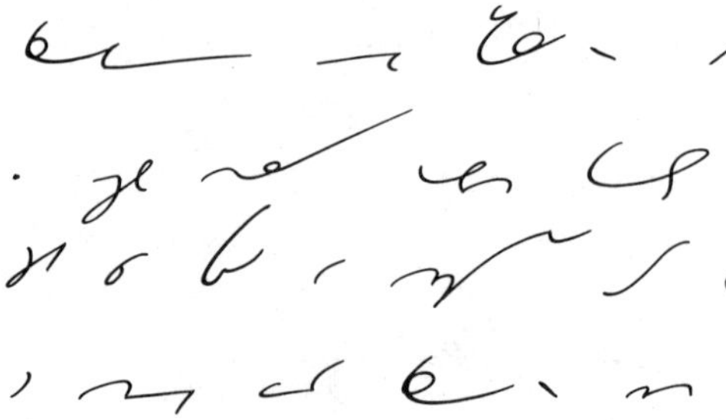

(262)

259 Mr. Fred Zimmerman, Connor Hotel, Third and Grand, Laramie, Wyoming 82070.

(184)

TRANSCRIPTION PACER

260 ▸ Mr. Harold L. Carney, District Sales Manager, National Products, Inc., 433 Walnut Street, Salt Lake City, Utah 84118. 13 24

33 42 51 61 68 79 89 99 110 122 135 147 156 169 175

lesson

55 BUILDING TRANSCRIPTION SPEED

SUSTAINED SPEED BUILDER

Practice the following vocabulary preview, and then see how well you can sustain your reinforcement and control speed.

Vocabulary Preview

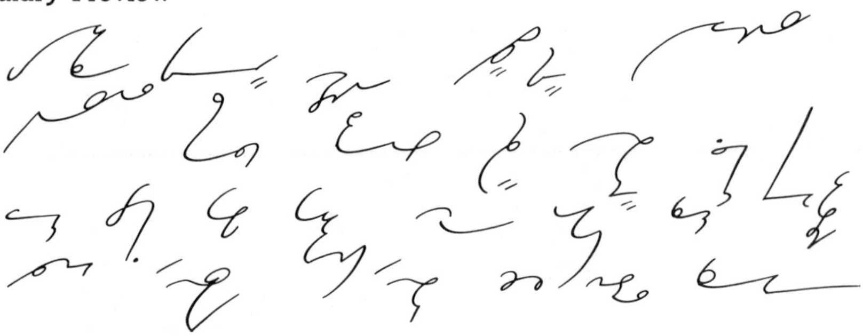

Automobile, Beaumont, computer, DataPhone, demonstrate, dilatory, evaluation, exploration, February, Gibson, hinges, judgments, omissions, packaging, preshow, prospective, quality, representative, serious, specialist, technician, transcribed, transcription, weekly, unnecessary, salesmen.

Speed Builder

261 To: All Salesmen, Subject: Dictation Record of All Calls.

Recently some of you have become dilatory about mailing your daily report of calls. The belts containing[1] each day's dictation must be put in the mail every night so that they reach the headquarters office within[2] two days after the call.

As you know, our headquarters typing pool transcribes your notes into a weekly report that[3] is released, along with complete weekly sales figures, every Tuesday to the sales manager and the[4] appropriate regional sales manager. A carbon copy is sent to each of you as a reference record. If[5] your dictation belts are not received every day, we cannot schedule transcription to ensure that weekly[6] reports will be available to provide necessary information in time for it to serve the purposes[7] for which it was planned.

Apparently, some of you are of the the opinion that since sales orders are sent from our[8] five district offices by DataPhone every morning, the daily report of calls is unnecessary.[9] Actually, it is one of our most valuable reports, for it gives an experienced salesman's on-the-spot[10] evaluation of local business conditions, prospective customers' needs, credit ratings, reasons for[11] buying or not buying, and other value judgments that computers can never tell us. Your value to the[12] company hinges on the quality of the information you supply in this daily report.

Please follow these[13] suggestions:

1. Keep your dictation unit in your automobile. Make a habit of dictating your report[14] immediately after you call on a prospect. Follow the outline pasted inside the cover of your[15] dictation machine when reporting a call.

2. Retain any notes used during the dictation until you receive[16] your transcribed weekly report. Sometimes the equipment fails and your dictation is not recorded. When your weekly[17] report arrives, check for any omissions or serious transcription errors before you destroy the notes.

3.[18] Follow the practice of "reporting by exception." This new management practice stresses the inclusion of[19] any material that does not follow the expected pattern. For instance, if a customer places an[20] unusually large order for some item or fails to give an anticipated order, the report should[21] contain the reason for his action. On the other hand, routine reorders would require no comment. (438)

262 ▸ Harwood Manufacturing Company, Bayou Lane, Beaumont, Texas 77701.

Gentlemen: The booklet that you requested, "Let Your Packaging Sell Your Products," was sent to you several[1] months ago. We hope that it gave you some new ideas for innovations in packaging your frozen foods[2] to meet increasing competition.

A report in Business Week of a recent survey conducted by a[3] marketing organization states that changes in packaging account for more increases in sales volume than do[4] changes in the product itself. A new package can generate new demand for an item by creating a[5] new image in the mind of the consumer. Incidentally, the new package costs a good deal less than a change[6] in the contents of the box.

During the first week in February, our representative in your area,[7] Mr. Mark Gibson, will be in Beaumont. He would like to call—without obligation to you—to discuss your[8] packaging problems and to demonstrate a new packaging idea that will be put on the market by NATIONAL[9] PRODUCTS in April. It is our policy to preshow such items to selected customers.

Mr.[10] Gibson will telephone you soon after he arrives in Beaumont to inquire about a time convenient for him[11] to call at your plant. He is a specialist in the packaging field and is unusually competent in[12] solving special customer problems.

After you have made a preliminary exploration of our product[13] in terms of your needs, you may wish to arrange a group conference with your technicians and Mr. Gibson to[14] discuss your requirements in depth.

We hope that you will enjoy talking with Mr. Gibson and that you will be as[15] pleased with the new product he will demonstrate as we think you will be. Yours cordially, (315)

TRANSCRIPTION CHECKPOINT

263 Lumsden Knitting Mills, Old Fort Road, Asheville, North Carolina 28800, Attention: Mr. Abraham C. Lumsden, Purchasing Agent.

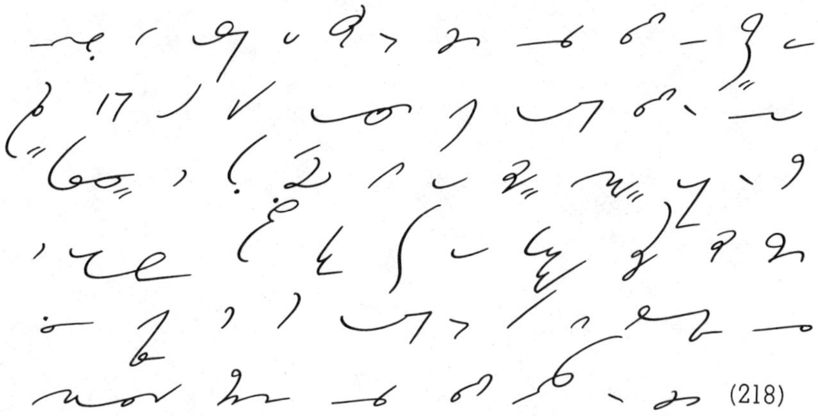

(218)

264 ▸ Mr. Jack Bowman, Shamrock Hotel, 2712 Oak Springs Drive, Houston, Texas 77015.

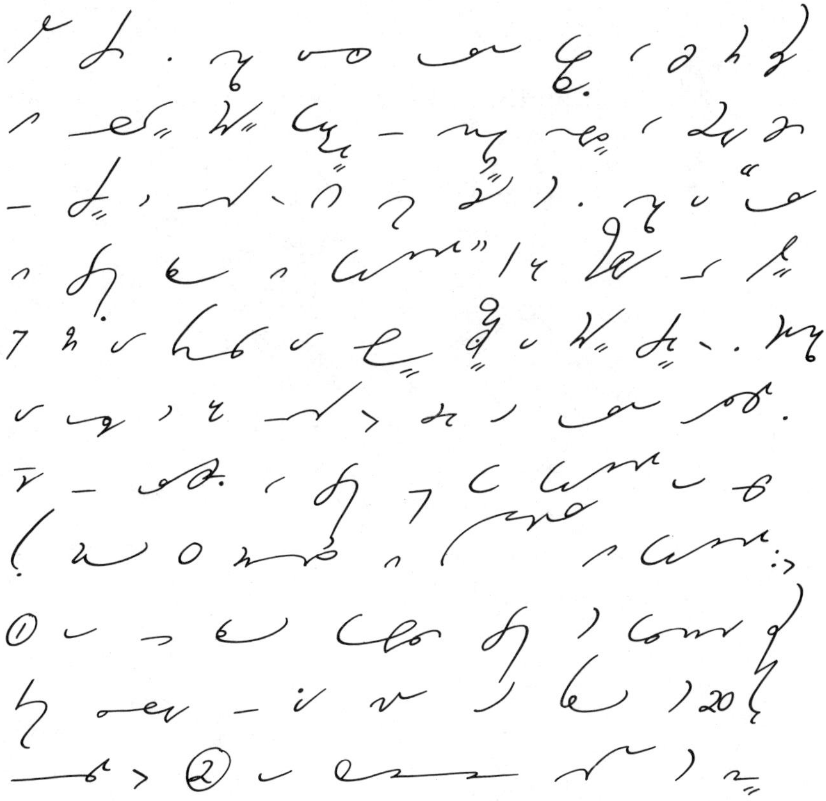

(229)

265 Memo to Stuart Henderson, Manager, Advertising Department.

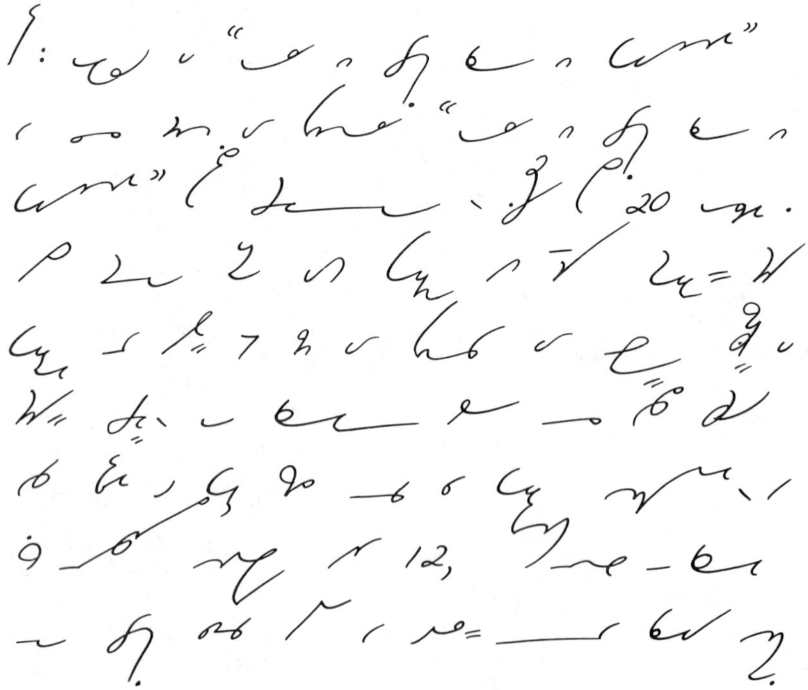

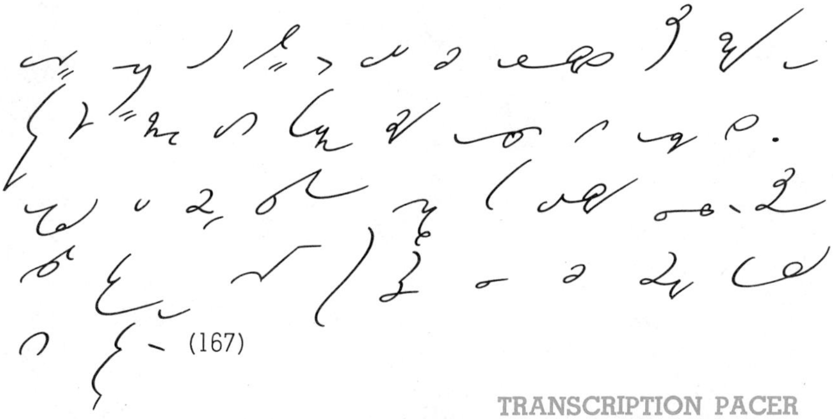

(167)

TRANSCRIPTION PACER

266▸ Mr. Walter C. Forbes, 725 Buena Vista Drive, Raleigh, North 12
Carolina 27600. 15

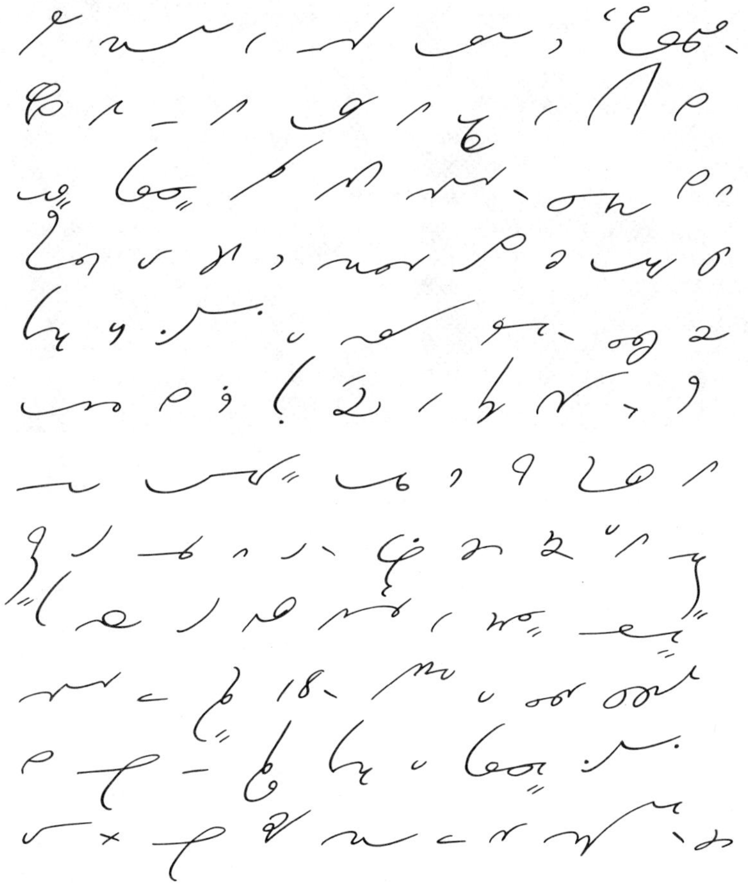

27
39
50
62
73
85
93
107
115
127
138
151

Traffic management is concerned with such questions as these: (1) How are purchased goods transported from a supplier? (2) How are sold goods transported to customers? (3) How are delayed shipments traced? (4) How are claims for loss or damage processed? Just how these questions are answered is governed by the size and the nature of the business organization.

In small companies a shipping clerk and a receiving clerk work separately or jointly in receiving and shipping goods and materials.

In large companies the head of the traffic department is the traffic manager. He furnishes guidance to department heads regarding supply coordination, transportation, traffic, and warehousing. Not only must he have expert knowledge of all these technical matters, but he must also represent the company in its negotiations with carriers and appear before state and Federal commissions, such as the Interstate Commerce Commission, the Federal Maritime Board, and the Civil Aeronautics Board.

unit 12

TRAFFIC

Secretarial Assignment

In this unit you are secretary to James R. Russo, manager of the Traffic Department. All letters are signed by him over his title, Traffic Manager.

SPECIALIZED TERMINOLOGY

You will transcribe Mr. Russo's dictation more efficiently after you have become familiar with the specialized terms he uses.

Affidavit • Signed written statement sworn to before an authorized officer.

Bill of Lading • A combination contract and receipt given by the common carrier to the person shipping certain goods. A straight bill of lading is prepared if the customer has established credit. If the shipper must use a local bank as a collection agent for a C. O. D. shipment, an order bill of lading and a sight draft are executed. When the sight draft is paid, the bank endorses the bill of lading to the customer so that he can obtain the shipment.

Consignee • Person or company to whom a shipment is sent.

Consignor • Person or company shipping goods to a consignee for sale.

K. D. Goods • Knocked-down goods that must be assembled before they can be sold.

L.c.l. Shipment • Less-than-carload shipment.

Piggyback Shipment • Loaded truck sent by rail to a certain point, from which it is driven to its destination.

S. U. Goods • Setup or assembled goods ready for sale.

Shook • A set of the parts of a box, piece of furniture, or other goods, ready to be put together.

Spur Track • Rail siding belonging to the shipper. It connects a railroad directly with a business concern.

Tariff • Any table of charges, as of a railroad.

Waybill • Routing instructions to accompany the shipment. The waybill usually routes the goods by the most expeditious route.

CONFUSED WORDS AND TRANSCRIPTION PRACTICE

The following similar-sounding and similar-looking words contain two types of word groups: (1) words that are pronounced exactly alike, though spelled differently, and for which the shorthand outlines are identical; and (2) words that look and sound somewhat alike, and for which shorthand outlines are very nearly the same.

precede to go before
proceed to advance

emigrate to leave a country
immigrate to enter a country

caret writers' and proofreaders' mark indicating an insertion
carat a unit of weight for precious stones, especially diamonds
karat a unit of fineness for gold

adverse opposing; unfavorable
averse unwilling; disinclined

emigrant one who leaves a country
immigrant one who enters a country

farther used when speaking of measurable distance (space)
further moreover; in addition (refers to time, quantity, or degree)

Transcribe the following sentences, preferably at the typewriter, until you can differentiate the confusing words that appear above.

lesson

56 BUILDING TRANSCRIPTION QUALITY

TRANSCRIPTION POINTERS

Uses of the Quotation Mark

1 When the words of a writer or a speaker are directly quoted, they are enclosed in quotation marks.

> The telegram read, "Order being shipped airexpress today."
>
> "Tariff schedules should be filed for quick reference," fumed the traffic manager.

2 When the words of a writer or a speaker are indirectly quoted, they are not enclosed in quotation marks.

> The traffic manager said that all tariff schedules should be filed for quick reference.

3 The period and the comma are always placed inside the closing quotation mark. The semicolon and the colon are placed outside the closing quotation mark. The question mark and the exclamation point are placed inside the closing quotation mark if they are part of the quotation; otherwise, they are placed outside the closing quotation mark.

> He said, "I am going."
>
> He said, "I am going"; but he didn't make a move.
>
> He asked, "Where is the contract?" (Sentence is a statement.)
>
> Did he say, "I shall continue to support you"? (Sentence is a question.)

Check your understanding of quotation mark usage by transcribing the following sentences, preferably at the typewriter.

1 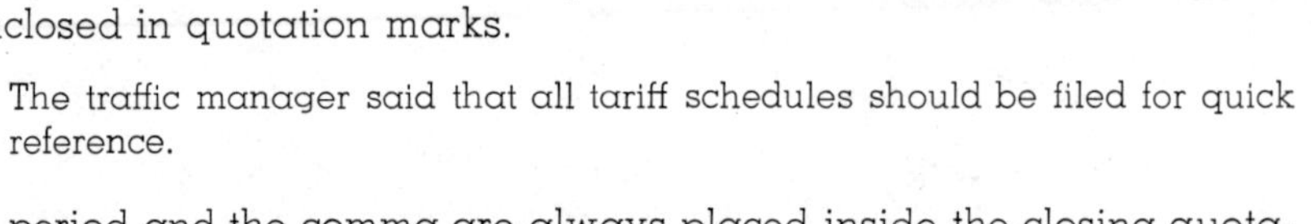

2 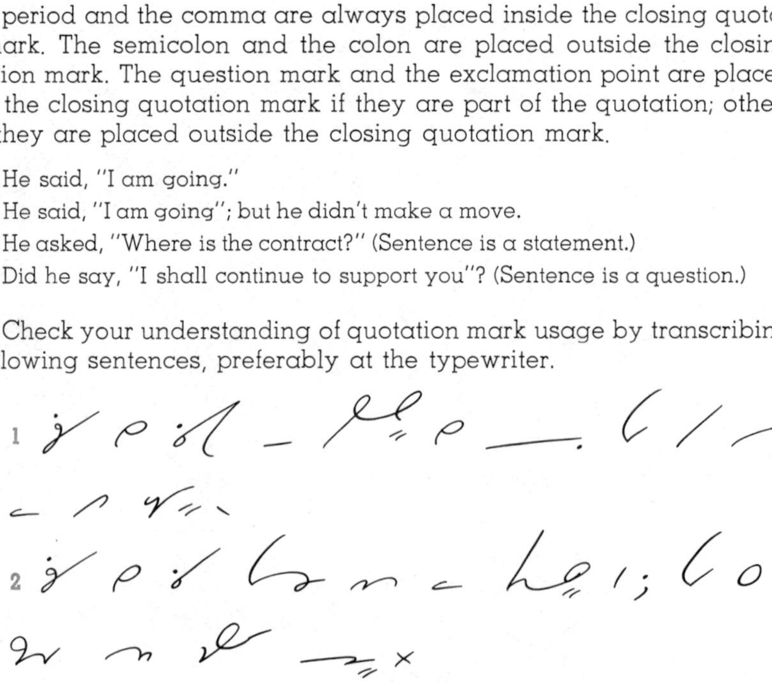

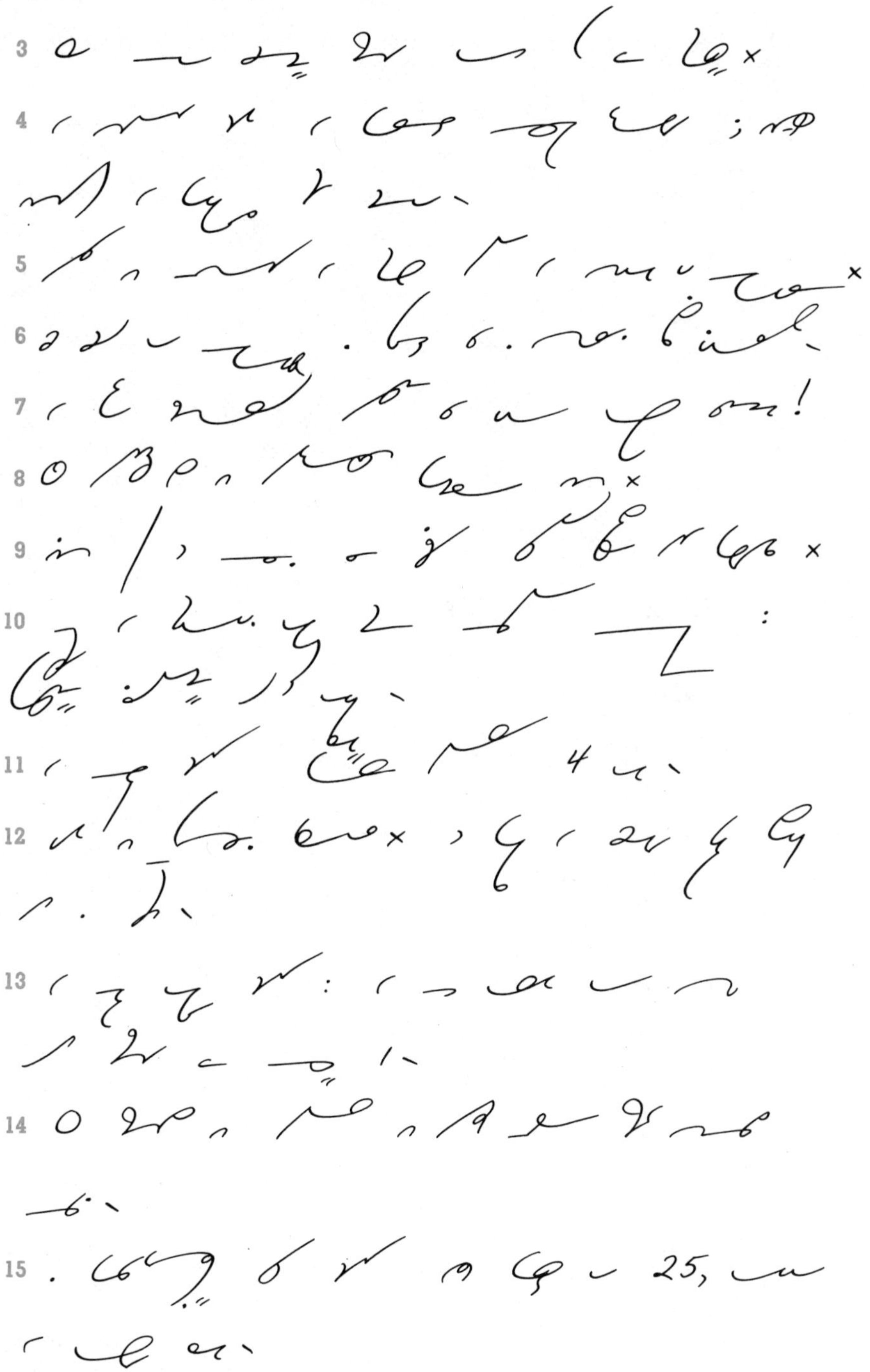

267 ▸ The Miller Mart, 3174 Jefferson Avenue, Davenport, Iowa 52803.

(172)

268 ▸ First National Bank, 433 River Street, Dubuque, Iowa 52001.

(131)

269 ▸ Mr. Walter J. James, Manager, Furniture Fixtures, A Division of National Products, Inc., High Point, North Carolina 27260.

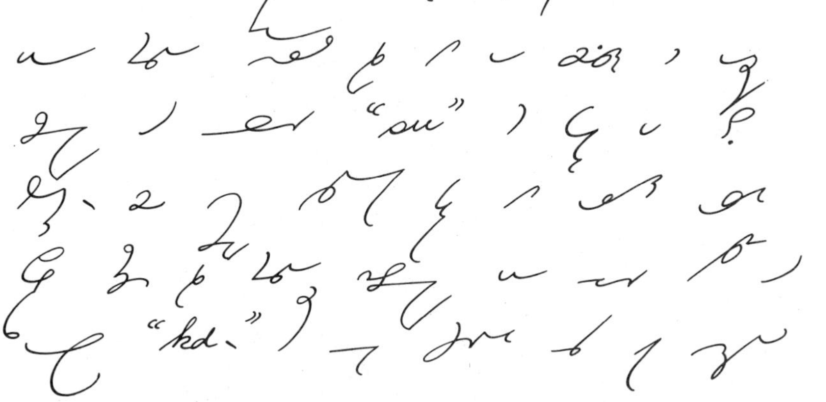

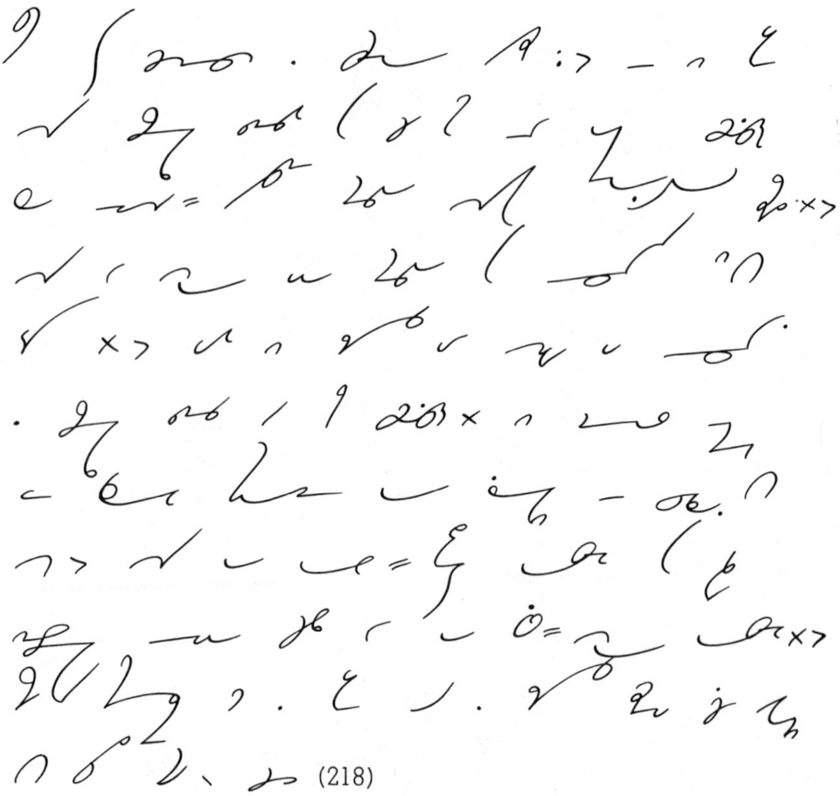

(218)

270 To: Mr. Ralph C. Akin, Sales Manager.

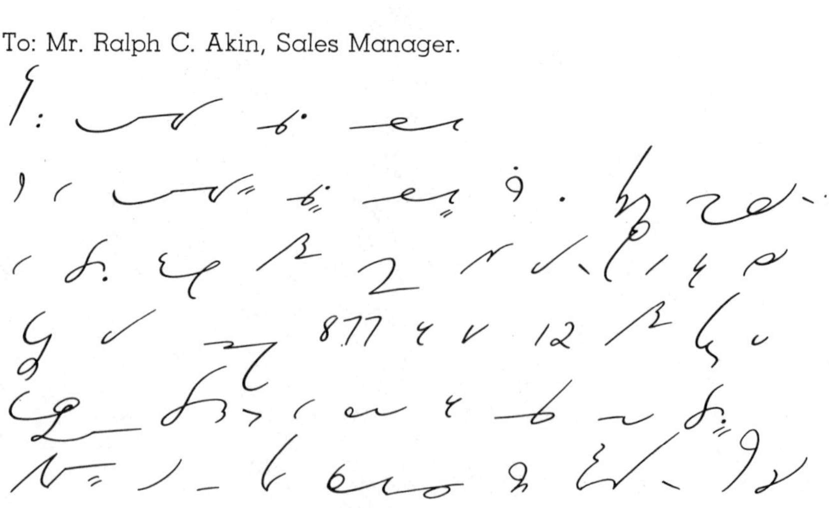

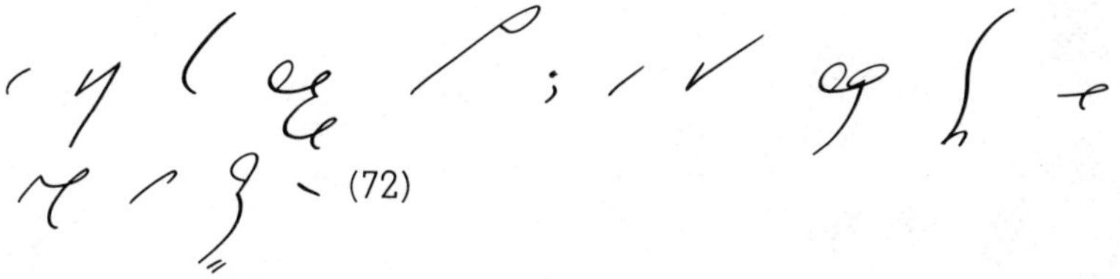

(72)

271▸ The J. L. Johnson Farm Products Company, 411 Railroad Street, Wichita, Kansas 67219.

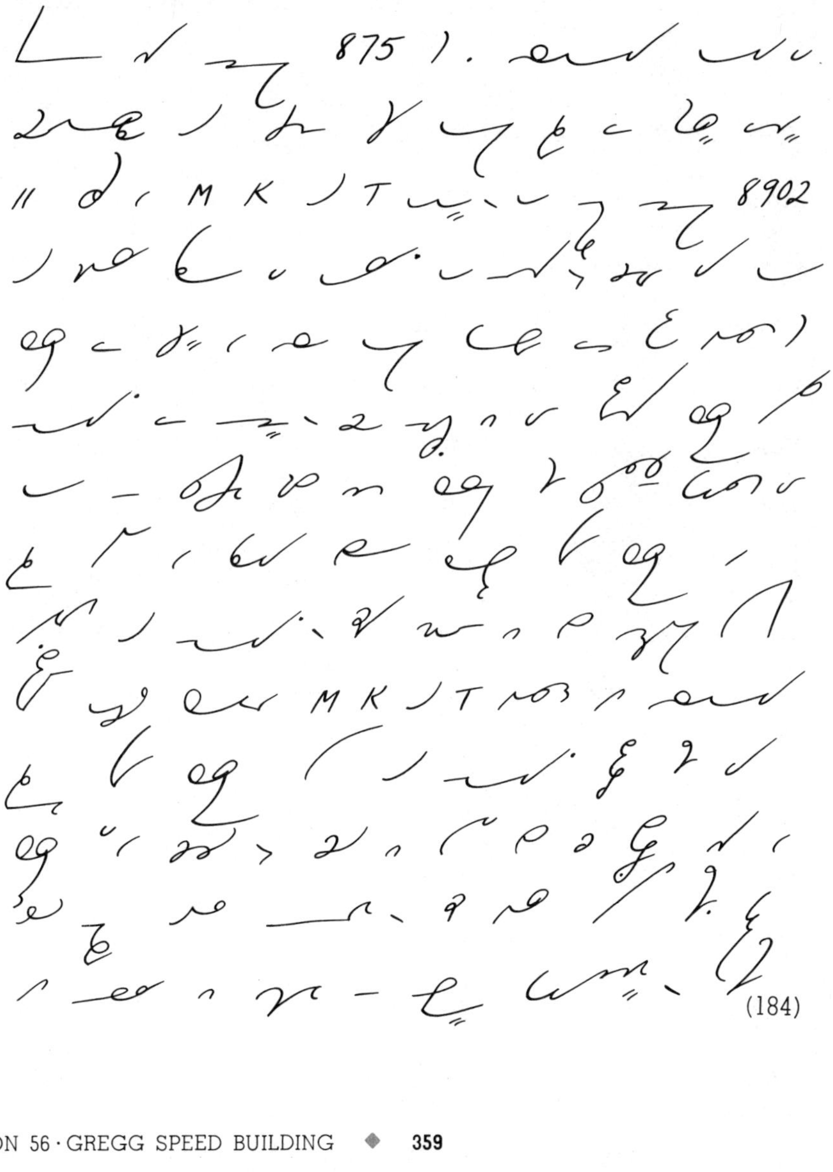

(184)

Lesson 57

MASTERING SHORTHAND THEORY

NAMES OF ALL STATES

Ala.
Alas.
Ariz.
Ark.
Calif.
Colo.
Conn.
Del.
Fla.
Ga.
Hawaii
Idaho
Ill.
Ind.
Iowa
Kans.
Ky.
La.
Maine
Md.
Mass.
Mich.
Minn.
Miss.
Mo.
Mont.
Nebr.
Nev.
N. H.
N. J.
N. Mex.
N. Y.
N. C.
N. Dak.
Ohio
Okla.
Oreg.
Pa.
R. I.
S. C.
S. Dak.
Tenn.
Tex.
Utah
Vt.
Va.
Wash.
W. Va.
Wis.
Wyo.

272 To: Helen Marie Brady, Secretary to Mr. Robert L. Simpson.

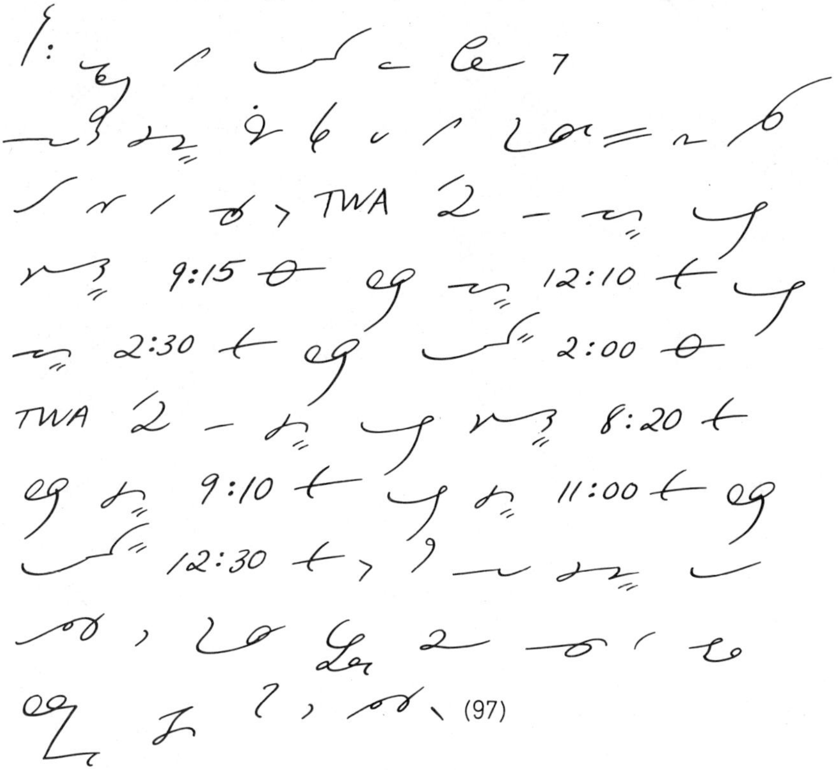

(97)

273 To: Mr. James M. Walsh, Production Manager.

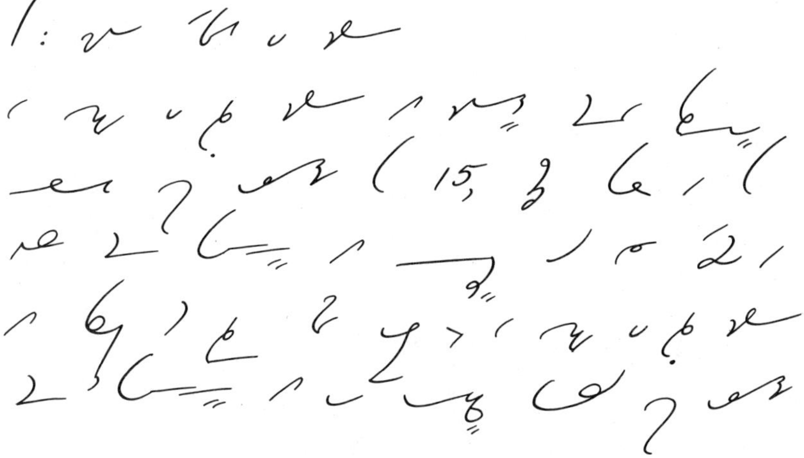

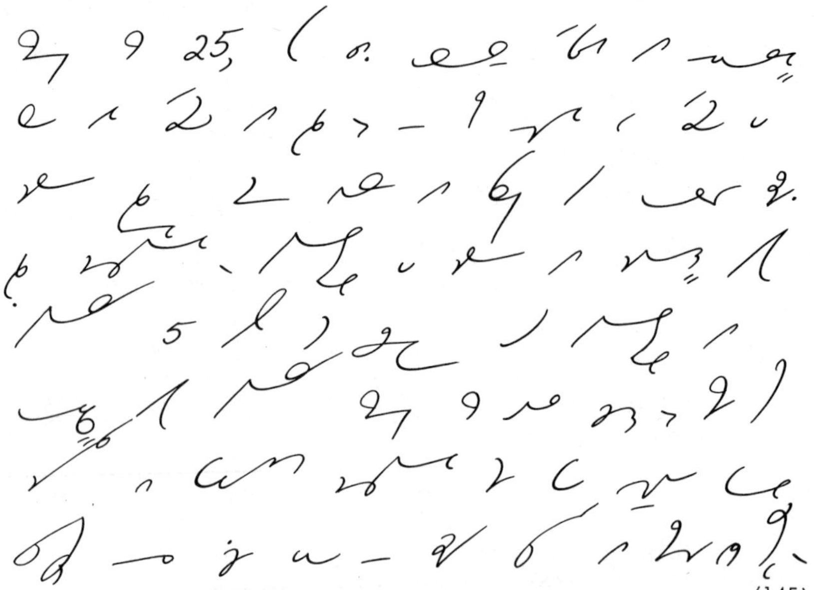

(145)

274 The Mervin Furniture Company, 700 Oak Street, Hasting, Nebraska 68901.

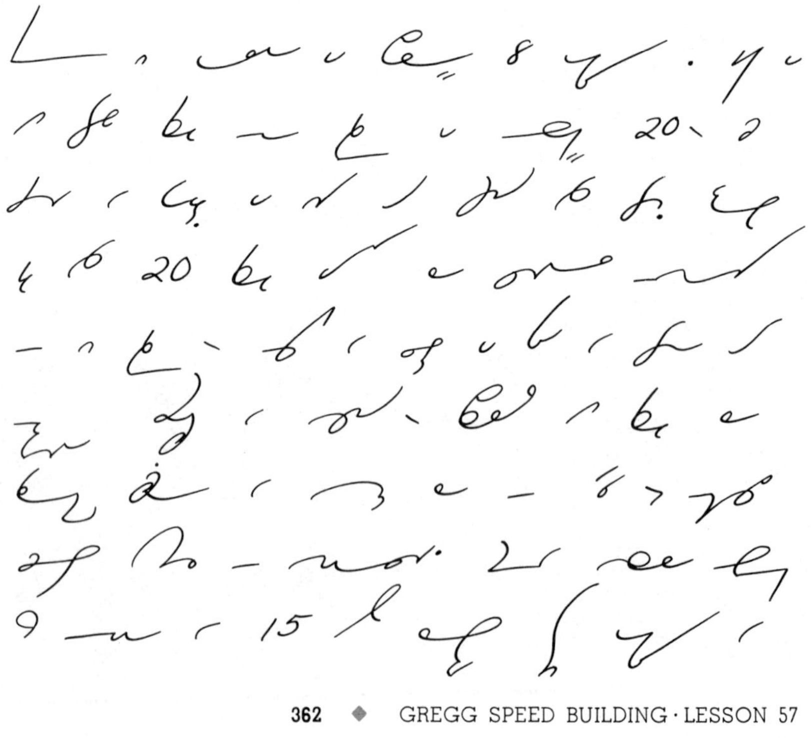

(160)

275▸ Claims Department, Union Pacific Railroad, Union Station, St. Louis, Missouri 63100.

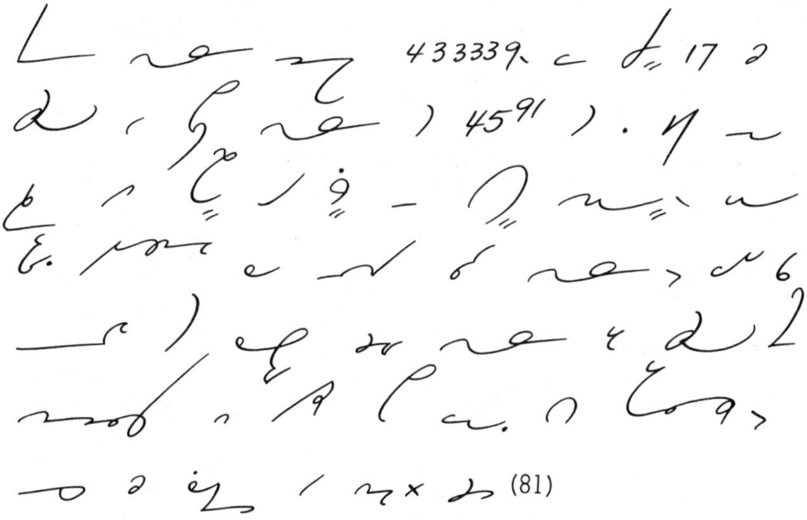

(81)

276▸ Pennsylvania Railroad, Pennsylvania Station, Seventh Avenue at 33 Street, New York, New York 10036, Attention of Freight Department.

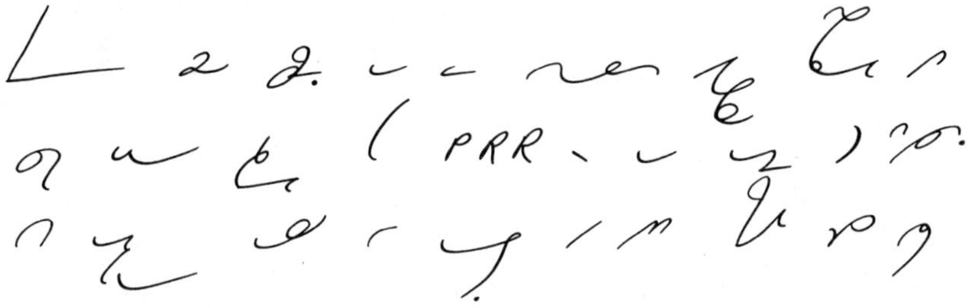

(172)

277▸ Kennedy, Martin, and Willing, Attorneys at Law, 412 Eye Street, N. W., Washington, D. C. 20014.

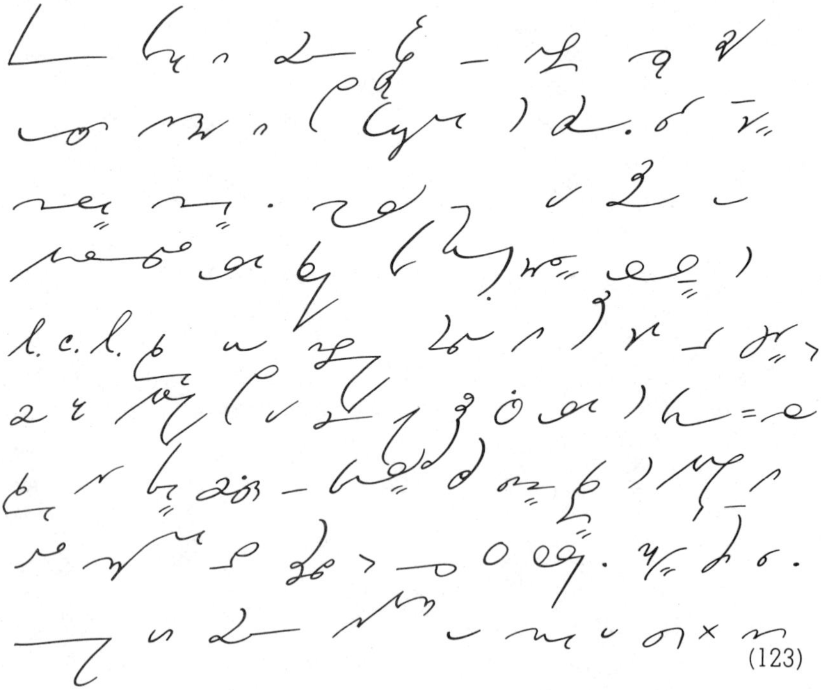

(123)

lesson

OFFICE-STYLE DICTATION 58

YOUR SHORTHAND NOTES

Simplify the handling of dictation problems by becoming thoroughly acquainted with proper shorthand notebook procedures.

1 When a dictator frequently restates his thoughts, write the dictation in the left-hand column of the shorthand notebook page to allow ample room (the entire right-hand column) for insertions, reminders, and instructions.

2 Date each day's dictation with the day, month, and year at the bottom of the page so that any day's notes can be located easily.

3 Use a symbol, such as a question mark, to identify doubtful items, ambiguous expressions, and points to be verified.

4 Clarify all matters relating to the dictation before you leave the dictator's office.

5 Draw a line through all transcribed material, and use an elastic band to secure the transcribed material.

TRANSCRIPTION SPEED BUILDER

278▸ To: All Rate Clerks.

(182)

279 ▸ Waxman Packing Box Company, 700 St. Louis Road, St. Charles, Missouri 63301.

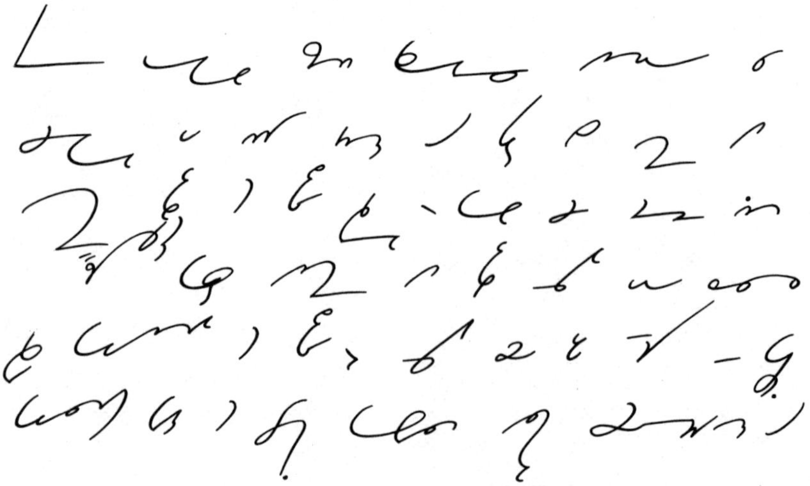

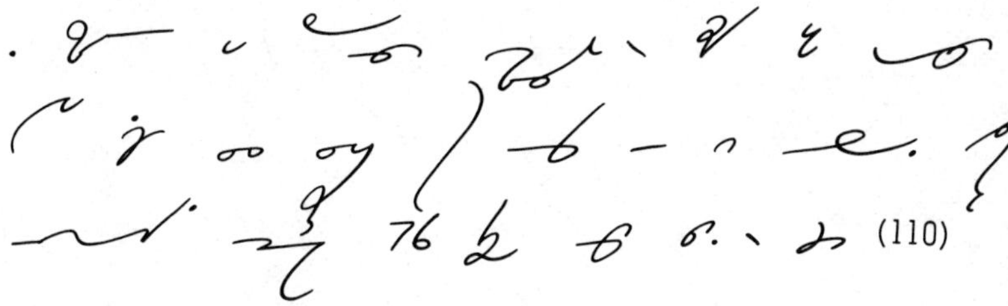

280 To: Edward R. Harmon, Director, Personnel Department.

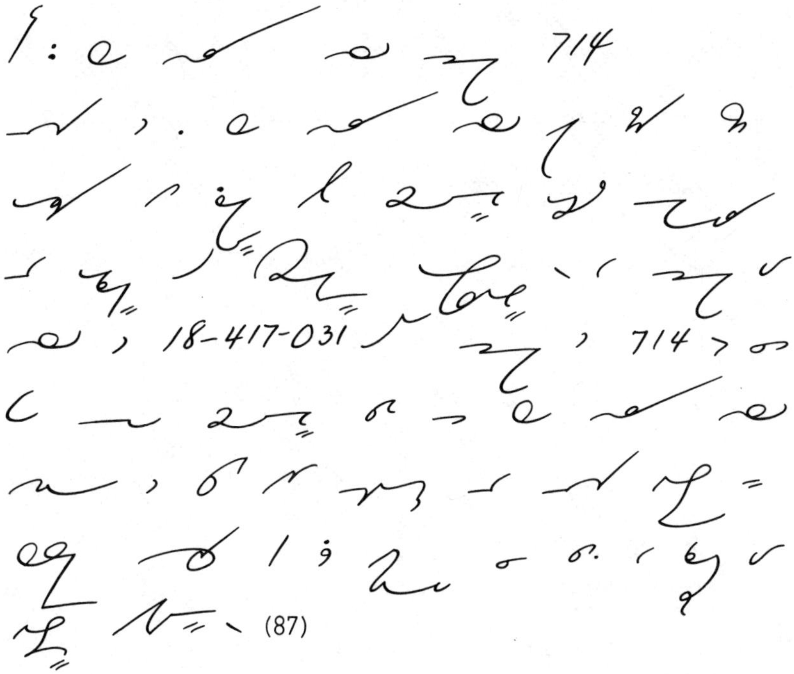

281 ▸ To: Harmon Jones, Purchasing Agent; Allen Shearer, International Division.

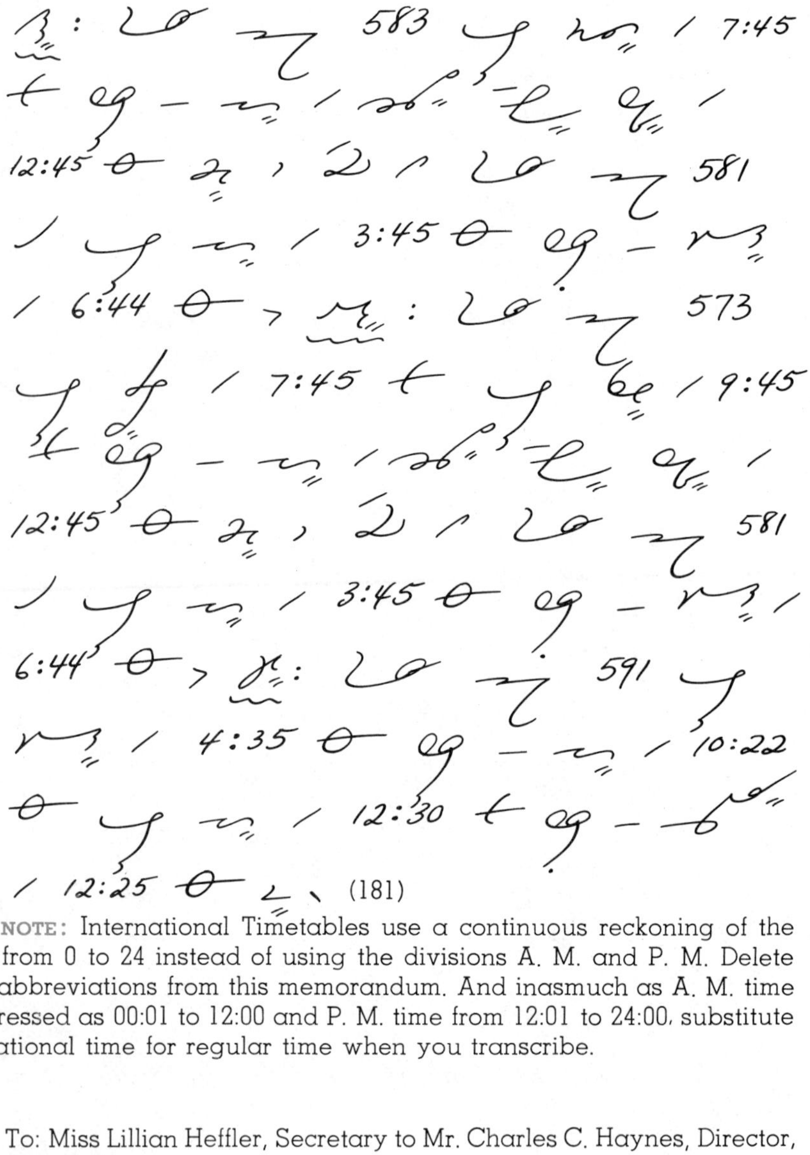

(181)

NOTE: International Timetables use a continuous reckoning of the hours from 0 to 24 instead of using the divisions A. M. and P. M. Delete these abbreviations from this memorandum. And inasmuch as A. M. time is expressed as 00:01 to 12:00 and P. M. time from 12:01 to 24:00, substitute international time for regular time when you transcribe.

282▸ To: Miss Lillian Heffler, Secretary to Mr. Charles C. Haynes, Director, Research and Development.

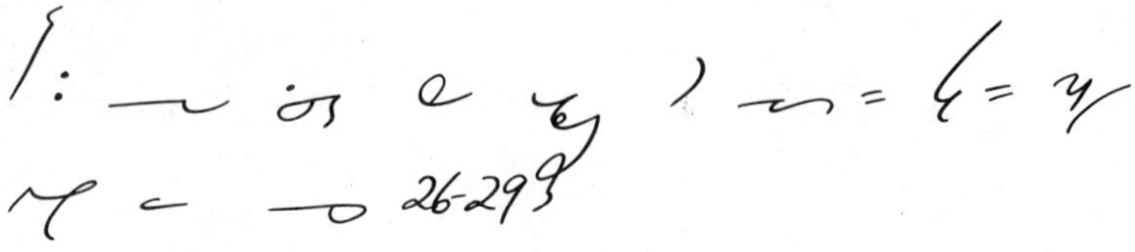

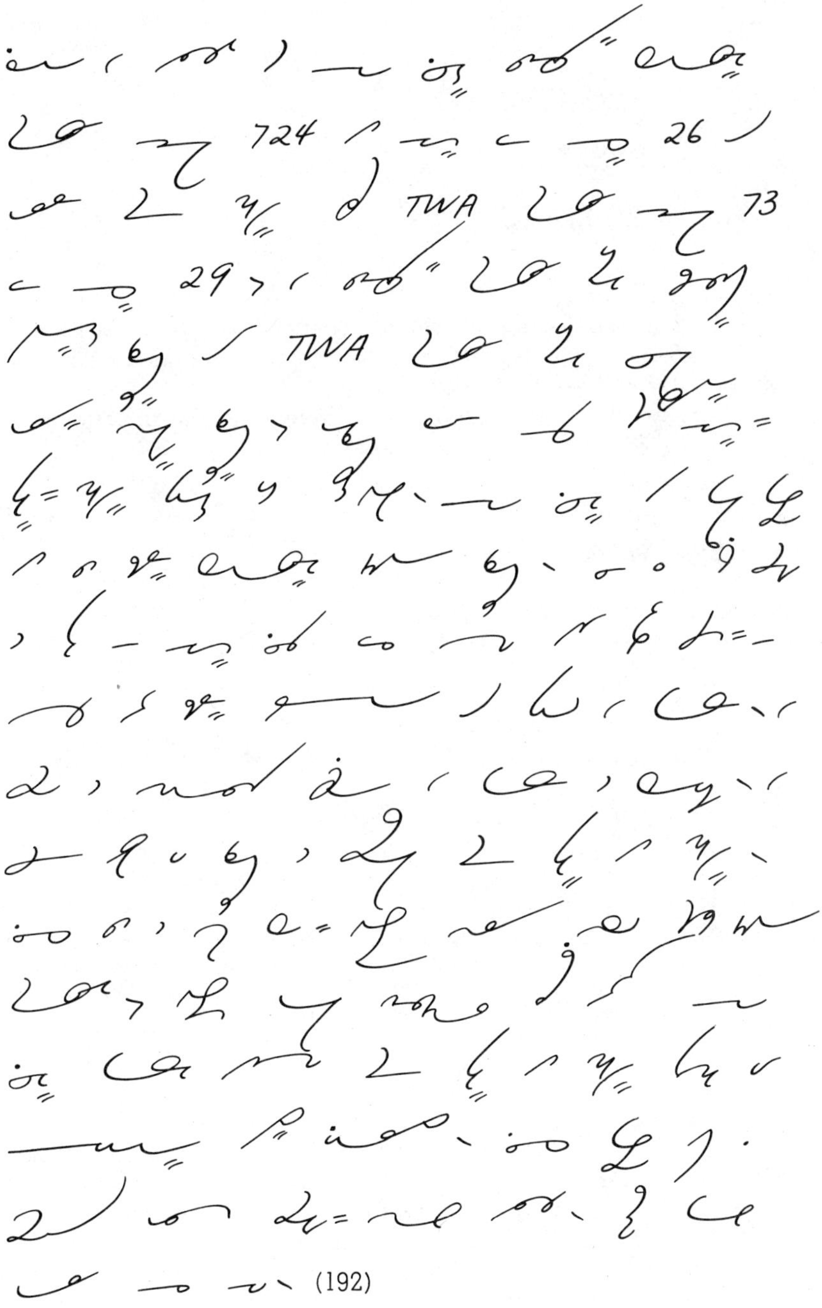
724
26
TWA
73
29
TWA
(192)

lesson

59 PROGRESSIVE SPEED BUILDING

In this lesson the one-minute speed-forcing letters will be dictated at 120, 130, and 140 words a minute; the two-minute reinforcement and control letter will be dictated at 130 words a minute.

Review the vocabulary before attempting the dictation.

SPEED-BUILDING LETTERS

Vocabulary Preview

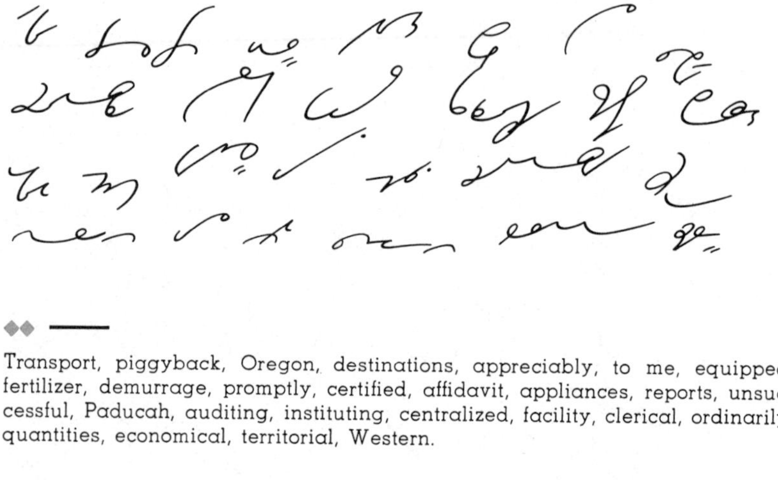

Transport, piggyback, Oregon, destinations, appreciably, to me, equipped, fertilizer, demurrage, promptly, certified, affidavit, appliances, reports, unsuccessful, Paducah, auditing, instituting, centralized, facility, clerical, ordinarily, quantities, economical, territorial, Western.

Speed Forcing

(1 Minute at 120)

283 Gentlemen: The enclosed proposal for using piggyback cars to transport our loaded truck trailers covers service for 50 cars a month for the next twelve months. These/ piggyback cars would be consigned to Portland, Oregon, where truck cabs would be attached to the trailers and driven to destinations throughout the Northwest. We estimate that//this arrangement will reduce transportation costs appreciably, especially across the mountains.

Please check the proposal covering this service; if you approve/// it, return it to Mr. Henry, who will draw the contract. If you do not approve it, please indicate the changes you desire and return it to me. Sincerely yours, (1)

(1 Minute at 130)

284 ▸ Gentlemen: Please deliver one freight car equipped with a closed hopper to our spur track for loading on Monday morning, December 8. We expect to have the car fully loaded with/fertilizer and ready to move to Omaha by four o'clock on the afternoon of the 8th.

On our fertilizer shipments recently, you have not "spotted" the cars promptly//at destination so that the consignee knows the track number and other details. Therefore, he cannot unload within the 48-hour free time and thus avoid demurrage/// charges.

We must insist that you supply this information promptly so that service to our customers will be improved and so that we may avoid extra shipping costs. Yours truly, (2)

(1 Minute at 140)

285 ▸ Gentlemen: A bill of lading, a certified copy of Invoice 89336, and an affidavit signed by the consignee are enclosed as proof of a shipment of an order of/electrical appliances to the Jones-Laughton Hardware Company in Nashville, Tennessee.

The consignee reports that this l.c.l. shipment was never delivered, although it was made five weeks// ago. Both the consignee and our Traffic Department requested a tracer, but neither of us received any satisfaction from your agent. Our own attempts to trace the shipment were///unsuccessful after the goods left Paducah.

Unless you have a receipt signed by the Jones-Laughton Hardware Company, please remit the amount covered by the invoice to cover our loss. Yours truly, (3)

Reinforcement and Control

(2 Minutes at 130)

286 ▸ To: All Branch Managers: Beginning on June 1, all branch operations will mail all copies of transportation bills to headquarters for auditing and payment. We have assigned two/auditing clerks to full-time jobs on this operation.

Our reason for instituting this specialized service at the centralized facility is that we believe that we can//save much more than two clerical salaries by concentrating on detecting errors that ordinarily are overlooked by members of the Traffic Department.

These clerks will be///responsible for verifying that:

1. Quantities charged for agree with packing slips.
2. Weights agree with those on bills of lading and express receipts.
3. Most economical and (1) fastest routing has been used.
4. Goods are properly classified. (In many cases, goods that are entitled to commodity rates are being sent by class rates.)
5. The correct rates/are charged and agree with the latest tariff schedules of rates and classifications.
6. The lowest rate by territorial classification is used. (For instance, we have found//a number of bills on which Western rather than Offi-

cial territorial classification rates were charged, although we ship all goods from the headquarters to the East from East///St. Louis, Illinois, rather than from St. Louis, Missouri.)

We hope that all managers will agree that this new procedure is a good one that will reduce transportation costs. (2)

TRANSCRIPTION SPEED BUILDER

287▸ Missouri Public Service Commission, Capitol Building, Jefferson City, Missouri 65101.

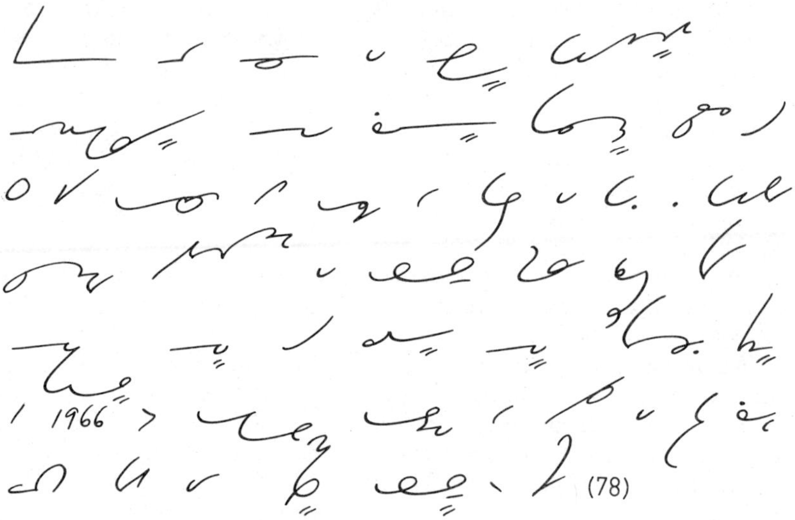

(78)

288▸ Freight Agent, Chicago, Burlington, and Quincy Railroad, Cedar Rapids, Iowa 52404.

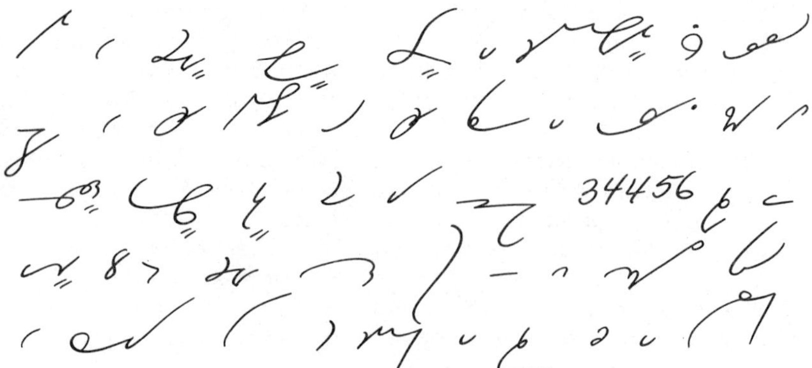

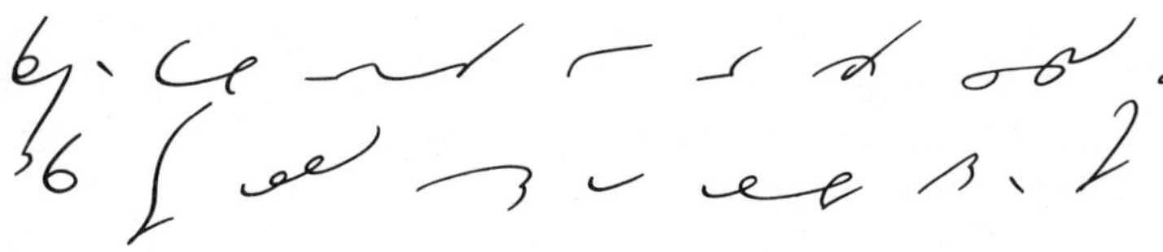

(80)

289 ▸ Mr. Herman Briggs, Attorney, 433 Walnut Street, Moberly, Missouri 65270.

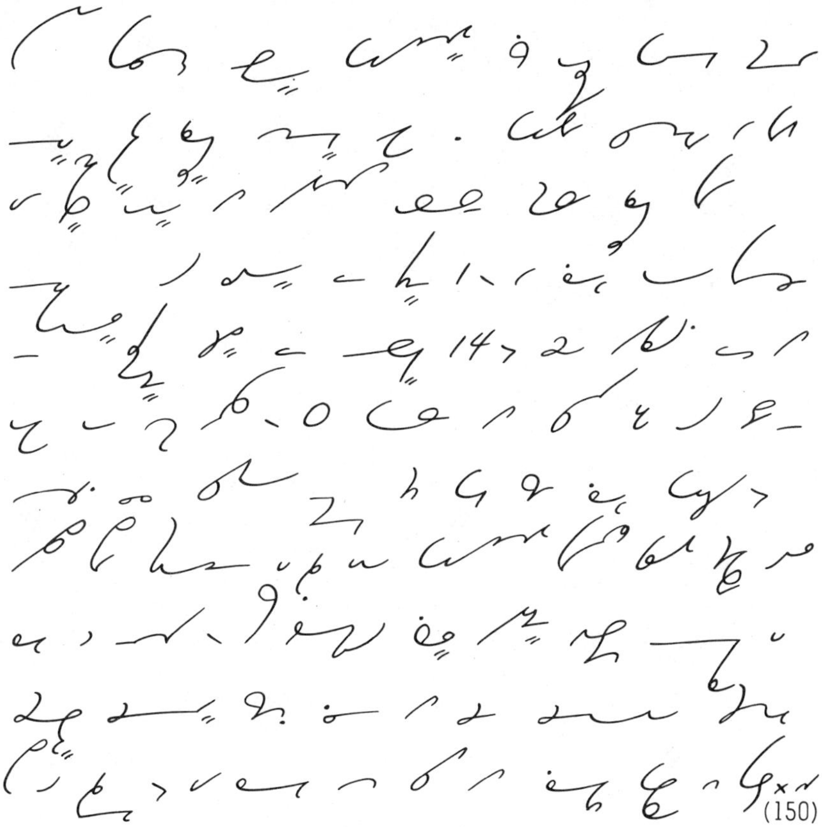

(150)

TRANSCRIPTION PACER

290 ▸ Mr. Monroe Wendt, Traffic Manager, Evans Manufacturing 11
Company, 87655 St. Charles Road, Overton, Missouri 63203. 23

34

46

55
70
78
90
101
113
126
137
149
158
170
184
194
209
218
229
241
251
257

lesson 60

BUILDING
TRANSCRIPTION
SPEED

SUSTAINED SPEED BUILDER

Practice the following vocabulary preview, and then see how well you can sustain your reinforcement and control speed.

Vocabulary Preview

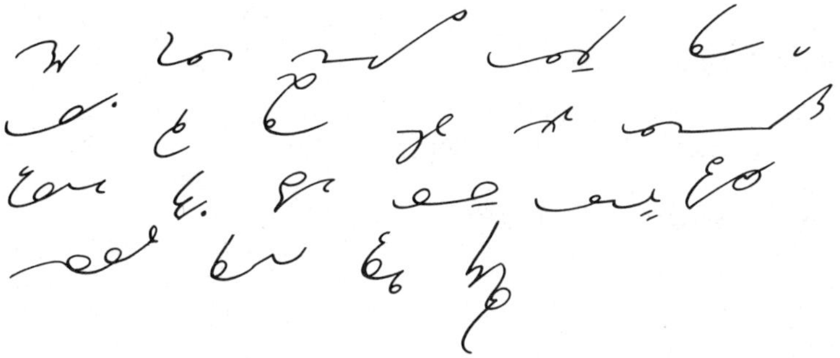

Consult, frequent, commodity, liquid, bill of lading, shipper, waybill, unsatisfactory, quantities, recommendations, operator's, posting, assistance, railway, Leonard's, expedite, guarantees, chartered, sparsely, justifiable.

Speed Builder

291 ROUTINES TO BE FOLLOWED IN SENDING GOODS BY FREIGHT.

A. BY THE RATE CLERK.

1. Consult rate card file for customer or city with frequent shipments of merchandise[1] covered by same classification. THIS FILE MUST BE UPDATED EVERY TIME NEW TARIFFS ARE ISSUED.

2.[2] Seek to classify at commodity rate (low-grade materials, such as coal, sand, grain, ores, lumber, oil, and[3] acids) rather than class rate, which is higher. Most manufactured goods will be at class rate.

3. Identify as[4] crude, rough, finished, set up or knocked down, loose, in bulk, boxed or otherwise packaged, liquid or dry, etc.

4. Send[5] to packer.

B. BY THE PACKER.

1. Attach rate information to assembled goods.

2. Select appropriate[6] container after studying illustration and directive posted above packing tables.

3. Check quantity[7] and description of merchandise against packing slip.

4. Pack securely, filling all unused space with shredded[8] paper.

5. Approve packing slip by initialing, and enclose in package.

C. BY THE INSPECTOR.

1. Approve[9] the shipment by initialing packing slip only after checking accurately.

2. Seal package, following[10] instructions posted above sealing station.

D. BY THE MARKING CLERK.

1. Check to see that boxes having a girth[11] of more than 144 inches are metal-strapped and that smaller packages are securely fastened[12] by gummed tape.

2. Weigh package and mark weight on top with Magic Marker.

3. Stencil address on box or crate, using[13] stencil brush.

4. Stencil name of carrier, customer's purchase order number, and code for classification[14] of goods beside the other information.

E. BY THE ROUTING CLERK.

1. Prepare three copies of bill of lading.[15] Send original to customer as notice of shipment, release second (shipper's order) to freight agent, and[16] file memorandum copy.

2. Prepare waybill,· indicating shortest and most expeditious route.

3.[17] Release to loader.

F. BY THE TRACING AND CLAIMS CLERK.

1. When customer reports delay, locate file copy[18] of bill of lading and ask railroad to trace shipment.

2. If results are unsatisfactory, communicate[19] by fastest method with first railroad freight agent and with subsequent agents until goods are located. If[20] necessary, go to point where car might be found.

3. If claim is necessary, report to traffic manager[21] necessary information for preparing documents and communicating with customer.

G. BY THE[22] AUDIT CLERK.

1. Check all transportation bills by verifying quantities, weights, routing, classification, rate,[23] and computations.

2. Approve by initialing and forward all bills to headquarters for final auditing[24] and payment. (482)

292▸ To: Systems and Procedures Department, Subject: Posting Copy of Freight Shipment Routines.

The enclosed copy of proposed routines for making freight shipments follows your recommendations. Details for each[1] clerk will be developed later for inclusion in his operator's manual.

The posting copy would be[2] typed on a legal-sized sheet so that all routines can be included on one page. The copy would be laminated[3] so that it would retain a neat appearance.

Please check the material. If you approve it, we shall go ahead[4] and post the routines. If not, please indicate further suggestions, keeping in mind the desirability[5] of confining the copy to one long sheet.

A similar posting copy of the routines for express and[6] parcel-post shipments will be prepared just as soon as approval is given for the one covering freight.

Can you give[7] me some idea of the amount of time your department would require to develop the detailed procedures for[8] each clerk? Also, can you tell me now when you can fit the time-and-motion studies into your schedule? We will try[9] to adjust our own operations to conform to your wishes. Thank you very much for your assistance. (199)

TRANSCRIPTION CHECKPOINT

293 To: Branch Traffic Clerks.

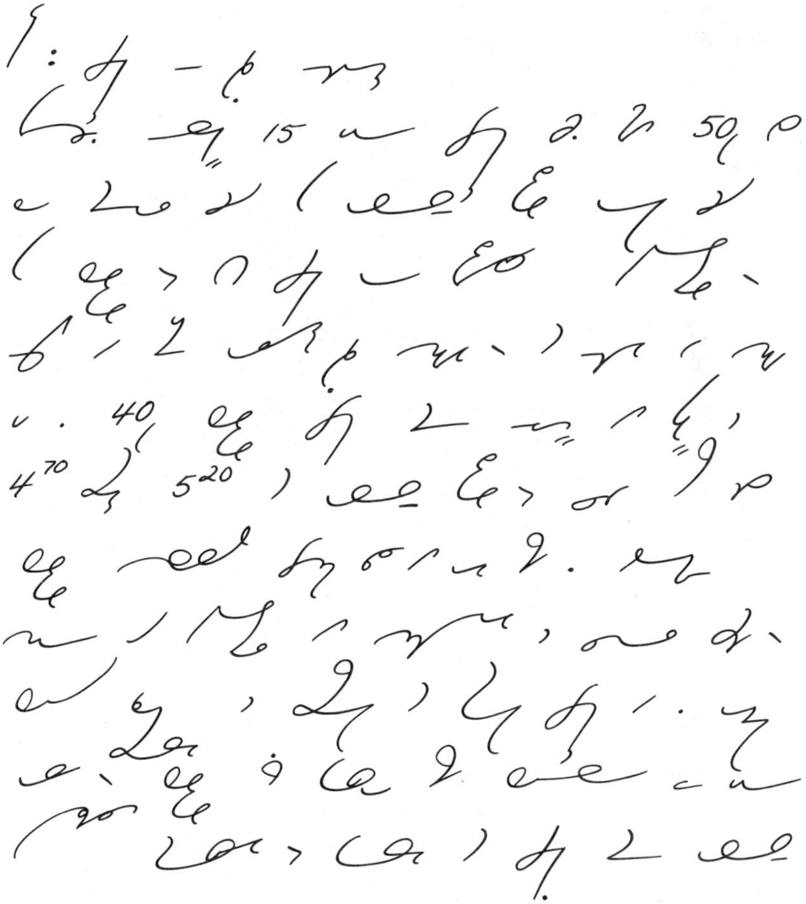

(214)

294 ▶ Memo to Systems and Procedures.

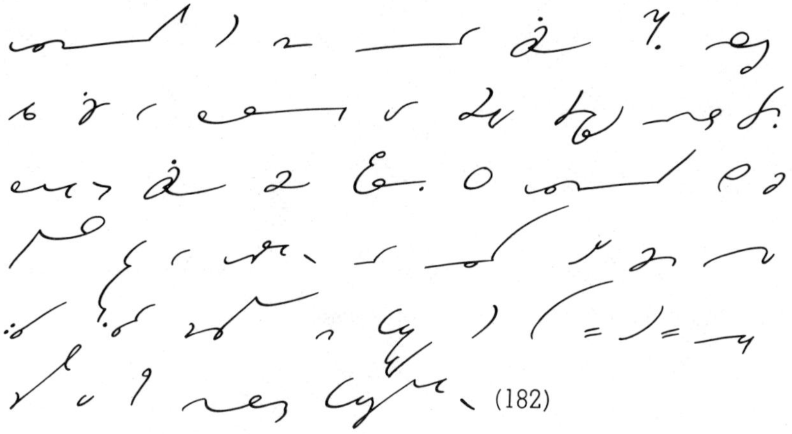

(182)

295▸ Air and Marine Travel Service, Mayfair Hotel, 810 Locust Street, St. Louis, Missouri 63101.

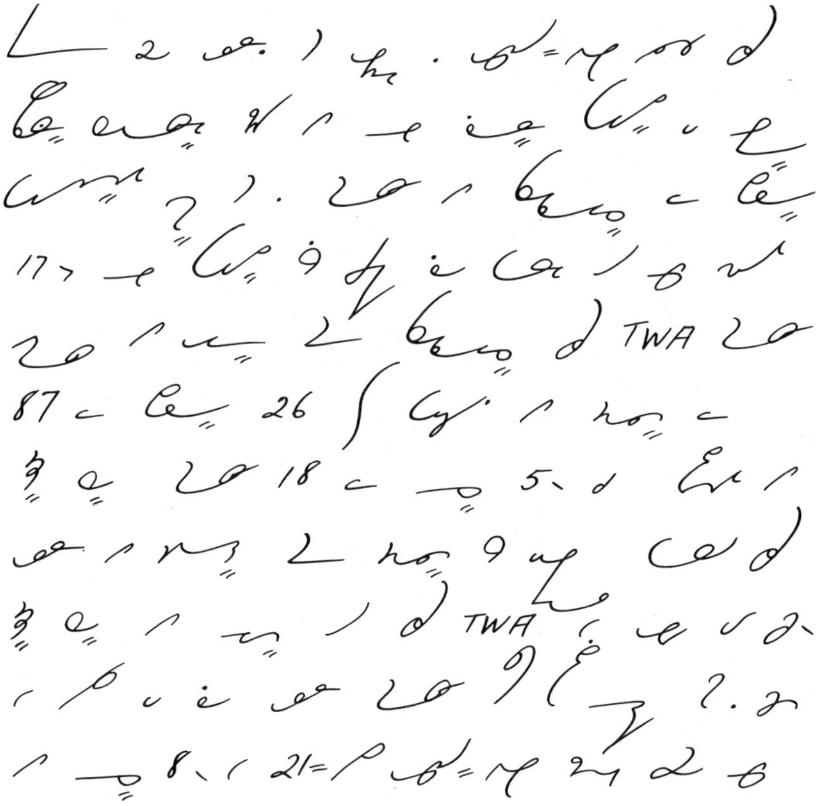

(175)

TRANSCRIPTION PACER

296 ▸ To: Ralph C. Akin, Sales Manager. 8

19
29
39
48
59
70
82
94
103
113
123
134
147
150

PART THREE Specialized DICTATION AND TRANSCRIPTION

Part Three, consisting of Lessons 61 to 80, deals with specialized types of secretarial positions. You will become acquainted with the types of material and many of the terms and expressions that are peculiar to four specialized areas of professional and business activity.

UNIT	SPECIALIZATION	EMPLOYER
13	Medicine	Herbert L. Kane, M.D.
14	Science and Technology	Bruno C. Haun, Ph.D.
15	Law	William G. Mancini
16	International Trade	Paul J. Vetter

You will not be expected to qualify as one of these specialized secretaries after one unit of instruction. However, you can –

1▸ Gain some insight into the nature and significance of each secretarial position so that you can decide whether you want to prepare for one of them.

2▸ Learn to recognize, spell, and use appropriately an extensive list of specialized terms and to some extent gain some insight into the nature of specialized vocabulary.

3▸ Develop some proficiency in writing special shorthand forms for frequently used specialized terms.

The practice of medicine is more than an honored profession; it is business in action. In the office of the physician, attention must be given to collections, expenses, public relations, communications, and other procedures and practices that are of concern to all business offices. Thus, the medical secretary is an important member of the medical team—doctor, nurse, secretary, and laboratory technician. The physician, the captain of the team, needs a specialized secretary so that he can confidently delegate responsibility for most nonmedical office activities and many semitechnical medical functions. Only when he is assisted by a competent medical secretary can the physician devote the maximum time to professional activities directly related to the examination and treatment of patients.

The secretary in the physician's office is expected to perform the same business duties as a qualified secretary in a typical business office. In addition, she must have (1) a fundamental grasp of medical etymology, (2) competence in processing unit

13

medical records and forms,
(3) skill in secretarial procedures and techniques
hat characterize the spe-
cialized scope of her work,
(4) an empathetic under-
tanding of people, partic-
larly sick people, and
(5) personal qualities of a
ery high standard.

MEDICINE

Secretarial Assignment

The objective of this unit is to familiarize you with frequently used medical word beginnings and word endings, with emphasis on compounding and combining word elements, and the function of the various word elements. Study the following list of word beginnings and word endings that are likely to arise frequently in medical dictation.

WORD BEGINNINGS

Element and Meaning		Illustration
Ab-	Away from, off	**abduct**
Ad-	To, toward	**adduct**
Adeno-	Gland	**adenopathy**
Aort-	Aorta	**aortic**
Arterio-	Artery	**arteriogram**
Auto-	Self	**autopsy**
Bi-	Two	**bifocal**
De-	Down, from	**delirium**
Dys-	Bad, difficult	**dystrophy**
Entero-	Intestines	**enterograph**
Ex-	Out, away from	**exhale**
Inter-	Between	**intercostal**
Intra-	Within	**intravenous**
Neuro-	Nerve	**neurosis**
Para-	Beside, beyond	**paracentesis**

Element	Meaning	Illustration	
Peri-	Around	**pericardium**	
Pheno-	Show	**phenomenon**	
Phlebo-	Vein	**phlebitis**	
Physio-	Nature	**physiologist**	
Post-	After, behind	**posterior**	
Pre-	Before	**preoperative**	
Re-	Back, again	**respiration**	
Sub-	Under, near	**subconscious**	

WORD ENDINGS

Element	Meaning	Illustration	
-edema	Swelling	**myxedema**	
-graph	Instrument for recording	**cardiograph**	
-itis	Inflammation of	**nephritis**	
-logy	Science, study of	**neurology**	
-oid	Like, resembling	**ethmoid**	
-oma	Tumor, swelling	**carcinoma**	
-ose	Carbohydrate	**glucose**	
-osis	Process, disease of	**neurosis**	
-pathy	Suffering, disease	**osteopathy**	
-scope	Instrument for seeing	**microscope**	
-tome	Cutting instrument	**myotome**	
-tomy	Cutting into	**tonsillectomy**	

lesson

61 MEDICAL SPEED BUILDER

SPECIALIZED TERMINOLOGY

Uses of Weights and Measures

Metric measures are used by those in the medical profession. Metric units are formed by combining the words *meter* (distance), *gram* (weight), and *liter* (capacity) with six numerical prefixes—*milli-* (one-thousandth), *centi-* (one-hundredth), *deci-* (one-tenth), *deca-* (ten), *hecto-* (one hundred), and *kilo-* (one thousand).

Length (*meter*)

Outline	Metric Unit	Abbreviation	Meters
	kilometer	km.	1,000.
	hectometer	hm.	100.
	decameter	dkm.	10.
	meter	m.	1.
	decimeter	dm.	.1
	centimeter	cm.	.01
	millimeter	mm.	.001

Weight (*gram*)

Outline	Metric Unit	Abbreviation	Grams
	kilogram	kg.	1,000.
	hectogram	hg.	100.

Weight (*gram*)

Outline	Metric Unit	Abbreviation	Grams
	decagram	dkg.	10.
	gram	gm.	1.
	decigram	dg.	.1
	centigram	cg.	.01
	milligram	mg.	.001

Capacity (*liter*)

Outline	Metric Unit	Abbreviation	Liters
	kiloliter	kl.	1,000.
	hectoliter	hl.	100.
	decaliter	dkl.	10.
	liter	l.	1.
	deciliter	dl.	.1
	centiliter	cl.	.01
	milliliter	ml.	.001

Check your understanding of metric weights and measures by transcribing the following sentences, preferably at the typewriter.

1 

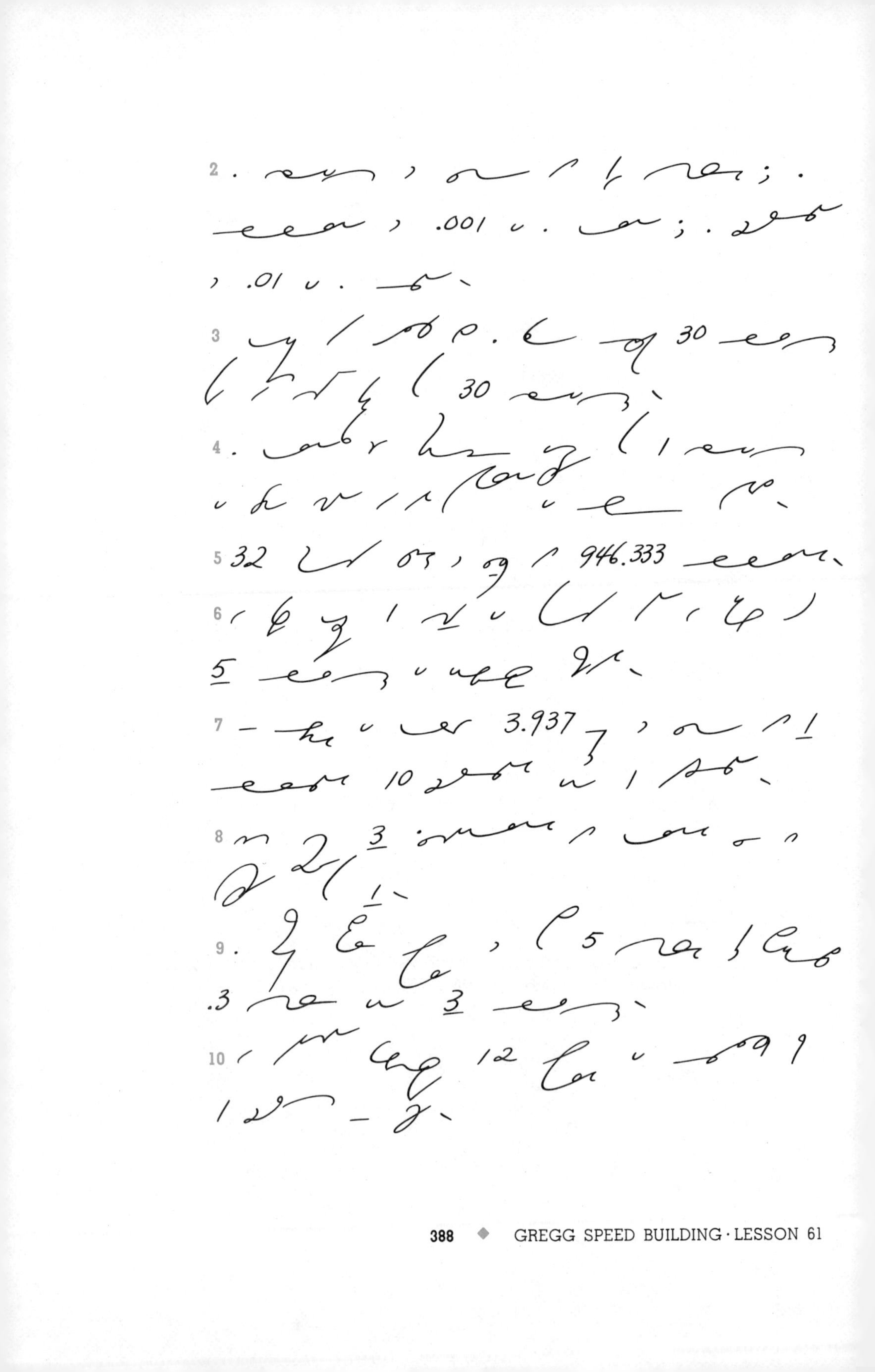

2.

3

4.

5

6

7

8

9.

10

Vocabulary Preview

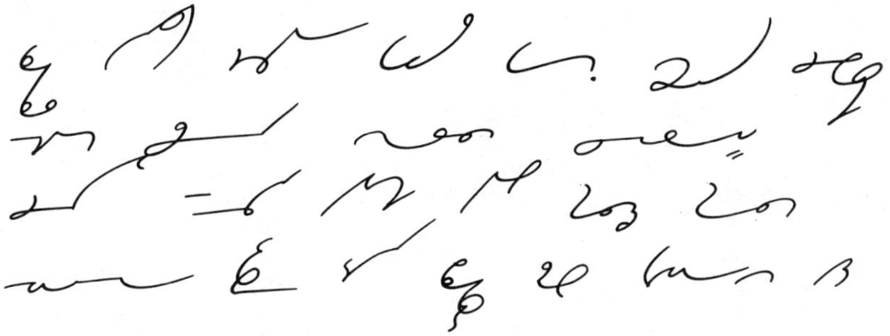

Surgery, tentative, schedule, promptly, progressing, confirmed, semiprivate, instruction, examined, clinic, Amarillo, symptoms, intermittent, discomfort, duration, frequency, flexion, normal, spasm, sustained, exercises, X rays, pathological, to us.

Sustained Dictation

297 Miss Catharine M. Talbott, 1240 24th Street, Lubbock, Texas 79406.

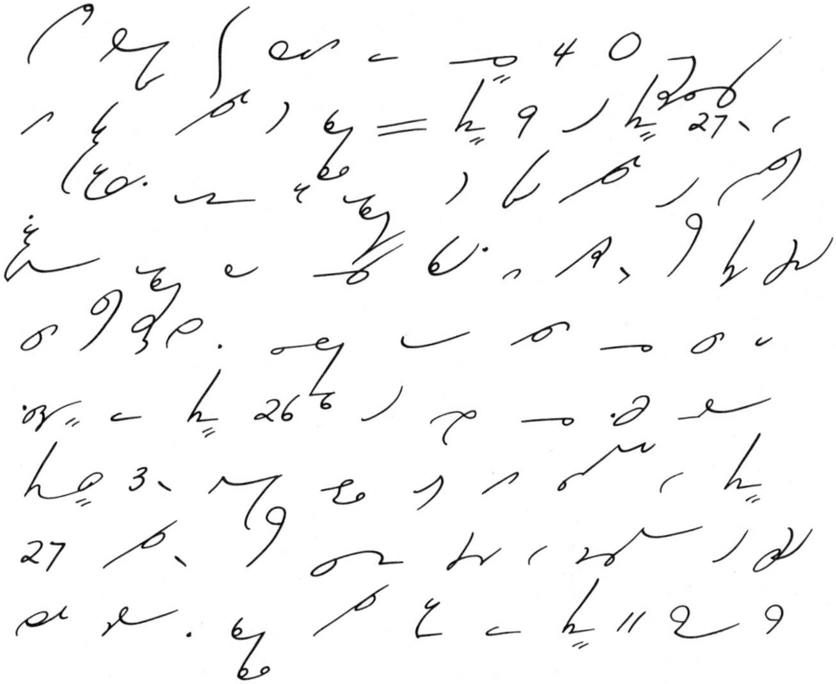

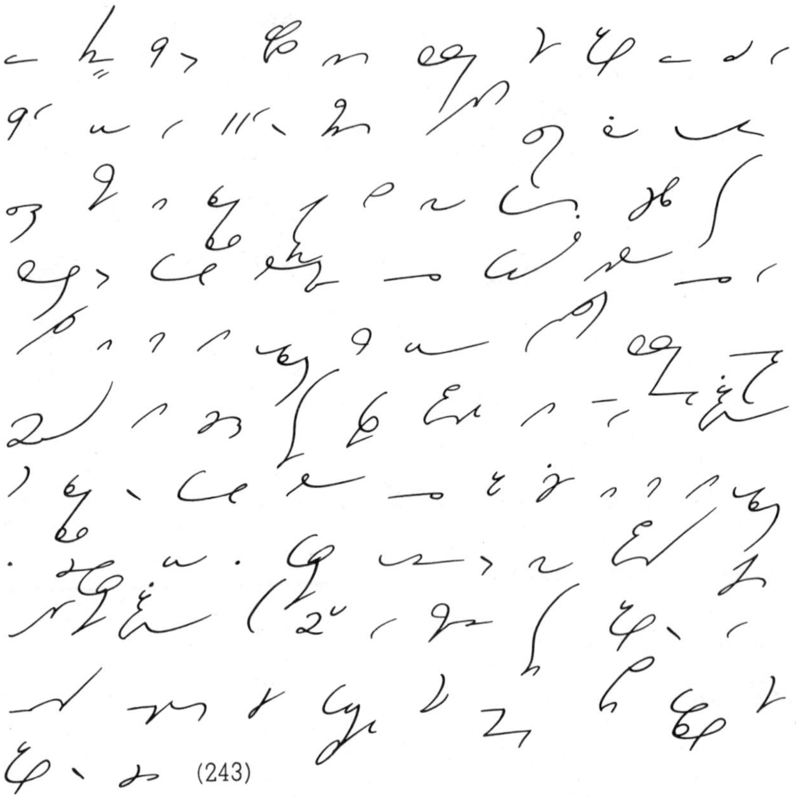

(243)

298 Dr. Warren C. Smith, Medical Plaza, Amarillo, Texas 79103.

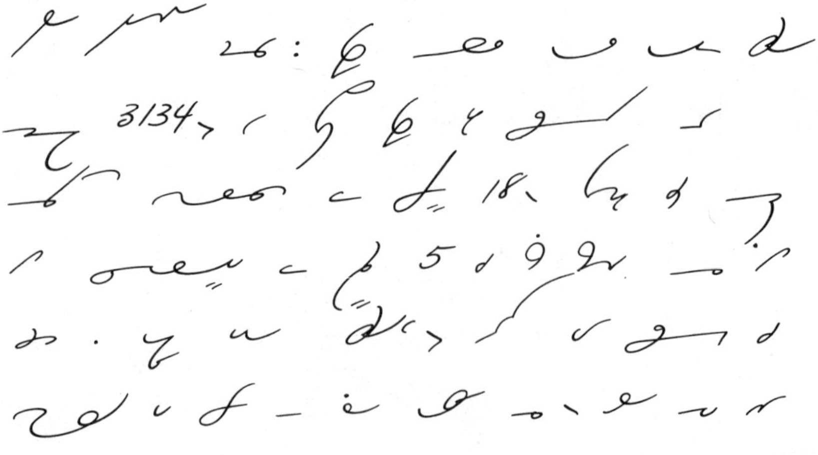

(217)

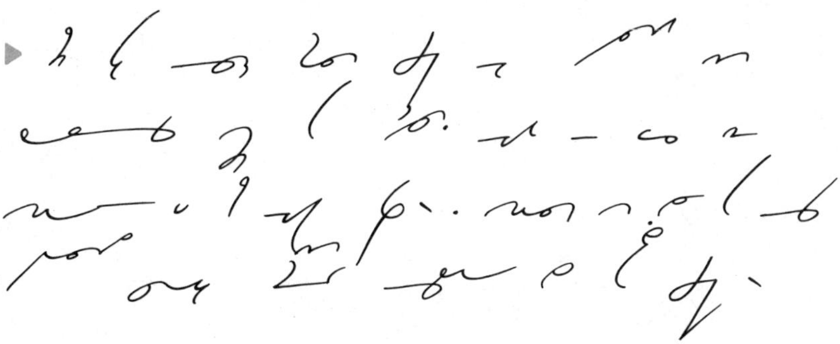

Lesson 62

MEDICAL SPEED BUILDER

SPECIALIZED TERMINOLOGY

Outline	Word and Pronunciation	Meaning
	phlebotomy fle-bot'o-me	The opening of a vein for bloodletting.
	phlebosis fle-bo'sis	Inflammation or irritation of a vein.
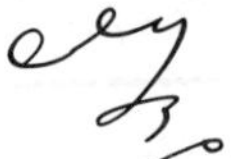	arteriovenous ar-te're-o-ve'nus	Both arterial and venous.
	enterectomy en'ter-ek'to-me	The excision of a part of the intestine.
	enteritis en'ter-i'tis	Inflammation of the intestine.
	adenoma ad'e-no'mah	An epithelial tumor with a glandlike structure.
	adenoid ad'e-noid	Resembling a gland.
	aortic a-or'tik	Of or pertaining to the aorta.
	aorta a-or'tah	The large vessel arising from the left ventricle and distributing blood to every part of the body.

TRANSCRIPTION SPEED BUILDER

Vocabulary Preview

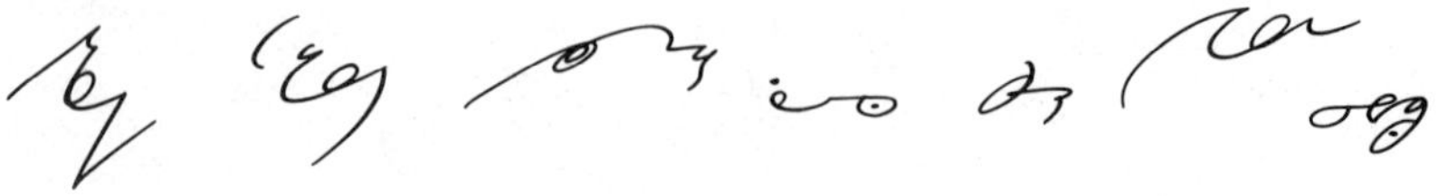

Discharged, postoperative, diagnosis, hernia, sinus, temperature, anaesthesia, recurrence, complications, outpatient, superficial, metabolism, oxygen, autopsy, hemorrhage, trauma, fracture, cranial, institution.

Sustained Dictation

299 Dr. Alvin R. Christian, 411 Main Street, Big Spring, Texas 79722.

(143)

300 ▸ Lone Star Insurance Company, 141 South Sixth Street, Fort Worth, Texas 76117.

(100)

301 ▸ Mrs. Wilma A. Whiter, 432 Jackson Street, Dallas, Texas 77414.

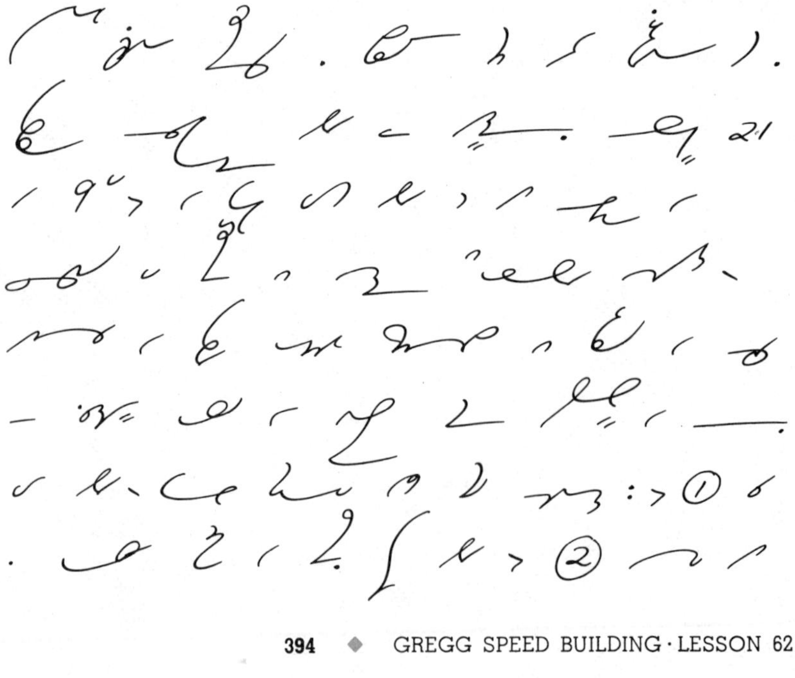

(170)

302 ▸ Mr. Wesley J. Higgins, 1419 Oak Lane, Galveston, Texas 77551.

(132)

303▸ Mr. Henry E. Barnett, District Director, Federal Bureau of Investigation, Room 322, Federal Building, Dallas, Texas 75200.

(94)

304▸ Miss Emily Weber, Oakdale Convalescent Home, 766 Oakdale Terrace, Norman, Oklahoma 73069.

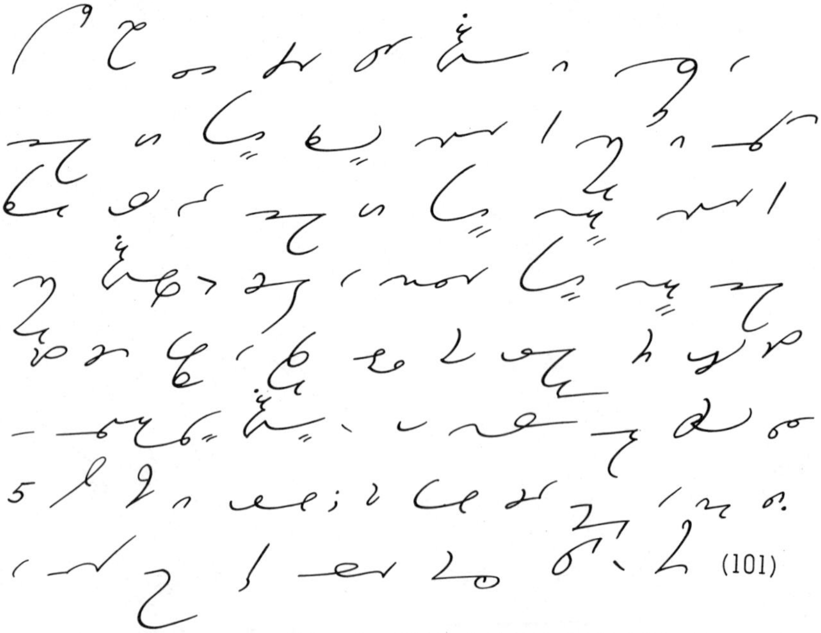

(101)

MEDICAL SPEED BUILDER

Lesson 63

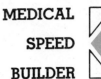

SPECIALIZED TERMINOLOGY

Outline	Word and Pronunciation	Meaning
	**neurologist** nu-rol'o-jist	An expert in the treatment of nervous diseases.
	**neuroma** nu-ro'mah	A tumor made up of nerve cells and fibers.
	**orthopedic** or'tho-pe'dik	Pertaining to the correction of deformities.
	**orthopedist** or'tho-pe'dist	An orthopedic surgeon.
	**physiologic** fiz'e-o-loj'ik	Normal; not pathologic.
	**physiological** fiz'e-o-loj'i-kal	Pertaining to physiology.
	**dysemia** dis-e'me-ah	Deterioration of the blood.
	**dysentery** dis'en-ter'e	Disorder marked by inflammation of the intestines.
	**bronchitis** brong-ki'tis	Inflammation of the bronchial tubes.
	**bronchus** brong'kus	Either one of the two main branches of the trachea.

TRANSCRIPTION SPEED BUILDER

Vocabulary Preview

Consultant's, diagnosis, intercostal, epilepsy, grand mal, seizures, to focus, irritability, Rorschach, epileptic, neurotic, anxiety, negativism, external, integration, reality; confusion, apperception, dynamic, corroborate, immaturity, hostility, realism, intellectual, significant, protocol, similarity, components, predominating, strength, impending, psychosis.

Sustained Dictation

305 ▸ Dr. Harold C. Shelley, First National Bank Building, Dallas, Texas 75201.

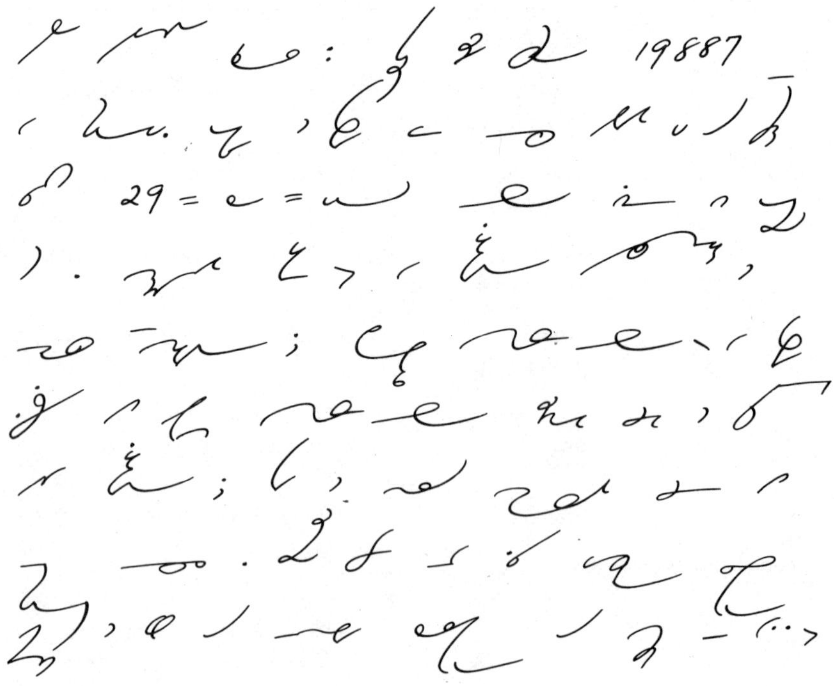

(520)

306 ▸ INCIDENCE OF SURGERY IN DIABETES.

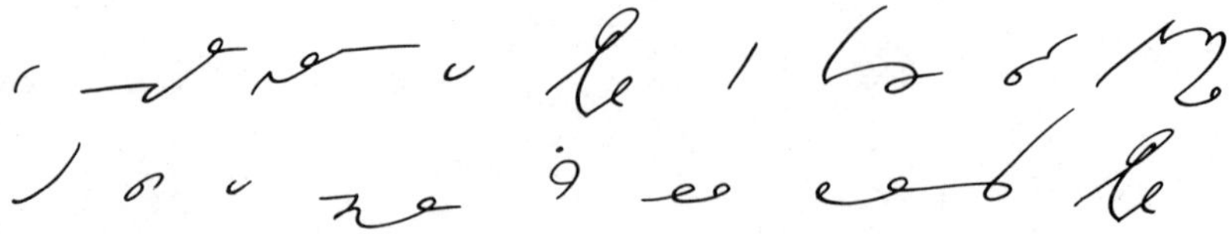

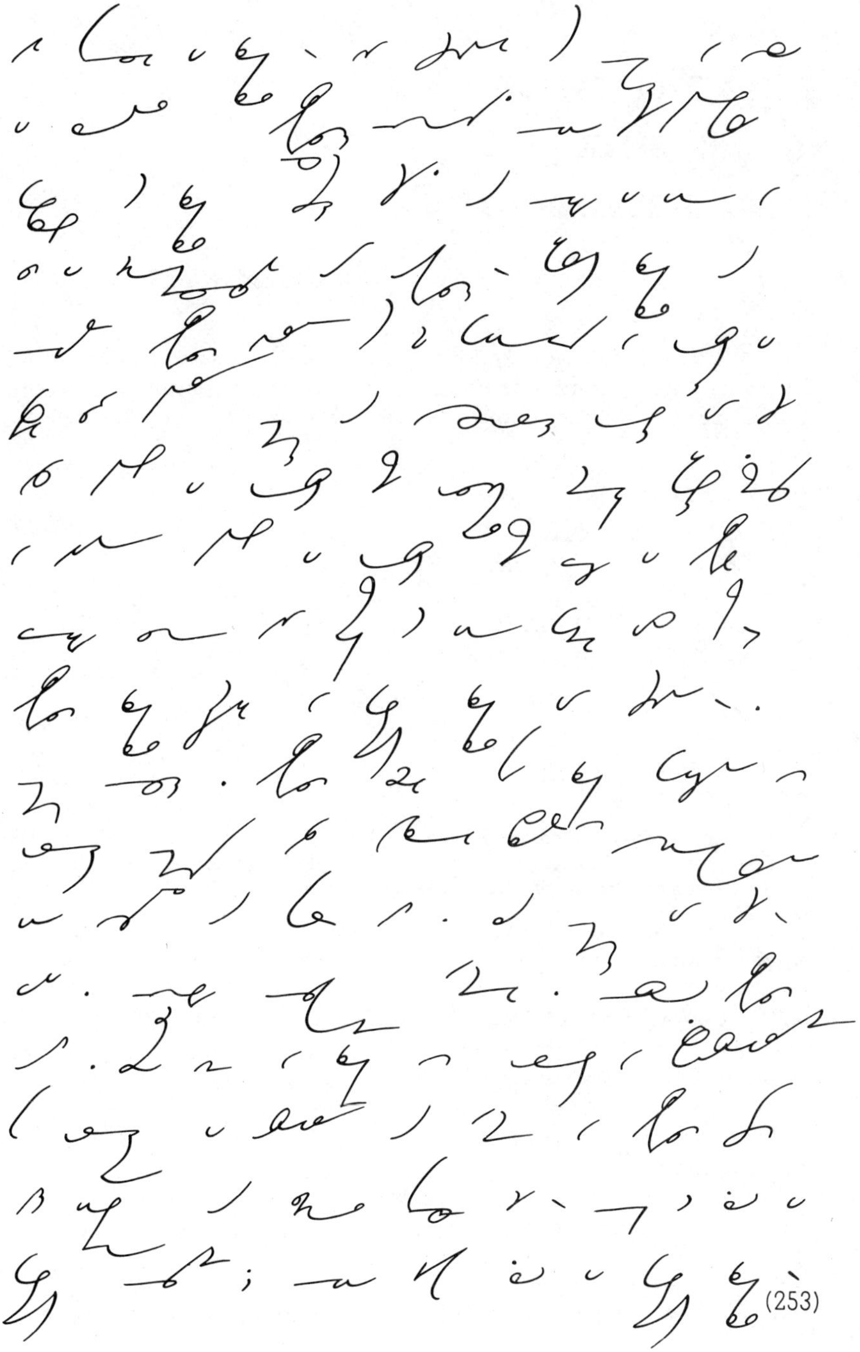

(253)

lesson

64 DICTATION SPEED BUILDER

SPEED-ESCALATION PRACTICE

Practice the vocabulary preview before working on the Speed Builder. The first minute is counted at 70 words a minute; the second minute, at 80; the third minute at 90; and the remainder of the letter, at 100.

Vocabulary Preview

Psychological, evaluation, schizophrenic, reaction, ulcers, intelligence, performance, Multiphasic, validating, comprehend, personality, Rorschach, anatomic, embodied, circumstances, identify, disorder, depressive.

Speed Forcing

(1 Minute at 70)

307 Dear Doctor Green: This is my report on Mr. Gray, whom you referred to me for psychological/ evaluation on the basis of your initial impression of schizophrenic reaction//latent.

The patient is under the impression that he came to the hospital because of///ulcers. He did not object to the interviews and tests that the psychological unit conducted. (1)

(1 Minute at 80)

In his first interview he stated that he finds it difficult to get along with people, especially men,/in almost all situations. He seems to feel that he is often unnecessarily "picked on" or discriminated//against by the men with whom he comes in contact, especially in a work situation.

On the///intelligence scale, the patient scored as follows: verbal, 94; performance, 90; full scale, 92. (2)

(1 Minute at 90)

These scores indicate an intellectual level within the average or low-average range. There is nothing/ unusual in the patient's performance on this test, and it is felt that the results represent a valid index of his present//capabilities.

On the Minnesota Multiphasic administered by our experts, five of the nine scales show scores above ///normal limits. A deviant score on the validating F scale, however, makes the whole profile very questionable. (3)

(2 Minutes at 100)

It is probable that the patient is not intelligent enough to comprehend many of the test items. Despite these factors, it is/felt that the results of this test do suggest a fairly severe degree of personality disturbance.

The patient gave a total//of six responses on the Rorschach test. Four of these were anatomic percepts, and none of the responses embodied particularly///good form. At the conclusion of the free association and inquiry, the cards were all spread out in front of the patient for testing of (4) the limits. He proceeded to try to arrange several of the cards into a combination to establish some type of form. In testing/the limits, the patient was able to see all the suggested percepts quite easily. This whole combination of circumstances is//somewhat unusual; and despite the patient's ability to identify all the suggested responses, it is felt that this record///represents a serious disorder. There may be a strong depressive drive that could be contributing to this disorder. Sincerely yours, (5)

TRANSCRIPTION REINFORCEMENT PRACTICE

Vocabulary Preview

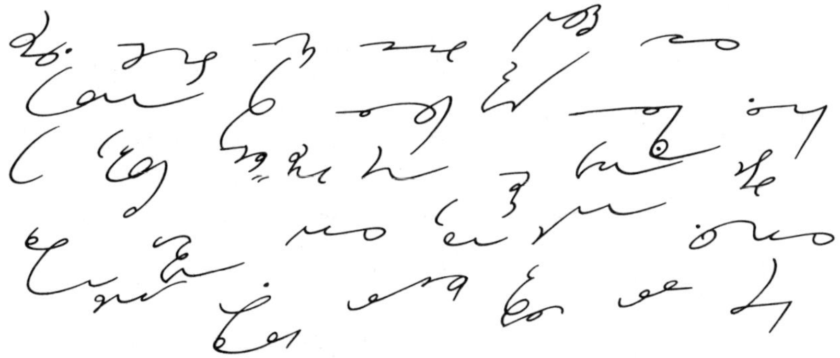

Fascinating, insignificant, unconscious, numbness, drowsy, coma, bilateral, Babinskis, negative, suspected, meningeal, hemorrhage, burr, postoperatively, seizures, focal, incisions, pathology, stiffness, cerebellar, occipital, trauma, posterior, subdural, hygroma, extraordinary, rehabilitation, reeducation, spastic, return, very much.

TRANSCRIPTION PACER

308 Dr. Joseph Foley, Department of Neurology, Boston City Hospital, Boston, Massachusetts 02116. 11 19

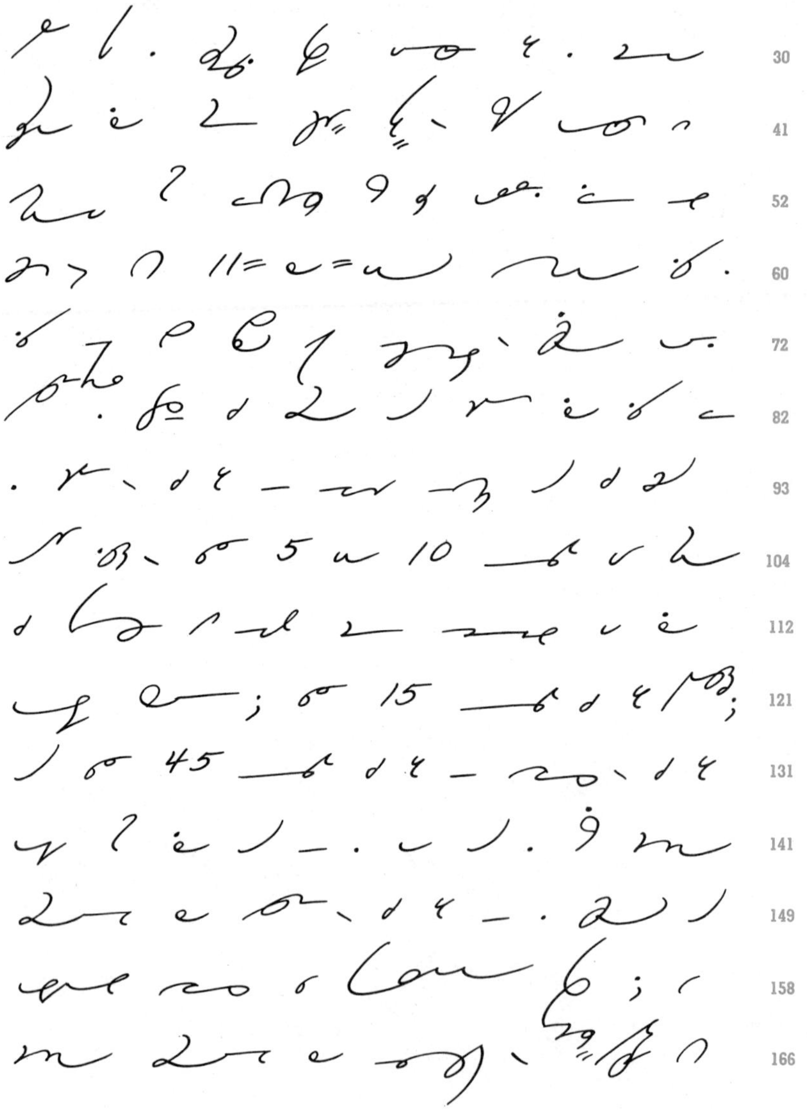

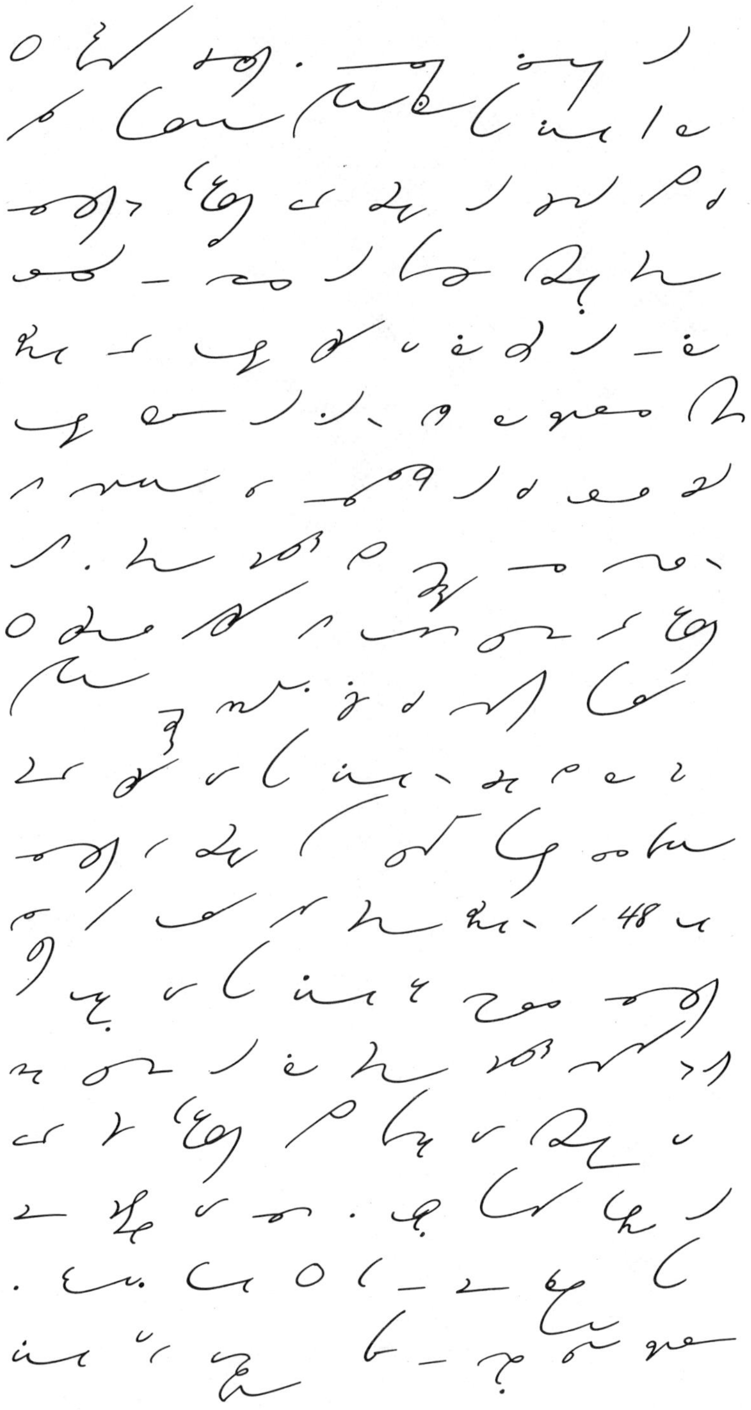

177
186
199
208
217
228
237
246
256
267
278
290
301
313
325
339
350
359
371

383
394
405
414
427
439
451
464
478
487
496
507
517
531
540
545

lesson

TRANSCRIPTION SPEED BUILDER 65

SUSTAINED SPEED BUILDER

The sustained speed builder is a medical case history and discharge summary dictated by Dr. Herbert L. Kane. Be sure to practice the vocabulary preview.

Vocabulary Preview

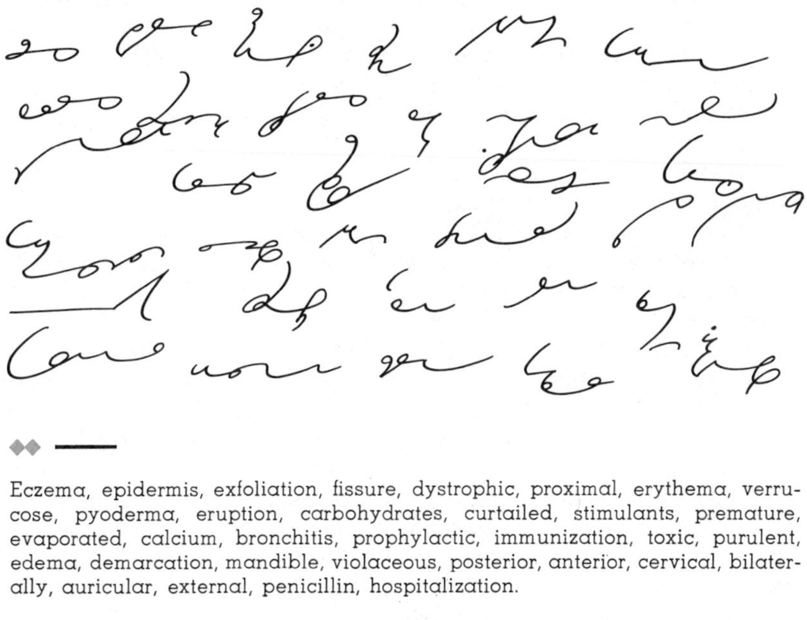

Eczema, epidermis, exfoliation, fissure, dystrophic, proximal, erythema, verrucose, pyoderma, eruption, carbohydrates, curtailed, stimulants, premature, evaporated, calcium, bronchitis, prophylactic, immunization, toxic, purulent, edema, demarcation, mandible, violaceous, posterior, anterior, cervical, bilaterally, auricular, external, penicillin, hospitalization.

Speed Builder

309 CASE HISTORY – William Wilson, File Number 3427.

Chief Complaint: Eczema.

Present Illness: The skin of both hands extending to the wrists has a rather pinkish[1] appearance with some areas of epidermis suggesting the appearance of the skin after exfoliation.[2] There is a scaly, crusted fissure patch between one or two of the fingers. The nails show considerable[3] dystrophic change, and one of them is partially detached in the proximal end. On the back is a diffused[4] erythema with mild scaling around the edge. On the lower half of the legs and part of the ankles, the[5] skin is quite thickened, showing verrucose patches covered with scales. The feet are quite moist and have a distinct odor.[6]

Treatment: The treatment for this condition will be along general lines toward building up the patient's resistance.[7] Since the pyoderma seems to be a very important factor in the eruption, the teeth and tonsils should[8] be looked over for a possible focal point of infection; and if such is found, it should be eliminated.[9]

A diet low in carbohydrates and without fried foods is prescribed. Smoking should be curtailed, and the patient[10] should discontinue the use of coffee and other stimulants. Injections of vaccine to buoy up the[11] patient's resistance against infection are to be given. (230)

310 DISCHARGE SUMMARY

History: This was the first admission of this 11-year-old white male, who entered with the chief complaints of[1] fever and a swollen face, six hours' duration. He had been perfectly well until three days before, when he[2] had developed a cold. The evening before admission his temperature was 101.8[3] degrees. On the morning of admission the left cheek was noted to be swollen and reddened. The left eye was noted[4] to be red, and there was a pus-like discharge. The child refused foods and fluids.

Past History: He was a[5] premature baby born at seven months, weighting five pounds, four ounces; hospitalized for two months. His formula was[6] evaporated milk and water. Calcium salts were added to the formula. Two months before admission,[7] he had had bronchitis. He had received his course of prophylactic immunization.

Family History: One[8] of the oldest children had a sore throat at the time of admission.

Physical examination: Temperature,[9] 104 degrees; pulse, 160, respiration, 30. He was well-developed and[10] well-nourished, drowsy, and toxic. Face was quite tender. The right eye showed slight swelling. The left eye was swollen. There was[11] a moderate purulent discharge. There was much brawny edema over the face with poor demarcation,[12] extending over the left cheek and the ramus of the left mandible to the neck and ear. The overlying skin[13] was hot and red. Several hours after admission it became violaceous. There were enlarged, tender[14] posterior and anterior cervical nodes bilaterally, more so on the left. There was a left anterior[15] auricular node. The external canal of the left ear was red. The throat was slightly red. The neck was[16] supple. Chest was clear except for a few loud rhonchi. The abdomen was not remarkable. The heart was negative.[17]

Progress Notes: He was treated with 600,000 units of penicillin a day. The temperature fell[18] to normal in the first 24 hours. The swelling and redness rapidly subsided.

The patient ate[19] heartily and appeared well during the last three days of hospitalization. He was then discharged to his home and[20] to the care of his local doctor. (407)

TRANSCRIPTION CHECKPOINT

Vocabulary Preview

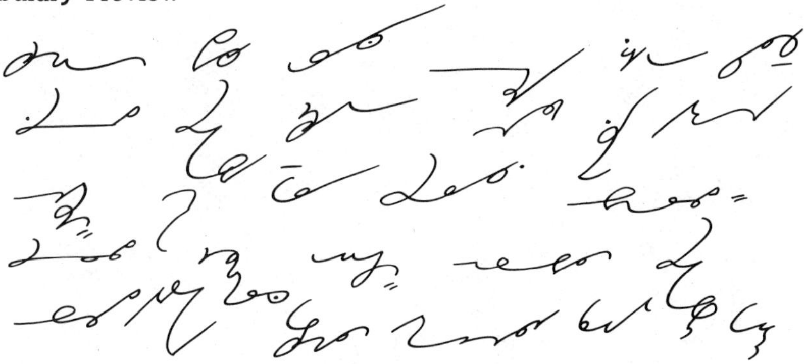

Psychologic, appetite, radiated, manifested, hostility, adequate, vehemently, verbalized, suicidal, continuation, behavior, disorganized, Multiphasic, questionable, interpreted, validating, masculinity-femininity, schizophrenia, Rorschach, unrealistic, verbalizations, markedly, disturbed, prepsychotic, to fluctuate, periods, processes.

TRANSCRIPTION PACER

311 CLINICAL RECORD PSYCHOLOGICAL DATA 8

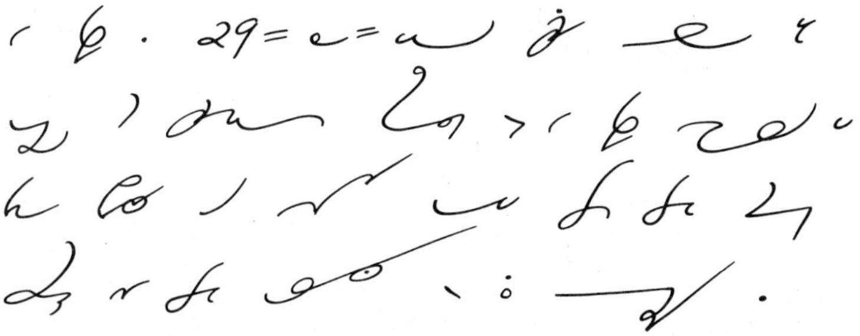

17

30

40

50

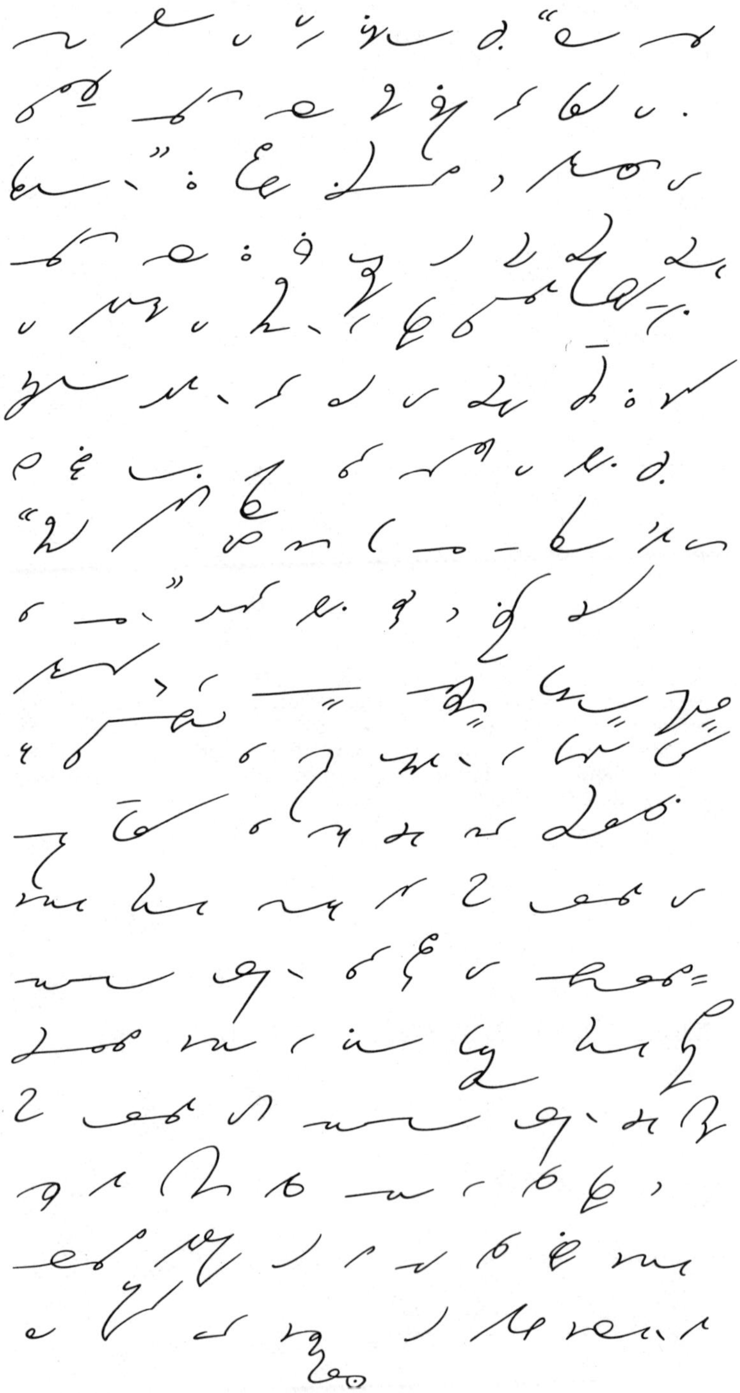

60
71
82
94
102
115
129
142
155
168
182
194
203
213
224
235
246
257
270

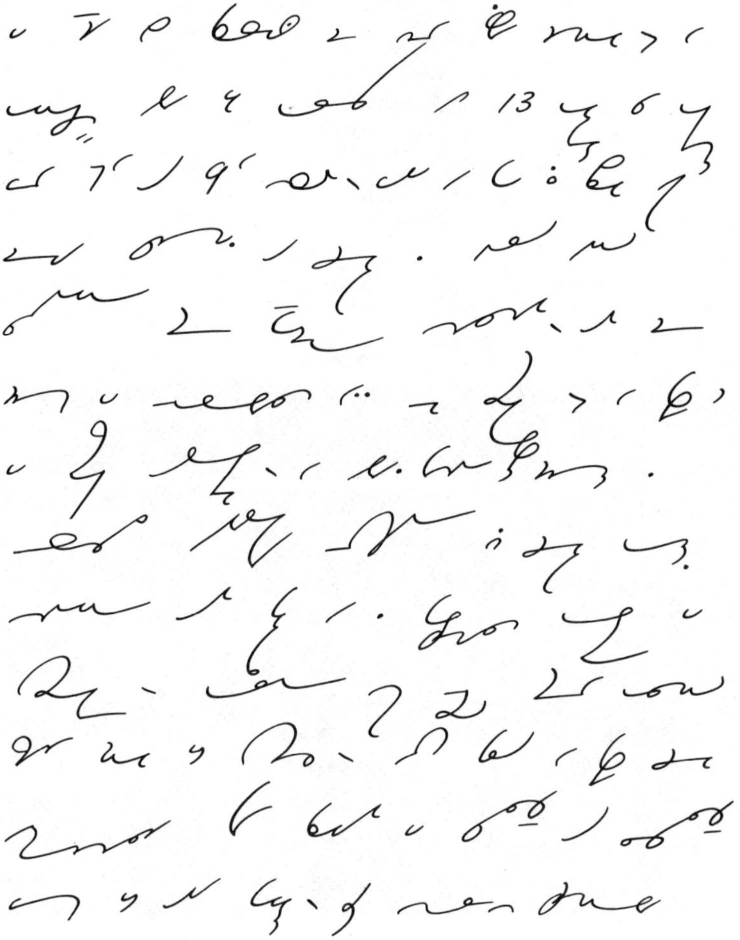

283
296
310
321
332
347
358
369
379
389
403
414
428

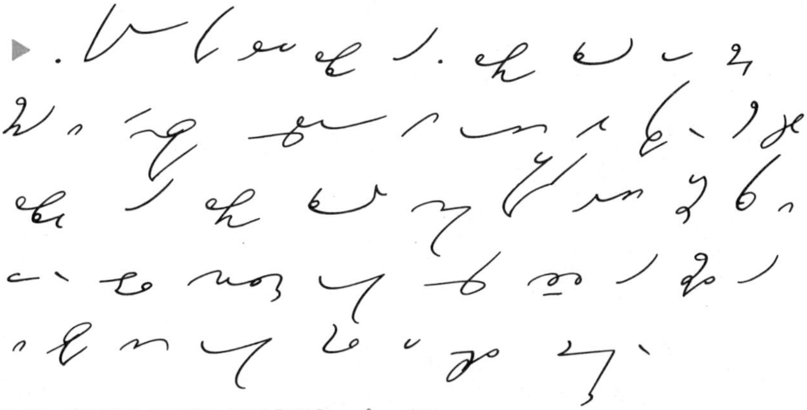

Advances in the fields of science and technology have created a need for different kinds of knowledge and skill and talent. The success of the work accomplished in different technological fields depends in no small measure on the availability of trained specialists, such as the data analyst and the systems engineer, and supporting personnel, namely, technical secretaries.

The technical secretary must be thoroughly trained in basic secretarial skills, like any other secretary. In addition, however, she must possess other specialized skills and abilities. She must have an understanding of technical terminology; a facility in processing and retrieving technical data; an ability to record technical dictation and to transcribe it; an understanding of statistical tables, charts, and graphs; and an appreciation of the role of technology in the world in which we live.

Only by possessing qualifications such as these can the technical secretary complete assignments accurately and efficiently.

unit 14

SCIENCE AND TECHNOLOGY

Secretarial Assignment

The objective of this unit is to familiarize you with dictation that samples scientific and technical vocabulary. Study and expand upon the following list of abbreviations that appear frequently in technical literature.

ABBREVIATIONS FOR TECHNICAL TERMS

air horsepower	air hp	freezing point	fp
alternating-current (adj.)	a-c	fusion point	fnp
ampere-hour	amp-hr	gallons per minute	gpm
Angstrom unit	A	gram	gm
antilogarithm	antilog	greatest common divisor	gcd
atomic weight	at wt	horsepower	hp
avoirdupois	avdp	indicated horsepower	ihp
azimuth	az	inside diameter	ID
Baumé	Bé	kilograms per cubic meter	kg per cu m; Kg/m^3
boiling point	bp	kilowatt-hour	kwhr; kw-hr
centigram	cg	low-pressure (adj.)	l-p
centimeter	cm	mean effective pressure	mep
centimeter-gram-second	cgs	molecular weight	mol wt
cosecant	csc	National Electrical Code	NEC
cubic feet per minute	cfm	outside diameter	OD
decibel	db	parts per million	ppm
degree centigrade	C	pounds per square foot	psf
degree Fahrenheit	F	reactive kilovolt-ampere	kvar
degree Kelvin	K	revolutions per minute	rpm
degree Reaumur	R	root mean square	rms
direct-current (adj.)	d-c	specific gravity	sp gr
electromotive force	emf	specific heat	sp ht
feet per minute	fpm	standard	std

temperature	temp	volt	v
tensile strength	ts	watt	w

NOTE: If technical abbreviations occur frequently, the periods are usually dropped; but in ordinary work, the periods are usually retained. In either case, the same abbreviation is used for the singular and plural (*g* for *gram* or *grams*).

Check your understanding of technical abbreviations by transcribing the following sentences, preferably at the typewriter.

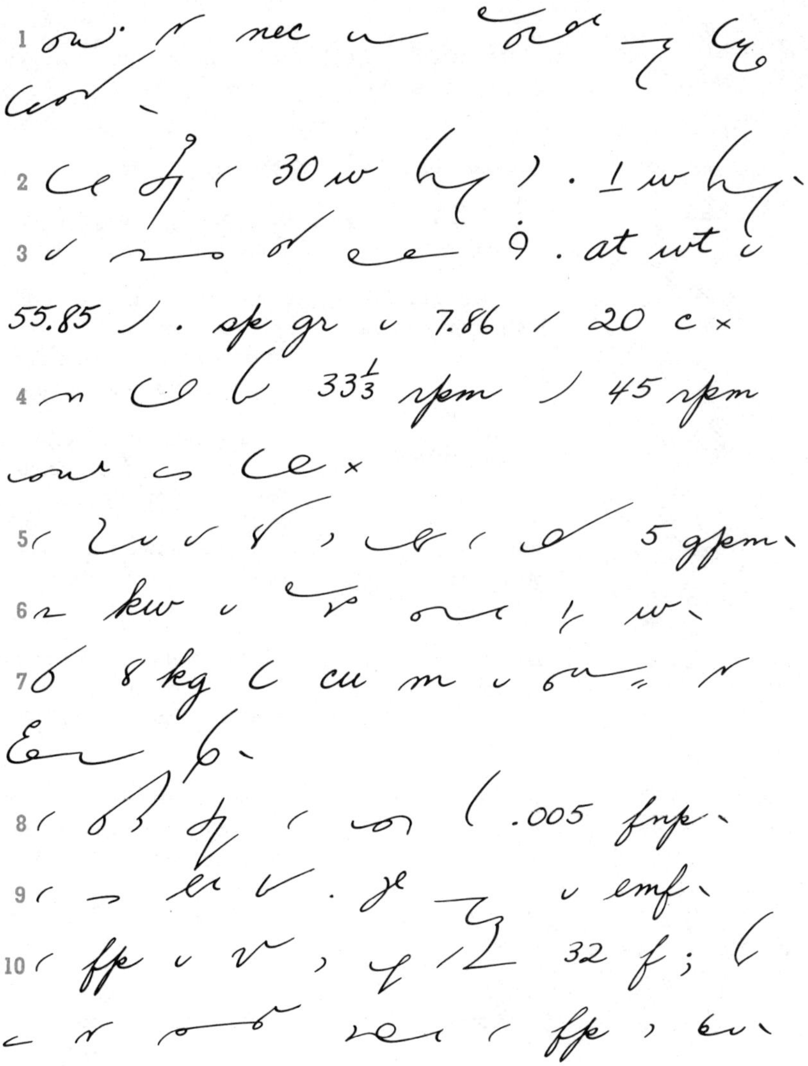

lesson

66 TECHNICAL SPEED BUILDER

SPECIALIZED TERMINOLOGY

To better understand the dictation in this lesson, you will need to study each of the following terms:

Outline	Word and Pronunciation	Meaning
	**hypothesis** **hi-poth'e-sis**	Tentative assumption for the explanation of certain facts.
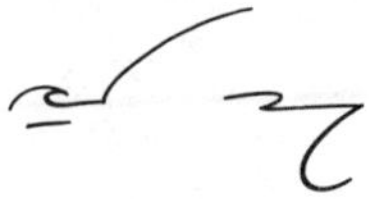	**quantum number** **kwan'tum num'ber**	One of the values or units of energy characteristic of the theory that radiation and absorption of energy take place in discrete quantities.
	**phlogiston** **flo-jis'ton**	The supposed principle of fire and combustion, discontinued with the discovery of oxygen.
	**valency** **va'len-se**	The power of a substance to combine with, or to affect, some other substance.
	**lepton** **lep'ton**	A charged or uncharged elementary particle having a mass of the same order or smaller than that of the electron.
	**neutrino** **nu-tri'no**	A hypothetical neutral electrical particle of matter existing along with protons in the atoms of most elements.
	**photon** **fo'ton**	A particle (quantum) of gamma radiation.
	**meson** **mes'on**	A heavy electron having a mass intermediate between that of an electron and that of a proton.

Vocabulary Preview

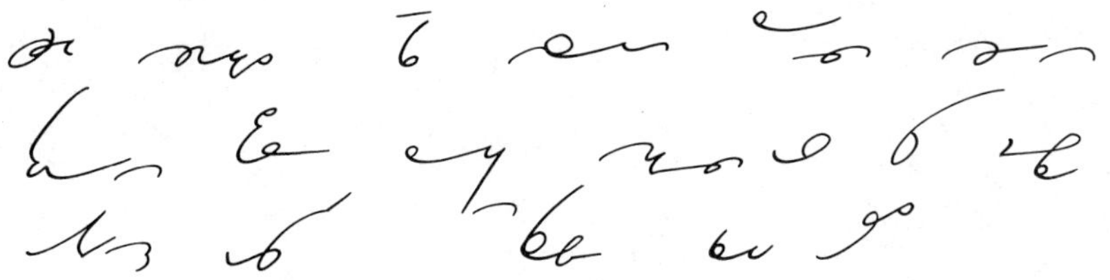

Science, curiosity, entropy, caloric, electronic, chemical, biological, experiment, illogical, cosmic ray, atom smasher, antiparticles, radiant, baryon, zero, entity.

Sustained Dictation

312 ASPECTS OF SCIENCE

(320)

313 MASS, ENERGY, AND MATTER

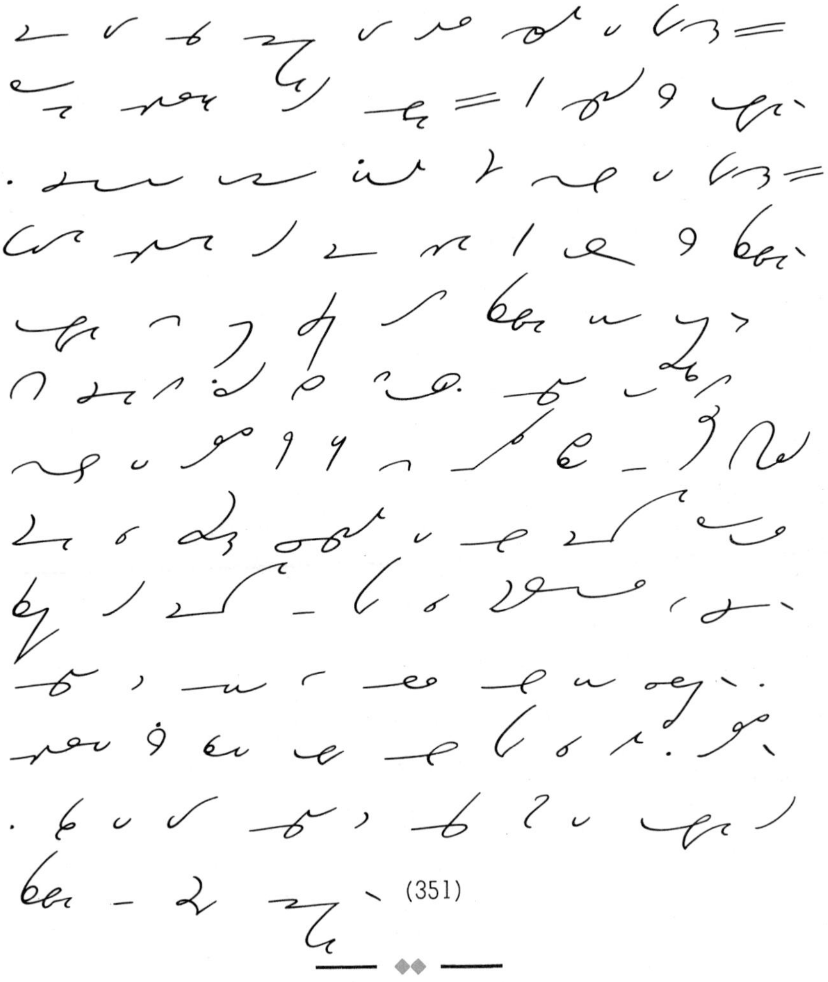

(351)

lesson

TECHNICAL SPEED BUILDER 67

SPECIALIZED TERMINOLOGY

Outline	Word and Pronunciation	Meaning
	biology bi-ol'o-je	The science of life.
	programmed pro'gramd	Arranged in a series of steps that follow one another according to a pre-established plan.
	analytical an-al-it'ik-l	Pertaining to analysis; separating into elements or component parts.
	component kom-po'nent	A constituent element or part.
	transistor trans-is'tor	Device having functions similar to vacuum tubes and used to amplify current.
	diode di'od	Vacuum tube containing two electrodes, which serve as a rectifier.
	rectifier rek'ti-fi'er	Something that makes or sets right; amends.
	germanium jer-ma'ne-um	A very rare white metal; symbol Ge.
	analogous a-nal'o-gus	Showing a likeness.
	cathode kath'od	The negative electrode or pole of a galvanic circuit.
	oscillate os'il-at	To swing backward and forward.

Vocabulary Preview

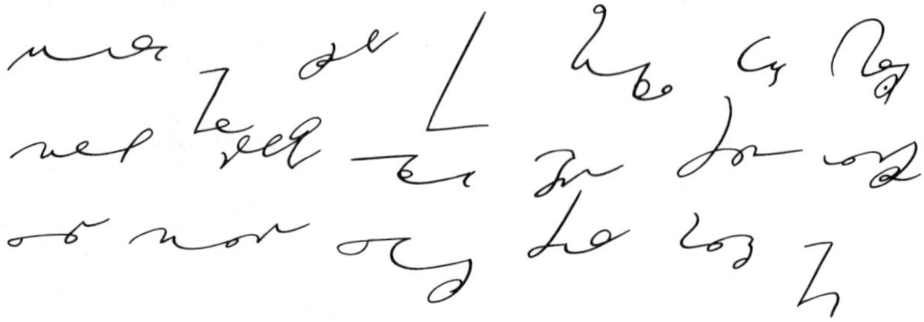

Tolerance, engineer, scientist, judgment, evolutionary process, differentiation, correlation, stereotyped, missiles, computer, vacuum, rectifier, emitter, collector, amplify, generate, frequency, injection.

Sustained Dictation

314 BIOLOGY AND ENGINEERING

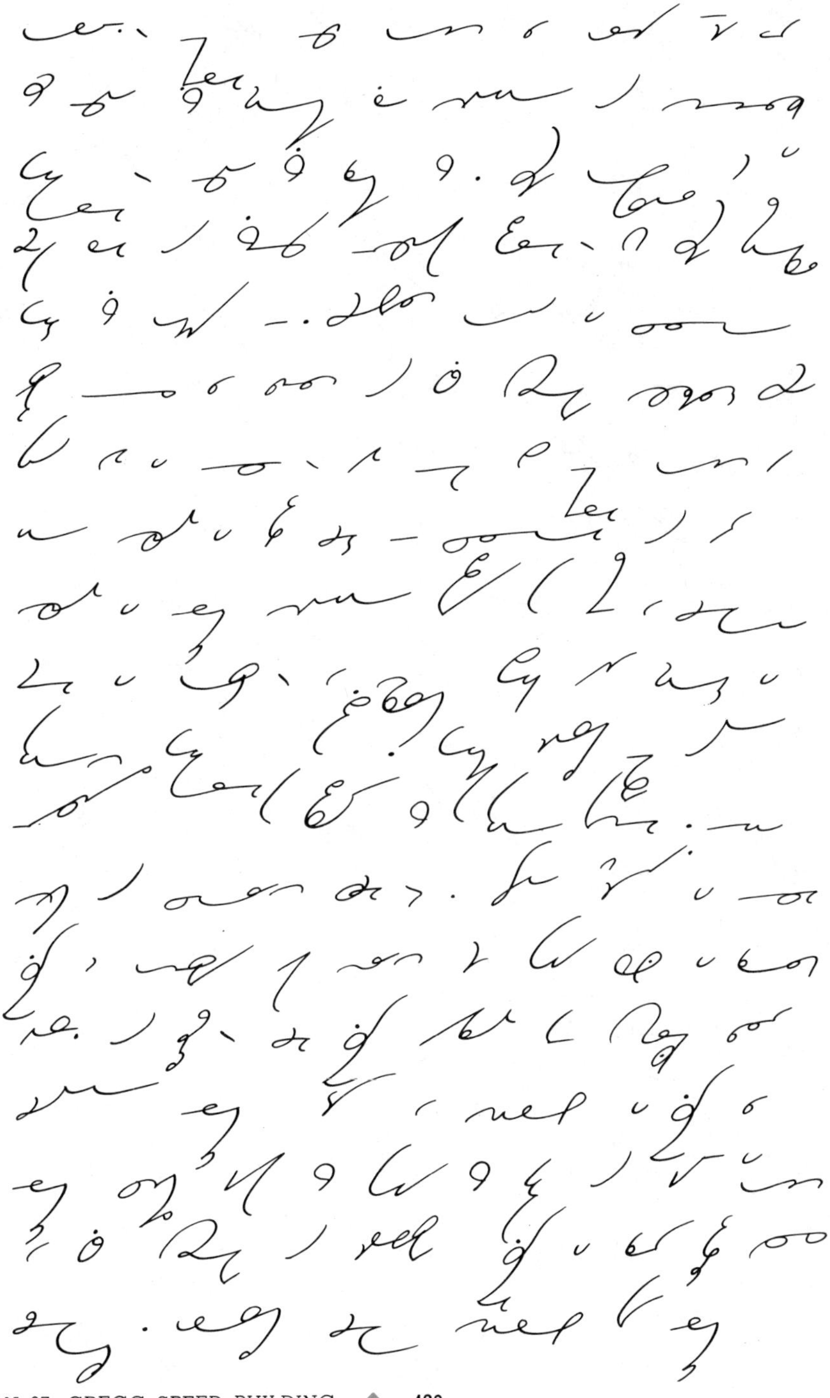

(487)

315 TRANSISTORS

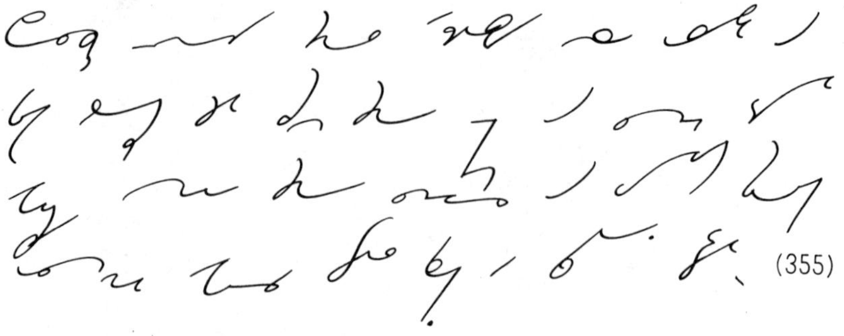

(355)

316▸ Memo to Arthur Williamson, Manager of Public Information.

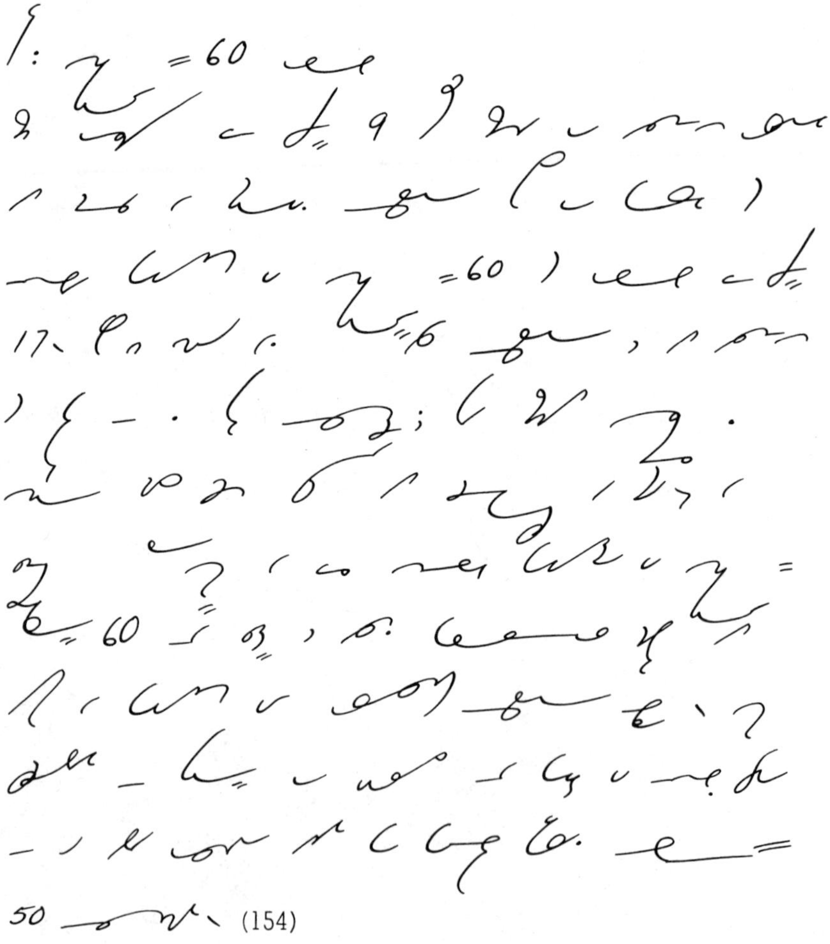

(154)

lesson

TECHNICAL SPEED BUILDER 68

SPECIALIZED TERMINOLOGY

Study each of the following terms:

Outline	Word and Pronunciation	Meaning
	**analogical** **an'a-loj'i-kal**	Founded on a relation of likeness between two things or of one thing to or with another.
	**significant figure** **sig-nif'i-kant**	Any digit in a number starting with the first which is not zero.
	**binary system** **bi'na-re**	Number system with base 2 based on the use of two symbols only – 1 and 0.
	**discrete** **dis-kret**	Separate; individually distinct.
	**nuclear dimension** **nu'kle-er di-men'shun**	Infinitesimal; exceedingly small.
	**synchronization** **sin'kro-ni-za'shun**	Happening or taking place at the same instant.
	**blanking pulse** **blangk'ing puls**	Square wave used to switch off a part of a television or radar set for a preestablished length of time.
	**sync** **singk**	Short for "synchronize" or "synchronization."
	**electron beam** **e-lek'tron**	Electromagnetic waves that radiate in a particular direction.
	**electron gun**	Group of electrodes that produce and focus on electron beam.

Vocabulary Preview

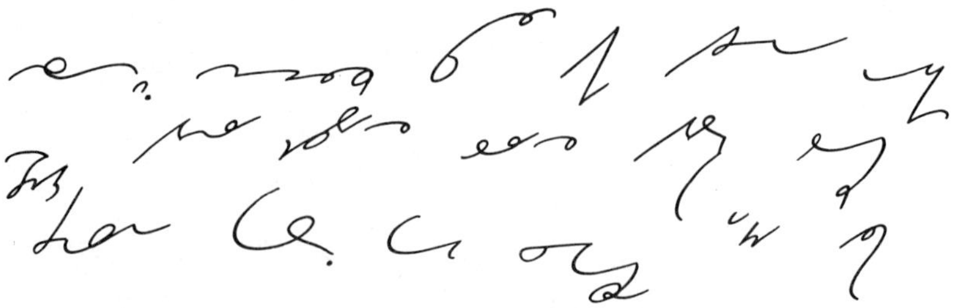

Calculating, communication, atomic, digit, decimal, logic, computations, discrete, statistically, theoretically, distinguishable, television, generator, blanking, pulse, amplifier, overshoot, tube.

Sustained Dictation

317 BINARY DIGIT

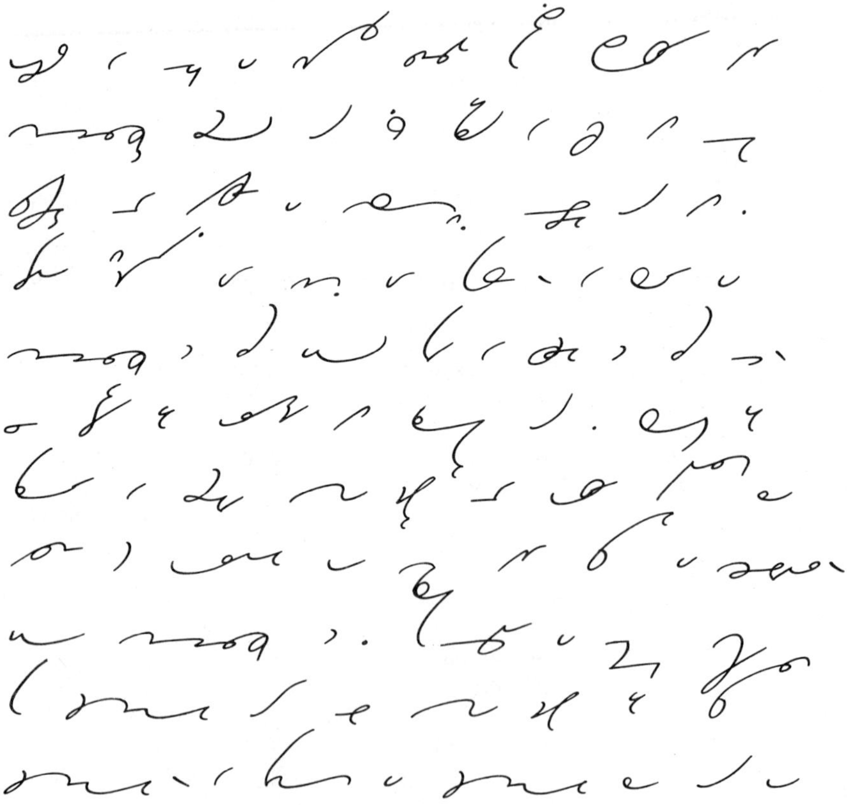

1 2 3 4 5 10 11
100 101

(533)

318 ▸ THE SIGNAL IN THE TELEVISION SET

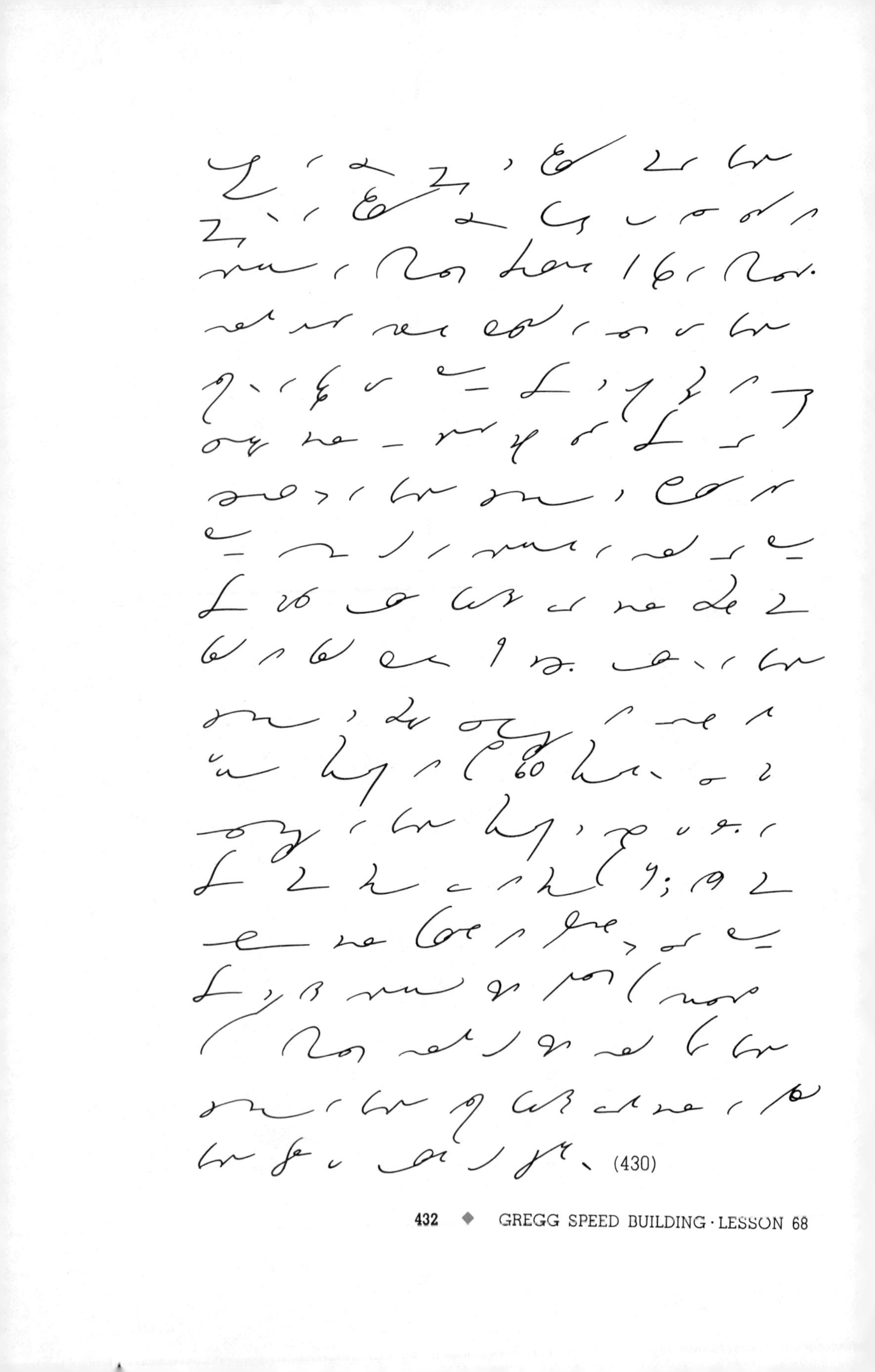

(430)

lesson 69

DICTATION SPEED BUILDER

SPEED-ESCALATION PRACTICE

Practice the specialized vocabulary and the vocabulary preview before writing the speed-pyramided article from dictation. The first minute is counted at 70 words a minute; the second, at 80; the third, at 90; and the remainder of the article, at 100.

SPECIALIZED TERMINOLOGY

Outline	Word and Pronunciation	Meaning
	**galaxy** **gal'ak-se**	The Milky Way; a group or cluster of stars.
	**interstellar** **in'ter-stel'er**	Space among the stars.
	**intergalactic** **in'ter-ga-lak'tik**	Space between galaxies.
	**spectrum** **spek'trum**	A charted band of wavelengths of electromagnetic vibrations.
	**metagalaxy** **met'a-gal'ak-se**	Space beyond the galaxy.
	**spheroidal** **sfe-roe'dal**	Having the form of a sphere; like a sphere.
	**Van Allen radiation belt**	A belt of intense radiations of electrons and protons that surround the earth.
	**aurora borealis** **au-ro'ra bor'ē-al'is**	A luminous phenomenon in the sky visible only at night. It is said to be of electrical origin.

Vocabulary Preview

Luminous, galaxies, constituents, dispersion, population, dwarf, subdwarf, external, globular, individual, nebulae, recognized, interstellar, intergalactic, molecules, particles, universal, captured, radiation, concentration, analogously, spectrum, entities, supergiant, metagalaxy, spheroidal, telescopes.

Speed Forcing

319 THE METAGALAXY

(1 Minute at 70)

In a vast but perhaps not limitless expanse of space and time, the common luminous units/have been defined as galaxies, of which the principal constituents are stars. The number of stars//in a galaxy seems to be in the range of 10,000 million. But there is a wide dispersion///in population. The Milky Way system may contain more than 200,000 million stars. (1)

(1 Minute at 80)

Some dwarf galaxies have scarcely more than 10,000,000. Indeed, there may be subdwarf galaxies of still smaller/population. Already there is convincing evidence that some of the external star clouds are probably no//more massive, or luminous, than the greatest of the globular star clusters.

Involved in the star fields of the ///individual galaxies are both bright and dark nebulae, and groups of stars in all degrees of organization. (2)

(1 Minute at 90)

Not so easily recognized as stars and nebulae is the widespread interstellar and perhaps intergalactic/ medium that is composed of electrons, atoms, molecules, and particles.

This universal medium may be the most//significant feature of the physical universe. The stars may be a phase that has captured human attention because///they generate a radiation, as a result of a concentration of mass, that happens to affect one human sense organ. (3)

(2 Minutes at 100)

Analogously, the little segment of the spectrum from violet to red which our eyes recognize has been overrated. To the short/of violet and the long of red are the energies that empower and reveal the universe.

All these material entities, from// interstellar atoms through stars to supergiant galaxies, are of interest in the study of the structure of the metagalaxy.///

There is considerable variety among the galaxies, especially in size and structural organization. But the (4) inaccessibility of most galaxies, and the scanty knowledge of those within range, have led to the classification of the/spheroidal, the spiral, and the irregular. Distance, with consequent faintness and small dimensions on photographic plates, hides the structures//of most of the galaxies that appear on the long-exposure photographs made with the telescopes best suited to the recording of galaxies.///The remote objects can be described only on the basis of shape and central concentration. Fortunately, a few thousand of the (5) galaxies are near enough to permit detailed analysis.

TRANSCRIPTION REINFORCEMENT PRACTICE

Vocabulary Preview

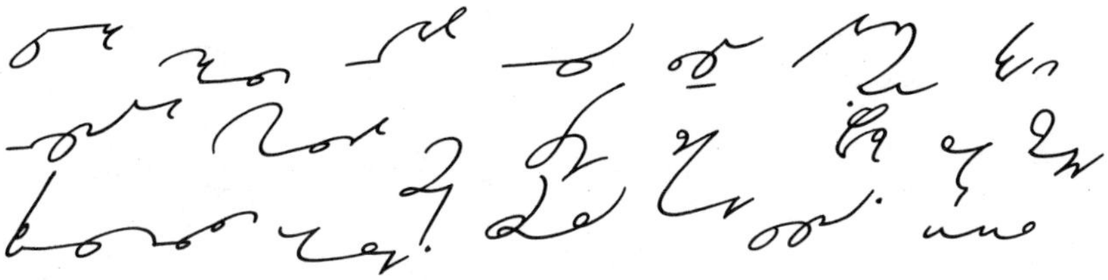

Atmosphere, cosmic, intensities, manned, equator, discoverer, postulate, encounters, deflects, converging, back-and-forth, established, hypothesis, eruption, as a result, geomagnetic, replenished, violent, accounting, aurorae.

TRANSCRIPTION PACER

320 LIMITATIONS OF SPACE FLIGHT 6

19

30

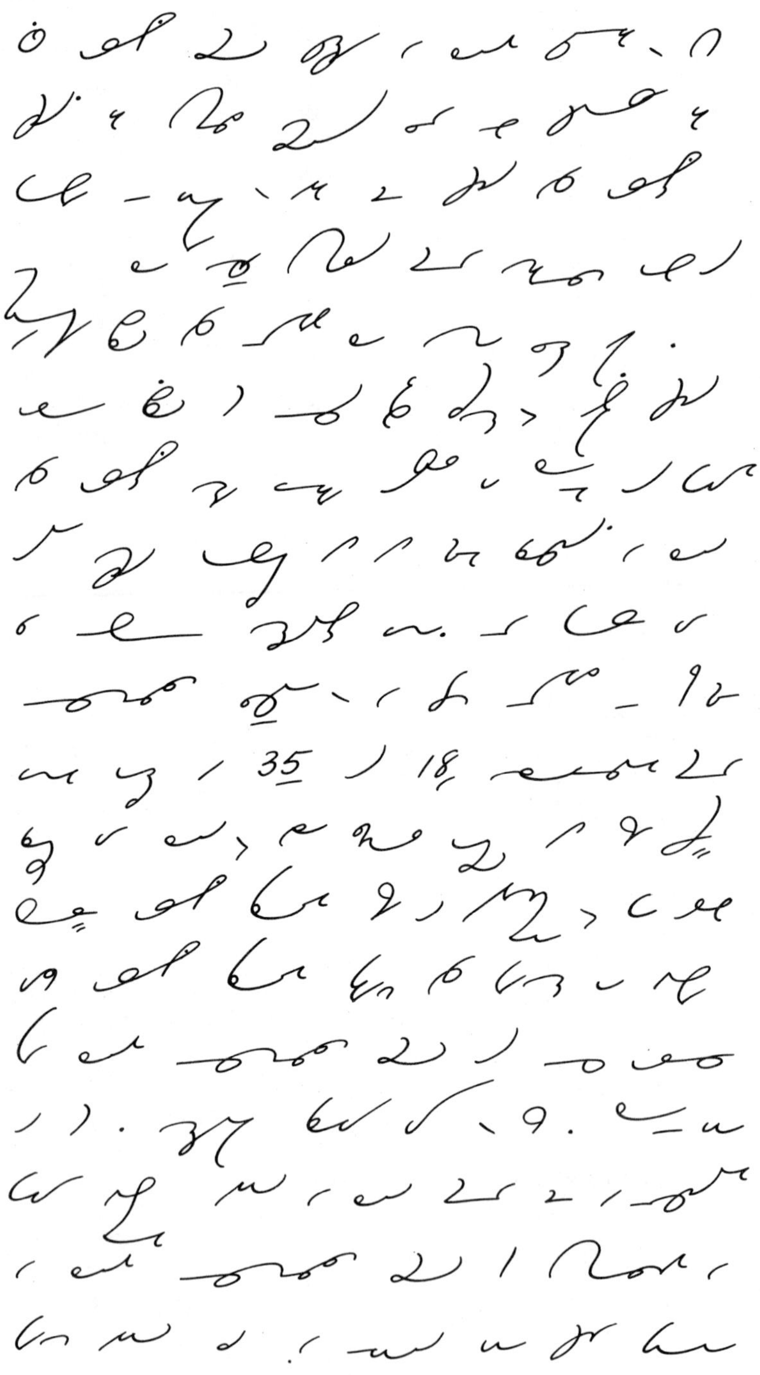

42
54
65
76
87
99
113
125
136
147
158
171
184
196
205
217
229
238
248

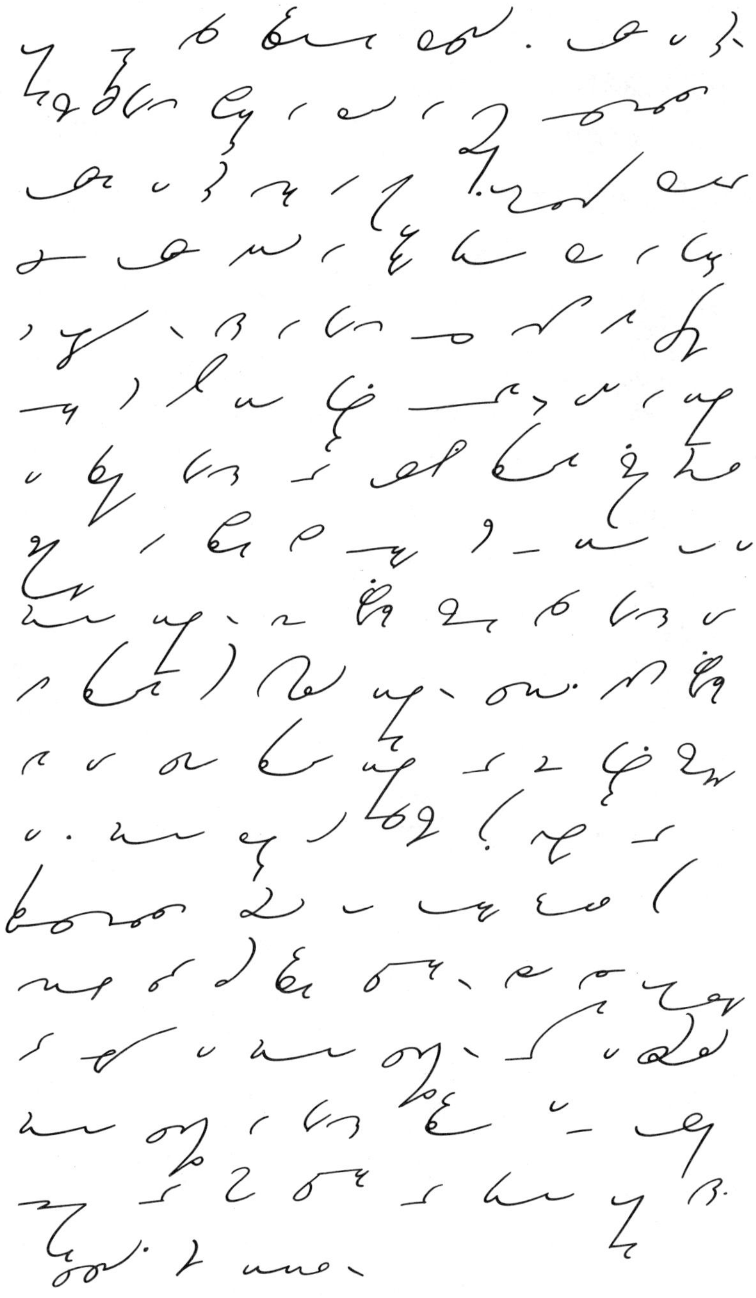

260
273
283
293
306
318
331
342
355
368
381
392
399
413
425
435
447
452

lesson 70 TRANSCRIPTION SPEED BUILDER

SUSTAINED SPEED BUILDER

The sustained speed builder is an article prepared by Dr. Bruno Haun for publication in Scientific Monthly. Practice the vocabulary preview, and then see whether you can sustain the highest dictation speed attained in the previous lesson.

Vocabulary Preview

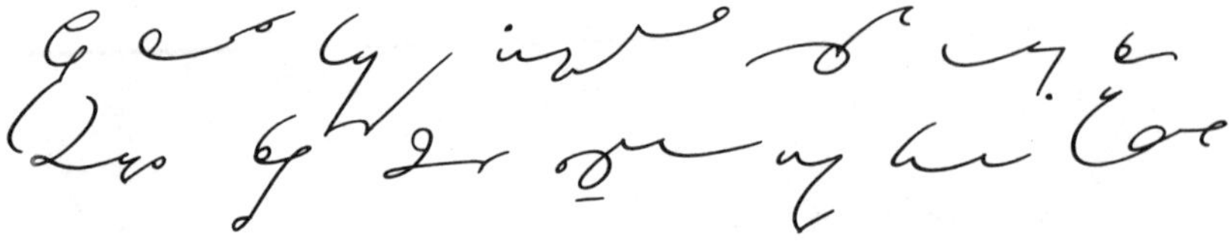

Appreciable, altitude, projected, horizontally, guidance, launching, circular, velocity, perigee, azimuth, equatorial, orbit, polar, oblateness.

Speed Builder

321 ARTIFICIAL SATELLITE

The creators of an artificial satellite are faced with a number of complex problems. First, the satellite[1] must be lifted to a point above the appreciable atmosphere, which means to an altitude at or[2] above 200 miles. Then it must be projected as nearly horizontally as guidance accuracy[3] will permit, and with sufficient velocity to ensure that the vehicle will remain above the[4] appreciable atmosphere throughout its orbit. By designing the propulsion system to give with certainty[5] more than enough velocity, one factor can easily be taken care of. However, the guidance problem[6] is more difficult. If, for launching with circular velocity at altitudes in the range from 200[7] to 300 miles, the angle of projection misses the true horizontal by as much as 2 degrees,[8] the perigee altitude will be roughly half the launching height.

Such an error occurring with the launching[9] altitude of 200 miles or less would cause the satellite to dip well into the denser parts of the[10] atmosphere and would, accordingly, cut short its lifetime.

If the launching direction of the vehicle misses in[11] azimuth, the consequences are not as serious as far as satellite lifetime is concerned. However,[12] locating observing stations on the ground is a problem. Different orbits are desired for different[13] experiments. These orbits may be classed roughly into three different types: equatorial, polar, and[14] intermediate. For the first case, the satellite moves around the equatorial plane, always above the[15] equator, and the earth's rotation simply causes a change in the apparent time of revolution. The placement[16] of observing stations on the ground is especially simple in this case. In the polar orbit, however,[17] the rotation of the earth causes the track of the satellite over the ground to spiral around in a[18] complicated fashion. Only at the poles can one always count on a passage of the satellite overhead once[19] per revolution. It is plain that the location of observing stations for a polar orbit presents some[20] great difficulties. For the intermediate orbit, the track of the satellite over the ground will wind[21] around in a sort of sine wave between a maximum latitude north and an equal maximum latitude south.[22] The equatorial crossing points, or nodes, will move around the equator in a fashion that depends mainly[23] on the earth's oblateness. (464)

TRANSCRIPTION CHECKPOINT

Vocabulary Preview

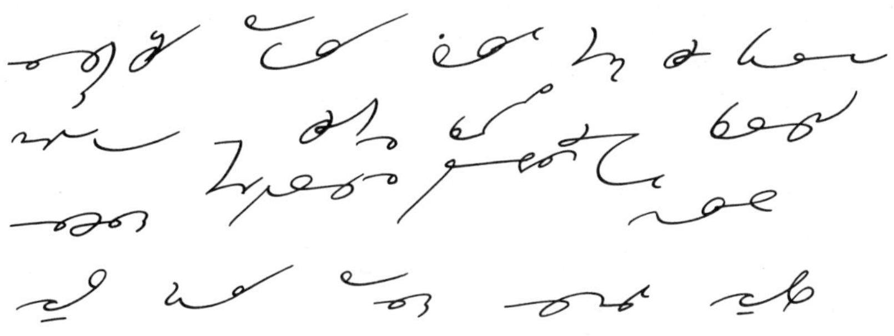

Negatives, oxide, electroplated, halides, focuses, cyan, polymer, unneutrality, invoked, scientifically, certainty, symbols, paramount, mechanics, dramatically, deterministic, climax, quanta, solid, electronics, magnets, quantization.

Sustained Dictation

322 ▸ 3M'S QUICK PROCESS DEVELOPS COLOR PRINTS THAT WON'T FADE, CURL, OR YELLOW WITH AGE

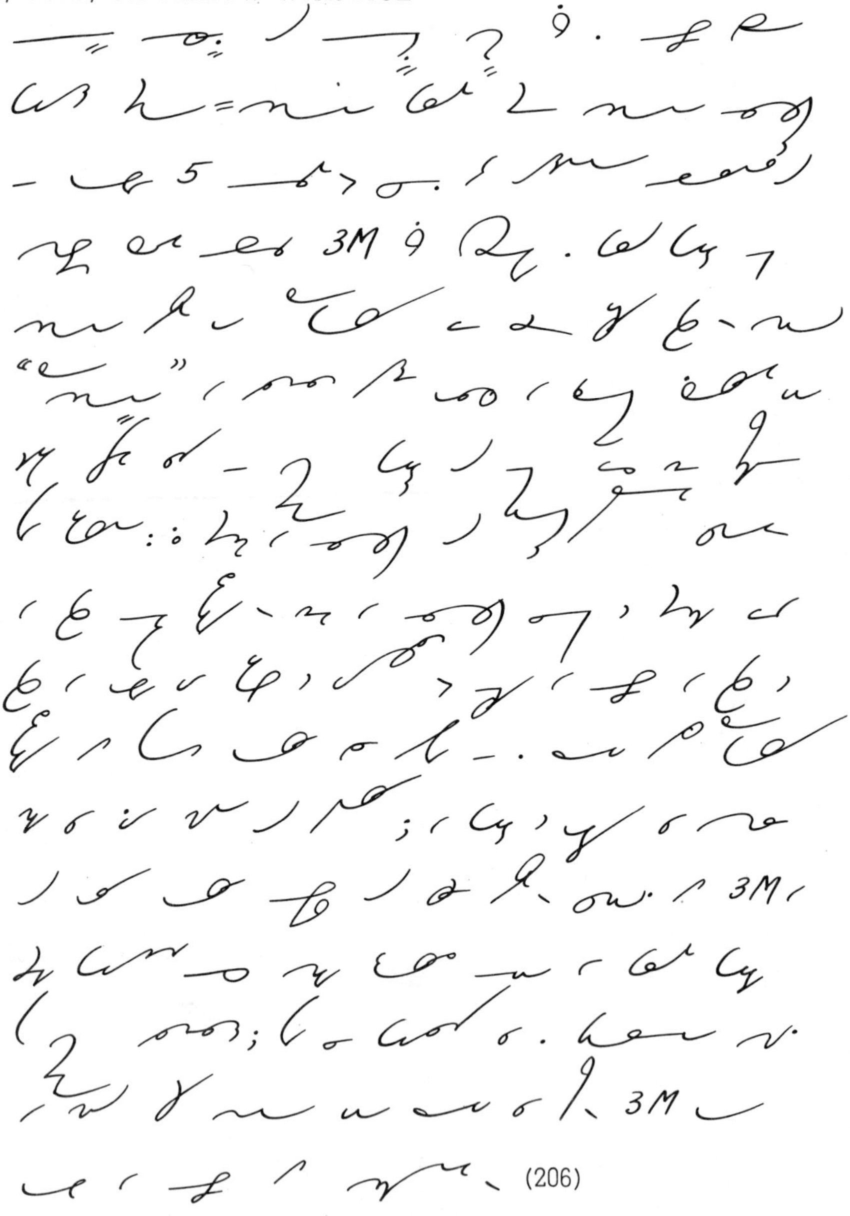

(206)

323▸ LIMITATIONS OF SCIENTIFIC CERTAINTY 8

21
31
43
52
64
74
86
98
107
119
130
141
152
164
176
190
199
209

219
229
241
255
265
275
289
300
312
325
334
345
356
369
379
391
402
414
427

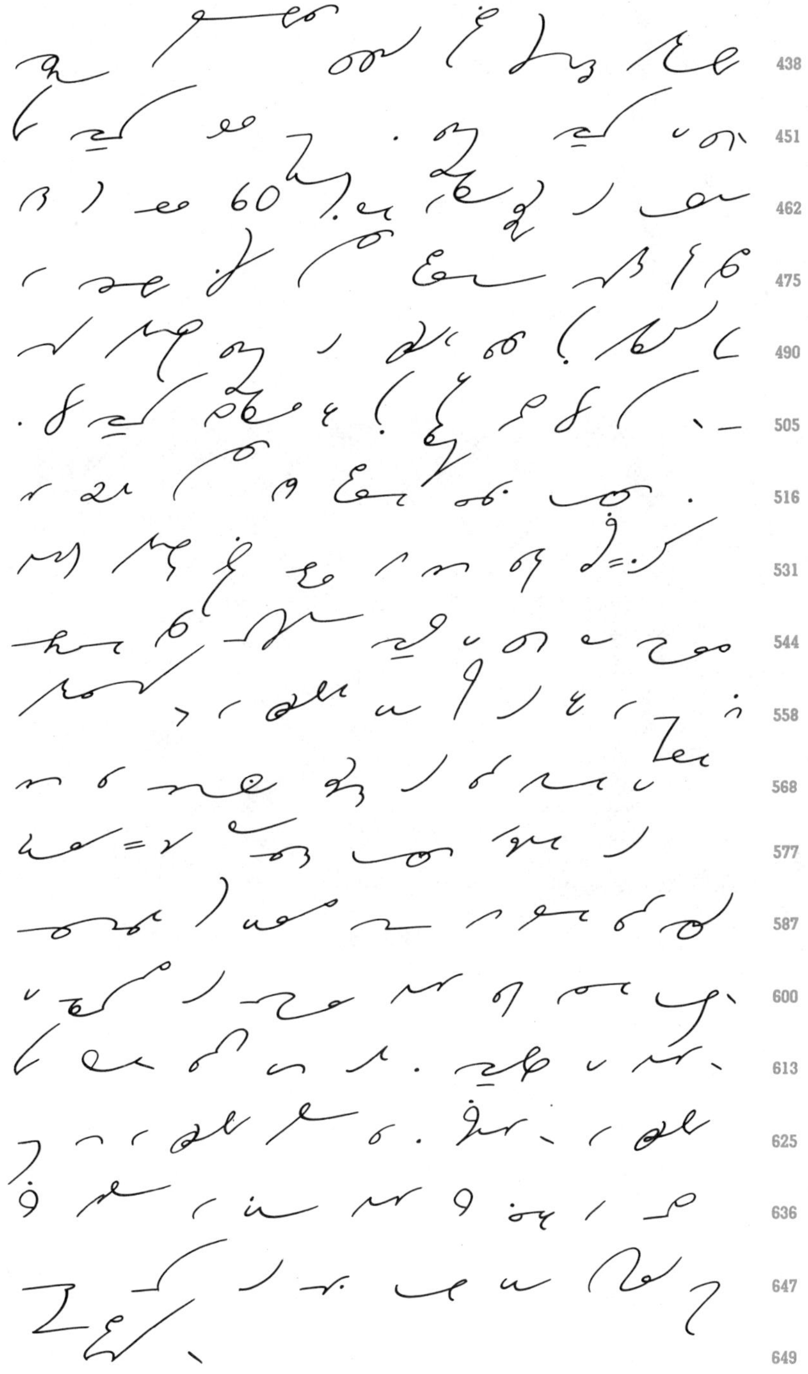

In our social system, a legal framework places the economy and all personal relations under regulatory control. The body of law that makes up this framework has expanded over the years with the passage of new legislation. Its applicability to human rights as well as to the economy has become more extensive through decisions made by enforcement agencies and the courts.

The attorney is a specialist who is educated in the profession of the law; it is his job to think, plan, and solve legal problems. He is an officer of the court, duly qualified to represent clients in a legal action.

The legal secretary is expected to enhance the image of the law office and the personality of the attorney. She wears simple, pleasing clothes, avoiding extremes of every kind. She is vitally interested in her work and is prepared to work under pressure. The typical legal secretary is alert to the need for sufficient legal training to meet the demands of the law office

unit 15

and assignments of the future that will demand entirely new capabilities. She has discovered that command of a foreign language, extensive reading in diversified fields of interest, and travel reflect the kind of versatility the emerging new era will demand.

LAW

Secretarial Assignment

The form employed in transcribing legal correspondence differs only slightly from the form used in other correspondence. The following guidelines should be followed in preparing legal papers and the correspondence that accompanies them.

Concise Wording

Use:	Rather than:
Name of party	Party of the first part
Made	Made and entered into
Date	Day and year
The title to the goods	The title and ownership of the goods

Subject Line

A subject line is usually employed either as part of the printed letterhead or below the salutation. Although the trend is toward typing the subject line without an introductory word or phrase, *Re, In re,* and *Subject* are frequently used to introduce the subject.

Contract Between Builtwell Homes, Inc., and Mark L. Massey and M. Margaret Massey, July 9, 19—.

Re: Simpson v. Simpson.

In re: Wilson Atwell (No. 1831) and Stella T. Atwell (No. 1832), Bankruptcy.

Subject: Account No. 18712—Seller, William Wilson; Buyer, Henry Blatner.

Figures

Except in land titles, there is a general tendency toward the elimination of the written repetition of numbers in legal papers.

Payable in 30 days.	NOT	Payable in thirty (30) days.
The sum of $693.33.	NOT	The sum of six hundred and ninety-three dollars and thirty-three cents ($693.33).

Signatures

A good legal signature consists of three full names — first, middle, and surname — and it should be written in ink for lasting quality. The name should be typed beneath the signed signature, even if the signature is legible and the name appears elsewhere in the letter or document.

"By," rather than "Per," should precede the written signature when a person is simply signing for a company, or as the representative of another person.

Sincerely yours,

RICHARDSON, QUINN & HEARCH

By: *William H. Meade*
William H. Meade

"Per" or "P.P." is used when the person signing is a lawful agent.

A "seal" may be written or drawn by the signer after his signature, or it may be printed or typed. The letters "L.S." (the place of the seal) are often used as a seal.

lesson

71 LEGAL SPEED BUILDER

SPECIALIZED TERMINOLOGY

To better understand the sense of the dictation in this lesson, you will need to study each of the following terms:

Appellate • Having the power and authority to retry or review an issue that has already been heard in a court of lesser jurisdictional power.

Appurtenance • That which belongs to something else, but which has not belonged to it immemorially; for example, buildings are appurtenances to land.

Assignment • The transfer of one's rights to another. The assignor transfers to the assignee.

Attachment • The taking of a debtor's property into the legal custody of an officer by virtue of the directions contained in a writ of attachment.

Bankruptcy • State of insolvency in which the property of the debtor is taken over by a receiver for the benefit of creditors.

Bill of Exchange • An unconditional order in writing by one person to another, signed by the person writing it, requiring the person to pay on demand, or at a fixed time, a certain sum of money to order or bearer.

Brief • A statement of the facts and points of law of a case that are to be pleaded in a court.

Foreclosure • An action to close out a mortgagor's interest when he has defaulted in his payments on the mortgage.

TRANSCRIPTION SPEED BUILDER

Vocabulary Preview

Mortgage, foreclosure, proceedings, delinquent, institute, wife, adjuster, résumé, nontechnical, Indiana, Edgar, Herbert, default, defendants, verification, Albert, obligated, contract, luxury, validated, majority, emancipated, consumed.

Sustained Dictation

324 Mr. Clyde N. Smith, 2274 Ohio Avenue, Richmond, Indiana 47374.

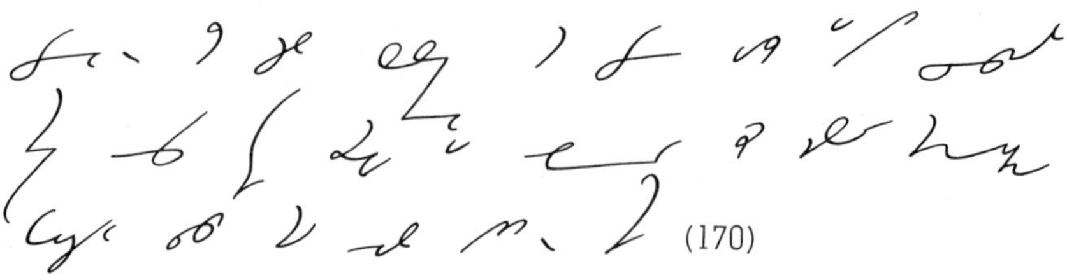

(170)

325 ▸ Dr. Harry L. Wilson, 1272 Medical Arts Building, South Meridan Street, Indianapolis, Indiana 46201.

(146)

326 ▸ Mr. William H. Hamilton, 346 Oak Street, Gary, Indiana 46402.

(141)

327 ▸ Hill Brothers, 235 Locust Street, Cameron, Missouri 64429.

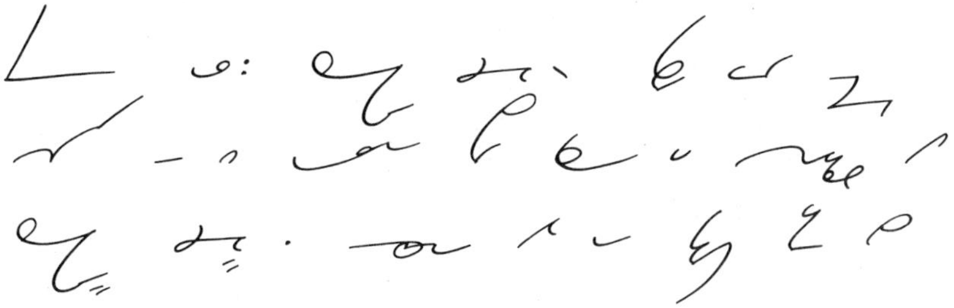

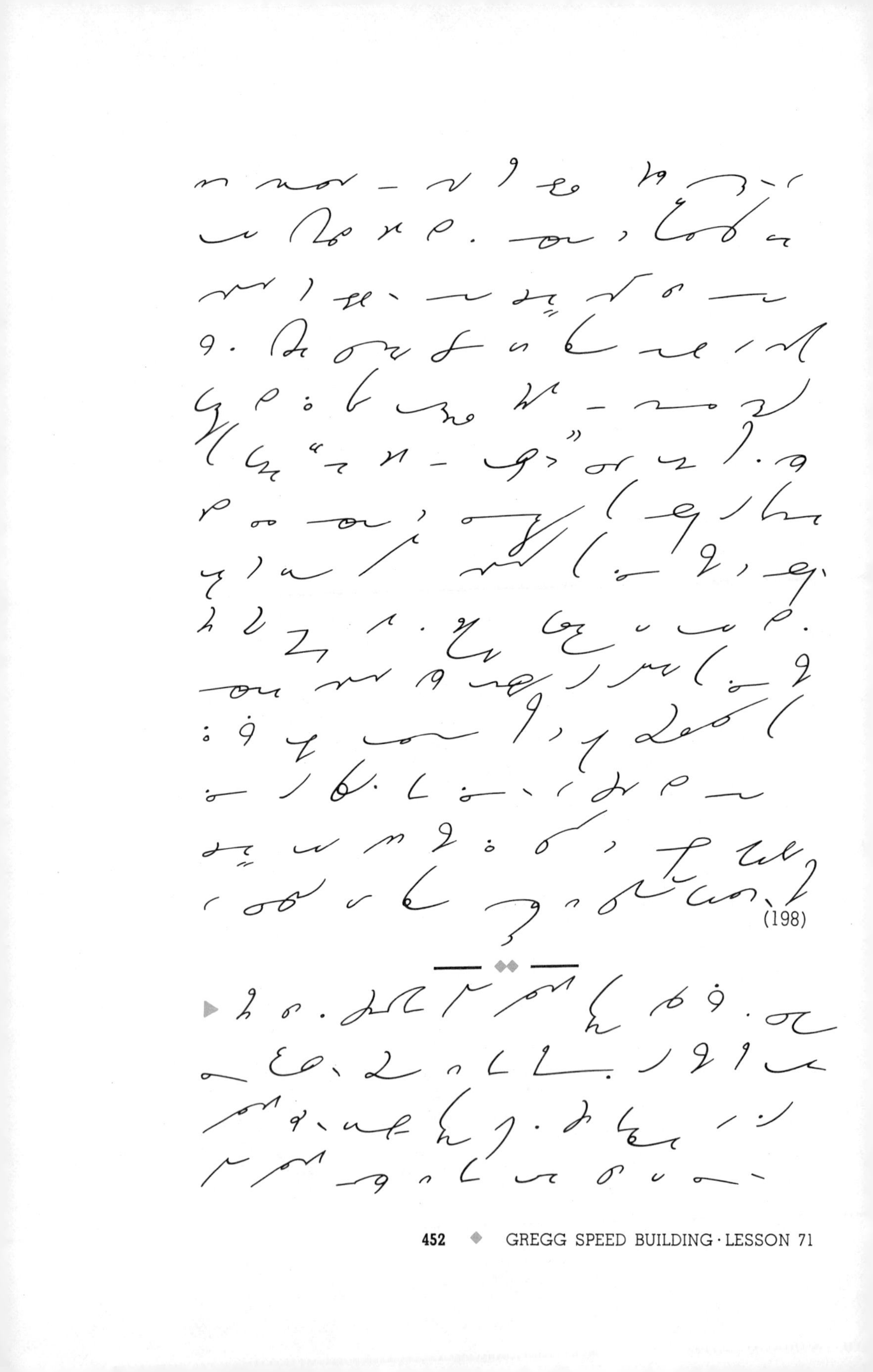

(198)

lesson

LEGAL SPEED BUILDER 72

SPECIALIZED TERMINOLOGY

Civil Law • The law that governs the rights of citizens among one another, as distinguished from criminal law, which deals with crimes.

Complaint • The allegations made by one who institutes suit at law.

Covenant • A formal agreement of legal validity; to make such an agreement.

Defendant • The person required to answer in a legal action or suit.

Docket • A brief entry or the book containing such entries. A list of lawsuits to be tried by court.

Garnishee • One who has money, usually wages, or property belonging to the defendant and who is served with notice not to deliver or pay it to the defendant but to the appropriate officer of law.

Litigation • A suit at law or legal action

Surety • One legally bound for the debt of another.

Waiver • A voluntary relinquishment of a right or privilege.

TRANSCRIPTION SPEED BUILDER

Vocabulary Preview

Disputes, substantiate, investigating, judgment, transcript, Justice of the Peace, attorney, execution, levied, covenants, demonstrator, installments, hereunto.

Sustained Dictation

328▸ Mr. Morris T. Fellows, 142 Exchange Building, Richmond, Virginia 23216.

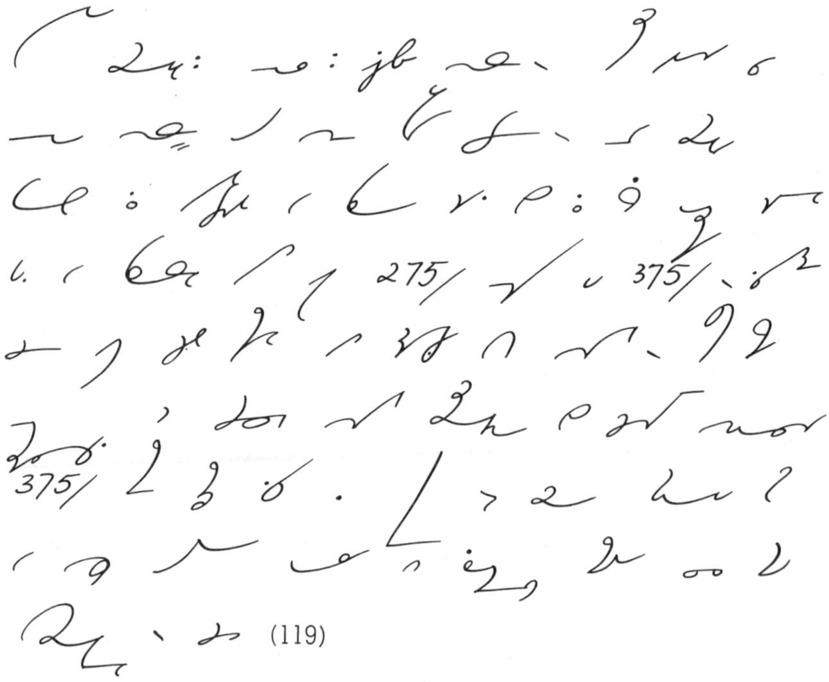

(119)

329▸ Mr. James W. Langston, Johnson Sales Agency, 378 Barker Building, Cincinnati, Ohio 45225.

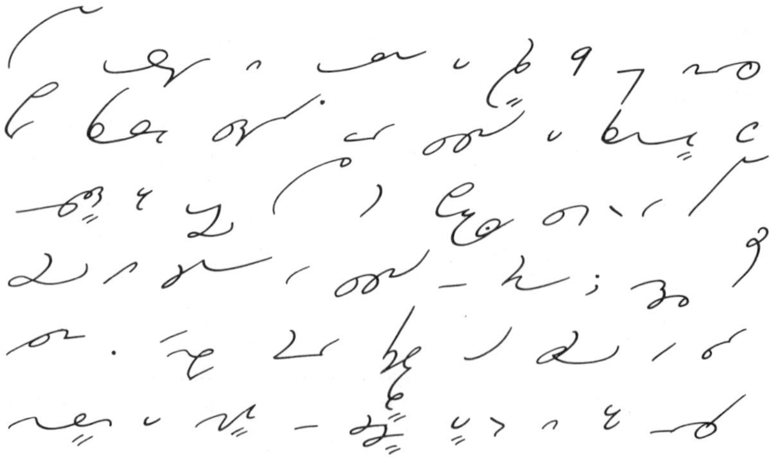

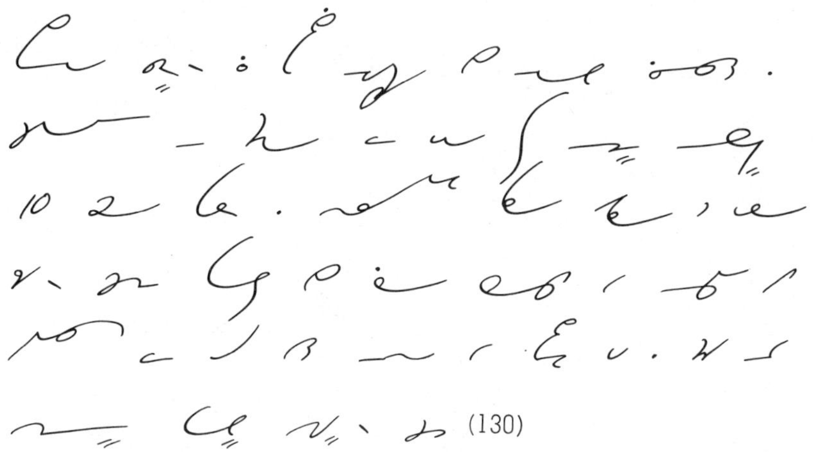

(130)

330 ▸ Messrs. Nutley & Cromwell, 118 Front Street, Tallahassee, Florida 32301.

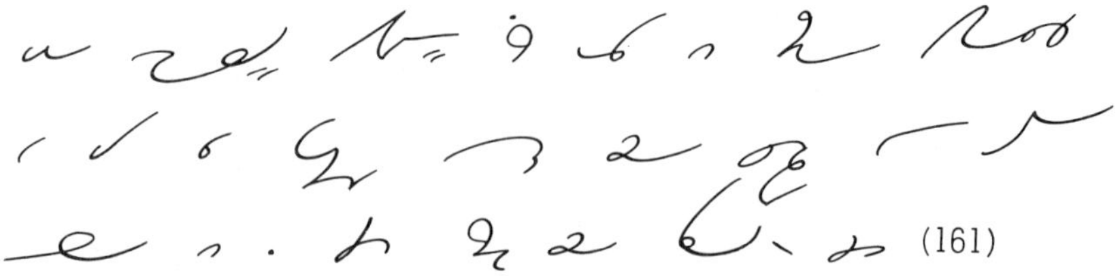

(161)

331 ▸ The James K. Little Company, 267 North Broad Street, Philadelphia, Pennsylvania 19101.

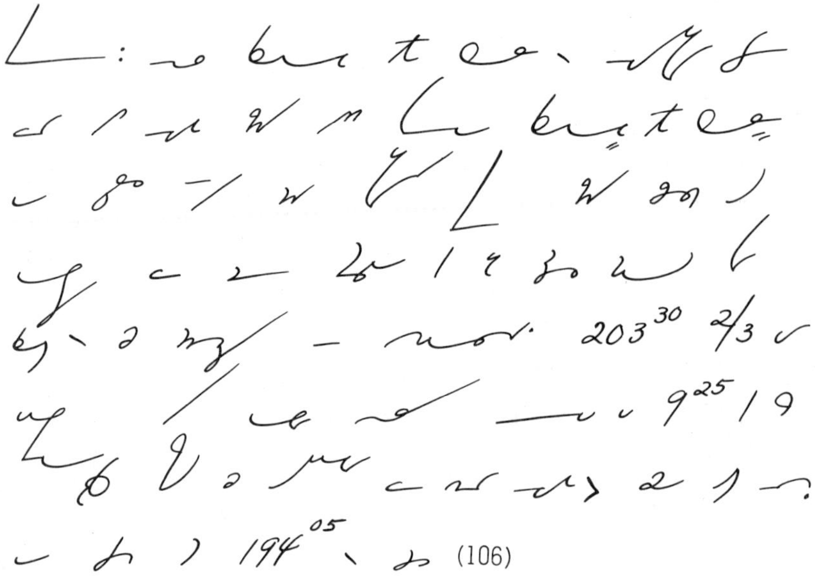

(106)

332 ▸ CONTRACT

(263)

333 Mr. Frank S. Ferris, 262 Green Avenue, Tarrytown, New York 10591.

(230)

lesson 73

LEGAL SPEED BUILDER

SPECIALIZED TERMINOLOGY

Lease • A written agreement or oral contract giving the right to use property for a certain length of time, usually gained by paying rent. The lessor rents the property to the lessee.

Mortgage • A document representing a claim on property in favor of the lender of money. The mortgagor borrows from the mortgagee.

Negotiable Instruments • Written contracts, such as promissory notes, drafts or bills of exchange, bank checks, and other commercial paper, that circulate almost as freely as money and may be transferred from one person to another by endorsement and delivery, or by delivery only.

Plaintiff • The person bringing suit.

Ratification • The subsequent approval of an act that previously had not been binding.

Revocation • A withdrawal; an annulment; a repudiation. The recall of some power or thing granted.

TRANSCRIPTION SPEED BUILDER

Vocabulary Preview

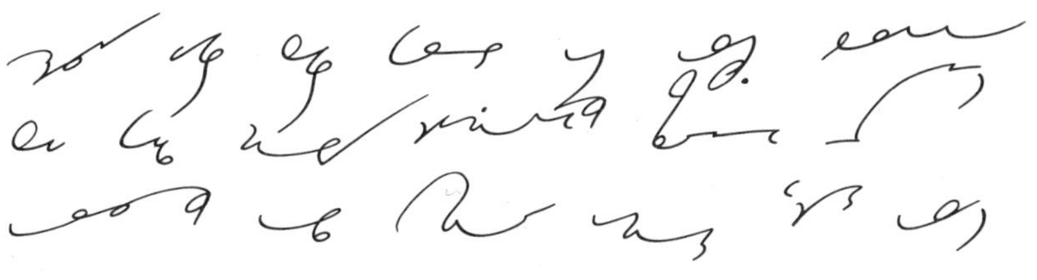

Constituted, whatsoever, wheresoever, premises, revocation, ratifying, territorial, whereof, proxy, solicited, stockholders, adjournments, indemnification, litigation, lessee, default, resolutions, circumstances, ratification.

Sustained Dictation

334 APARTMENT LEASE

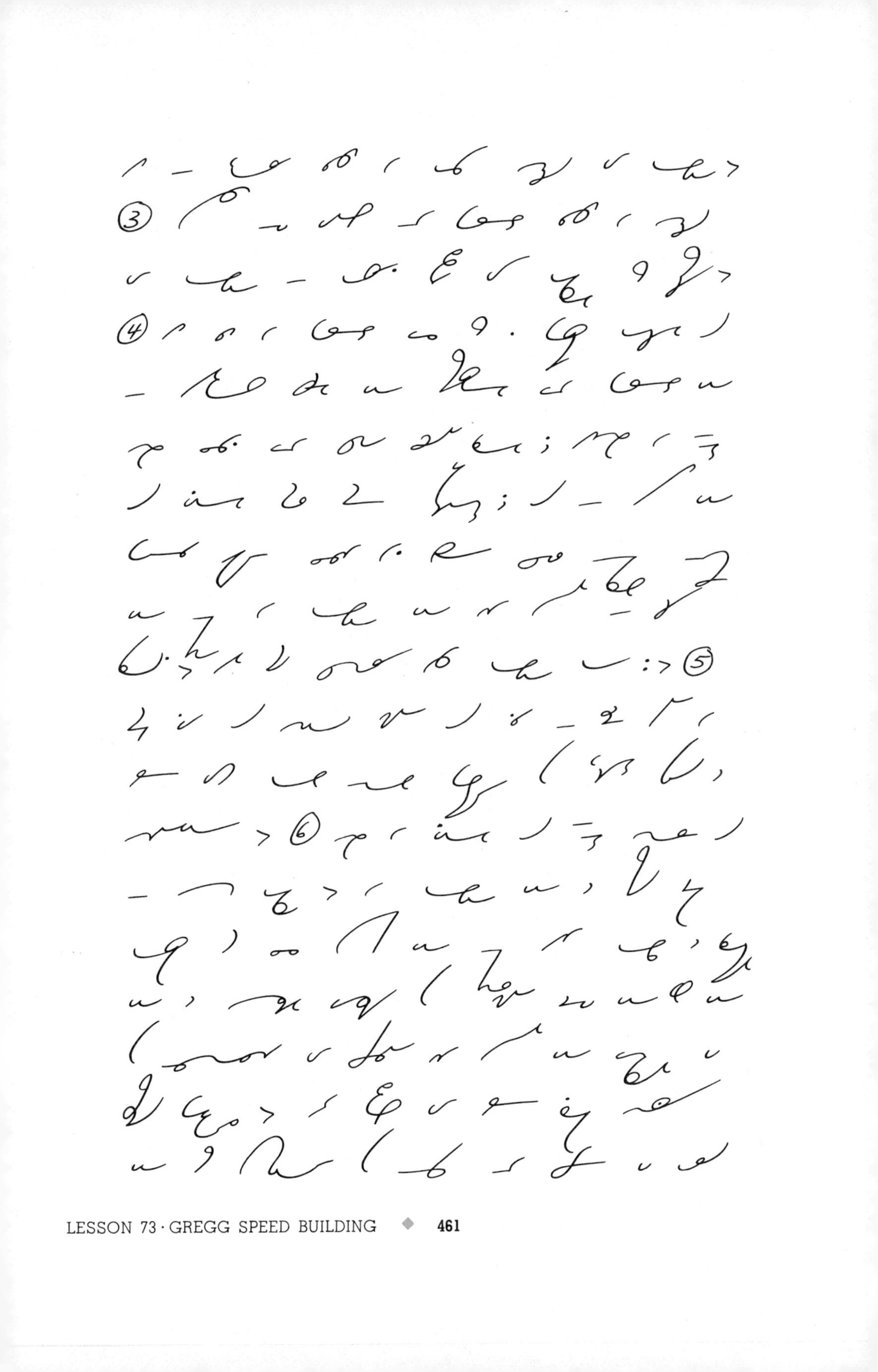

(500)

335▸ PROXY

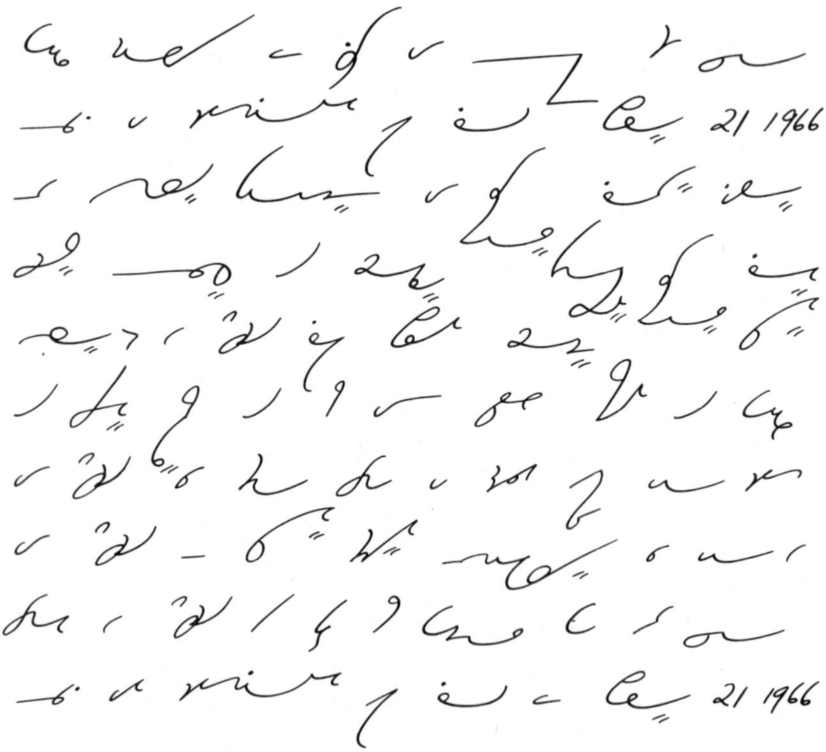

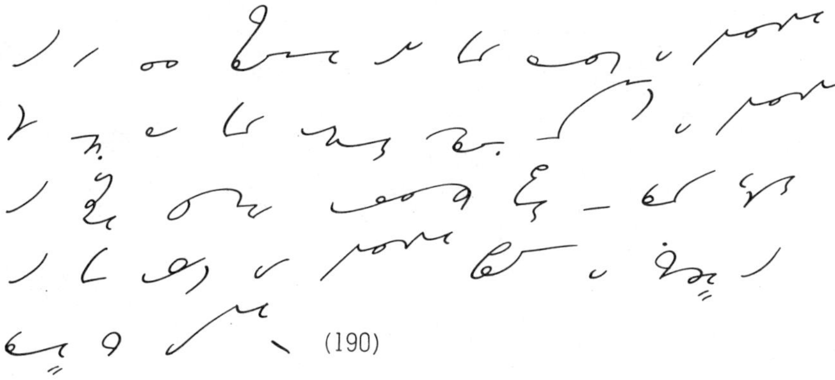

(190)

336▸ POWER OF ATTORNEY

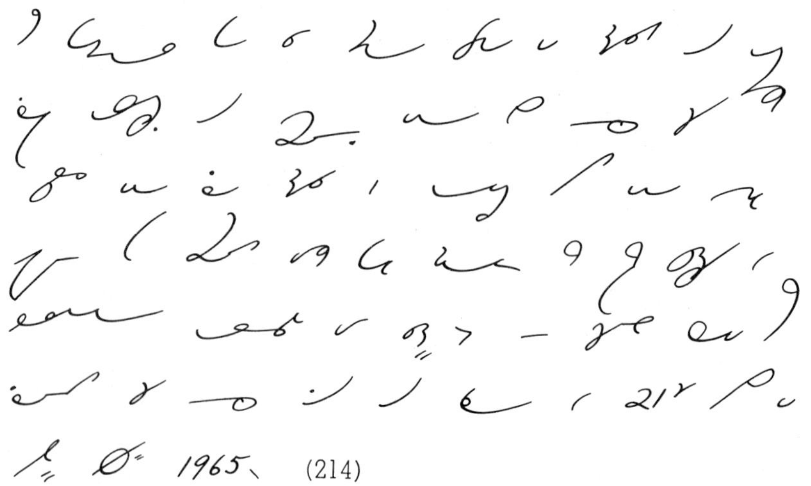

(214)

337 Mr. Bryon S. Mead, 87 Chimney Road, Stamford, Connecticut 06902.

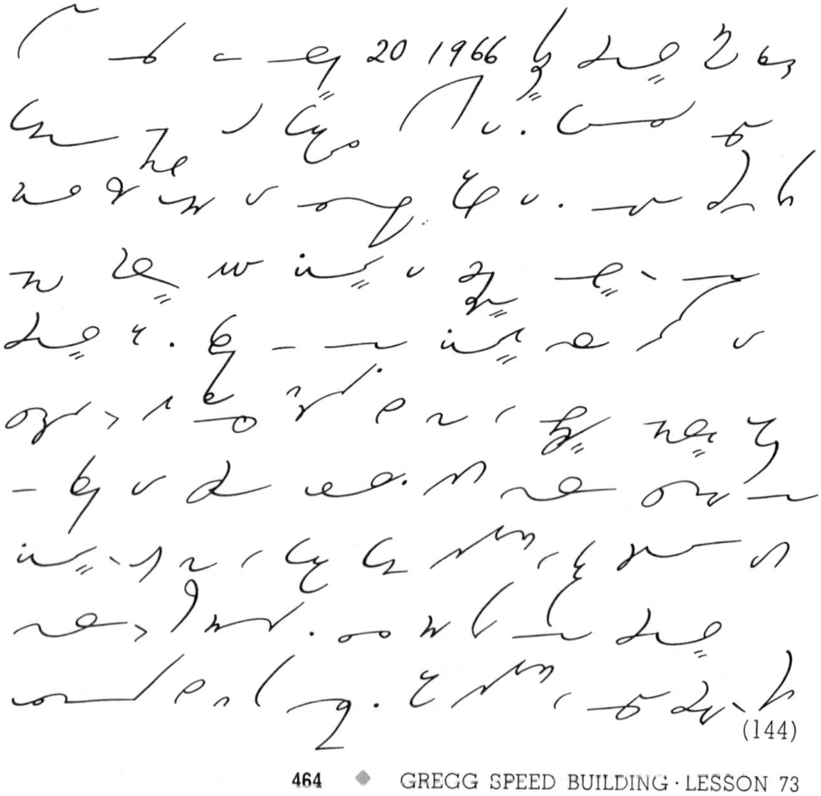

(144)

lesson

DICTATION SPEED BUILDER 74

SPEED-ESCALATION PRACTICE

Practice the vocabulary preview before writing the speed-pyramided letter from dictation. The first minute is counted at 80 words a minute; the second, at 90; the third, at 100; and the remainder of the letter, at 110.

Legal Shortcuts

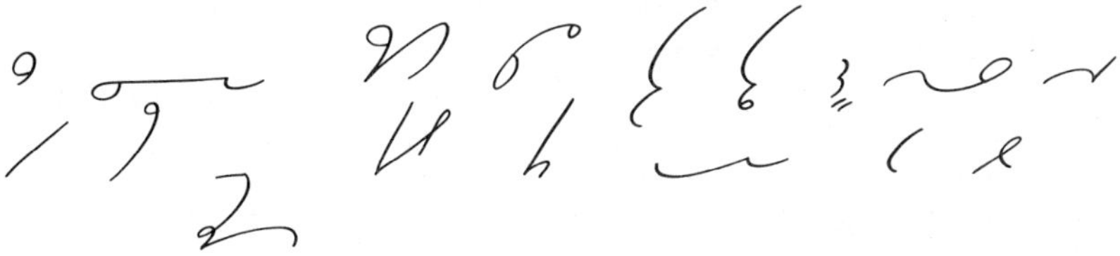

Accident, administrator, affidavit, attorney, bankrupt, bankruptcy, Civil Service, claim, court, defendant, evidence, investigate, judicial, jury, lawyer, plaintiff, testify—testimony.

Vocabulary Preview

Maxwell, hereinafter, sewerage, Okinawa, Ryukyu, Pacific, performed, aforesaid, capacity, furnished, temporarily, in the world, satisfaction, of course, forward, political, subdivisions, compensation, prorated, departure, withhold, security, designated, remainder, annual, accumulate, remuneration, inclusive, foreign, transportation, termination, interpreted, expenditures, 300 pounds, continue, actually, required, foregoing, signify, let us.

Speed Forcing

(One Minute at 80)

338▸ Dear Mr. Gross: The firm of Pearson, Lambert & Maxwell, with address of 122 Broadway, New York, New York/10006, hereinafter called the "Employer," is engaged in engineering work in connection with//the improvement of sewerage system facilities at Okinawa, Ryukyu Islands. Said work will/// be performed for the firm of Pearson, Lambert & Maxwell and Pacific Engineering, of Okinawa, (1)

(One Minute at 90)

both are under a contract to the U. S. Army Corps of Engineers, Okinawa District, an agency of/the U. S. Government, hereinafter called the "District."

We should like to retain your services as an engineer in//connection with the performance of the aforesaid work and of any other work that the employer may undertake in///the area of Okinawa; and, to that end, we hereby offer to employ you on the following terms and conditions: (2)

(One Minute at 100)

DUTIES—You are to be retained as an engineer in the performance of work in and about Okinawa and shall perform all such/services in said capacity as may be required. All services are to be furnished by you at Okinawa and elsewhere as may be//directed, whether within Okinawa or temporarily anywhere in the world.

It is understood that you will render services///for your employer only during the term of this agreement; that such services shall be performed to the employer's satisfaction. (3)

(6 Minutes at 110)

We shall, of course, look forward to your cooperating with us, as well as with any of the representatives of the Government of Okinawa/or any of its political subdivisions or agencies in rendering such technical and expert services as will be required of you//in your capacity named above.

COMPENSATION—You will receive as basic salary for your services the sum of $693.33///a month, or a prorated portion thereof for services of less than one month, for each and every month during which you actually (4) perform services under this agreement. You will receive, in addition, $350 a month living allowances for services/in Okinawa, or temporarily elsewhere, under this agreement.

Payment of the aforesaid basic salary and living allowance shall// begin on the date of your departure from the United States for Okinawa. Your entire monthly salary, less deductions for Federal///Withholding, Federal Social Security, group insurance, Blue Cross-Blue Shield membership dues, and New York State Workmen's Compensation, will be sent to a bank (5) in the United States designated by you for deposit to your account; or, if you so designate, a portion of your salary in United States/dollars will be sent to you in Okinawa, and the remainder will be deposited to your account as prescribed above.

In addition, you//will be entitled to annual vacation of two weeks each year, with basic salary at the rate stated above, which vacation may be allowed///to accumulate. Should your vacation accumulate, no extra remuneration will be paid to you; but when you take such vacation leave, basic salary (6) will be paid to you at said rate stated above.

Said salary is inclusive of all income taxes and other forms of taxes, foreign and/domestic; and you will, of course, be liable for the payment of such taxes on salary, including any taxes on such portion of said compensation//as represents the aforesaid benefits.

TRANSPORTATION AND TRAVEL EXPENSES—You will be paid normal traveling expenses from New York City///to Okinawa, Ryukyu Islands; and upon the termination of this agreement, you will be paid normal traveling expenses for the return (7) trip from Okinawa to New York City.

Normal traveling expenses shall be interpreted to mean expenditures actually made for/air transportation by most direct route, food and lodgings while en route, and transportation of baggage by airfreight not exceeding 300 pounds.

Should your//employment continue under this agreement for a period of more than two years, then at the end of said two-year period the employer agrees///to pay your normal traveling expenditures actually made for a round trip from Okinawa to New York City.

TERM—The term of this agreement shall (8) be the period during which your services as an Engineer in Okinawa shall be required, which is estimated to be not less than two/ years from this date, unless sooner terminated.

If the foregoing offer correctly expresses our understanding, please signify your approval thereof//by signing this letter in duplicate, thereby making this a binding agreement. You may then retain a signed copy for your files and return the///other signed copy to us. Let us assure you that we are looking forward to the pleasure of having you work with us for some time to come. Sincerely yours, (9)

TRANSCRIPTION REINFORCEMENT PRACTICE

Vocabulary Preview

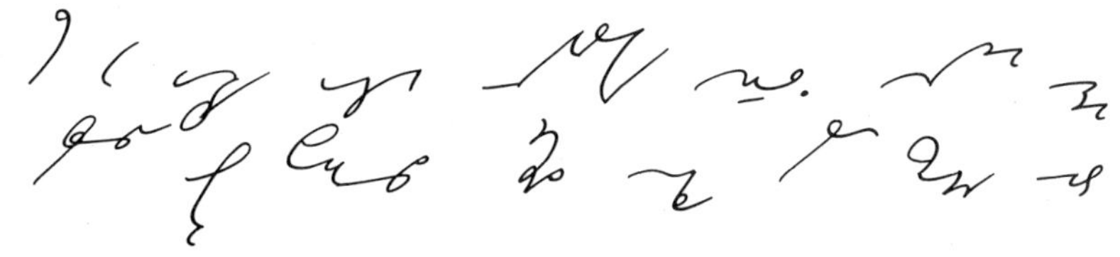

Evidence, plaintiff, occupied, residential, undisturbed, quarrying, continuance nuisance, diameter, thereabouts, approximately, sufficiently, crusher, derrick, as a result, noises.

Sustained Dictation

339 Mr. Louis C. Fletcher, Publisher, Direction Magazine, 29 Chandler Drive, New York, New York 10007.

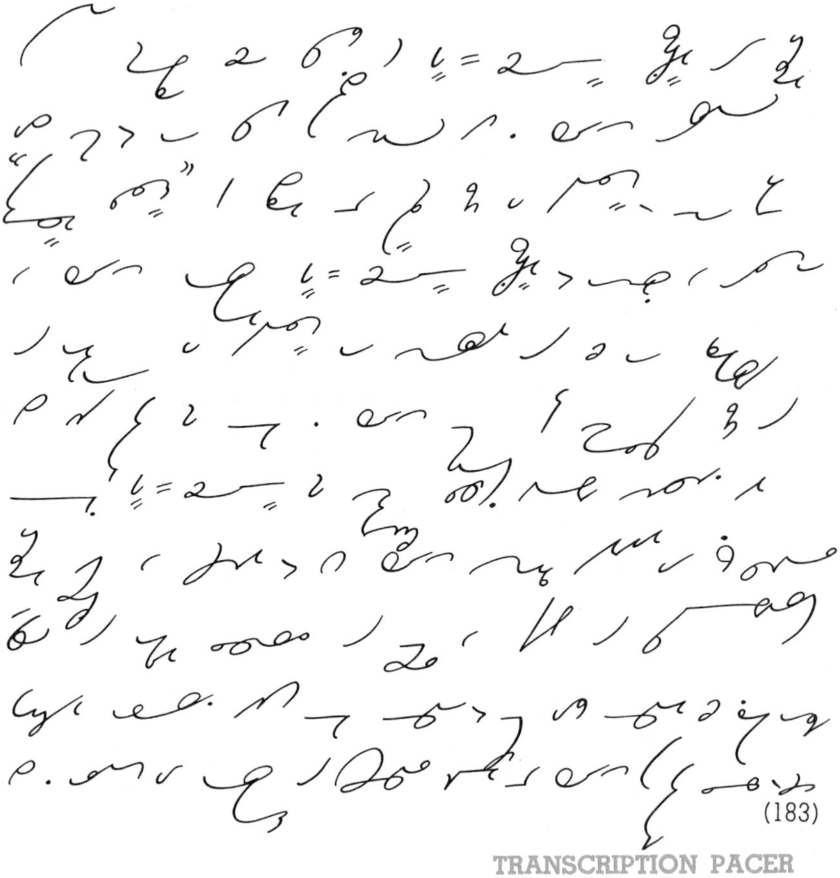

(183)

TRANSCRIPTION PACER

340 OPENING STATEMENT 4

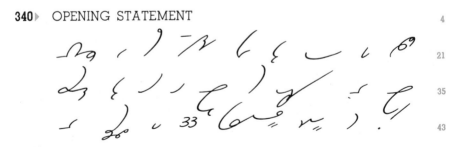

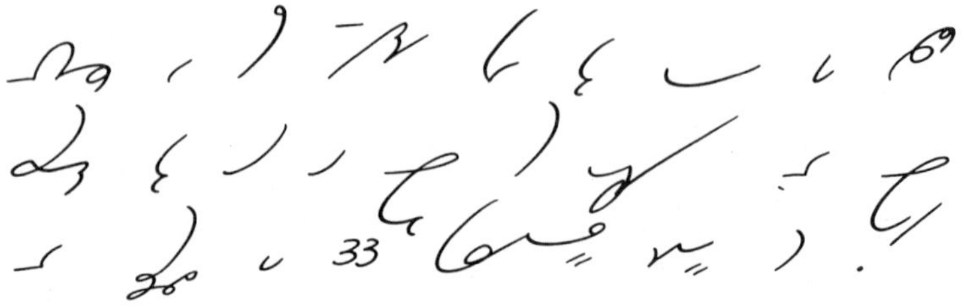

21

35

43

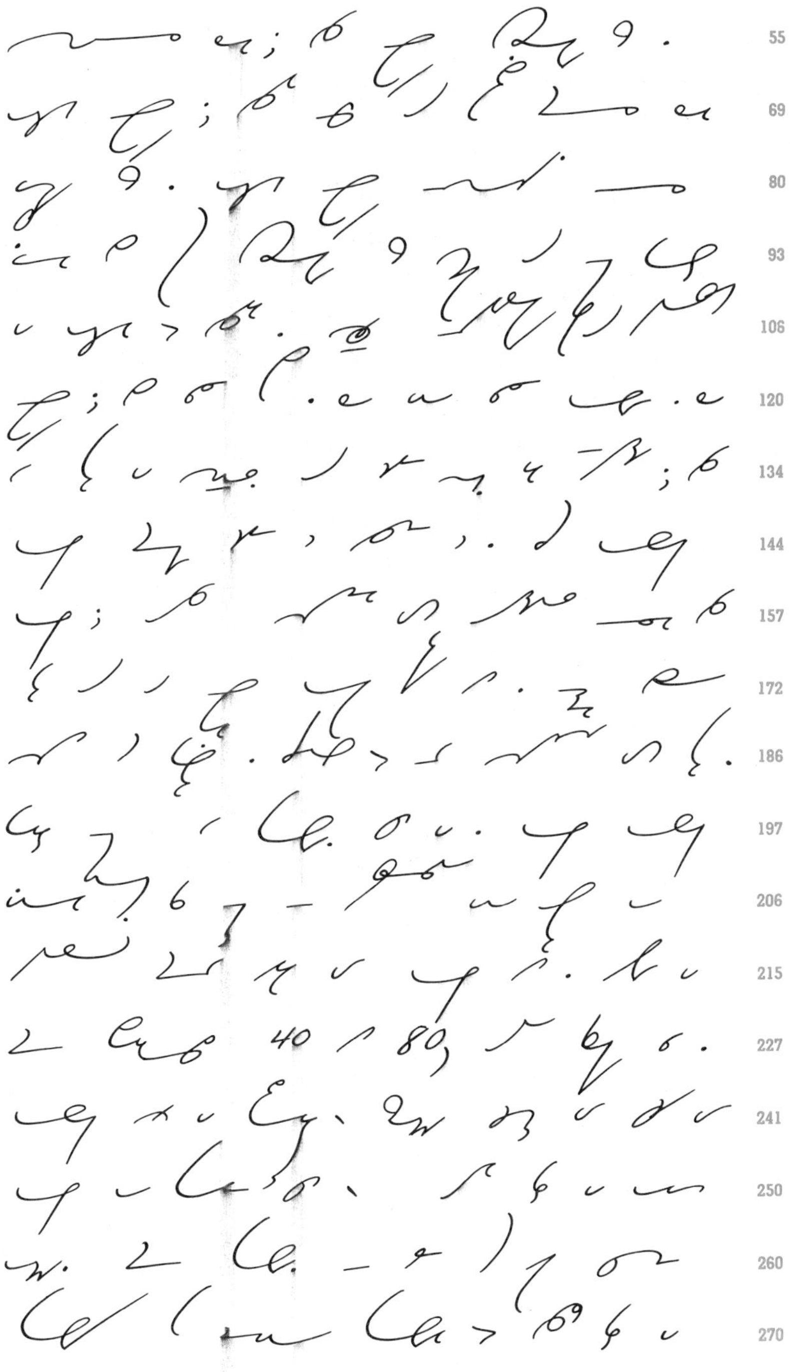

280
290
298
307
318
327
336
352
365
379
390
401
414
425
436
449
463
476
479

lesson 75

TRANSCRIPTION SPEED BUILDER

SUSTAINED SPEED BUILDER

The sustained speed builder is a will prepared by William G. Mancini. Practice the vocabulary preview, and then see whether you can sustain the highest dictation speed attained in the previous lesson.

Vocabulary Preview

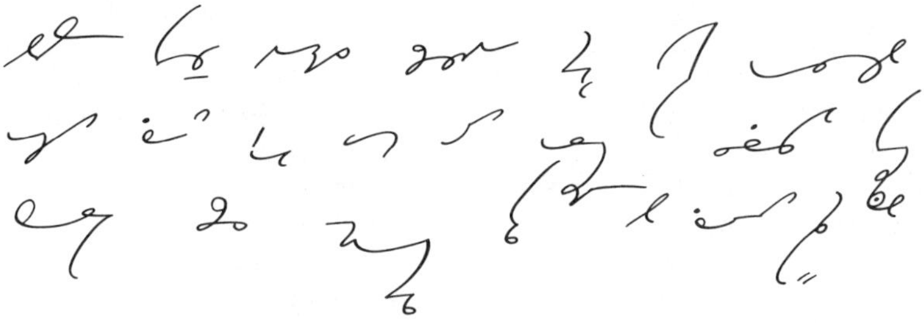

Testament, bequeath, trustee, executor, furnishings, tangible, legatees, residue, hereunder, sureties, auction, thereto, reinvestment, inheritance, beneficiaries, alienable, assignee, insolvency, bankruptcy, testimony, hereunto, February.

Speed Builder

341 I, Elmer E. Macy, of Stamford, Fairfield County, Connecticut, being of sound and disposing mind and[1] memory, do make this my last will and testament revoking all wills by me at any time heretofore made.[2]

After the payment of my just debts and funeral expenses, I give, devise and bequeath all the property and[3] estate, both real and personal, of which I shall die seized and possessed, and to which I shall be entitled at the[4] time of my decease, as follows:

1. I give and bequeath to my trustee, hereinafter named, the sum of twenty[5] thousand dollars to pay the income quarterly to my sister Sarah Macy Littlefield, of Kenne-

bunk, Maine,[6] during her natural life and upon her death to divide three-quarters of the principal of said trust fund[7] among the heirs of my brother James N. Macy, being his children Carrie Sands Lord, of said Kennebunk, William Macy,[8] of Brockton, Massachusetts, and Frank Macy, of Lynn, Massachusetts, in equal shares. The remaining one-quarter[9] of said trust fund shall be paid to my nephew Howard Mason, of Cleveland, Ohio.

2. I give and bequeath[10] to my said trustee the sum of twenty thousand dollars in trust to pay the income quarterly to my sister[11] Elizabeth Macy Mason, of Cleveland, Ohio, during her natural life; at her decease one-half of[12] the principal of said trust fund shall be paid to the President and Fellows of Harvard University to[13] be used for the work of the Cancer Commission of Harvard University in memory of my wife Mary[14] Winslow Macy.

3. I direct my executor to distribute all my house furniture and furnishings,[15] all my personal belongings and tangible personal property not otherwise disposed of, in accordance[16] with a paper bearing the same date as this will duly executed and deposited with it.

4. All[17] expenses of packing and shipping articles to the various legatees shall be paid out of the residue[18] of my estate.

5. I nominate Elliott B. Church to be the executor of this will and the Rockland[19] Trust Company of Stamford to be the trustee hereunder, and I request that both be exempt from giving[20] sureties upon their official bonds.

6. I give both executor and trustee full power and authority[21] to sell both real and personal estate by public auction or by private sale and to convey the same by[22] such deeds or other instruments as may be necessary to transfer the legal title thereto. But no[23] purchaser, either from my said executor or trustee, shall be required to see to the application of[24] the purchase money. I give to my executor and trustee, respectively, all powers with reference to[25] the management, sale, conversion, investment and reinvestment of my estate, both real and personal, which I[26] should have if personally present and acting. Both executor and trustee may make distributions and[27] diversions in kind, and the valuations of both executor and trustee upon such divisions shall be[28] final.

All inheritance taxes shall be paid out of the principal of the residue of my estate.

I[29] direct that the interest of the beneficiaries hereunder shall not be alienable by them or[30] any of them, either by assignment, or any other method, nor shall the same be anticipated by[31] them or be subject to be taken by their creditors under any legal process whatever, nor shall the[32] same pass in any event to any assignee or trustee under any trust deed that may be executed[33] by them or any of them or under any insolvency or bankruptcy law, state or national.

IN[34] TESTIMONY WHEREOF, I hereunto set my hand this fifth day of February, 1966.[35] (700)

Vocabulary Preview

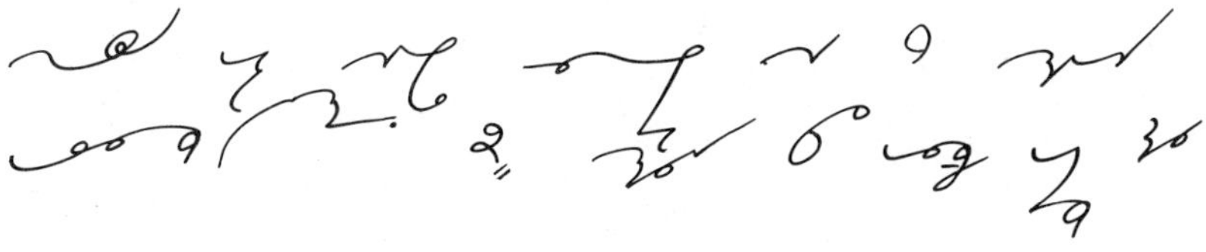

Client, responsible, contributory, negligence, court, accident, construed, litigation, time-consuming, Essex, constituted, attorney, requisite, revocation, substitute.

Sustained Dictation

342 Williams & Andrews, Attorneys at Law, The First National Bank Building, Danville, Indiana 46122. 12 19

28 37 52 63 73 85 96 107 121 131 144

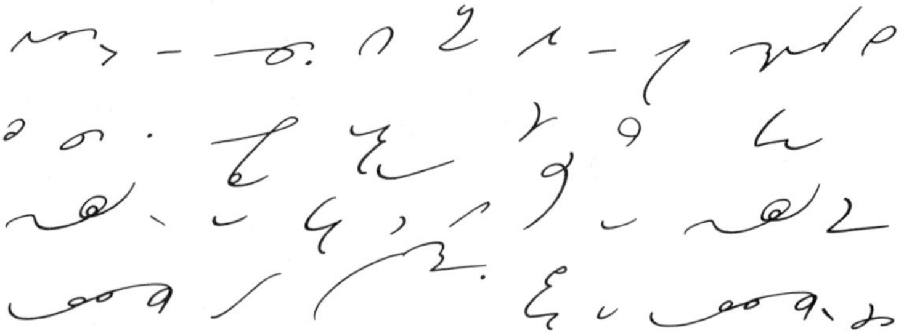

156
169
179
194

TRANSCRIPTION PACER

343 POWER OF ATTORNEY 4

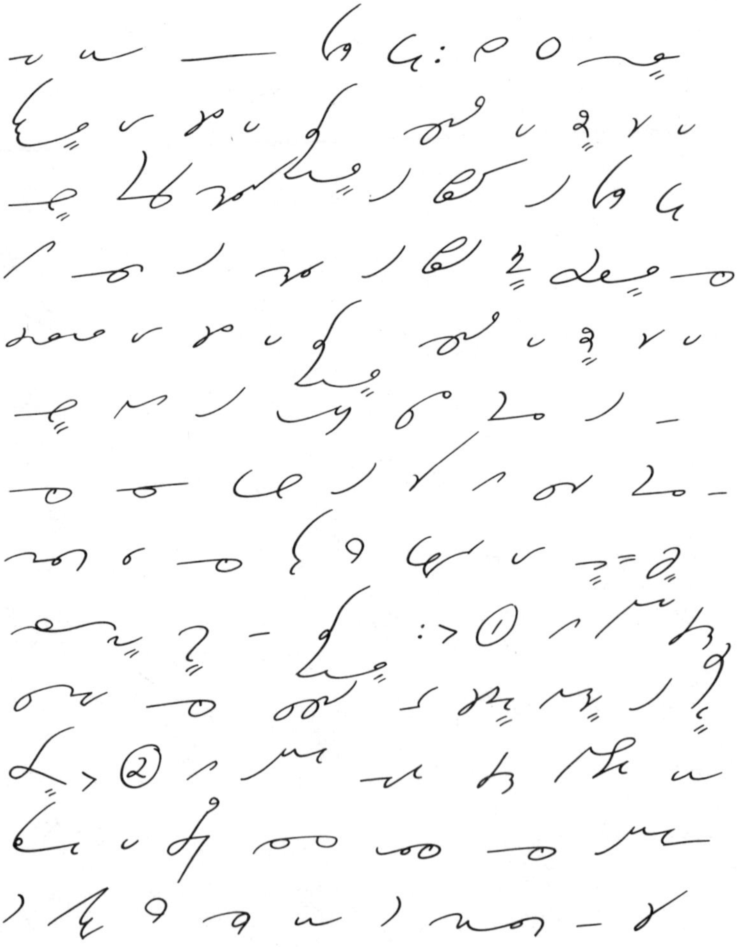

14
26
41
52
64
75
83
94
105
116
125
135
144

153
163
172
182
196
206
216
230
240
251
261
272
279

One of the most interesting and complex developments facing the American businessmen today is the challenge presented by the European, African, and Latin American economic communities. They are trying to develop strength so that they can compete favorably in world trade. In each instance, the procedures used are the pooling of industrial and agricultural resources by sharing one another's raw materials and the free movement of capital and labor. The results of their efforts portend (1) a more even distribution of wealth over a larger percentage of the population and (2) a switch from saving to spending for the necessities of modern-day living.

These two trends spell but one thing to the alert businessmen — new international markets.

Businesses in the United States are attempting to expand their markets, to purchase raw materials at advantageous prices, and to produce goods in locations that provide reduced labor costs. Practically every American business engages in international trade of one kind or another. The secretary assigned to a department involved in international trade will find herself concerned with the many facets of this exciting job — geography, currency, import-export regulations, Washington lobbies, maritime trade, international

unit 16

relations, to mention only a few. She may even find herself on a plane bound for Kuwait or Madrid to work in a foreign operation of her United States-based company. She may find a mastery of foreign languages essential to her work. Whether home-based or foreign-based, though, she will find her horizons broadened through her daily contact with world trade.

INTERNATIONAL TRADE

Secretarial Assignment

The methods of writing sums of money in most foreign countries is similar to that practiced in the dollar economies. The symbol or abbreviation designating the basic unit is placed before the sum, and a period, comma, or space appears before the fractional part.

INTERNATIONAL MONEY UNITS

Country	Basic Unit	Fractional Unit
Great Britain	Pound	Shilling, penny
Australia		
Ireland		
New Zealand		
Union of South Africa		
Egypt	Pound	Piaster
Lebanon		
Syria		
Israel	Pound	Prutah
France	Franc	Centime
Belgium		
Luxembourg		
Monaco		
Morocco		
Switzerland		
Canada	Dollar	Cent
British Honduras		
Ethiopia		
Hong Kong		
Liberia		
Malaya		
Singapore		

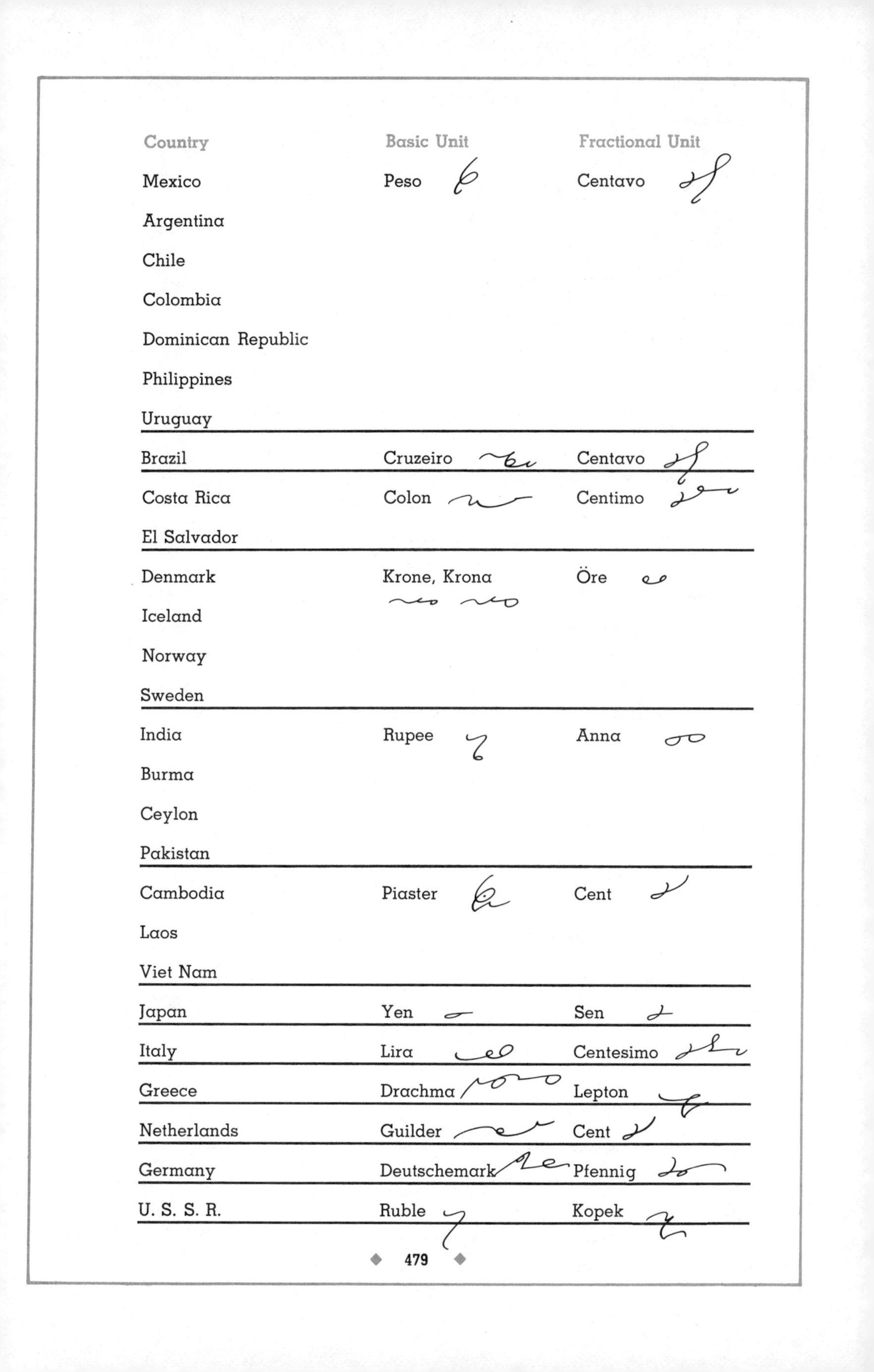

Country	Basic Unit	Fractional Unit
Mexico	Peso	Centavo
Argentina		
Chile		
Colombia		
Dominican Republic		
Philippines		
Uruguay		
Brazil	Cruzeiro	Centavo
Costa Rica	Colon	Centimo
El Salvador		
Denmark	Krone, Krona	Öre
Iceland		
Norway		
Sweden		
India	Rupee	Anna
Burma		
Ceylon		
Pakistan		
Cambodia	Piaster	Cent
Laos		
Viet Nam		
Japan	Yen	Sen
Italy	Lira	Centesimo
Greece	Drachma	Lepton
Netherlands	Guilder	Cent
Germany	Deutschemark	Pfennig
U. S. S. R.	Ruble	Kopek

lesson

76 INTERNATIONAL SPEED BUILDER

SPECIALIZED TERMINOLOGY

To understand the sense of the dictation in this lesson, study each of the following terms:

British Crown Colony • Area comprising Kowloon, the New Territories, Hong Kong Island, ruled by a governor representing the Queen.

Certificate of Origin • Statement of country in which goods were produced. In this case the certificate must state that the goods were not manufactured in China or North Korea.

Clipper Cargo Horizons • Airline's publication provided to augment foreign trade and thus increase both passenger and cargo traffic.

Keyed Advertisement • An advertisement that does not divulge the identity of the advertiser. Answers are sent to a number, not a company or a person.

TRANSCRIPTION SPEED BUILDER

Vocabulary Preview

Pan American, Horizons, languages, components, inquiries, Thailand, Africa, distributor, Hong Kong, comprehensive, certificate, Korean, Treasury, brocaded, originates, China, Territories, Kowloon, New Delhi, Orly, airport, Frankfurt, Wiesbaden, Oslo, London, Baltimore.

Sustained Dictation

344 To: Mark C. Lambert, President, From: Manager, International Sales.

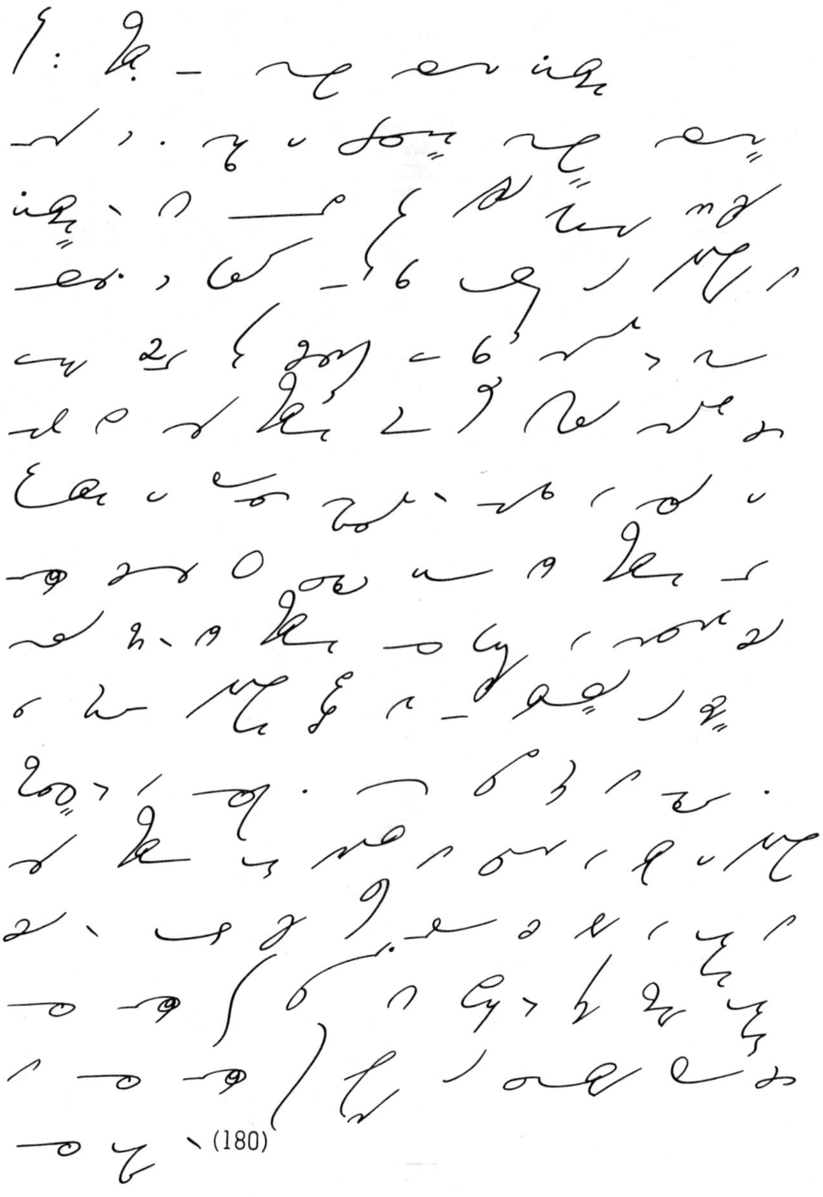

(180)

345 ▸ Mr. Wilbur R. Adams, Peninsular Hotel, Hong Kong, British Crown Colony.

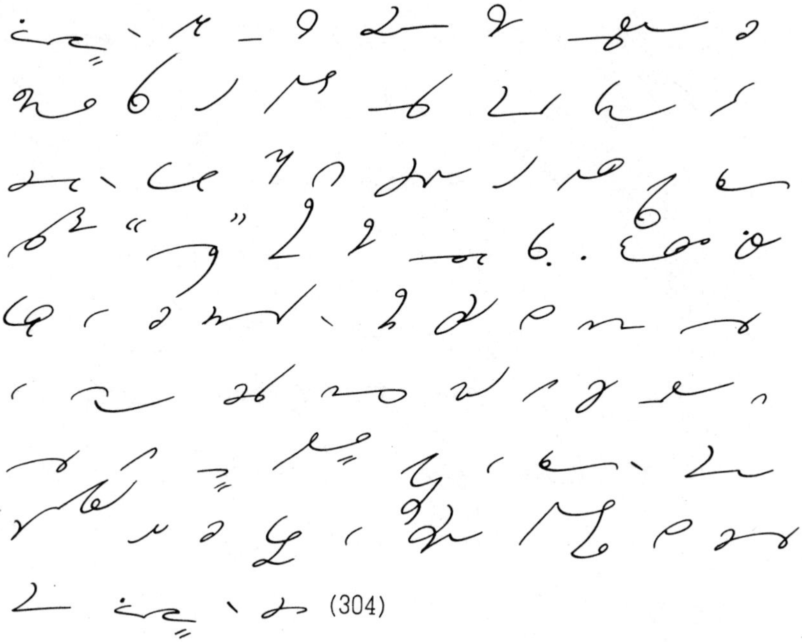

(304)

346 Air France, 683 Fifth Avenue, New York, New York 10019.

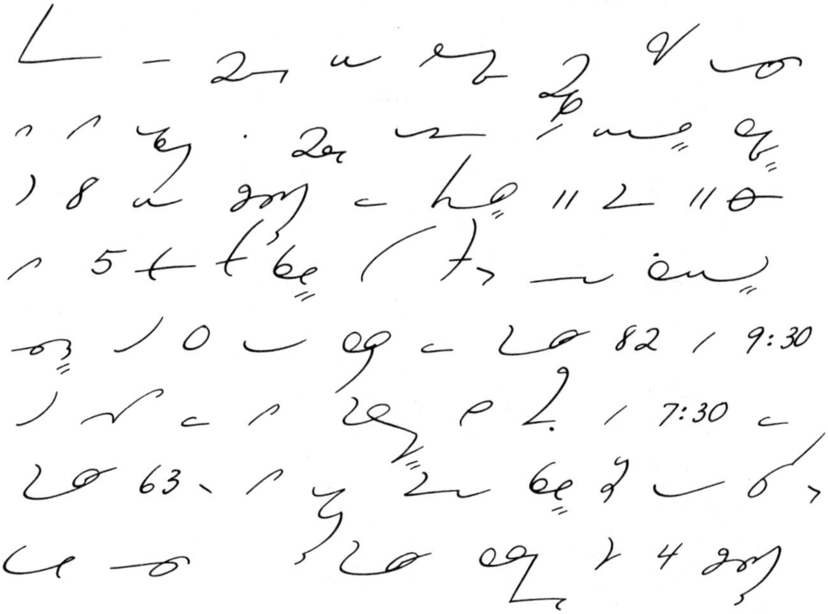

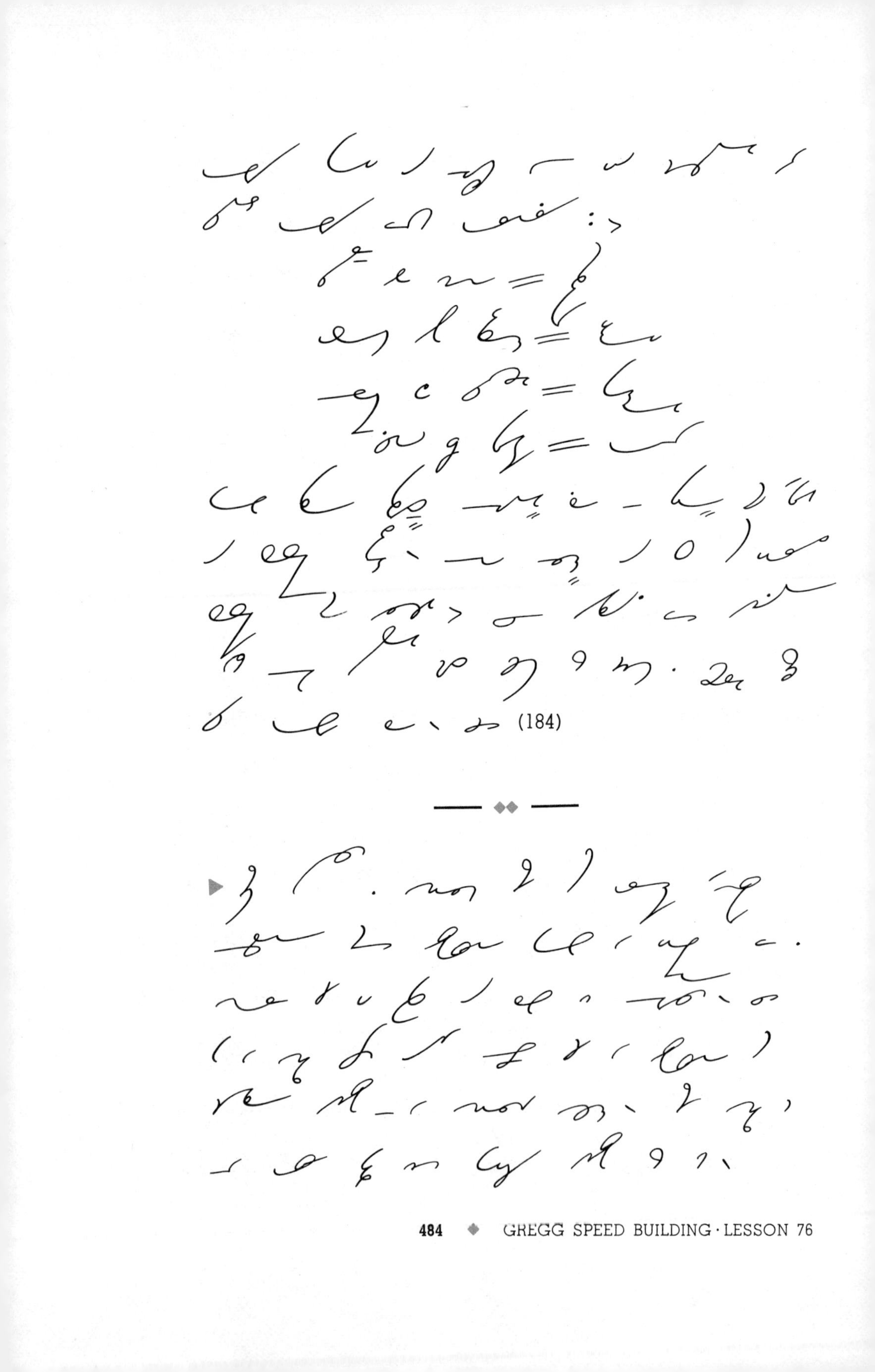

(184)

Lesson 77

INTERNATIONAL SPEED BUILDER

SPECIALIZED TERMINOLOGY

Euratom • Certain European countries have developed this agency for coordinating the development of peaceful uses of atomic power.

European Coal and Steel Community • Competition in coal and steel is eliminated between the countries in the Common Market.

European Economic Community or Common Market (EEC) • Six countries have eliminated trade barriers, travel restrictions, etc., and are sharing their economic development. The members are France, Italy, West Germany, and the Benelux countries.

Administrative City • A new development is being built in the heart of Brussels in which EEC, EC&S, and Euratom are housed.

European Free Trade Association or Outer Seven (EFTA) • An organization somewhat looser than the Common Market and one having the same general purposes. The members are Austria, Britain, Denmark, Norway, Portugal, Sweden, and Switzerland.

Imported Components vs. Local Components • In an effort to build up their economy, many countries place restrictions on the percentage of imported components that may be used by a foreign manufacturer. This is one of the most controversial issues between the country permitting foreign factories and the country owning the factory.

TRANSCRIPTION SPEED BUILDER

Vocabulary Preview

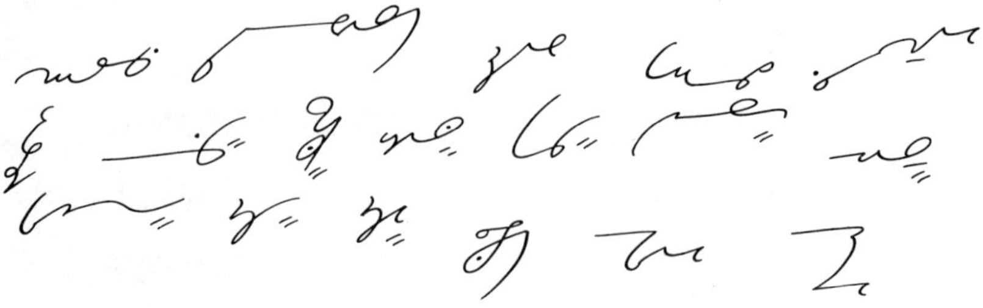

Mexican, United States, industry, Commerce, automobile, diesel, construction, equipment, political, calculator, Brussels, European, Community, Italy, Belgium, Luxembourg, Netherlands, Euratom, coordinating, administrative, subsidiaries, proximity, headquarters, specialist, Manhattan, Association, Austria, Britain, Denmark, Norway, Portugal, Sweden, Switzerland, initiative, importers, movements.

Sustained Dictation

347 To: Millard D. Weston, Vice-President for International Trade, From: Manager, International Sales.

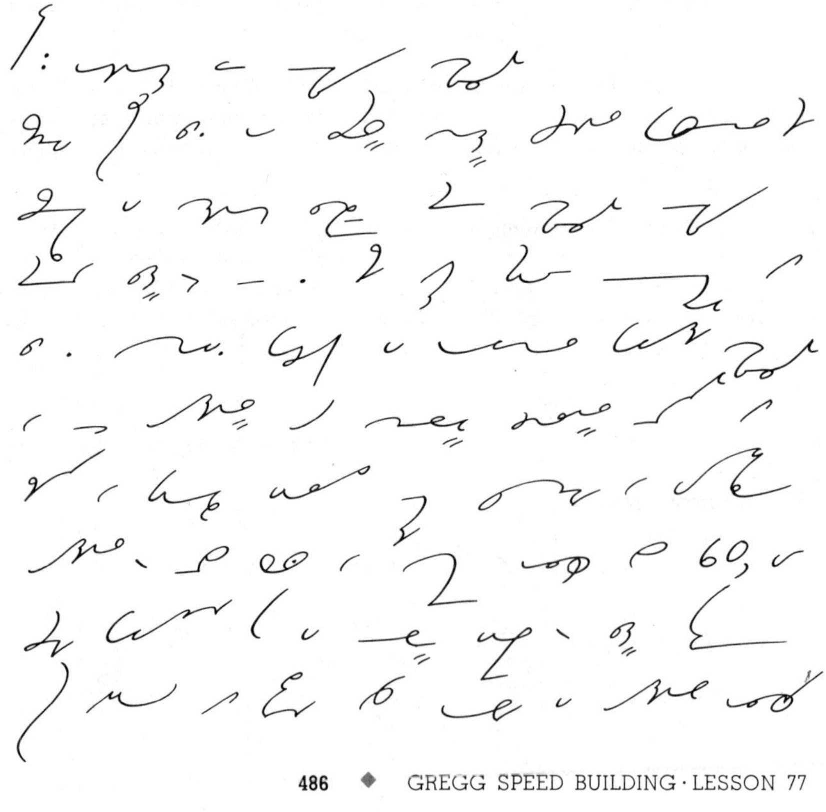

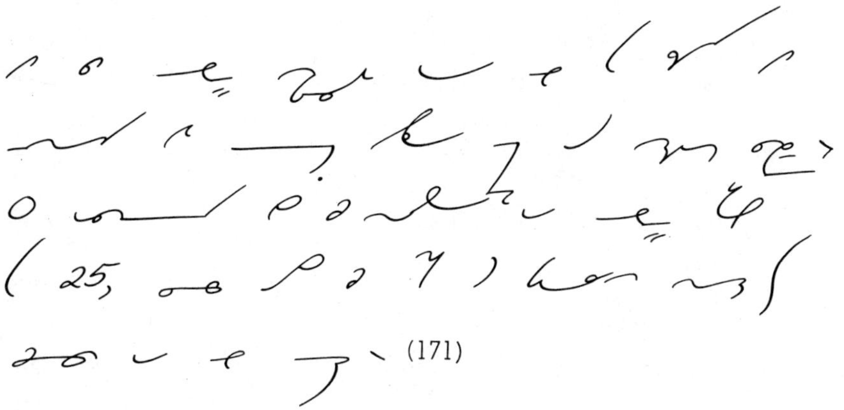

(171)

348 ▸ Mr. Arnold G. Thompson, Administrative Assistant, Modern Office Equipment, Baltimore, Maryland 21204.

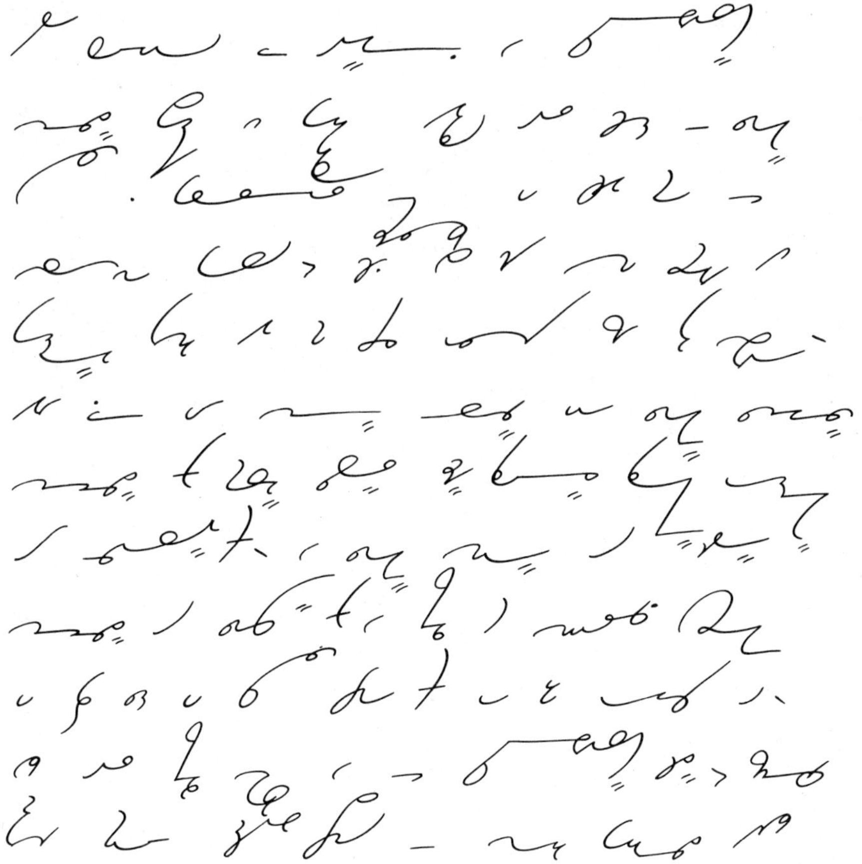

(356)

349 To: William P. Shea, President, From: Manager, International Sales.

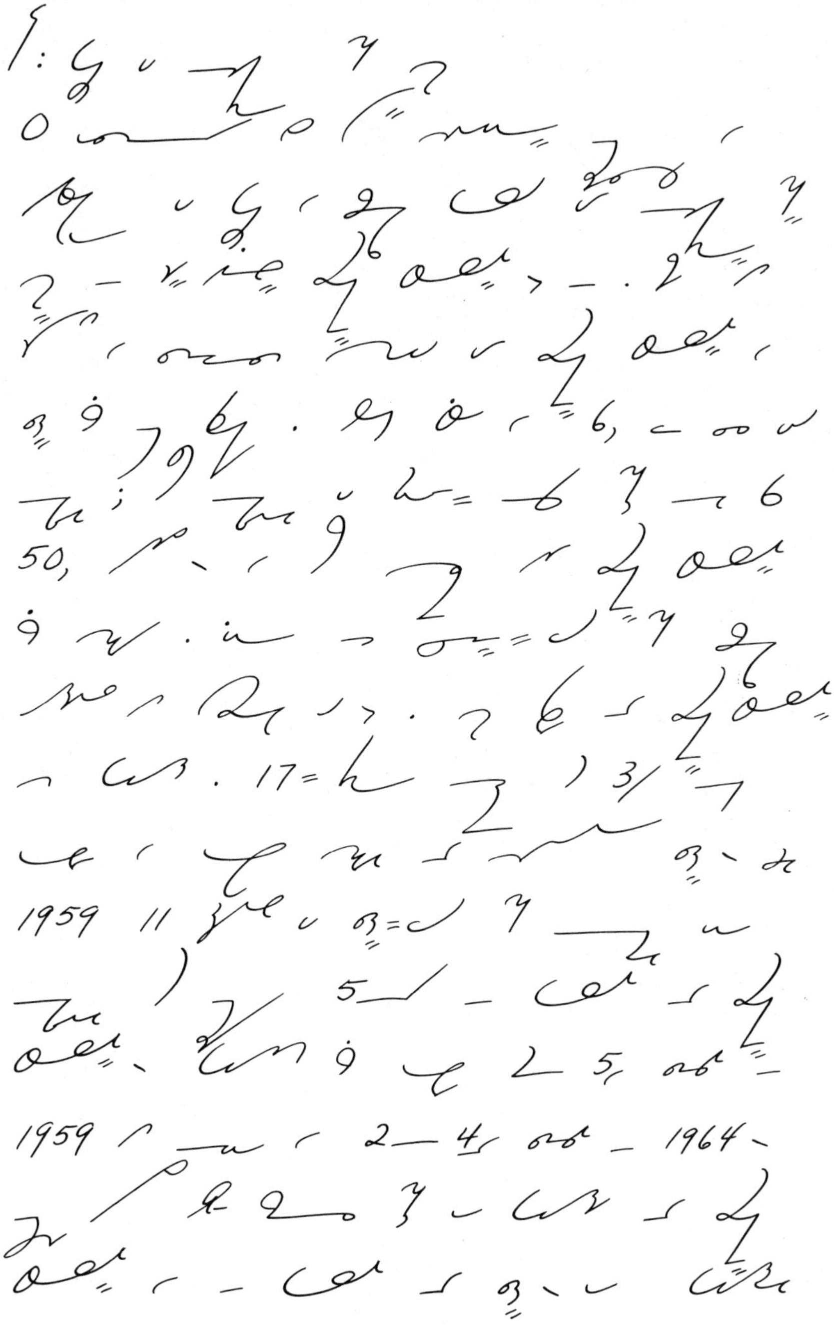

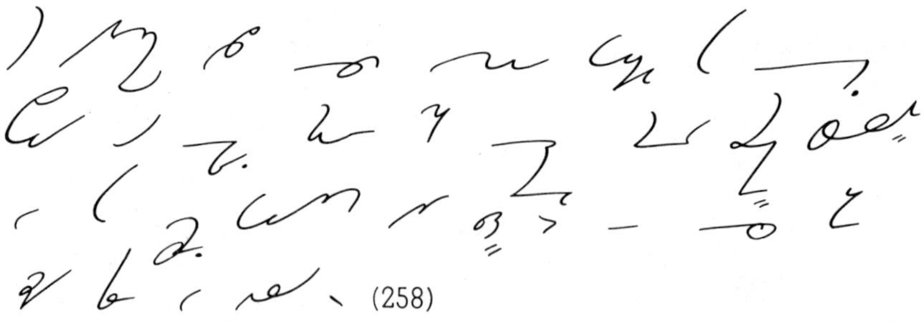

(258)

350▸ Aruba Trading Company, Nassaustraat 7, Oranjestad, Aruba, Netherlands Antilles.

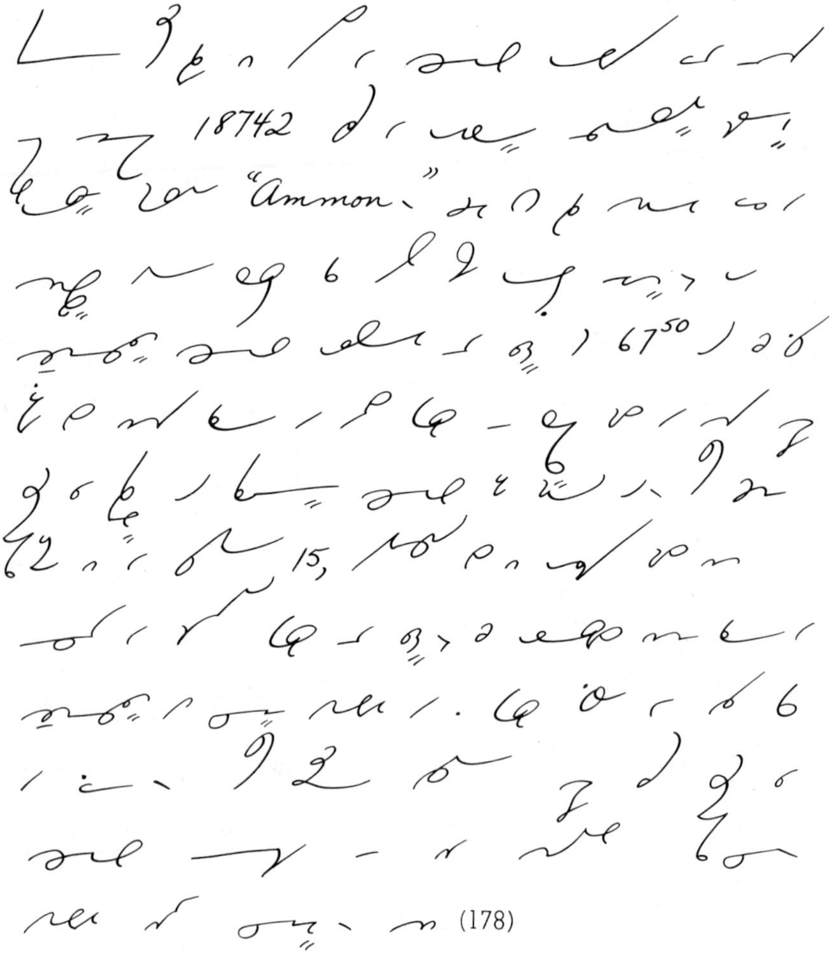

(178)

lesson 78

INTERNATIONAL SPEED BUILDER

SPECIALIZED TERMINOLOGY

Balance of Payments • A country strives to keep exports ahead of imports so that more money will be coming into the country than leaving it. If this does not occur, the government may prohibit certain types of spending.

Dun and Bradstreet • A top credit-rating agency.

Yen • The Japanese monetary unit. There are 360 yen to the American dollar.

Selling Yen for Future Delivery • This practice would be advantageous if there were a possibility that yen might depreciate in value.

Strike Hedging • Stockpiling materials in anticipation of a strike.

TRANSCRIPTION SPEED BUILDER

Vocabulary Preview

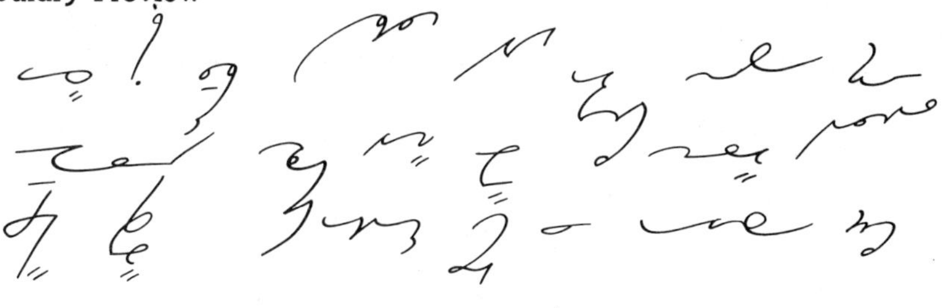

Omaha, hedging, equivalents, domestic, destination, respectively, curtail, foreign, implemented, conservative, Tokyo, Nippon, Commerce, directory, Interchange, Japanese, restrictions, conversion, yen, locale, successfully.

Sustained Dictation

351▸ Mr. Charles M. Goodson, Manager, Union Rubber Company, 12-2-16 Higashicho, Teramachi-Gashira, Kimikyo-ku, Tokyo, Japan.

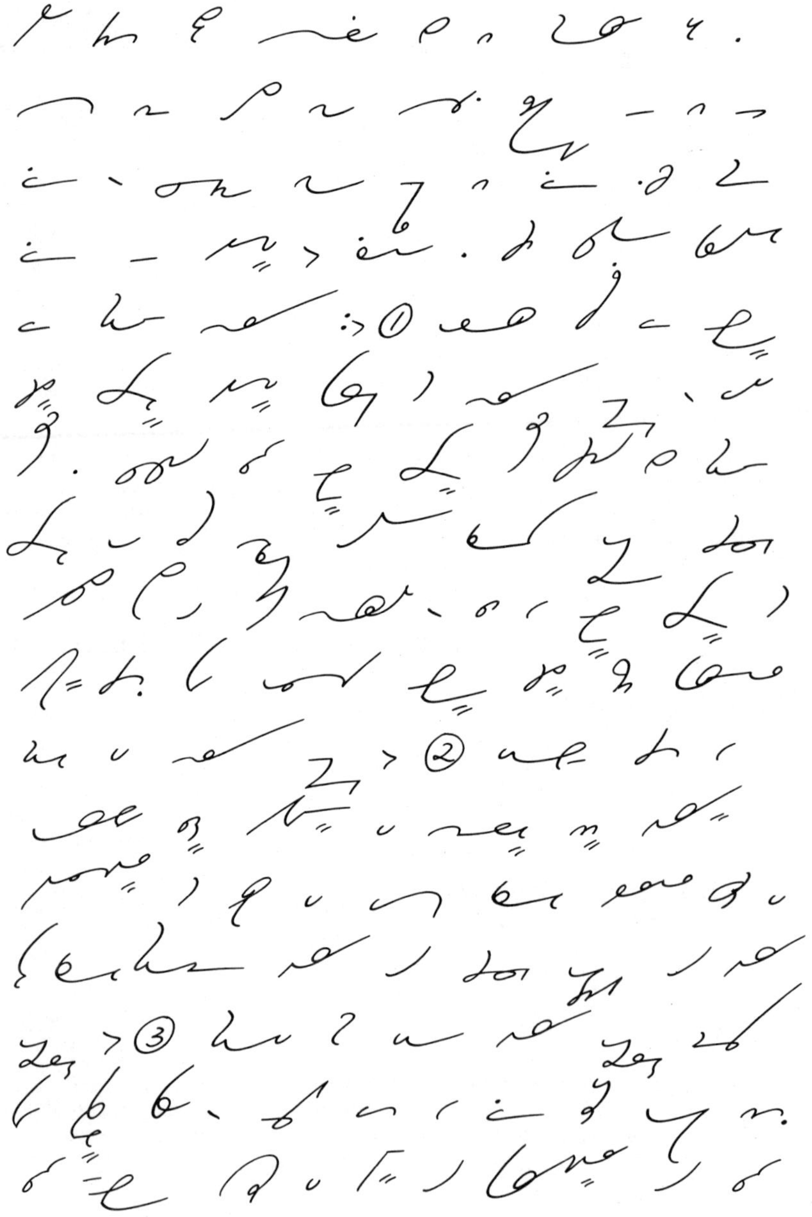

(349)

352▸ To: All Members of the Administrative Committee, From: Manager, International Sales.

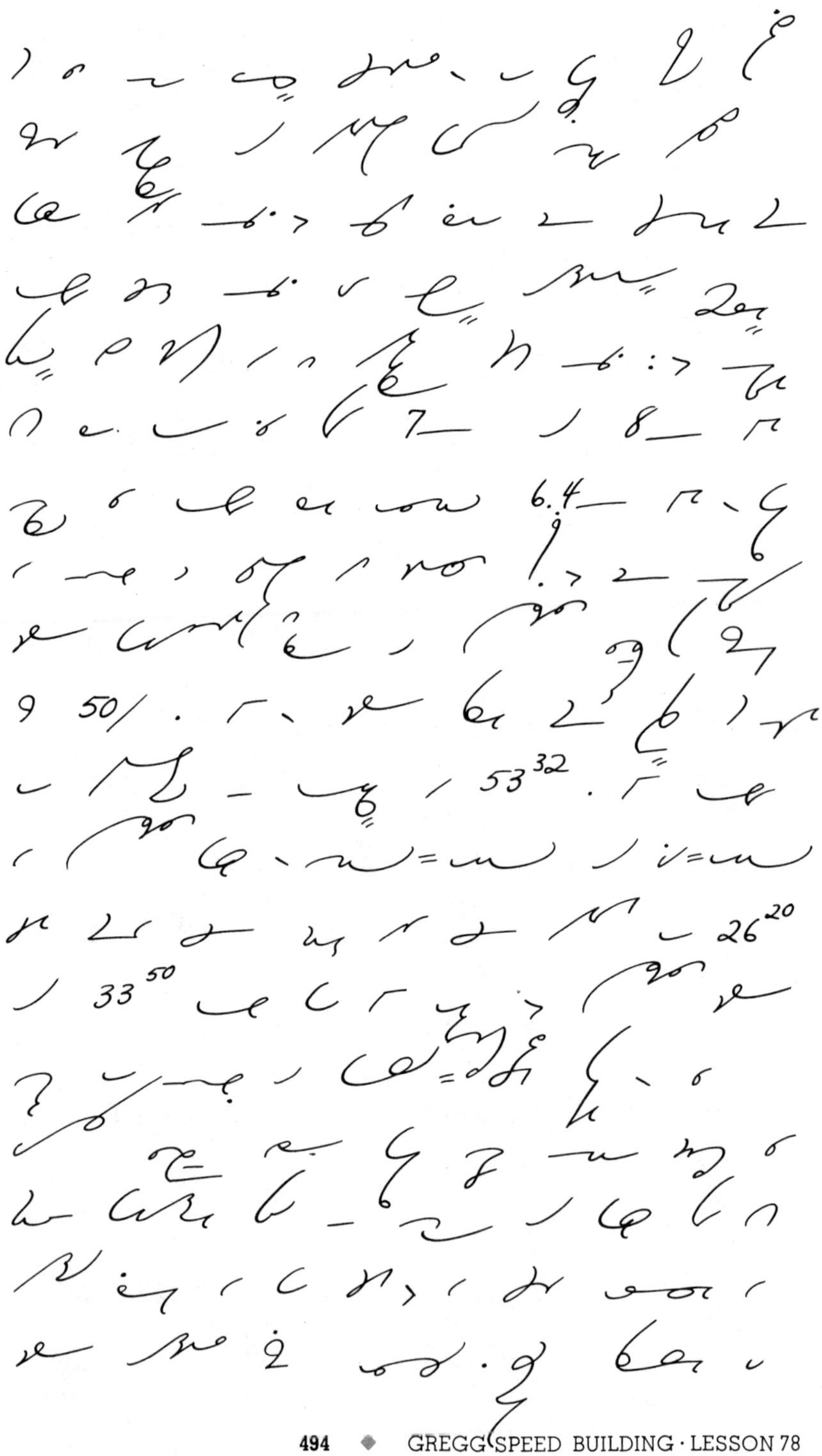

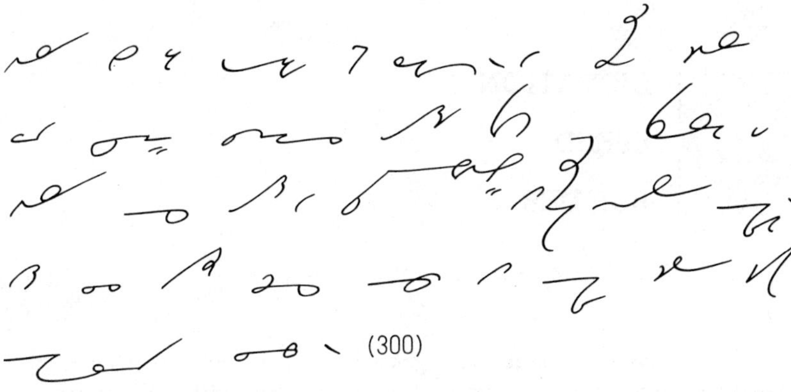

(300)

353▸ Aruba Trading Company, Nassaustraat 7, Oranjestad, Aruba, Netherland Antilles.

(150)

lesson 79

DICTATION SPEED BUILDER

SPEED-ESCALATION PRACTICE

Practice the vocabulary preview before writing from dictation the speed-pyramided letter. The first minute is counted at 80 words a minute; the second, at 90; the third, at 100; and the fourth, at 110.

SPECIALIZED TERMINOLOGY

Documentary Sight Draft • The exporter draws dollar drafts on his customers abroad, routing them and the title documents needed, through an American bank, which, in turn, sends them for collection to its branch office or correspondent bank in the buyer's country. When the buyer pays the draft "at sight," he gets the documents that entitle him to ownership of the goods.

Exchange Control Board • A government agency approving conversion of local currency into other types for export.

Forwarder • The agency at the border that takes care of sending a shipment abroad.

Letter of Credit • A letter of credit is bought at the bank or American Express in this country. The purchaser pays the issuer the amount of the letter plus a service charge of 1 percent or less. Along with the letter goes a booklet listing the cashing banks abroad.

Propaganda Material • What is called "advertising" here becomes "propaganda" there.

Trade Fair • A more important form of marketing in most foreign countries than in the United States.

Vocabulary Preview

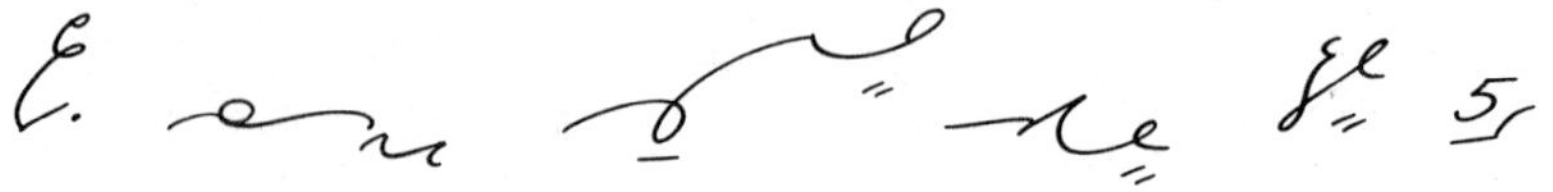

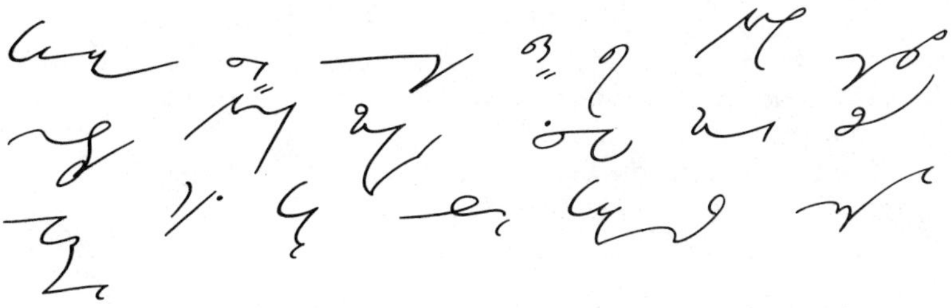

Exhibiting, calculators, Guatemala, Multiplex, Speedex, 500,000, promotional, English, manufactured, United States, usable, distribute, unfortunately, classified, discourage, exorbitant, hampered, solution, exempt, improvements, forwarding, purposes, markings, propaganda, customs.

Speed Forcing

(1 Minute at 80)

354 Gentlemen: Last September 21 we wrote you (our letter No. 620) about exhibiting/Diamond calculators at the Guatemala Trade Fair. A copy is enclosed just in case our first letter went astray.//

We plan to exhibit both your calculators, the Multiplex and the Speedex. An estimated///500,000 visitors are expected at the Fair; therefore, we shall need plenty of promotional material. (1)

(1 Minute at 90)

It would, of course, be best if the literature were in Spanish. If this is, not possible, English will do.

We do not know/yet whether the Multiplex can be exhibited. It is manfactured in Holland, and the Fair is being organized by//the United States Government to promote the sale of United States products. The material describing the Multiplex///may not, then, be usable. We do know, though, that we can expect to distribute 10,000 brochures describing the Speedex. (2)

(1 Minute at 100)

Unfortunately, advertising material is classified as propaganda. In an effort to discourage the sending of/propaganda into the Central American countries, an exorbitant duty is assessed on it. This factor has hampered us in the//past in getting an adequate supply of brochures describing Diamond office equipment. However, we have found a solution to our///problem in this particular case. Advertising material is exempt from import duties if it is consigned to the Fair Committee. (3)

(1 Minute at 110)

We enclose a form for filing your request for exhibiting the Multiplex. We shall be able to arrange for display models incorporating/the latest improvements if officials of the Fair approve your request.

Your display models of the Speedex and both brochures are to be sent to a forwarding//agent.

We shall need to have an invoice for customs purposes made out to the same name shown on the case markings. The material is to be described///as PROPAGANDA MATERIAL.

Time is short, as we must allow for red tape at the customhouse — sometimes as much as fifteen days. Sincerely yours, (4)

TRANSCRIPTION REINFORCEMENT PRACTICE

Vocabulary Preview

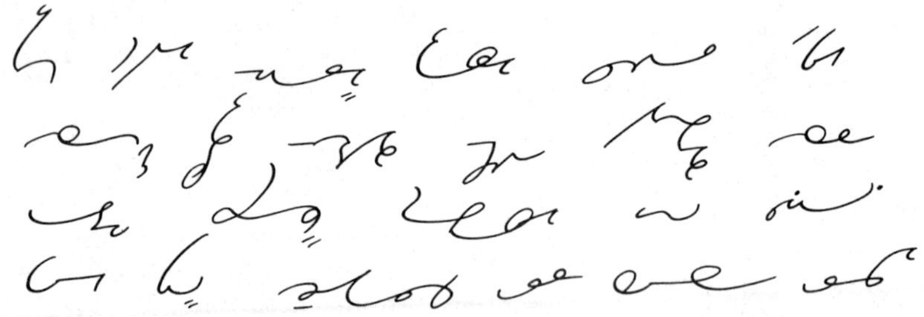

Objection, forwarders, New Orleans, suppliers, actually, transportation, calculations, specify, inconsistencies, in the future, discrepancies, carrier, let us know, Vargas, flashlights, occurred, withholding, permission, Board, quintuplicate, return, airmail, remittance.

Sustained Dictation

355 Diamond Office Equipment, Box 893, Geneva 6 Eaux-Vives.

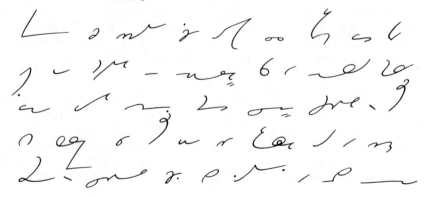

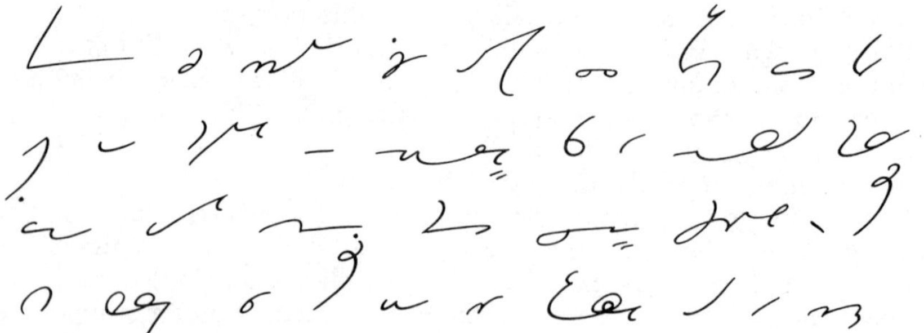

(224)

356▸ First Merchants Bank, 8 Boylston Street, Boston, Massachusetts 02116.

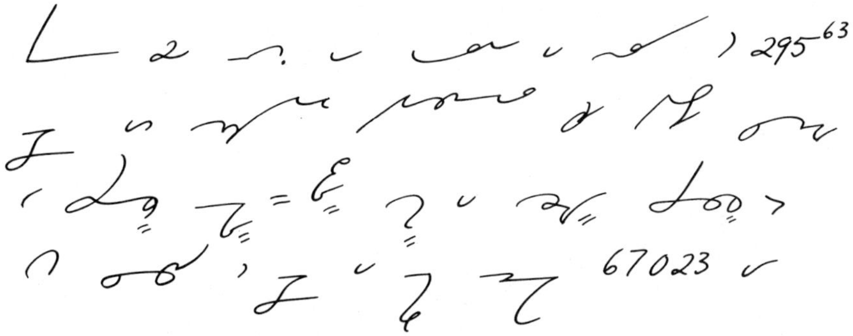

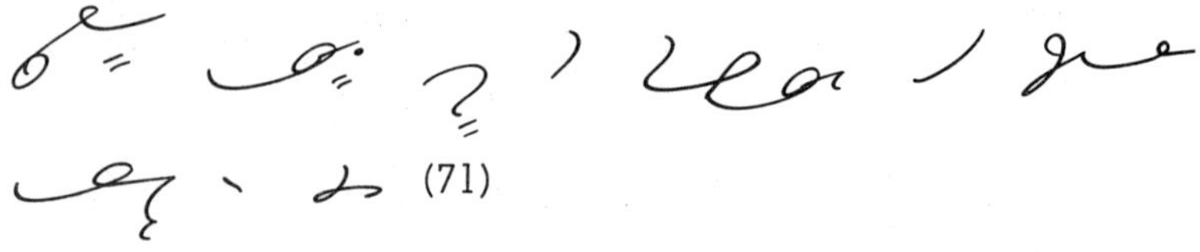

(71)

TRANSCRIPTION PACER

357 ▸ Diamond Office Equipment, Box 893, Geneva 6 Eaux-Vives, Attention of Mr. Michael Jones, Export Administration Supervisor. 11 24

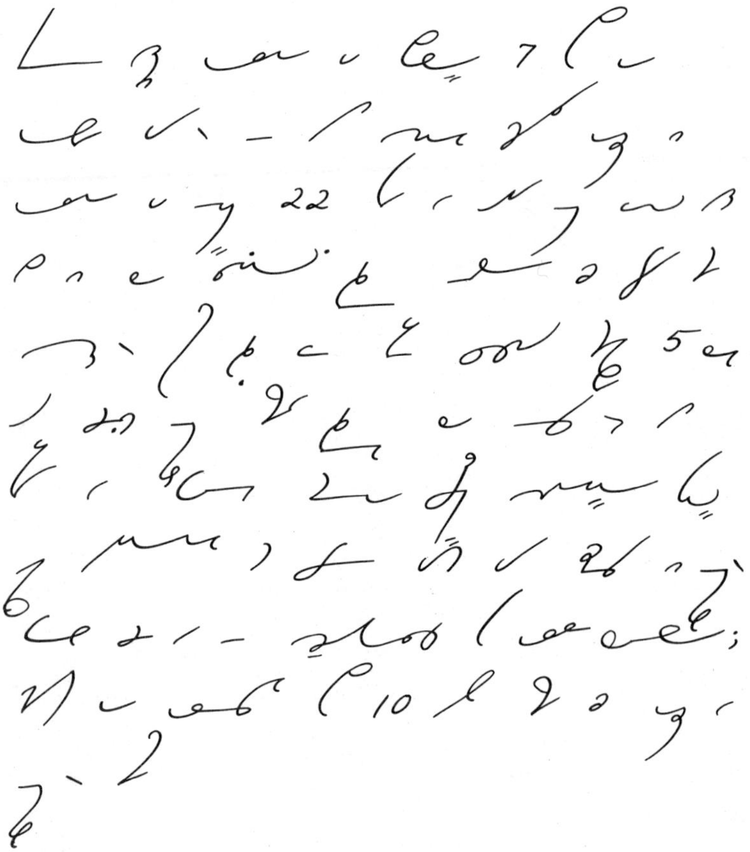

34 43 55 67 81 93 104 118 128 142 148

lesson 80

CERTIFIED PROFESSIONAL SECRETARY SKILLS EXAMINATION

As a final checkup, measure your shorthand competency on the secretarial skills section of the CPS (Certified Professional Secretary) examination—a 12-hour examination developed by The National Secretaries Association as one means of identifying top-level secretaries. The two and one-half hour secretarial skills test requires candidates to transcribe dictation given at speeds varying from 80 to 110 words a minute, to edit and retype a report, to compose a communication, and to design and tabulate a memorandum.

Sample Secretarial Skills Examination

Four samples of the eight items included in the secretarial skills test are reproduced here. They include a letter dictated at 80 words a minute, an uncorrected draft of a report, a telegram to be composed, and a memorandum with a tabulation.

Assume that you are secretary to Mr. E. R. Harper, head of personnel at Thomas Baker and Company, an industrial firm in Cincinnati, Ohio. Mr. Harper communicates with David T. McGrath. Also working in your office is Helen Johnson, a typist. Mr. Harper's letters are to be set up in any approved style, the closing lines should include his name and department, thus: E. R. Harper, Head of Personnel.

You are to decide on all matters of form, except that you will follow Mr. Harper's indicated style preference in typing memorandums. Use the current date on all correspondence. Make the appropriate number of carbon copies for each item, with one for your files. Address an envelope for the letter.

Your instructor will dictate the letter and allow you time to read, organize, and edit your shorthand notes and problem copy; then you are to produce usable copies of the four items.

Dictated Letter

358

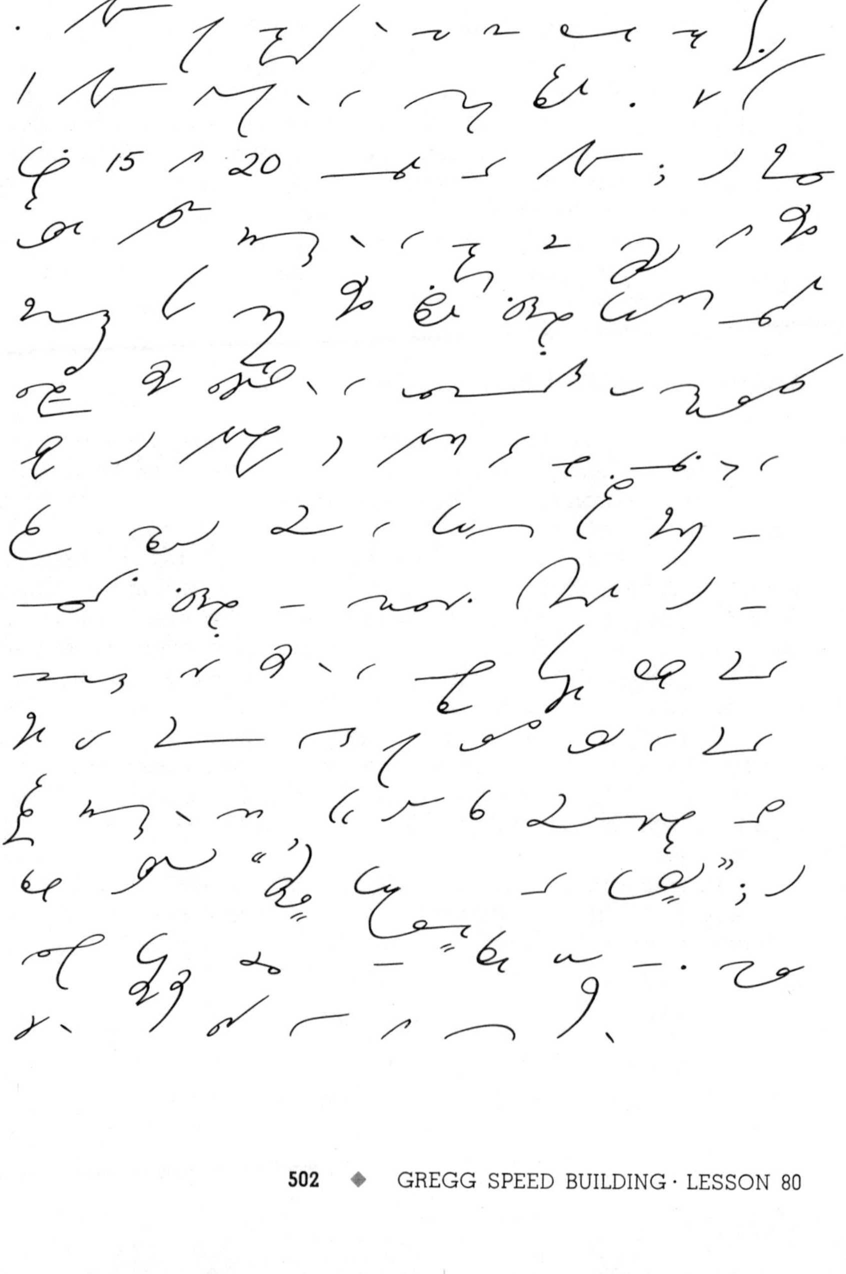

Report to Be Edited

359▸ DIRECTIONS: This is uncorrected copy of the first portion of a manual. Set it up in good typewritten form. Number the pages. Allow extra space for the left margin, because these pages, when reproduced, will be punched for a three-ring binder. Make all changes necessary for accurate spelling, punctuation, grammar, and diction. Change wording only when it is necessary. You may mark this printed copy in any way you wish.

RULES FOR PAY FOR TIME NOT WORKED

I. APPLICATION OF RULES

Only those payments that are specificly covered in this manual shall be made for time not worked for any reason.

For the purpose of applying these rules, the number of hours in a working day, a working week and a working month has been defined as following.

One working day	8.0 hours
One working week	40.0 hours
One working month	173.3 hrs.

These definitions do not constitute a schedule of working hours, as the actual working hours of field personal may vary considerable from one day to another.

If in any instants the application of these definitions should not be appropriate to the circumstances, the facts in the case shall be presented to the Vice-president concerned for review and decision.

II. ABSENCE

The provisions of this section refer to the affect of absence on payments of salary and on payments on cost of living bonus, where applicable. For special rules covering the effect of absence on semi-annual bonus payments, see pages 15 through 19, Paragraph IX.

A. Company Business

Time spent away from regular work because of company business shall not be considered time absent.

No deduction shall be made from the salary of an individual whom is away from regular work because of company business.

B. Holidays

See page nine, paragraph six.

C. Illness or Injury

Individuals absent because of non-occupational illness or injury shall receive a percentage of their salary based on their length of service, providing the absence is approved by the district manager in the case of representatives, or by the Vice-President concerned in the case of individuals on or above the district manager level of responsibility. For rules covering payments in the event of occupational accident or disease, see page 10, paragraph VII.

If the individual returned to work but subsequently suffers another period of illness from the same or related cause, his eligability for future salary payments shall be determined in the following manner:

1. If the individual returned to active employment for a period of three months or longer, the second period of illness shall be regarded as a new illness and salary payments handled accordingly.
2. If the individual returned to active employment for a period of fewer than 3 months, the second period of illness shall be regarded as a continuation of the first and salary payments made accordingly; beginning the first day of the second period of absence. If the individual received the maximum allowable salary under the schedule above during the first absence no further salary payments shall be made.

If an individual returns to work but subsequently suffers another period of illness from a different or unrelated causes, the second period of illness shall be regarded as a new illness and salary payments handled accordingly.

D. Jury Duty

An individual receiving a subpena for jury duty would be paid the difference between the sum received for such service and regular salary for the hours absent because of jury duty.

E. Marriage

An individual absent to be married shall be paid for the regular hours absent up to and including 5 regular working days, provided a leave of absence has been previously obtained form the department Head. The five days pay shall not be granted if a leave of absence of more than one calender week (excluding paid vacations and paid holidays) were taken for this purpose.

F. **Leaves of Absence Without Pay**

The amount by which the salary of a monthly pay roll employee shall be reduced in case of absence for which pay is not allowed shall be computed by dividing the salary for the month in which the absence occured by 173.3 hours. The resulting amount shall be deducted for each working hour for which pay is not allowed.

Telegram

360 ▸ DIRECTIONS: Mr. Harper is planning a business trip to South America and will be out of the office from May 10 to May 18.

Yesterday, May 5, a letter was received from Eugene Carletti, of your Sacramento office. He says he plans to come to Cincinnati on May 11 or 12, at which time he expects to discuss some matters on which he and Mr. Harper have been working. Mr. Harper is eager to get in touch with Mr. Carletti before leaving on his trip. Efforts to reach Mr. Carletti by telephone have been unsuccessful. You learn that he was called out of town on a family emergency of indefinite duration and cannot be located.

Mr. Harper asks you to send a message to Mr. Carletti's office (the address is 713 North 22 Street), requesting him to telephone before Mr. Harper leaves for South America. In case Mr. Carletti does not make contact, Mr. Harper would like to have the data that Mr. Carletti was compiling sent to your Cincinnati office immediately. Mr. Harper will leave instructions with you as to the disposition of the data in that case.

Type the message to send to Mr. Carletti. (The Sacramento office is open on Saturdays.)

Memorandum

361 ▸ DIRECTIONS: Assume that Mr. Harper dictated this memorandum to a machine. You are to transcribe the memorandum, which was dictated the way it is shown here.

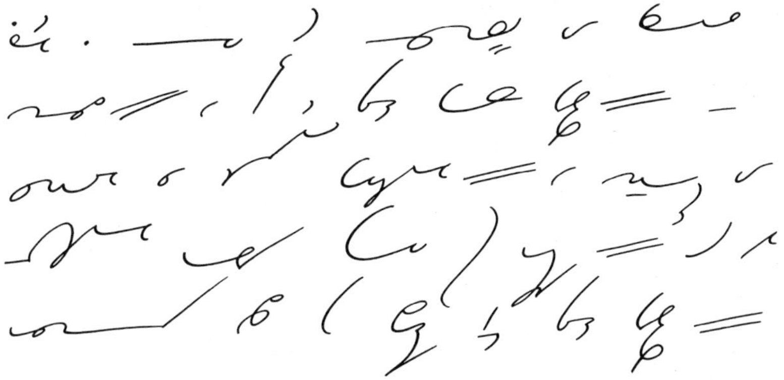

This is the information regarding the people eligible for the bonus:

Charles Bond, Salesman, 1-13-60
L. B. Kruse, Salesman, 2-20-60
James T. Fischerman, Salesman, 4-21-60
S. J. Jabowitz, Salesman, 5-5-60
Sam Petersen, Salesman, 5-16-60
Arthur Paine, Salesman, 6-16-60
Elizabeth Ann Eller, Secretary (District Mgr.), 10-15-53
Faye Keaner, Secretary (Controller), 4-8-57
Anne Marie Clarke, Secretary (Mgr.-Marketing), 6-3-58
Joan Lee Seaton, Secretary (District Mgr.), 3-18-59

recall drills

LIST OF JOINED WORD ENDINGS

1 -ment

2 -tion, -tial

3 -ly

4 -ily

5 -ful

6 -sume, -sumption

7 -ble

8 -ther

9 -self, -selves

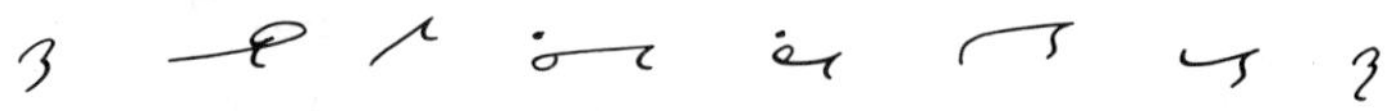

LIST OF DISJOINED WORD ENDINGS

10 -hood, -ward

11 -ship

12 -cle, -cal

13 -ulate

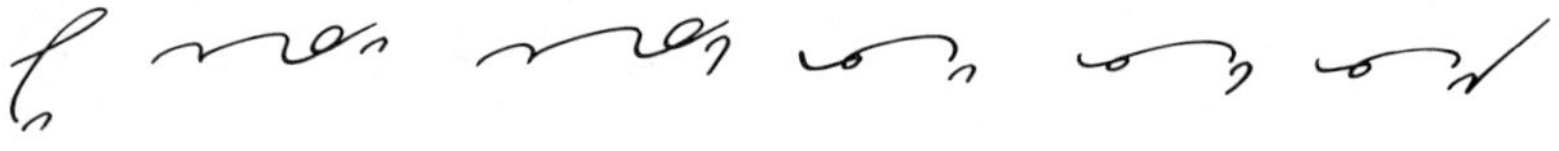

14 -ingly

15 -ings

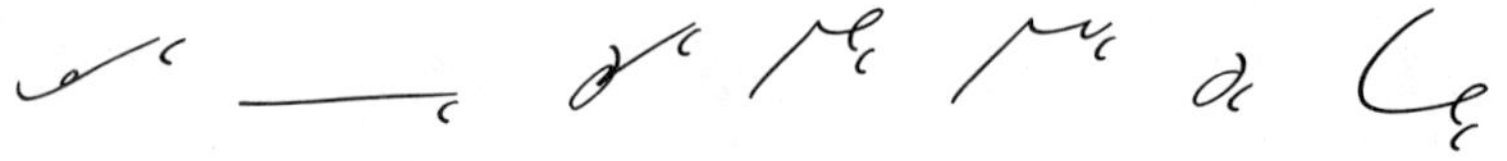

16 -gram

17 -ification

18 -lity, -lty

19 -rity

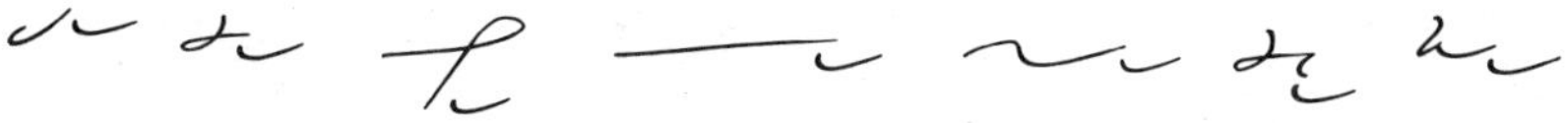

LIST OF JOINED WORD BEGINNINGS

20 Em-, Im-

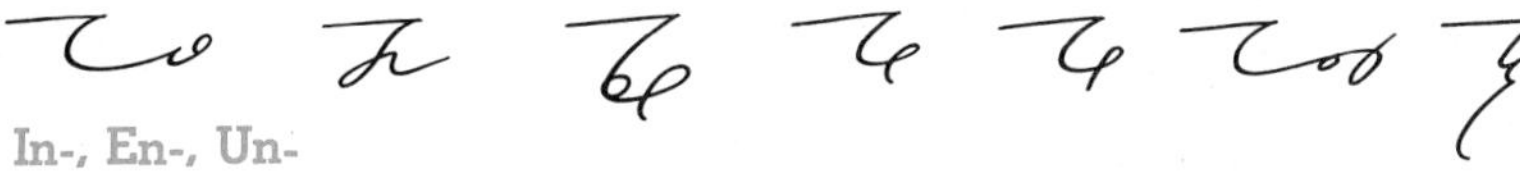

21 In-, En-, Un-

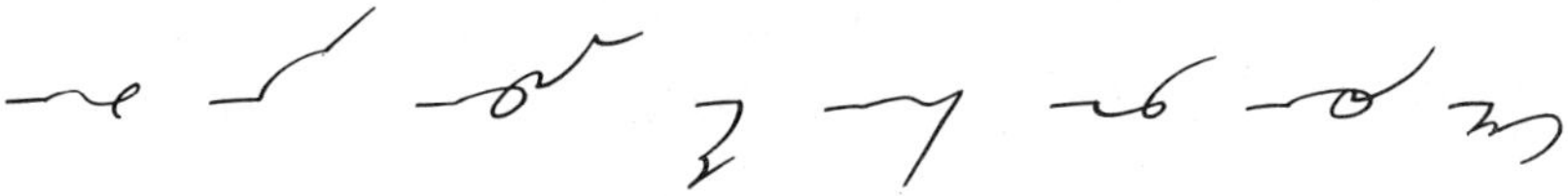

22 Re-

23 De-, Dĭ-

24 Dis-, Des-

25 Mis-

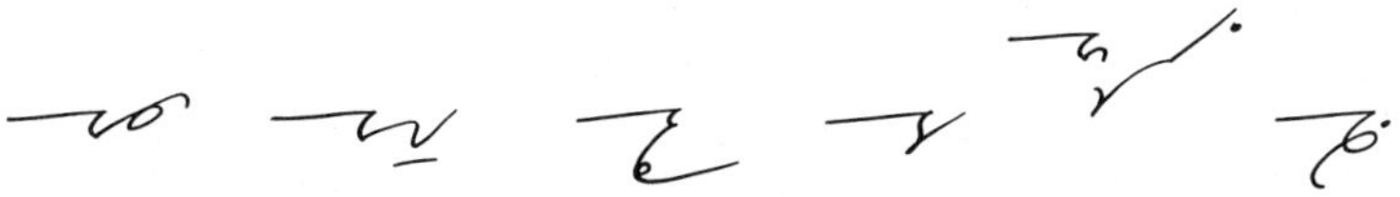

26 Com-, Con-

27 Sub-

28 Al-

LIST OF DISJOINED WORD BEGINNINGS

29 Inter-, Intr-, Enter-, Entr-

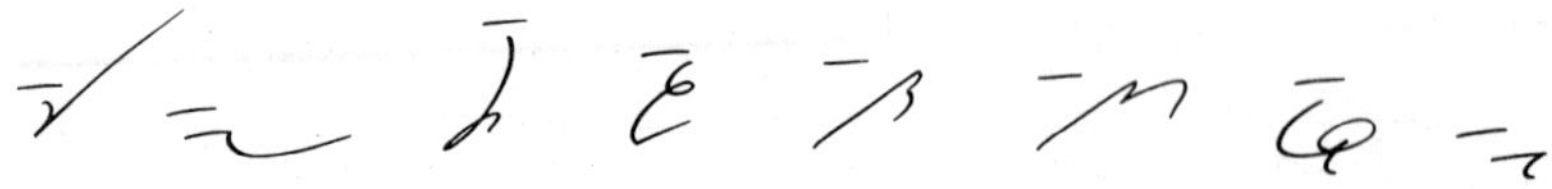

30 Electr-, Electric

31 Post-

32 Super-

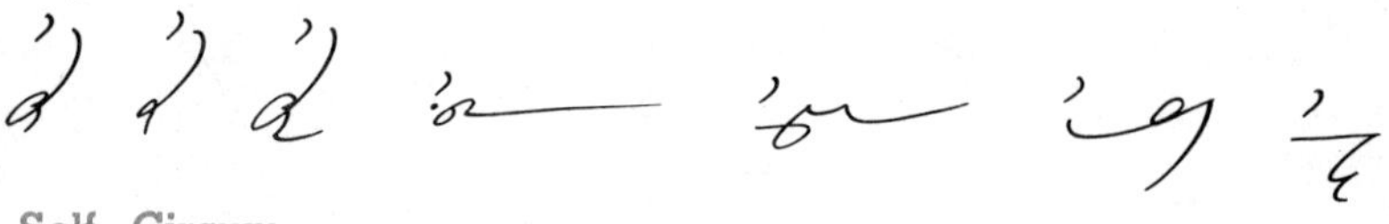

33 Self-, Circum-

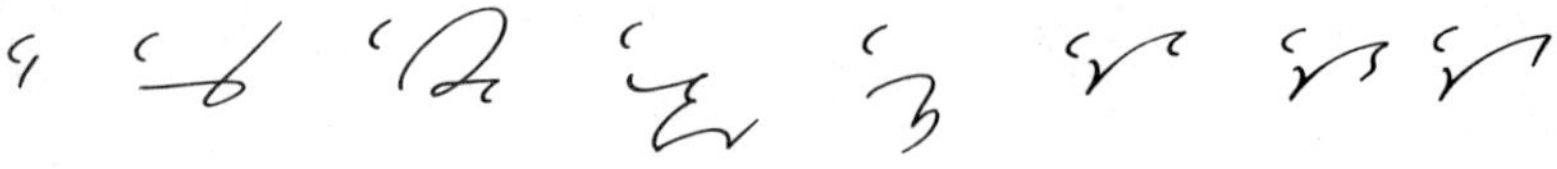

34 Trans-

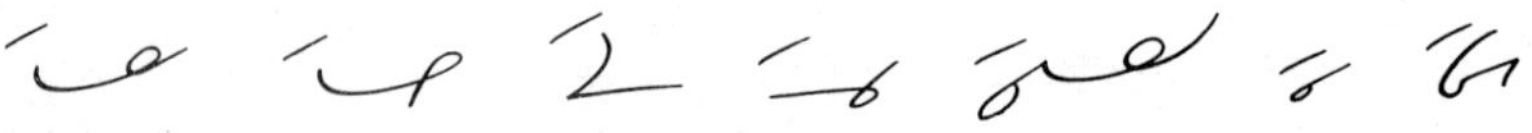

index